Protestant Empires

Protestantism during the early modern period is still predominantly presented as a European story. Advancing a novel framework to understand the nature and impact of the Protestant Reformations, this volume brings together leading scholars to integrate global Protestant experiences into accounts of the early modern world created by the Reformations. It seeks to compare Protestant concepts and practices with other world religions, to chart colonial politics and encounters, and to ask how resulting ideas and identities were negotiated by Europeans at the time. Through its wide geographical and chronological scope, *Protestant Empires* advances a new way of understanding the Protestant Reformations. Showcasing selective model approaches on how to think anew and pointing the way towards multi-national and connected accounts of the period, this volume demonstrates how global interactions and their effect on Europe have played a crucial role in the history of the "long Reformation" in the seventeenth and eighteenth centuries.

ULINKA RUBLACK is Professor of European History at the University of Cambridge. She is the author of *Reformation Europe* (2nd revised edition, 2017), and editor of *The Oxford Handbook of the Protestant Reformations* (2016) and *The Concise Companion to History* (2011).

Protestant Empires

Globalizing the Reformations

Edited by
Ulinka Rublack
University of Cambridge

Shaftesbury Road, Cambridge CB2 8EA, United Kingdom

One Liberty Plaza, 20th Floor, New York, NY 10006, USA

477 Williamstown Road, Port Melbourne, VIC 3207, Australia

314–321, 3rd Floor, Plot 3, Splendor Forum, Jasola District Centre, New Delhi – 110025, India

103 Penang Road, #05–06/07, Visioncrest Commercial, Singapore 238467

Cambridge University Press is part of Cambridge University Press & Assessment, a department of the University of Cambridge.

We share the University's mission to contribute to society through the pursuit of education, learning and research at the highest international levels of excellence.

www.cambridge.org
Information on this title: www.cambridge.org/9781108794978

DOI: 10.1017/9781108894449

First published 2020
First paperback edition 2024

A catalogue record for this publication is available from the British Library

ISBN 978-1-108-84161-0 Hardback
ISBN 978-1-108-79497-8 Paperback

Contents

Figures

Contributors

SUSANNA BURGHARTZ is Professor of Renaissance and Early Modern History at the University of Basel. She has published widely on early modern gender and sexuality, Reformation and confessionalization, material culture, and early globalization. Her publications include "The Fabric of Early Globalisation: Skin, Fur and Cloth in the De Bry Travel Accounts, 1590–1630," in *Dressing Global Bodies*, ed. Beverly Lemire, Giorgio Riello (2019); *Sites of Mediation. Connected Histories of Places, Processes, and Objects in Europe and Beyond, 1450–1650*, ed. Susanna Burghartz, Lucas Burkart, Christine Göttler (2016); "Covered Women? Veiling in Early Modern Europe," *History Workshop Journal*, 80/1 (2015); *Staging New Worlds/Inszenierte Welten. Die west- und ostindischen Reisen der Verleger de Bry, 1590–1630 / De Bry's Illustrated Travel Reports, 1590–1630* (2004).

RENATE DÜRR is Professor of Early Modern History at the University of Tübingen. She has written on Lutheran church spaces as contested spaces in the early modern period for her habilitation. In the past few years she has worked on Jesuit missions, on cultural as well as linguistic translations in these contact zones, and on the connection between the Society of Jesus and Enlightenment. Recently, she has started to look into the global dimensions of early modern German history. Her analysis of Lutheran baptismal sermons concerning Muslim prisoners of war and African slaves is part of this new research interest.

ULRIKE GLEIXNER is Head of the Research Department at the Herzog August Library in Wolfenbüttel, Germany, and is Professor of Early Modern History at the Technical University Berlin/Zentrum für Interdisziplinäre Frauen-und Geschlechterforschung. Her research fields include the cultural history of religion, especially Pietism; autobiographical writings; the gender history of knowledge and memory culture; the materiality of books. She is currently working on a book with the working title *The Pietist Empire in India. Millenarian Practices and the German supporter network*.

ANTHONY GRAFTON is Henry Putnam University Professor of History at Princeton University. He is the author of ten monographs that focus on major Renaissance intellectual figures and knowledge practices, and the co-author, editor, co-editor, or translator of nine other books, including *Defenders of the Text* (1991) and *Bring Out Your Dead* (2001). He has been the recipient of the Balzan Prize for History of Humanities (2002), and the Mellon Foundation's Distinguished Achievement Award (2003). Professor Grafton is currently finishing a monograph on the science of chronology.

DAVID D. HALL is Bartlett Professor, emeritus, Harvard Divinity School. He has written widely on religion and culture in early New England and, more recently, on early modern Britain. His books include *The Puritans: A Transatlantic History* (2019); *A Reforming People: Puritanism and the Transformation of Public Life in Early New England* (2011); and *Worlds of Wonder, Days of Judgment Popular Religion in Seventeenth-Century New England* (1989).

NEIL KAMIL is an associate professor in the department of History at the University of Texas at Austin. He is the author of *Fortress of the Soul: Violence, Metaphysics, and Material Life in the Huguenots' New World, 1517–1751* (2005).

CHARLES H. PARKER is Professor of History at Saint Louis University. His research interests focus on the religious and cultural history of early modern Europe and interactions in world history. He is currently finishing a book on Calvinism and empire in the early modern world entitled *Global Calvinism: Conversion and Commerce in the Dutch Empire*.

CARLA GARDINA Pestana, the Joyce Appleby Endowed Chair of America in the World at UCLA, researches religion and empire in the English Atlantic context. She is the author, most recently, of the *English Conquest of Jamaica: Oliver Crowell's Bid for Empire* (2017), as well as of *Protestant Empire: Religion and the Making of the British Atlantic World* (2009). Harvard University/Belknap Press will publish *The World of Plymouth Planation* in 2020.

ULINKA RUBLACK is Professor of European History at Cambridge University. Her books include *Reformation Europe* (2nd expanded ed. 2017, Cambridge University Press), and, as editor, *The Oxford Handbook of the Protestant Reformations* (2016), as well as *The Concise Companion to History* (Oxford University Press, 2011).

JON SENSBACH teaches early American and Atlantic history at the University of Florida. He is the author of *A Separate Canaan: The*

Making of an Afro-Moravian World in North Carolina, 1763–1840 (North Carolina, 1998), and *Rebecca's Revival: Creating Black Christianity in the Atlantic World* (Harvard, 2005). He is at work on the life of Mary Prince and on the Impressionist artist Camille Pissarro's images of Afro-Caribbean people.

JACQUELINE VAN GENT is an early modern historian at the University of Western Australia. She has published widely on early modern gender, colonial encounters, emotions and religion. Her publications include *Gender, Power and Identity in the Early Modern Nassau Family, 1580–1814* (2016) and *Dynastic Colonialism: Gender, Materiality and the Early Modern House of Orange-Nassau* (2016) (both co-authored with S. Broomhall); "Emotions and Conversion" (2015) as a special Issue of *Journal of Religious History* (ed. with S. Young); "Gender, objects and emotions in Scandinavian history" (2016) as a special Issue of *Journal of Scandinavian History* (ed. with Raisa Toivo). She is currently writing a book-length study on Moravian global encounters in the eighteenth century.

JAMES VAN HORN MELTON is Professor of History and Chair of the department of Spanish and Portuguese at Emory University. His books include *Religion, Community, and Slavery on the Colonial Southern Frontier* (2015) and *The Rise of the Public in Enlightenment Europe* (2001), both published by Cambridge University Press.

MERRY WIESNER-HANKS is Distinguished Professor of History and Women's and Gender Studies, emerita, at the University of Wisconsin-Milwaukee. She is the long-time senior editor of the *Sixteenth Century Journal*, and the editor-in-chief of the seven-volume *Cambridge World History* (2015). She is the author or editor of thirty books and many articles and book chapters that have appeared in English, German, French, Italian, Spanish, Portuguese, Greek, Chinese, Turkish, and Korean.

Introduction

Ulinka Rublack

This volume advances a novel framework to understand the nature and impact of the Protestant Reformations. It starts from the assumption that it will be fruitful for the next decades of scholarship to investigate religious change as multi-centric across Western and non-Western worlds. Protestantism during the early modern period is currently predominantly presented as a European story, and, despite a growing awareness of European networks of exchange as well as scholarship on the history of missions, much research remains confined to national boundaries. Further dialogue between scholars of the European Reformations and early Americanists, and scholars of the Caribbean, Asia, and Africa is needed to enrich the way the entire subject is conceived and taught. Historians have adopted the concept of a "long Reformation" during the past decades, but they are only beginning to substantially integrate global Protestant experiences into their accounts of the early modern world created by the Reformations, to compare Protestant ideas and practices to other world religions, to chart colonial politics and experiences, and to ask how resulting ideas and identities were negotiated by Europeans at the time. Through its wide geographical and chronological scope, *Protestant Empires* aims to contribute to this change and showcases selective model approaches on just *how* to think anew.

A Europeanized Reformation

During the past decades, university courses, textbooks, and handbooks have Europeanized the Protestant Reformations and globalized the Catholic Reformations.[1] There are several historiographical and institutional reasons for this development. First among these is the influence of the confessionalization paradigm which newly invigorated Reformation history for three decades after 1980 but focused solely on a European path

[1] For a discussion and new departure, see Ulinka Rublack, "Introduction," in *The Oxford Handbook of the Protestant Reformations*, ed. Ulinka Rublack (Oxford: Oxford University Press, 2016), 1–22.

towards modernity.[2] This paradigm proposed that Lutheranism, Calvinism, and Catholicism consolidated their confessional profiles in Europe in similar ways during the sixteenth and seventeenth centuries. It argued that this supported state-building processes by enshrining new disciplinary norms among the population. Developed by Wolfgang Reinhard and Heinz Schilling, the paradigm challenged an entire tradition of segregated scholarship that had focused on either the Protestant or the Catholic Reformations and tended to equate only Protestantism with the features identified with modernity, such as greater rationalization. It also departed from the often intensely local and short-term focus of social historical studies, which had been influential from the 1960s onwards and typically explored the local implementation and impact of the Reformation in specific urban or rural communities as well as territories.

Confessionalization historians were informed by sociological approaches and interested in broad structures and comparisons. This meant that they had little time for the new cultural history that took off during the 1970s and 1980s. New cultural historians were influenced by anthropological approaches which led them to investigate historical belief-systems and identities through the rituals, symbols, and everyday practices which made sense to people at the time. They were interested in tracing the relationship of popular and elite cultures, the transgressions and the conflicts. New cultural historians equipped themselves to study the importance of kinship as well as the household as microorganisms of government, ideas about femininity and masculinity, sexuality and the body. They were fascinated by the way in which ideas about the supernatural and "magic" merged with Christian ideas in idiosyncratic ways long into the eighteenth century. All of their research challenged teleological views of modernity as unilinear processes of rationalization or the decline of familial ties, for instance.[3] Inspired by microhistory, such research often deeply mined local archives, contextualized case-stories or focused on one particular theme. It intersected with a new cultural history of the book that studied the reception, circulation, and transformation of ideas through practices of reading, annotating, and communication, which

[2] For an influential summary in English, see Heinz Schilling, "Confessional Europe," in *Handbook of European History 1400–1600*, ed. Thomas A. Brady, Heiko A. Oberman, and James D. Tracey (Leiden: Brill, 1995), 205–47, free access on the web www.pro-europa.eu/europe/schilling-heinz-confessional-europe/.

[3] For general approaches, see Peter Burke, *What Is Cultural History?*, 3rd ed. (Cambridge, UK: Polity, 2018), for the field of religious history more specifically, see Alexandra Walsham, "Migrations of the Holy: Explaining Religious Change in Medieval and Early Modern Europe," *Journal of Medieval and Early Modern History*, 44/2 (2014): 241–80.

were rooted in specific life-worlds.[4] The confessionalization paradigm, by contrast, intended to chart the authoritative standardization of ideas through catechisms, for instance, and to map the social disciplining of entire populations by multiple churches and states. It advanced long-term and comparative perspectives of change, but soon invited sustained debate. This eventually led to comprehensive criticism of its top-down nature, its focus on specific definitions of "modernity," and of its rigid framework and chronology. This debate was at its most vibrant between 1980 and 2010 and involved scholars on the continent, particularly in Germany and Switzerland.[5]

During the same period, it continued to be a major advance for British Reformation historians to transcend national frameworks in order to research the links between English and continental Reform ideas.[6] North American history remained a separate field of inquiry that often charted the history of one faith tradition in a specific locale, but its specialists became increasingly interested in popular beliefs and everyday religious practices.[7] Meanwhile, however, the study of Catholic missions, global encounters, and entanglements attracted enormous interest from the 1990s onwards. The field of Jesuit studies, in particular, began to witness remarkable growth. Such research documented how robust institutions and hierarchical structures, such as the Inquisition and bishoprics, or robust networks, such as the correspondence mandatory among Jesuits, fared in an early modern globalized world.[8]

Europeanists felt they could tell no comparable Protestant story, as Protestant powers during the early modern period were less insistent on converting indigenous people than their Catholic counterparts and implemented few of the institutional structures of its main confessions – Lutheranism and Reformed Calvinism – abroad. Protestant powers were primarily interested in trade and settlement. They did not conduct mass

[4] Here the scholarship of Carlo Ginzburg, Robert Darnton, Anthony Grafton, and Lisa Jardine has led the field. For a summary, see Burke, *Cultural History*.

[5] For a valuable overview, see Stefan Ehrenpreis, Ute Lotz-Heumann, *Reformation und konfessionelles Zeitalter* (Darmstadt: WBG, 2002), 62–74; for a review of debates since then, see Birgit Emich, "Konfession und Kultur, Konfession als Kultur? Vorschläge für eine kulturalistische Konfessionskulur-Forschung," *Archiv für Reformationsgeschichte* 109 (2018): 375–88.

[6] See the landmark publications by Diarmaid McCulloch, *Thomas Cranmer: A Life* (New Haven, CT: Yale University Press, 1996); *Reformation: Europe's House Divided 1490–1700* (London: Penguin, 2004).

[7] For a wide-ranging landmark study, see David D. Hall, *Worlds of Wonder, Days of Judgement: Popular Religious Belief in Early New England* (New York: A. Knopf, 1989).

[8] For an incisive discussion, see Simon Richard Ditchfield, "Catholic Reformation and Renewal," in *The Oxford Illustrated History of the Reformation*, ed. Peter Marshall (Oxford: Oxford University Press, 2015), 152–85.

baptisms, and they worked with far fewer clergymen through a far more dispersed church structure in Europe that furthermore had abolished religious orders. In contrast to Catholicism, Protestant churches also played a less substantial role as property owners and in the credit markets of local societies outside Europe during the early modern period. Hence, Reformation historians have held Protestantism to be primarily interesting as a European phenomenon, sidelining the story of dissenting traditions.

Disciplinary boundaries shaped this research landscape. Most dialogue between European and US historians of the Reformations continued to focus on European history, and early Americanists seemed only rarely to join the conversation. Protestant Reformation historians in the United States were often tasked to teach European history only, while early modern Europeanists based in European universities rarely attended to religious dimensions in the history of the Dutch Empire or of Britain and British America, let alone of other parts of the world.[9] The history of Protestant "missions" was treated as a separate field and focused on the "modern" period from 1800 onwards.

New Comparative Approaches

Slowly, a new field of inquiry and different approaches began to emerge. In 1995, Natalie Zemon Davis used the lens of a historian trained in micro-history and the analysis of ego-documents to tell the parallel stories of three women. One of them was Glückel von Hameln, a Jewish woman in Hamburg; another Marie de l'Incarnation, a Catholic nun who migrated to Quebec; and the third of these women was Maria Sibylla Merian, a Protestant artist who observed flora and fauna in the Dutch colony of Suriname. Davis explored how a turn to naturalistic observation, movement, and migration shaped novel experiences, practices, and religious ideas, and showed how global travel had become a possibility even for women. Indigenous natives and slaves shared their knowledge about the uses of plants with Merian, who belonged to the Labadists, a radical Protestant faith group centered in the Netherlands. In contrast to father Labadie, Merian never once referred to those she encountered in Suriname as "savages" and she trusted the authority of her "go-betweens."[10] This approach showed that highly local encounters could reshape views of

[9] For an excellent insight into these, see Philip Benedict, "Global? Has Reformation History Even Gotten Transnational Yet?," *Archiv für Reformationsgeschichte – Archive for Reformationhistory*, 108/1 (2017): 52–62.

[10] Natalie Zemon Davis, *Women on the Margins: Three Seventeenth-Century Lives* (Cambridge, MA: Harvard University Press 1995).

humanity, race, religion, and the imprint of God's nature on the globe that were mediated through Merian's work in Europe.

In 2000, Merry Wiesner-Hanks – initially a historian of Reformation Germany – contributed to the widening scope of comparative research in her landmark account *Christianity and Sexuality in the Early Modern World*. This charted how Christianity regulated the sexual and marital lives of both Europeans and their colonial subjects. The book included separate chapters on Catholicism and on Protestantism in early modern Europe as well as on their global impact on North America, Latin America, Africa, and Asia. It highlighted, for example, the ways in which the Dutch Empire could markedly interfere with local attitudes to promiscuity or female animist prophetesses in colonies such as Formosa. The Dutch attempted to establish a society based on male religious experts, married couples, and households. At the same time, Wiesner-Hanks also outlined the problems in staffing that beset the project, and the way in which Protestant messages were adapted in catechisms and altered in response to indigenous ideas.[11] Above all, this showed that historians of the Reformation could widen their scope from Eurocentric discussions and think about parallel movements.

The European fear of and debate about old women as witches, for instance, directly related to the ways in which Dutch Calvinist ministers would look at *inibs*, elderly women on Formosa who were associated with greater spiritual power than priests and were tasked with ritually asking for rain through drinking alcohol while standing naked on top of roofs, urinating and vomiting. Chiu Hsin-Hui's 2008 monograph on Dutch Formosa further detailed that by 1651, after twenty years of missionary efforts, 250 of these women were banished, 202 had died, while 48 survived banishment and were placed under the supervision of clergymen. Local elders could collaborate in these policies, but their implementation was often improvised, marked by uncertainty about which spiritual authority to adopt, and resistance to missionary efforts.[12]

As the influence of global and transnational history grew after the 1990s, interest in "connected" histories became ever more marked. Jorge Cañizares-Esguerra's influential *Puritan Conquistadors* (2006) argued that the British Protestant expansion shared much in common intellectually with the Iberian Catholic expansion. In search for these

[11] Merry Wiesner-Hanks, *Christianity and Sexuality in the Early Modern World: Regulating Desire, Reforming Practice*, 2nd ed. (Abingdon, VA: Routledge, 2010).

[12] William M. Campbell ed., *Formosa under the Dutch: Described from Contemporary Sources with Explanatory notes and a Bibliography for the Island* (Taipei: SMC Publishing, 1992); Chiu Hsin-Hui, *The Colonial "Civilising Process" in Dutch Formosa, 1624–62* (Leiden: Brill, 2008), esp. 212.

similarities, Cañizares-Esguerra particularly focused on ideas about chivalrous conquest as well as on religious idioms in a selection of Puritan sermons and Protestant literary works that equated wilderness with the heretical, for instance by evoking spiritually charged imagery of planting and weeding. This approach sought to newly conceptualize an American Atlantic history as Pan-American, and more broadly investigated the role of religion in US American historical myths of nationhood and Western achievement, which consolidated a patronizing attitude towards Catholic Latin America and its heritage. Cañizares-Esguerra's challenge of narratives of Western supremacy as rooted in Protestant traditions and values of freedom was echoed by many others who highlighted the extent of Protestant people's involvement with colonialism and slaveholding.[13] David Armitage's groundbreaking *The Ideological Origins of the British Empire* (2000) meanwhile had already deconstructed the idea that British imperial ideology was underpinned by exclusively Protestant ideas – he pointed to the importance of classical traditions in Catholic and Protestant writers' justifications for empire building.[14]

Sir John Elliott's *Empires of the Atlantic World*, also published in 2006, compared practices of state-building and its ideologies in Spanish and British America by scrutinizing the role of religion and churches and by taking a closer look at similarities and differences than Cañizares-Esguerra had done. A shared theological inheritance indeed led to many points of convergence and related imagery – not least in ideas about an omnipotent God and the nature of the demonic. Yet in practice, as Elliott pointed out, malefic magic seemed to have been given greater prominence in New England than in New Spain. The financing of the churches utterly differed – nothing in the Protestant world equalled the massive accumulation of real estate by the church in Spanish America. Protestants, moreover, were bound together by their rejection of papal authority in the name of the superior authority of the biblical word. This meant that diverse interpretations of the Bible led to different Protestant creeds; this "fissiparous character of Protestantism was compounded in British America by the fissiparous character of the process of settlement and colonization."[15] By the end of the seventeenth century, Elliott concluded, British American religion "stood in a very different relationship to

[13] Jorge Cañizares-Esguerra, *Puritan Conquistadors: Iberianizing the Atlantic, 1550–1700* (Stanford, CA: Stanford University Press, 2006).

[14] David Armitage, *The Ideological Origins of the British Empire* (Cambridge: Cambridge University Press, 2000).

[15] John Elliott, *Empires of the Atlantic World: Britain and Spain in America 1492–1830* (New Haven, CT: Yale University Press, 2006), 207 and especially his chapter 7 on "America as Sacred Space," 184–219.

both society and the state from that which prevailed in the American territories of the Spanish crown." Religious diversity was interlinked with political plurality. British America appeared as "an atomized society in a continuous state of political turmoil," marked by tensions about ideas of liberty. These, in Elliott's reading, could be resolved to some extent in a shared commitment to a biblical culture that also encouraged greater literacy. Just like Cañizares-Esguerra, Elliott criticized the idealized portrayals of Protestant British America that emerged during the eighteenth-century, linking it to liberty and cultures of ingenuity. These, he remarked, "easily air-brushed" indigenous and African people "out of the picture," and long remained foundational in accounts of the Spanish Empire as locked in tyranny.[16]

While Elliott, nonetheless, admitted to focusing on settlers rather than on the indigenous populations, Carla Pestana's *Protestant Empire* (2009) broke new ground by asking central questions about the ways in which all religions changed as a result of movement and cultural encounters across 300 years in the British Atlantic – European Christianity no less than Native American or Afro-American spirituality – and how they responded to the coming together of different Protestant, Catholic, and Non-Christian traditions in particular locales. Yoruba and biblical myths of origin, for example, needed to be explored side-by-side, as did ideas of progress. The "act of moving," she posited, "changed people and their beliefs."[17] Pestana hence highlighted the importance of give and take through negotiations in religious encounters and explored in detail how different beliefs clashed or blended, for what reasons and with which results. As in her essay for this volume, she underlined the different face of the Church of England in the colonies: church buildings, books, communion plates, and vestments all required a daunting investment. Worship services based on prayer books became its most robust structure. As religious diversity grew between the 1640s and 1660s among different Protestant faith groups, transatlantic radicalism among Quakers particularly flourished from its early centers in Barbados and on Rhode Island and helped to generate key ideas in debates about religious liberty. Millennial ideas actioned social change before the second coming of Christ and the imminent end of the world, and led to connections with European Jews as well as to the growth of Jewish settlements in the English colony of Suriname, Jamaica, and Rhode Island. Hope that missionizing might convert those who belonged to other religious

[16] Elliott, *Empires*, 403–5.

[17] Carla Gardina Pestana, *Protestant Empire: Religion and the Making of the British Atlantic World* (Philadelphia: University of Pennsylvania Press, 2009), 7.

traditions now also extended to the Indians, who were often categorized as descendants of Jews. The impact of such missions was highly local but stood in marked contrast to the much longer reluctance to Christianize slaves or convert Catholic slaves to Protestantism. Above all, Pestana detailed the extraordinary picture of Protestant colonial diversity in North America, which by 1683 included the Labadist community of "New Bohemia" as a first separatist experiment, alongside Mennonites, French Huguenots, Swedish or German Lutherans, German Pietists, Walloon Calvinists, Dutch Reformed believers, among others. All of them transplanted and transformed their own traditions in ways that could link to contingency and local adaptation as much as to systemic economic interests and political shifts.[18] An emphasis merely on the similarities between these traditions and Catholicism would be insufficient to capture the dynamic of Protestant practices and ideas.

The purpose of this book is to build on Pestana's and Wiesner-Hanks's pioneering works. This entails mapping out a wider geography of plural *Protestant Empires* and explains the book's title. Further, the title is intended to suggest that empires of the mind, or failed and short-lived practices, are as interesting as long-term and politically stable structures. Given the limited amount of comparative research and in order to be able to more precisely map out similarities and differences in relation to Catholic Empires or other faith traditions, it is crucial to sharpen our understanding of the scope and nature of Protestant experiences through their encounter with other faith traditions in the Americas as much as in Asia, the Mediterranean, or the Ottoman Empire from the sixteenth century onwards. In an overview article "The Reformation in Global Perspective," published in 2014, Charles H. Parker observed that "the study of Protestants in overseas environments" for the early modern period was "not nearly as extensive or theoretically well developed as it is for Catholic missionaries or institutions." "According to standard narratives," he elaborated, "Protestants were either uninterested or incapable of converting native peoples outside of exceptional and short-lived episodes in Massachusetts and Taiwan, until the great Pietistic revivals of the nineteenth and twentieth centuries."[19] Yet Parker also pointed to recent Dutch studies that had argued for far more significant successes given the limited resources available, especially in Batavia and the Molucca Islands. The Reformed Church in Batavia, for instance, is now estimated to have had around 5,000 members by 1700, most of

[18] Pestana, *Protestant Empire,* here 6–7.

[19] Charles H. Parker, "The Reformation in Global Perspective," *History Compass* 12/12 (2014): 924–34, here 926.

whom were Portuguese-speaking freed slaves who were converted from Catholicism. D. L. Noorlander has recently built on such research to argue that the Dutch Reformed Church was integral to Dutch colonization and that the WIC's religious activities were interrelated with its secular goals: "a deep religious sensibility and social, institutional commitment to the Dutch Reformed Church and its politics permeated the WIC and influenced its plans and activities." Lay clergy supported the small number of paid, ordained ministers. Their ratio in relation to the size of the population was not too dissimilar from staffing in the Dutch Republic.[20] Dutch missionary power reached its modest highpoint during the 1640s. It missionized among the Tupi in Brazil as well as among black slaves. In Africa, there "was a new school at Elmina, a few clergy and schoolmasters in Luanda, and a foothold in the kingdom of Kongo."[21] Parker's contribution in 2014, however, also underlined the importance of looking at Protestant experiences in or through global settings aside from this focus on conversion. As he further explores in his contribution to this volume, major intellectuals, including the Dutch philosopher Hugo Grotius, constructed an "ecumenical and ethical Christianity as a response to both domestic and global points of reference."[22] An understanding of how religious knowledge was created in Europe can therefore be globalized.

The most recent research, moreover, continues to turn up new and unexpected aspects of Protestant translations and brokerage that emerged from the remarkable intersections of several cultures and faiths in global locales. The ethnomusicologist David R. M. Irving, for instance, has shown that the Genevan Psalter was translated into several local Asian languages in and for eighteenth-century Indonesia and Sri Lanka. The Psalter with its Swiss musical settings was based solely on the Psalms of David and translated "into Portuguese (a language traditionally associated with Catholicism), Tamil (associated with Hinduism), Sinhala (associated with Buddhism) and Malay (associated with Islam)." It was printed by the presses of the Dutch East India Company in the two major port cities of Java and Sri Lanka for use by Asian and Eurasian communities.[23] The slim and portable Tamil version was printed in Colombo and translated by Philippus de Melho (b. 1723), a Sri Lankan Tamil who was the first native minister of Ceylon's Dutch Reformed Church. The result was a musical hybrid that attributed indigenous

[20] D. L. Noorlander, *Heaven's Wrath: The Protestant Reformation and the Dutch West India Company in the Atlantic World* (Ithaca, NY: Cornell University Press, 2019), 218, 225.

[21] Ibid., 180. [22] Ibid., 929.

[23] David R. M. Irving, "The Genevan Psalter in Eighteenth-Century Indonesia and Sri Lanka," *Eighteenth-Century Music*, 11/2 (2014): 235–55, here 235.

syllables to each note. Melho acted as a go-between who knew how to combine European staff notation with South Asian musical *nomenclatura* to further the reach of congregational singing among the indigenous population. For Calvinists, psalm singing provided the most direct communication with God. It was an embodied practice that crucially linked to ideas about measured emotions and civility. The Psalter's melodies were correspondingly measured, and thus regarded by Calvinists as "pure" music in contrast to other types of music they feared as inciting lasciviousness and other ungodly sentiments.[24]

This volume's principal focus on Protestantism is therefore not directed against attempts to provide more unified accounts of religious change in the age of Protestant and Catholic Reformations or comparisons of the Protestant and Catholic Reformations. These have recently successfully focused on themes such as the greater awareness of normative relativism which emerged from encounters with the Americas, or the importance of exile and social purification. Lee Palmer Wandel's *The Reformation: A New History* (2011) demonstrates how the intellectual dislocation caused by the Reformation ran parallel to the unsettling of European views about the sacred through an encounter with the New World, and was mediated by print.[25] Nicholas Terpstra's "alternative history of the Reformation," published in 2015, shows that the Catholic and Protestant Reformations were "Europe's first grand project in social purification." Its account of Christian experiences nonetheless overwhelmingly focuses on how elites enforced exile and how this reshaped European society, rather than integrating, for instance, the history of British America to show how Protestant refugee experiences reshaped wider parts of the globe.[26] By using the methodological insights of pioneering studies on the later Protestant missions, this volume seeks to contribute to building better foundations for comparison and for further work interlinking research on the early modern period.[27]

[24] Ulinka Rublack, *Reformation Europe*, 2nd ed. (Cambridge: Cambridge University Press, 2017), 233. The experience in borderlands rather than contact zones could be very different, as Lutheran missionaries in Scandinavia sought to root out Sami traditions of drumming, which they likewise thought of as heathen, see Cat., *Der Luthereffekt* (Berlin: Deutsches Museum 2017).

[25] Lee Palmer Wandel, *The Reformation: A New History* (Cambridge: Cambridge University Press, 2011).

[26] Nicholas Terpstra, *Religious Refugees in the Early Modern World: An Alternative History of the Reformation* (Cambridge: Cambridge University Press, 2015).

[27] For an important book series in this area, founded in 2013, see Crawford Gribben and Scott Spurlock eds., *Christianities in the Trans-Atlantic World* (New York: Palgrave Macmillian, 2013–); as well as Sujit Sivasundaram, *Nature and the Godly Empire: Science and Evangelical Missions in the Pacific, 1795–1850* (Cambridge: Cambridge University Press, 2005).

Entanglement and Its Limits

A commitment to understanding "entanglements" and "connected histories" remains key for all contributions. Put simply, the goal is to highlight the ways in which existing attitudes framed practices and ideas and then shifted in new locales, which in turn reflected back upon European understandings. The concept of such "entanglements" in encounters has replaced the idea that cultures were necessarily entirely separate from each other, that they clashed or had to be forcefully acculturated. "Rather," as Sanjay Subrahmanyam has put it, "what usually happened was approximation, improvisation, and eventually a shift in the relative positions of all concerned." People of other cultures could be as involved in building bridges or functioning as go-betweens as Europeans themselves, and historians have increasingly charted their motives and investment in those processes.[28] For the history of Protestant faiths, as several contributions to this volume document, it has thus been important to recognize how many indigenous women and slave women gained new social roles and types of authority through their involvement in churches, and to examine their role as translators.

A striking biographical example of a male go-between is offered by the short-lived Jacobus Eliza Joannes Capitein (1717–1747), who was born as a slave in Ghana, taken to Holland aged eleven, and eventually studied theology at Leiden (Fig 0.1). Having justified slavery in his dissertation, Capitein returned to Ghana in 1742 as a minister and translated the Lord's Prayer and the Ten Commandments into local languages with the inclusive rendering "Father of all of us" at the start. He enthusiastically ran and extended a multi-racial primary school in the town of Elmina that included black and mixed-race children. He became more critical of slavery and struggled with the control mechanisms imposed by the Dutch church, which prohibited his marriage to a local black woman who was not Christianized. Capitein was forced to marry a Dutch woman, but he continued to ask questions which confronted his Dutch superiors with the inconsistencies in their ideas about sexuality, religion, and race.[29]

[28] Sanjay Subrahmanyam, *Courtly Encounters. Translating Courtliness and Violence in Early Modern Eurasia* (Cambridge, MA: Harvard University Press, 2012), 29; see also Simon Schaffer et al. eds., *Go-Betweens and Global Intelligence, 1770–1820* (Segamore Beach: Watson publishing, 2009).

[29] For a brief treatment of this, see Charles R. Boxer, *The Dutch Sea-Borne Empire 1600–1800* (London: Penguin, 1965), 170–71, 180, for a recent and highly interesting reading, see Christine Leveq, "Jacobus Capitein: Dutch Calvinist and Black Cosmopolitan," *Research in African Literatures*, 44/4 (Winter 2013): 145–66.

Fig 0.1 Pieter Tanje, *Jacobus Eliza Joannes Capitein 1742*, Rijksmuseum

As critics of entangled approaches have noted, it remains crucial to carefully investigate to what extent experiences in a colonial locale really did influence European policies and perceptions elsewhere or at home. If "ideas and concepts only operate in a particular historical and cultural context and in so doing are transformed," historians need to explain whether and how they were communicated beyond that specific context to precisely outline their reach.[30] Jonathan Israel, for instance, has argued that the unusual amount of tolerance the Dutch conceded to Jews and Catholics during their twenty-four year interlude in Brazil (1630–1654) seems to "have had very little, if any, symbolic significance either for the late seventeenth-century European toleration debate where this topic, seemingly, is virtually never mentioned or indeed for the Enlightenment proper." Sephardic Jews were granted greater liberties in Dutch Brazil because of their language skills, money, and experience with the sugar industries. Lutherans, by contrast, were excluded from tolerant policies. After Governor Johann Mauritz's departure, tolerance was further restricted, while Catholics were banned from worshipping in Suriname, for instance, until 1787 (Fig 0.2). "Even in the case of the Jews, the specific toleration prevailing after 1667 in Suriname did not entail the extension of comparable Jewish privileges, on a lasting basis, to the West Guyana colonies of Berbice, Essequibo, and Pomeroon."[31] As historians of Europe have likewise stressed, "tolerance" was therefore certainly founded on pragmatism, and its framework needs to be explored in its own right. Yet on the other hand, as Charles Parker argues in his contribution, we can certainly observe crucial shifts in the intellectual framework towards Enlightened debates, which would have been unthinkable without the need for university professors of oriental languages or theology who sought to more successfully train colonial missionaries to respond to experiences in the Dutch Empire. A broader range of texts needs to be taken into consideration to explore closely contextualized discursive changes.

Protestantism, of course, is often equated with the mythical movement towards tolerance, freedom of conscience, free inquiry, democracy, and believers' more "individual" relationship with God.[32] Several chapters in this volume further contribute to our understanding of how global perspectives can challenge this narrative. As Renate Dürr, Ulrike Gleixner, and Jon Sensbach underline, Protestantism needs to be confronted with its deep entanglement with slavery and forced migration in the Mediterranean as much as in the Atlantic world and Asia. Susanna Burghartz meanwhile shows how the mediation of ideas was linked to market forces in publishing. From the sixteenth century onwards, for

[30] Shruti Kapila, "Preface," in *An Intellectual History for India*, ed. Shruti Kapila (Cambridge: Cambridge University Press, 2012), vii.

[31] Jonathan Israel and Stuart B. Schwartz, *The Expansion of Tolerance: Religion in Dutch Brazil (1624–1654)* (Amsterdam: Amsterdam University Press, 2007), 1–32.

[32] Alec Ryrie, *Protestants: The Radicals Who Made the Modern World* (London: William Collins, 2008).

Fig 0.2 Theodor Matham after Frans Jansz Post, *Portrait of Johann Moritz van Nassau-Siegen with his motto "As Far as the World Extends,"* 1635–1676, engraving, Rijksmuseum

instance, European religious identities could be sustained by the medialization of images of abhorrent non-European idolatry. Anthony Grafton and Neil Kamil moreover stress that an understanding of books by Protestants was not necessarily individualized but could be strongly shaped by family traditions, as annotated books were bequeathed over generations and libraries formed the learned reputation of descendants. Alchemical thinking, moreover, was central to elite and artisanal making and thinking in France and England as much as in North America.

By challenging unilinear narratives of change towards modernity, the volume thus chooses not to approach a global history of Protestantism through a comparison of "world civilizations" via a selection of theological writings.[33] Rather, it highlights the importance of densely researched case studies of cultural and intellectual encounter informed by questions derived from the history of knowledge and the anthropology of religion. These, in sum, suggest that there is fruitfulness in the following lines of inquiry: How were global Protestantisms formed in particular sites and through particular interpretative communities, institutions, and media of communication that were rooted in interaction with symbols and the imaginary of the time; and how did they connect with other locales and undergo processes of translation? How can we move away from an institutional history of European missions towards a connected cultural history? Who created knowledge about religion and where? How could this authority be claimed and defended, and how was this knowledge organized, disseminated, and controlled? How contested was it inside and outside of movements, and what new forms of inquiry, explanation, and argument did such knowledge-making generate? How can we investigate the cultural and emotional meanings behind ideas of the divine, and how did Protestant perceptions and practices shape everyday life, demarcations of the feminine or masculine, ethnic stereotypes, commercial practices, notions of temporality, of violence, spatiality, the sensuous, and of visual and material culture? Protestants went on different paths in marking difference to or excluding specific groups, in mapping out internal hierarchies, inter-faith relations, attitudes towards science and commerce, or moral discourses on issues such as social inequality or ethnicized politics. These plural histories in global interactions and their effect on Europe form part of a history of the "long Reformation" in the seventeenth and eighteenth centuries properly conceived (Fig 0.3).

A commitment to this novel framework connects contributors and lends the volume its coherence and momentum. Eleven contributions present major case studies. These begin with a challenging new account of "Puritans" in early America and end with a fundamental reworking of the famous story of Mary Prince, the nineteenth-century

[33] This approach is attempted by Heinz Schilling and Silvana Seidel Menchi eds., *The Protestant Reformation in a Context of Global History: Religious Reforms and World Civilisations* (Berlin: Dunker und Humblot, 2017).

Fig 0.3 Gesina ter Borch, *Hillegonda Louise Schellinger in Curaçao*, 1680, Rijksmuseum

abolitionist who became the first black woman to publish an autobiography and lived in London. The volume broadly follows chronologies, but certainly does not take them as a structuring feature with which to map the march of Protestantism around the world. Instead, as we have seen, it asks centrally about the circulation and translation of ideas, the role of media, and of sermons or performances in providing imagined or real contact zones, as well as the accommodation and pluralization of beliefs and practices in local milieus.

Protestant Empires does not aim to be comprehensive in its coverage of all strands of Protestantism, but it significantly extends the scope beyond research on the British Atlantic by including scholarship, for instance, on German Lutheranism, French Huguenots, or on Calvinists employed by the United East India Company. It therefore moves past an institutional history of missions by incorporating questions about the ways in which other faiths were imagined by Protestants, or how, for instance, the conversion of Muslims was ritualized and medialized in Europe. Questions about the nature of religious encounters among people of different Christian faiths in relation to their European traditions are richly explored. Several contributions show how conceptions of resistance, gender, or the supernatural were worked out in distinctive ways; how different religious emotions were learned and made to matter. These emphasize that visual and object cultures played a key role in translating faith. Alongside this interest in practices of belief the volume consistently looks at the importance of learned traditions, which included artisanal or alchemical knowledge in particular milieus. A repudiation of "mentalist" in favour of "materialist" approaches towards the study of religious cultures is unhelpful. Instead, our contributors analyze how Dutch university scholars shaped attitudes towards Muslims in Southeast Asia, how European humanism could be accommodated, adapted, and expanded in North America, or how French Huguenots invented new material aesthetics in relation to their beliefs. The importance of millenarianism in Pietist missions and its links to Enlightened thought are likewise brought out, while the story of Mary Prince reveals how the genre conventions of a spiritual autobiography concealed far more complex spiritual worlds. Taken together, this underlines the importance of a broadly conceived intellectual history of global Protestantism which investigates the circulation of ideas and their framing in nuanced ways.

Connectivities and Comparisons

Carla Pestana begins the volume by exploding one of the most influential Protestant myths of origin in an examination of the English religious migrants who first settled in Leiden and then in Plymouth Plantation in 1620. Cast as "forefathers" and "pilgrims" since the eighteenth century, their alleged purity amidst hardship and the fight for religious freedom became the major building block of a US national mythology that remains foundational in the celebration of Thanksgiving to this day. Pestana closely examines the sources to reveal that these migrants confronted the same structural difficulties as any migrant church, battling with issues of adequate staffing of ministers and the definition of membership. For the first nine years of their settlement they had no minister at all and were not exacting in their demands for "purity" among those who attended gatherings. Many more people arrived with the Great Migration in 1630. This created its own difficulties in deciding which practices should be followed and which boundaries between the "pure" and "impure" should be drawn. Meanwhile, Plymouth, like other Atlantic locations, proved an attractive prospect for predators: in at least one known case a minister who raped a number of parishioners had to be brought to court in England. Pestana concludes: "Even the best-known colonies – the easily categorized places – in practice had complex and contingent relationships to their purported identities." The Leiden church was not transplanted, rather it was a "mixed community struggling to gain common ground." Attempts to monumentalize its members as heroes of piety, tolerance, and dedication appear to have been hopelessly overblown.

David Hall's contribution turns to Massachusetts and to the exceptional source material of lay people's "relations" in Cambridge during the decade 1638–1648 as well as to sermons preached by Thomas Shepard, a graduate of the "old world" Cambridge. Hall underlines that these men and women often felt profoundly alienated from their churches and from ineffective pastors in England, and they therefore practiced alternative forms of worship for the "precise" through prayer meetings and psalm singing in conventicles. Cambridge, Massachusetts meant church building, and this brought with it tensions about the control of "pure" behavior and thus membership. Hall examines the psychological costs of this process. Above all, the uneasy feelings of "spiritual deadness" were mixed with anxiety about hypocrites and a deep insecurity about what might make one worthy to receive God's grace. These reveal the continuities between old and New England as well as new urgencies in an Atlantic locale. As this community's minister, Thomas Shepard, too, had different voices within him that were linked to his English upbringing and education as much as to the people he now had to guide through life as his flock. His stress on humility, repentance, and the difficult road to salvation formed a tension with his message of mutual love and his "children's innocence." Parishioners responded to these registers in different ways. Their experiences cannot be easily slotted into the commonplace notion that Protestantism furthered greater "rationalism" or a more individualized relationship to the divine. Just as in Europe, the church, with its entrenched mechanisms of inclusion and exclusion, and its male ministers, powerfully shaped faith and religious struggles in ways which were linked to doctrinal questions of sin and grace as much as to ideas about gender and authority.

Social Histories of Protestant Knowledge

Anthony Grafton's contribution continues to highlight the importance of drawing a far more complex and nuanced map to show how the old world interlinked with the new. He turns to the later seventeenth and eighteenth centuries to examine the ways in which attitudes to a wide variety of books and reading that were shaped in Europe significantly influenced the lives of New Englanders. The history of how these men and women read and of how they worked with the books they sourced from Europe has barely begun to be written. Grafton focuses on Francis Daniel Pastorius, a German lawyer who had studied in Altdorf and founded Germantown; on James Logan, a fur-trader and powerful Pennsylvanian, who built a collection of almost 4,000 books; and on the Winthrop family and their uses of books. Protestant late humanist practices of systemic, interpretive reading, and of annotating and excerpting as a way to manage knowledge and gain orientation in the world guided these avid readers. Pastorius (1651–1719) drew on books in classical languages as well as in German, Dutch, and English. These were not mere dusty tomes: reading could be politically explosive. For instance, a seventeenth-century Dutch book informed Pastorius's radical stance that all humans around the globe were divinely created and that slavery must be abolished. Needless to say, not all books led to the same ideas, and their reception was embedded in the different practices of sharing them. Pastorius, for instance, discussed his ideas with women and was more flexible in spirit than the Winthrops. John Winthrop and his circles, by contrast, saw reading in part as an exercise through which he might fortify himself against the lure of mad love and evil feminine temptation. A practice which appeared to make him fear the threat of witchcraft all the more. His son Wait was one of the judges at the trials in Salem in 1692, and Grafton suggests that John's library helped to create his own reputation as learned man. Book annotations reveal that much of this learning was not about a more "rational," "modern" religion in spirit, but was rather concerned with the invisible power of the unseen – devils, angels, witches, and divine providence.

This explains why it remains a crucial part of study to attend to the complex spiritual crucible of early modern Protestant ideas as they made sense of their own worlds. Alchemical ideas about the transmutation of matter and spirit were extremely influential. This was true for elites, who paired libraries with laboratories, as well as for many artisans, who made these ideas their living. Protestantism has often been seen as a movement that repudiated the material world as profane, but this view can easily be challenged. Instead, we need to ask how ideas about the material and nature were spiritualized and how they were made to matter and by whom in particular contexts. Neil Kamil's essay focuses on the little-known entrepreneur Jacques Fontaine (1658–1728), a Huguenot refugee who left behind a lengthy account of his life. Together with his wife and sister-in-law, Fontaine invented a small, portable fire machine to produce a cheap imitation-silk finish on woolen textiles. Cheap, "little" materials, such as wool, could be ennobled through their surface treatment. Such ingenuity in spirit led to polished appearances, and these "New Luxuries" were manufactured by highly skilled refugee Huguenot artisans scattered throughout the Atlantic after the Revocation of the Edict of Nantes (1685). Fontaine modelled himself on St. Paul and the Huguenot potter Bernard Palissy (1510–1590), both of whom were artisans and preachers. Kamil shows that Fontaine and his descendants formed a multi-generational, transatlantic link to Palissy, who is best known for his earthenware dishes which featured many casts of earth-bound, "lowly" animals, such as snakes and worms. Kamil traces the influence of his origin story as "the first Reformed artisan from the 'primitive church' of Saintonge to represent alchemical death and rebirth as the pious artisan's way to achieve material and spiritual translucency in refuge." Fontaine instructed his transatlantic family to follow this as a strategy for self-improvement over a century later. Ten thousand French religious refugees traveled across the Atlantic or further afield to the Indian Ocean, and most of them settled in British America. Atlantic networks of knowledge, alchemical, and religious ideas thus fired a Protestantism that led to technological change and merged with strong ideas about politeness that were at the heart of the consumer and industrial revolutions. Material objects, from textiles to furniture, constituted Protestant identities in ways that interlinked Europe and British America in their quest to define taste. This tells a far more interesting story than the traditional focus on the reduced aesthetics of Puritan meetings houses or Shaker styles has allowed us to see.

Protestant commercial activity was, of course, also linked to activity in the burgeoning book market. Susanna Burghartz's essay is about the most famous Protestant cultural entrepreneurs in the business, the de Bry family. Theodor de Bry, his sons, Johann Theodor and Johann Israel, and their son-in-law, Matthäus Merian, chronicled the European expansion in elegant folio volumes, replete with fine illustrations. Much movement had shaped the de Brys' experience before they settled in Frankfurt in 1590 to produce this first global Protestant travel collection. Their enterprise used to be seen as a Calvinist vehicle to denounce the Catholic expansion as dehumanizing and motivated by greed, but recent research has challenged this view. Building on such research, Burghartz demonstrates how the de Brys used Calvinist migrant knowledge but aimed their work at a broad readership beyond all confessional barriers. The essay then focuses on the de Brys' conflicted attitude to images – both in print and as "idols." Fascinated by South American goldwork, Burghartz explains how the de Brys valued their indigenous colleagues as equal while harshly condemning the production of idols and idolatrous images and rituals by heathens as well as by Catholics. Yet their own use of images was not just didactic, but also sensuous and aesthetic in its refinement. It turned readers into eyewitnesses, secured the book market, and continues to define our pictorial archive of the beginnings of the European expansion. These findings correspond to Bridget Heal's recent work on Protestant uses of the image in the seventeenth and eighteenth centuries, which likewise questions the notion that Protestants so feared the power of images that they reduced them to didactic tools to "rationalize" their power and appeal.[34] Protestantism has often been linked to the importance of print as a cultural sphere so as to imply that books only consisted of words. The printed image and arguments about Protestant uses of the visual beyond Reformation broadsheets is clearly a fertile field of enquiry. Burghartz emphasizes the need for Calvinists to also distance themselves from the Muslim hostility to images: "If they wished to be successful on the European market," she thus concludes, "Calvinist goldsmiths and publishers like the de Brys had to adopt a rather paradoxical stance, at once positioning themselves critically towards idolatry and emphasizing the particular significance of the skillful artistic portrayal of God's wonders."

Burghartz therefore shows how relevant the notion of "entanglement" is to unlock European Protestant identities in new ways. In 1599, for instance, the Protestant German duke Frederick I of Württemberg built a public entertainment that closely referenced the de Brys' recent depiction of Virginia. The Lutheran ruler himself paraded as Queen America and was accompanied by his politically influential officers, all of whom were clad in skins and American featherwork. The Württemberg court went to great lengths to source authentic American featherwork via the Netherlands and then recreated further items. The de Brys' travel books therefore interlinked with the trade and collecting that furnished elite cabinets of curiosities, but in this case also helped to make a far wider point. The duke used knowledge about America to project his ambition as a leading Protestant ruler who was curious about the world and sought to

[34] Bridget Heal, *Magnificent Faith: Art and Identity in Lutheran Germany* (Cambridge: Cambridge University Press, 2017).

integrate the commercial benefits of cultural encounters. This was not merely an age of traditional, navel-gazing Lutheran "orthodoxy" in the German lands.[35]

Islamic Encounters

Protestantism hence continued to unfold within an international Eurasian context characterized by imperial expansion and revived long-distance trade. Charles Parker explores what this meant for Dutch Calvinist attitudes towards Islam. The United East India Company (VOC) traded with and sometimes fought Muslim rulers in the East Indies throughout the seventeenth and eighteenth centuries. The company's fundamental goal was profit, but many of their investors were pastors and the company also employed missionaries who cared for employees and sought to convert Muslims. Although they regularly complained about being understaffed, they still managed to set up schools, preach, and teaching the catechism. Historians have often taken such complaints as evidence that the Dutch neglected missions. Yet, as Parker explains, the "company objectives aligned perfectly with Calvinist conversion efforts with one sizeable category of peoples in the East Indies: those who had been baptized by Catholic priests." The numbers here are significant – in addition to lay chaplains, between 700 and 1,000 missionary pastors worked in the Dutch Empire to convert thousands of non-Europeans. Parker traces the fluidity of evolution in these missionaries' views. Initially, he writes, missionaries simply dismissed Islam through conventional stereotypes. Just like the early Luther in relation to Jews, they expected large-scale conversions upon proclaiming the Word of God. Yet they failed to attract a significant number of Muslims and soon understood that proper learning was needed to engage in debate. University theologians at Utrecht and Leiden in the mid-1600s therefore comprehensively compared the Qur'an with the Bible in order to better equip their students when they went overseas. Just as in New England, then, learning had practical uses, and applications and books were not made just for ivory towers or sealed off libraries. This new learned tradition changed the missions in the East Indies. Calvinist and indigenous linguists in the second half of the 1600s translated large sections of biblical texts, and a Malay Bible appeared in 1730. The ministers still

[35] See my forthcoming article on this subject in Susanna Burghartz, Lucas Burkart, Christine Göttler, and Ulinka Rublack eds., *Materialised Identities* (2021) which relates to a Swiss National Foundation funded project, www.materializedidentities.com/.

failed to convert Muslims, and meanwhile the VOC's economic success slowly contracted.

Just as in the case of Pastorius in New England, the gifted Utrecht linguist Adriaan Reland's more tolerant understanding was brought about through his own learning in the early eighteenth century. Reeland was a professor of oriental languages at the University of Utrecht and from an orthodox Calvinist milieu. His highly influential 1705 publication *On the Mohammedan Religion* was not just an exercise in Enlightened learning, it was also directly linked to his frustration that the success of missions in the Dutch Empire had been so limited. Reeland argued that Christians had to understand and even appreciate Islam before they could engage Muslims successfully. They should learn Arabic and explore similarities between the faiths. Reeland's work significantly helped to reshape learned European views of Islam in the age of Enlightenment. The faith was flawed, but reasonable, he suggested; no new religious truth could be imposed in a spirit of ignorance and arrogance. Entanglement hence means in this case that the European Enlightenment was propelled by a sustained experience of encounter in which the resistance of the population in the Dutch Empire through debate was as important as the collaboration of learned local informers. This is a particularly important aspect in emphasizing how local populations of different faiths played an active part in reshaping European attitudes.

Of course, European Protestants frequently encountered Muslims closer to home. Reeland's book asked rhetorically: "Do we not have much contact" with Muslims in "Constantinople, along the borders of Hungary and Turkish lands, on the coasts of Africa, in Syria, Persia?" Renate Dürr's chapter draws attention to the fact that Europeans abducted and enslaved Muslims, and even celebrated their conversion at home through elaborate baptisms. Like Burghartz's chapter, Dürr's essay deconstructs the image of early modern Protestant Germany as provincial and uninterested in global issues. Indeed, the numbers significantly undermine that notion: the Holy League captured over 2,000 prisoners in Buda alone during the 1680s who were then given away or sold in the German heartland of the Holy Roman Empire. Dürr analyzes the printed baptismal sermons as tools of Lutheran self-assertion and concludes that they "became a divine symbol of an explicitly Lutheran universalism." This, in short, was "global Lutheranism that did not need to embark on missions"; it was "glocal" in nature and anchored in small towns or even villages; it focused on individuals and celebrated local territorial rulers to reach a broad audience through print: through stories of single individuals, "small-town Germans learned about the wider world." We know of some Muslims who voluntarily entered Protestant lands, and, as in

Parker's case, it is important to highlight that the knowledge interlocutors from different faiths offered propelled Western culture in new directions. One example for such an entanglement is Haq Virdī, a man in mid-life who accompanied a Persian embassy to northern Germany and up to his death in 1650 helped the scholar Olearius to compile a dictionary of Persian, Arabic, Turkish, German, and Latin. This served to translate Persian texts into German, such as a collection of poems entitled "Persian Rose Valley" in 1654.

Pietist Empires

During the eighteenth century, one of the best-known missionary efforts in German-speaking lands traveled from Salzburg to Georgia. Here, a Pietist pastor named Johann Martin Boltzius served more than thirty years in Ebenezer, a small community made up of refugees from Catholic Salzburg on the southernmost frontier of Britain's North American empire. Boltzius also sought to convert Georgia's indigenous population. Pietism actively promoted what James van Horn Melton describes as a "program that aimed at nothing short of evangelizing the world and bringing forth the Kingdom of God." This was interlinked with Luther's early hope that Jews might be saved through conversion once Protestantism had reformed the Christian Church. Pietists at Halle University during Boltzius's student days regarded St. Paul's unrealized prophecy of Jewish conversion as imminent. Just as in the Dutch republic, university learning in subjects such as oriental languages shaped these young missionaries. At Halle, Johann Heinrich Callenberg taught Greek, Arabic, Hebrew, and Yiddish explicitly in order to train a future generation of missionaries both abroad and in Europe. In 1728, he founded an institutional center for the first organized Protestant mission to Jews in Germany. It included a printing house and distribution center for Hebrew and Yiddish dictionaries, grammars, and translations of the Christian gospels. Van Horn Melton hence shows that when Boltzius settled in Georgia he not only sought to convert the indigenous Yuchi people, but also the German-speaking Jews as well as the enslaved Africans who arrived in far greater numbers after 1750. He mines Boltzius's journals, which were published in Germany at the time, as well as his diaries and letters, which reflected on these efforts as they evolved and ultimately failed. The "dimmer the prospect of conversion," Melton explains, "the more threatening non-Christians appeared in the pastor's eyes." The Yuchi resisted by refusing much contact. In relation to slaves in households and on plantations, Boltzius was assured by Samuel Albinus, a Halle-trained Pietist preacher at the German court chapel in London, that Christian education was entirely compatible with slaveholding. Like the Dutch missionaries, Boltzius's attitude in regard to this issue proved remarkably fluid. His initial pessimism turned into a perception that slaves were "distinct individuals with souls amenable to salvation," and by 1763 he was calling for the abolition of slavery altogether, most likely as a result of reading Quaker abolitionist literature. Key to this was the notion that slaveholding was a result of Christian greed. Boltzius was ambivalent about Ebenezer's new prosperity – he was replaced by a minister who was both wealthy and a major slaveholder. For Boltzius, slavery "had become a symbol of how Ebenezer, once chosen and thus exceptional in God's eyes, had succumbed to worldly temptation."

In order to answer the question of how German Pietists fared in other parts of the globe, Ulrike Gleixner turns her attention to the South Indian missions during the early eighteenth century. She argues that millenarian expectations – the idea that Christ would establish a messianic kingdom on earth after his second coming and would reign over it for 1,000 years before the Last Judgment – shaped the fundraising for these missions as much as their planning and medialization. During the late seventeenth century, Pietists began to believe that educational activities and conversion work among Jews and other non-Christians benefitted a better society which would gradually realize God's Empire on earth. Gleixner analyzes sources from a transnational network of those who organized and staffed missions to South India. She furthermore explores the correspondence between Halle and male and female donors for the mission in Europe as well as Halle's published mission journal. During the eighteenth century these efforts resulted in a narrative of progress which tied in with Enlightenment ideals. August Hermann Francke (1663–1727) campaigned for a "universal social reform" and institutionalized it in Halle. Orphanages and schools based on the Halle model developed in the German-speaking lands, in Britain, Eastern Europe, North America, and in India. As in the case of Boltzius, many of the university graduates influenced by Halle Pietism regarded themselves as active ambassadors sent to expand the Empire of God on earth. The South India project lasted from 1706 until 1845. It was initiated and supported by the Danish court, London's "Society for Promoting Christian Knowledge (SPCK)," and by the Halle Orphanage. The Danish crown held the colonial trading post in Tranquebar, paid the salary of the missionaries, and oversaw a supervisory committee. Halle educated the missionaries and brought in donations through a "constant flow of information" in letters and a mission journal. Middle-class women from highly educated officeholding families were prominent in organizing regional support groups, while a noble abbess of a Protestant convent paid for two Indian schoolboys to be educated, and established a "fund for widows" in her birthplace as well as in Tranquebar. Gleixner explains that this endowment can be seen as a practice which expanded the Protestant Empire geographically, while the abbess's "paralleled charitable activities made Europe and India appear as one territory in which she acted as a sovereign." Such activities stabilized Protestant identities through much enthusiasm about the tangible extension of God's Kingdom. The first Tamil was converted in 1733. Schooling relied on local men and women as helpers, and intercultural collaboration in the mission field was a common practice. As in earlier essays in the volume, we can see that indigenous people transferred their knowledge about languages, religious philosophies, medicine, and local conditions in ways which reshaped European expertise. Gleixner concludes: "The core of millenarianism required social, educational, and religious creative initiative and activism; the concept resulted in practices," which influenced the globalization of Protestantism through Danish, German, and British collaborators "to a high degree."

Moravian Encounters

Just as there were European efforts to reform "popular religion," indigenous cultures likewise reinterpreted the messages they received from missionaries through local cosmologies and social values. To explore this indigenous response, Jacqueline Van Gent turns to Moravian missions – one of the earliest and fastest growing mission movements. Moravians were present in Danish colonies (1733 Greenland, 1734–1736 Lapland, 1737 Guinea, and from 1758 Tranquebar), in Dutch colonies (1738 Suriname, 1737 South Africa, and 1739 Ceylon), and English colonies (from 1735 in Georgia and after 1740 in New York and Pennsylvania). Their history reached back to the Hussite movements in fifteenth-century Bohemia, and their experiences of repression and exile since the sixteenth century powerfully shaped Moravian faith across the generations. Van Gent's contribution focuses methodologically on new approaches from the history of emotions towards the study of verbal and non-verbal communication between missionaries and those they attempted to convert. Missionaries took the performance of a repertoire of "appropriate" emotions to indicate successful internal conversion or, at least, a readiness for baptism. They perceived the heart as the center of feeling and a vehicle for a connection with Christ's love and suffering. This idea was linked to a metaphorical use of temperature – a believer's "warm" or even "melting" heart indicating proper connection and aliveness. Van Gent highlights the important role played by indigenous Christian converts in these religious encounters. This leads her to focus on the intricate power relations that were formed between missionaries, converts, and communities that reshaped emotional practices and emotional communities. Missionaries, she writes, "sought to promote a shared understanding of spiritual love and the experience of Christ's suffering, while also maintaining social distance and superiority by reinforcing shame and patriarchal obedience." Converts were socialized into new emotional styles and communities in a life-long process which constituted and re-affirmed belonging through the performance of specific emotional repertoires regarded as pious. This particularly centered on annual rituals of spiritual "awakening," which took place at night, in the wilderness, and were experienced through weeping to acknowledge one's own worthlessness. Van Gent returns us to Tranquebar, also the focus of Gleixner's essay, to tell the story of Maria Magdalena Malabar. Maria was born in 1774 to a slave woman and was baptized. Rituals such as the awakening, but also rituals of "speaking" faith from her childhood onwards shaped her faith with its notions of sincere emotional intensity. Moravian encounters with the Inuit, by contrast, show how difficult it could be to map emotional repertoires on to local populations, especially if they had very different conceptions of "love."

Resistance, conflict, and negotiation thus once more highlight the active part that indigenous people played in the transformations of global Protestantism. Jon Sensbach provides a re-reading of the story of a famous Caribbean woman, Mary Prince. The first slave woman to write an autobiography, Prince's book, *The History of Mary Prince* (1831) helped to galvanize the British antislavery movement. Before settling in Britain, Prince had belonged to the Moravian Church in Antigua, then part of the British West Indies. Methodists and Moravians started their unusually successful missions among slaves in the 1750s. The colony seemed so much the "favorite of heaven" that John Wesley visited in 1758. Women recruits were particularly active in spreading these Protestant faiths, so that by the early nineteenth century they claimed to have 15,000 members. Sensbach for the first time uses Moravian manuscripts to reveal how Prince's narrative was shaped by her British editors in order to strategically conceal her reliance on African-derived spiritualities, which flourished alongside and within evangelical worship in Antigua. Prince's *History* streamlined the narrative of her Christian faith, which was actually rooted in a multi-layered religious culture that challenged or even ignored specific Christian practices and concepts. Prince was therefore the product of a larger culture of West Indian slavery and thus emerges as a person "immersed in several overlapping sacred worlds in conversation, and often at odds, with her providential narrative."

African-American Christianity in the West Indies, North America, and England developed through those like Prince who left the colony and carried their Afro-Caribbean spirituality with them. Yet the court records of the Moravian church in Antigua also paint a disturbing picture of a violent colonial society in which slaves themselves reproduced violence in order to fight for their role in the congregation. Missionaries, moreover, used punitive exclusion mechanisms in order to uphold discipline on sugar plantations. Sensbach thus maps out the hidden history of a very different emotional community that formed between European Christians and their colonial congregations – a community in which gender deeply mattered and one that was marked by fear and jealousy about authority and rage.

Reciprocal Comparisons

Merry Wiesner-Hanks closes this volume by linking the findings of several essays in the collection to central themes in the historiography of gender and religion. She builds on Sensbach's and Van Gent's interest in emotional communities and on the interest across several contributions to include a wider range of historical actors, in particular European women and indigenous men and women. Wiesner-Hanks's contribution emphasizes the importance of embedding an analysis of Protestants through "reciprocal comparison" across global cultures, which views each case "from the vantage point of the others." This makes it urgent, as Sensbach and Van Gent likewise suggest, to investigate non-Western concepts of mood, mind, or heart, and the practices of physical enactment or literary expression linked to them. This can equally inspire historians of European Protestantism, as competing concepts of emotions also co-existed in European societies, and their adaption or contestation has not been sufficiently explored by historians of religion. Wiesner-Hanks then addresses research that has contributed to the "spatial turn," and in particular to the subject of migrations in the Atlantic world as a site of complex interactions among gender cultures and different diasporas. As this volume shows, this research strand has done much to add to the previous research that overwhelmingly focused on Puritan experiences. The most recent research on Quakers, for instance, demonstrates a need to re-think gendered accounts of godly households as domesticated, patriarchal spheres. This approach has become particularly influential through work on the early Reformation in Germany. But it might not fit later developments. As Naomi Pullin has recently shown, it certainly does not fit the situation of Quakers in eighteenth-century Britain and British America.[36] Here, women became transcultural brokers of religious ideas and identities by making their households meeting points and by forming bonds among themselves. Quakers were the most influential Protestant religion in British America during this period, and – just as among Moravians – within it women were extremely influential. This in turn means that historians of Europe, as in the case of Gleixner's essay, must continue to re-assess the significant role of women as supporters and mediators of faith through mutual bonds in order to nuance the notion that this was a straightforwardly patriarchal religion.

As indicated above, Wiesner-Hanks's book on *Christianity and Sexuality*, published in 2000, pioneered a global history of religion which sufficiently integrated early modern Protestant experiences in Europe and abroad. Her contribution here underlines the need for the historiography to further attend to the experiences of indigenous people as actively producing and reproducing spiritual worlds, knowledge, and life-worlds of wider consequence. As I hope this introduction has made clear, there is no reason to confine accounts of Protestantism to Europe without considering the ways in which identities and knowledge inflected with the global, first predominantly through print, but from the early seventeenth century onwards increasingly through settlement and encounter as well as through sustained intellectual debates.[37]

This volume arose from a conference held at the Huntington Library in December 2017 – a year that marked the commemorations of 500 years of Protestantism. These predominantly focused on Martin Luther, who disseminated his 95 Theses against the indulgence trade in 1517. I am grateful to all contributors to the conference and to this volume for their willingness to take part in a continued effort to avoid a narrowing of the history of Protestantism through a return solely to founding figures, and for embarking on an intellectual adventure which this book hopes to further sustain.

[36] Naomi Pullin, *Female Friends and the Making of Transatlantic Quakerism* (Cambridge: Cambridge University Press, 2018).

[37] On one of the most prominent results of such debates, see Lynn Hunt, Margaret C. Jacob, Wijnand Mijnhardt, *The Book that Changed the Europe: Picart & Bernard's Religious Ceremonies of the World* (Cambridge, MA: Harvard University Press, 2010).

1 Reworking Reformation in the Early English Atlantic

Carla Gardina Pestana

Plymouth Plantation – the first settlement permanently planted in the region the English dubbed "New England" – demonstrated the practical problems of exporting Reformation. In Plymouth, no less than elsewhere, migration to the Americas forced Christians to confront the problems at the heart of the Reformation. Even if this group's initial isolation and commitment to separatism set it apart from other English Protestants, the experiences of the Plymouth settlers were far from unique. Like all religious migrants, they struggled to recreate the fundamentals of the spiritual life they had known in Europe.

Some scholars have argued that mobility played a central role in the Reformation experience, as religious changes and the contentions over them set people in motion. While the journey to southern New England represented a particularly bold move, many religious individuals and communities migrated, finding "emigration … a necessary tactic in the strategies of adjustment and survival" during this ideologically fraught time.[1] Certainly, mobility forced a reconsideration of the Reformation project, by wrenching people and churches out of familiar contexts and thrusting them into a space in which they had both the freedom and the responsibility to define institutions and practices. Plymouth grappled with central issues: staffing (or the portability of ecclesiastical structures), membership (or the relationship of the church to the world), and praxis (or the exercise of faith in the routines of community). Considering each of these allows us to reassess Plymouth, its separatist heritage, and its relation to the larger currents of reform. In reconsidering the Protestant Reformations as global and multicentric phenomena, the portability of both faith and practice becomes paramount for understanding the potentially transformative effects of mobility.

[1] Douglas Anderson, *William Bradford's Books: Of Plimmoth Plantation and the Printed Word* (Baltimore, MD: The Johns Hopkins University Press, 2003), 20. The intersection of mobility and religious reformation has engendered much literature of late. For example, see Nicholas Terpstra, *Religious Refugees in the Early Modern World: An Alternative History of the Reformation* (New York: Cambridge University Press, 2015), 1–2, 3, 327, 180–82.

Before taking up the analysis of Plymouth church's effort to address these challenges, a word about the choice of this case. Though it was a small and relatively insignificant settlement, Plymouth Plantation nonetheless looms large in the history of early America as modern residents of the United States understand it. In the southeast corner of what is today the state of Massachusetts, Plymouth existed as a quasi-official jurisdiction from its settlement in 1620 until it was absorbed into its larger neighbor in 1692. During that time it never gained its own charter, but existed on a patchwork of authorizations that worked as an agreed upon fiction allowing it to subsist without full legal authority. That its neighbors accepted its existence helped it to survive as long as it did. First in the region, it was eclipsed by newer colonies – most notably Massachusetts Bay, but also Connecticut, New Haven, and Rhode Island – with more population and greater access to resources.

Despite its marginality, Plymouth gained prominence after the American Revolution. Various New Englanders – initially through the addresses delivered at annual celebrations of Forefathers Day – extolled its early history and presented it as exemplary of the founding of the United States. The first use of the term "Pilgrim" for the settlers dated from a 1793 address, and such worthies as John Quincy Adams contributed to the commemorations.[2] These promoters presented stories of the signing of an agreement on shipboard that laid out terms of self-government (the "Mayflower Compact"), the landing at Plymouth Rock, settlers meeting with a Native man "Squanto," and especially a Thanksgiving meal at the time of the first harvest. These vignettes became pivotal images in the American lexicon of foundational moments. School children learn about Squanto and the first Thanksgiving, families across the United States sit down for a Thanksgiving meal every November in commemoration of that event, and tourists travel to the shores of Cape Cod to view a rock. One of the unofficial patriotic anthems of the United States, "My Country, 'Tis of Thee,'" extolls the "Land of the pilgrims' pride" in its first verse; the lyricist of the 1831 song thus nodded to the Plymouth legacy. As one author of a popular history enthused, Plymouth migrants stood out as "the first successful European settlers." In doing so he intentionally dismissed Virginia and Bermuda and seemingly forgot the many accomplishments of a vast Iberian America.[3] Plymouth's outsized image defies its modest place in early English America.

[2] For Chandler Robbins's use of the term, see Ann U. Abrams, *The Pilgrims and Pocahontas: Rival Myths of American Origin* (Boulder, CO: Westview Press, 1999), 5; for John Quincy Adams, see *An Oration delivered at Plymouth, December 22, 1802, at the Anniversary Commemoration of the First Landing of our Ancestors* ([Plymouth, 1803]).

[3] Godfrey Hodgson, *A Great & Godly Adventure: The Pilgrims & the Myth of the First Thanksgiving* (New York: Public Affairs, 2006), 9.

The popular understanding of Plymouth's religious history hinges on the idea of freedom of religion. The commentators who promoted Plymouth's image emphasized that the migrants struggled to find a place to worship freely; they then equated the quest for personal liberty with a general commitment to freedom of religion for all. In that way, Plymouth settlers (even if they migrated in order to keep their own faith and practice pure) became advocates for the later US commitment to separation of church and state. While most modern Americans know about this connection in only vague terms, popular histories often detail Plymouth's association with English separatism and the English church in Leiden. These accounts – and indeed all accounts of Plymouth, whether they emphasize the religious issues or not – rely heavily on William Bradford's famous (and for a time lost) *Of Plimoth Plantation.* Written by a long-time governor, the first, shorter section of this manuscript account was composed in 1630, at a time when Bradford sought to underscore the plantation's religious roots. Fearful that the migration to Massachusetts then underway would overwhelm Plymouth and aware that the recently arrived contingent of Leiden residents was the last that Plymouth would receive, he presented a narrative of religious striving that has become the accepted Plymouth origins story.

Relying on Bradford, the standard narrative locates that first New England settlement in a context of separatism.[4] Bradford – and his many imitators – began with the Reformation and its supposedly limited influence on the process of reforming the English national church. The narratives then turn to the Cambridge educations of Leiden and Plymouth lay elder William Brewster and of Leiden pastor John Robinson. Next they consider the creation of a church at Scrooby in Nottinghamshire, the decision of the congregation to move to Holland

[4] See for instance the frequent invocation of Plymouth and, even more so, John Robinson, in Stephen Foster, *The Long Argument: English Puritanism and the Shaping of New England Culture, 1570–1700* (Chapel Hill: IEAH&C/University of North Carolina Press, 1991). While Michael P. Winship agrees on the role in *Godly Republicanism: Puritans, Pilgrims, and City on a Hill* (Cambridge, MA: Harvard University Press, 2012), 134–59, 159; Mark L. Sargeant diverges, questioning the role of Plymouth in shaping Massachusetts Bay; see "'The Best Parts of Histories': The Letters in William Bradford's of Plymouth Plantation," in *Lives out of Letters: Essays on American Literary Biography and Documentation, in Honor of Robert N. Hudspeth*, ed. Robert D. Habish (Madison, NJ: Fairleigh Dickinson University Press, 2004), 51–52. The standard narrative is contained in many histories of Plymouth. Tailored to an evangelical Christian audience are John Robert Broome, *In Search of Freedom: The Pilgrim Fathers and New England* (Harpenden, UK: Gospel Standard Trust Publications, 2001); David G. Fountain, *The Mayflower Pilgrims and their pastor* (Wothing, UK: Henry E. Walter, Ltd., 1970). Jeremy Dupertius Bangs favors the idea that they had to flee a deteriorating situation in Holland; his *Strangers and Pilgrims, Travellers and Sojourners: Leiden and the Foundation of Plymouth Plantation* (Plymouth, MA: General Society of Mayflower Descendants, 2009), 568.

in 1606, and its eventual settlement in the university town of Leiden. In 1620 some members, with the blessing of their leader, left the Netherlands to travel to North America, where they established Plymouth. Once in New England, according to Bradford and his followers, they attempted to maintain the church's principles in the face of various troubles: they were challenged by those outside the Leiden/Plymouth church, by the indigenous people who became their nearest neighbors, by greedy investors who wanted the settlement to yield returns quickly, and by a scattering of new arrivals to the Plymouth region who sought to upend their efforts. The advent of Massachusetts Bay Colony marked the beginning of the end of their story in such accounts. Numerous authors do pause to discuss how the separatist legacy shaped the congregationalist establishment created subsequently in the Bay Colony.

This emphasis is somewhat ironic for a number of reasons. First, the separatism of the most dedicated of Leiden or Plymouth members hewed closely to the moderate line adopted by Leiden pastor John Robinson (1575–1625). Unlike more extreme proponents who demanded that all religious interactions with established church members cease, Robinson encouraged communion with Church of England members. His many learned works articulated views amenable to others in the reform-minded wing of the Church rather than on its fringe. He published in support of the Synod of Dort and was closely associated with William Ames, the leading English theologian so dear to the hearts of non-separating but Reform minded Christians in England.[5] Depicting Plymouth as occupying an extreme position overlooks the denunciations Robinson and those associated with him aimed at "overstrained and excessive separation."[6] As Plymouth agent Edward Winslow averred, they hoped the king would accept them as loyal subjects and ignore those who defamed them as "Brownists, factious Puritanes, Schismatickes &c."[7] While such claims contained an element of disingenuousness, they were not outright lies,

[5] Keith L. Sprunger, *Dutch Puritanism: A History of English and Scottish Churches of the Netherlands in the Sixteenth and Seventeenth Centuries* (Leiden: Brill, 1982), 134–37, 341.

[6] See Leiden church member and Plymouth supporter Robert Couchman's [Cushman's] *The Cry of the Stone* (London, 1642), discussed in Stephen Foster, "The Faith of a Separatist Layman: The Authorship, Context, and Significance of *The Cry of the Stone*," *The William and Mary Quarterly* 3rd ser., 34 (1977): 375–403. For Robinson's theology, see Timothy George, *John Robinson and the English Separatist Tradition* (Macon, GA: Mercer University Press, 1982).

[7] Jeremy Dupertuis Bangs, *Pilgrim Edward Winslow: New England's First International Diplomat, A Documentary History* (Boston, MA: New England Historic Genealogical Society, 2004), 150.

given the moderate position adopted in both Leiden and Plymouth on relations with those outside the church.

Second, if separatists were ever a majority of the settlers, that moment was fleeting. Only a minority of Leiden church members made the journey to North America in 1620; most stayed behind. Although surviving church records do not allow a full accounting, Robinson remained in Leiden with the majority, sending ruling elder William Brewster with the minority who went in 1620. The Leiden migrants journeyed with other recruits (referred to by Bradford and in the subsequent historiography as "strangers").[8] These additional participants made up the majority of the *Mayflower* passengers and residents in the plantation thenceforth.[9] The Leiden church carried on without the departing group, surviving for at least a decade in Holland after the 1625 death of its pastor, Robinson. Additional Leiden church members made the sojourn to Cape Cod over the first decade. Perhaps sixty – mostly poor – passengers drawn largely from Holland arrived on the *Handmaid* in 1630, the last infusion of any notable numbers affiliated with the separatist church.[10] In the end, by one estimate, no more than one-third to one-half of all members of the Leiden congregation came to New England.[11] Meanwhile others, designated variously as strangers, servants, hired hands, "particulars," and even one "Merchant Adventurer," overwhelmed the Leiden people with their sheer numbers. Our understanding of Plymouth as a separatist outpost on the American strand elides the presence of these others. Non-separatists would ultimately make up the vast majority of all settlers in the

[8] William Bradford uses the term "strangers" to refer to those "discontented, & mutinous" among the passengers, who were "some of strangers amongst them" in discussing the need for a compact prior to disembarking. See his "Of plimoth plantation," in *History of the Plimoth Plantation containing an account of the voyage of the "Mayflower,"* facsimile edition (London, 1896), 125.

[9] While George F. Willison probably did over emphasize the number of strangers on the first ship in his *Saints and Strangers: Lives of the Pilgrim Fathers and Their Families* (1945; reprint ed., New Brunswick, NJ: Transaction Publishers, 2011), appendix, as asserted by Jeremy Dupertuis Bangs, *Strangers and Pilgrims, Travellers and Sojourners*, 277, it remains the case that the *Mayflower* included numerous "strangers," and that their numbers in the overall population would grow with time. Crispin Gill, *Mayflower Remembered: A History of the Plymouth Pilgrims* (Newton Abbot: David & Charles, 1970), 47, points out further that of those who came from Leiden to Plymouth, only seven had started in Scrooby, evidence of how that narrative arc follows the great men (Robinson and Brewster) not the church membership.

[10] See "Of plimoth plantation," 165. Winthrop reported on the arrival of the *Handmaid* with sixty passengers and the difficulty of its crossing; see *The Journal of John Winthrop, 1630–1649*, ed. Richard S. Dunn, James Savage, and Laetitia Yeandle (Cambridge, MA and London: Belknap Press of Harvard University Press, 1996), 40–41.

[11] Joke Kardux and Eduard Bilt, *Newcomers in an Old City: The American Pilgrims in Leiden, 1609–1620*, In den Houttuyn 7 (Leiden: Burgersdijk & Niermans, 1998; revised 3rd ed., 2007), 63, 74–76.

jurisdiction, and they may never have sunk to a minority at any point even in the first decade. Separatists, vocal and self-aware as they were, must be understood as a minority, despite the plantation's reputation as a separatist enclave. Bradford's writings may not have succeeded in schooling a younger generation in the history he wanted them to know, but it has shaped the understanding of Plymouth, New England, and American origins for modern readers.

From this perspective the importance of Plymouth was two-fold: their purity as demonstrated by their separatist position and the depth of their commitment to their faith. This account works well from the viewpoint of national mythology, because the separatists' principles brought them persecution, forced them to migrate, and allowed them to be seen as suffering in the interests of freedom of worship. In the context of the national myth, the religious component is rendered with varying degrees of subtlety. Paintings and other representations of the first Thanksgiving emphasize the piety of the participants. Scholars, appreciating that later commentators reshaped the Plymouth migrants to serve their later purposes, objected to the remaking of Plymouth to suit the needs of national mythology. Numerous scholars and others have pointed out that the migrants intended to ensure their own freedom of worship and not the general principle of religious liberty; that relations with the region's inhabitants were never conflict-free long before New England erupted into the violence of King Philip's War in 1675 – which started in their neighborhood; and that giving thanks on a predetermined date would have been incomprehensible to any seventeenth-century Christian. Plymouth gained pride of place in New England's (and eventually the nation's) origin myth, in part because Massachusetts Bay disqualified itself. Founded a decade later and the dominant colony in the region, it had an embarrassing record of killing Quakers and witches that eventually tarnished its reputation. For that reason, tiny Plymouth, never officially a full-fledged colony, took on the role of founders – the Forefathers, as nineteenth-century commemorations had it – of New England and by extension the United States.[12]

Plymouth, usually invoked to illustrate the mission of the United States as an exemplar of religious liberty and the dedication of the first

[12] On the origins myths, see Anna Brickhouse's insightful comment about the "zero-sum game" they represent; *The Unsettlement of America: Translation, Interpretation, and the Story of Don Luis De Velasco, 1560–1945* (New York: Oxford University Press, 2015), 219. Abrams recounts the contest between two colonial regions for primacy in *The Pilgrims and Pocahontas: Rival Myths of American Origin*. For the role of witches in shunting the focus to Salem, see Gretchen A. Adams, *The Specter of Salem: Remembering the Witch Trials in Nineteenth-Century America* (Chicago, IL: The University of Chicago Press, 2008).

generation of settlers, also revealed much about the process of transferring Reformed Christianity into an American context. Considered from this vantage point, the Plymouth case represented less a peculiarly American case of striving and liberty and more a broader example of the challenges besetting migrating Protestant churches. Plymouth experienced all the basic conundrums associated with founding distant and isolated churches, including those in the areas of staffing, membership, and practice.

Staffing and the Problem of Religious Expertise

Although Plymouth was occasionally accused of religious radicalism in its early years, the settlers were united in the view that the man who led their worship had to be educated. No one believed that an uneducated individual – much less a woman – could guide the church, and in that regard the church forswore the extremes associated with those who elevated lay preachers to the highest office. The Leiden church's leader, John Robinson, instructed his followers of the necessity of a university education in a minister, and those who had been members of his congregation held to that requirement. Adequate staffing therefore necessitated appointing a man trained at Oxford or Cambridge, well-versed in languages and Christian theology. A lay settler, regardless of his gifts, could not fill the post. Indeed, Robinson instructed William Brewster, who had spent time at Cambridge but never graduated, that it was "not lawfull for you" to administer sacraments when only a ruling elder.[13]

The church's problem finding a suitable pastor would have been resolved by the arrival of their Leiden minister, John Robinson. The leader of the English separatist church in Leiden never undertook the transatlantic journey. Cambridge educated, Robinson had developed a reputation as a thoughtful and serious proponent of Reformed Protestantism. Although frequently lumped in for his separatism with other radicals, his published theological works reveal him to fit comfortably on many points into the puritan wing of the Church of England. As Keith L. Sprunger noted, while at Leiden, Robinson wrote numerous theological treatises that gained him "an international Puritan reputation."[14] His intractable opposition to the practice of vesting great power in the office of bishop alone compelled him to separate.[15] Members

[13] Robinson to William Bradford, December 19, 1623, "Of plimoth plantation," 229. Also, his to William Brewster, December 20, 1623, 231.

[14] Sprunger, *Dutch Puritanism: A History of English and Scottish Churches,* 135–36.

[15] For his moderation, see Martha L. Finch, *Dissenting Bodies: Corporealities in Early New England* (New York: Columbia University Press, 2010), 25.

of his church knew they were fortunate to look to such a man for leadership. Those who sailed in 1620 regretted leaving him behind, even if (as they hoped) the separation would be only temporary, as the letters they subsequently exchanged with him make clear.[16] In the meantime, they relied on ruling elder Brewster to see to their spiritual needs. As Bradford would later eulogize Brewster: "when the church had no minister, he taught twice every Saboth, and y^t both powerfully, and profitably, to ye great contentment of ye hearers, and their comfortable edification, yea many were brought to god by his ministrie He did more in this behalfe in a year then many that have their hundreds a year doe in all their lives."[17] Despite the admiration expressed here, the church never elevated Brewster to the status of pastor. In the five years after their landing, Brewster, Bradford, and others held out hope that Robinson would eventually join them and that the Leiden church would be reconstituted in its entirety in Plymouth under their beloved pastor. It was only Robinson's death in 1625 that finally convinced them to search for another man to lead the community.[18] Separating from Robinson had clearly proved difficult for Leiden migrants among the Plymouth settlers.

Much ink has been spilt – especially by the settlers' modern admirers – on Robinson's failure to journey to Plymouth. Many authors assume he felt a strong desire to do so, even as he learned of the high death rate and other difficulties the migrants faced, but his commitment to the idea over time is difficult to gauge. In the evangelical circles where the story is frequently retold, his eagerness to be reunited with this sector of his flock is taken as axiomatic. He did assert his desire to do so in a letter to his brother in law John Carver in 1620, although subsequent letters addressed the matter only to explain why he was not doing so.[19] Such accounts blame the investors who backed the migrants but were unwilling to pay for the transportation of Robinson and others who had remained behind. According to a letter that Robinson wrote in 1623, the investors acknowledged no obligation to pay for additional church members' travel.[20] If they wanted to go, they would need to finance their own passage.

The Christian commentators on this question cast the investors as persecutors bent on thwarting the true church, but in fact they had

[16] See for instance his to the congregation, in "Governor Bradford's Letter Book", Collections of the MHS, for the Year 1794. III (Boston, 1810): 45; and those letters scattered through Bradford's "Of plimoth plantation."
[17] "Of plimoth plantation," 491.
[18] News of his death arrived March 1625/6. See "Of plimoth plantation," 281–82.
[19] Letter included "Of plimoth plantation," 97.
[20] Robinson to Bradford, December 19, 1623, "Of plimoth plantation," 229.

good economic reasons to hesitate. As with all early colonial investors, the Adventurers (as they were called for having adventured their money) found that they had made a bad bargain: they were among the first to learn that new settlements absorbed vast sums but never yielded quick returns. Sending those Leiden church members who had chosen not to go with the first sailing appeared a losing proposition, especially if age or infirmity had caused their initial hesitation. Their later Christian critics correctly surmised that reuniting the church was not their highest priority – indeed the Adventurers disclaimed having made any commitment to do so – but that had less to do with their hostility to religion and more to do with their interest in a return on their investment.[21] Later, the settlers themselves shouldered further expense in bringing other individuals from Leiden, but they were in no position to do so in the years before Robinson's death.[22]

The few English Protestant churches in the wider Atlantic in the 1620s all faced difficulties recruiting clergyman, but Plymouth had a special set of problems.[23] While the small struggling community had little to offer a prospective minister, the separatist leanings of the most dedicated meant that they could not be satisfied with the usual candidates likely to wash up on Plymouth's shores.[24] Given its opposition to episcopal ordination, the church refused to accept the idea that a minister could be assigned to it by any outside authority, but expected instead to issue its own call to the candidate of its choosing. One Church of England clergyman resided in the region briefly without a pulpit, but no evidence exists that he sought a relationship with the Plymouth church.[25] The first man in the settlement with the proper educational credentials to warrant consideration agreed to abide by the policy of awaiting a call from the

[21] Broome sees the investors as plotting to impose the Church of England, *In Search of Freedom*, 71. For a correction emphasizing the financial, see Norman K. Risjord, "William Bradford: Pilgrim," in *Representative Americans: The Colonists*, 2nd ed. (Lanham: Rowman & Littlefield Publishers, Inc., 2001), 26–47, 33.

[22] See "Of plimoth plantation," 315.

[23] In Virginia for instance, by 1620, one half of the boroughs had no minister to see to residents' spiritual needs. There were only three ministers and two deacons to see to the scattered population. Edward L. Bond, *Damned Souls in a Tobacco Colony: Religion in Seventeenth-Century Virginia* (Macon, GA: Mercer University Press, 2000), 114–15.

[24] In a slightly earlier era, Virginia seemingly had problems with fit as well, when residents avoided a specific minister when they found him "somewhat a puritane." See John Beaulieu to William Trumball, November 30, 1609, printed in Philip L. Barbour ed., *The Jamestown Voyages under the first charter, 1606–1609*, 2 vols., works issued by the Hakluyt Society, 2nd ser., 136–37 (London: Hakluyt Society, 1969), 2: 287.

[25] The failed trading endeavor at Wessagusset, the scheme of Thomas Weston, hosted Church of England clergymen, one of whom lingered briefly after the settlement failed. Charles McLean Andrews, *The Colonial Period of American History*, 1: *Settlements* (New Haven, CT: Yale University Press, 1934), 338, 339–40.

church, perhaps confident that one was imminent. As Robert Cushman (1577–1625) wrote to his friends in Plymouth via the same ship that brought John Lyford (ca. 1580–1634), "he knows he is no officer amongst you, though perhaps custome, and universalitie may make him forget him selfe."[26] Cushman was prescient, for later Lyford felt affronted when the church failed to appoint him. At the time, church leaders continued doggedly to insist that Robinson be sent, and they flatly refused to appoint another. Even after Robinson's death, the church remained committed to deliberating carefully about any prospective minister. Of one of them, "they perceived upon some trial, that he was crased in his braine." Sending him back to England, they resented having to foot the bill for his transport.[27] Finally in 1629 their caution was rewarded with a satisfactory minister, who first "exercised his gifts amongst them, and afterwards was chosen Into ye ministrie and remained for sundrie years."[28] After a decade of striving, Plymouth finally had its first pastor. Only in 1636 did the church install someone with some staying power, when John Rayner (or Reyner) took up the post. A graduate of Magdalene College, Cambridge, he arrived in New England in 1635, and remained in Plymouth until some unnamed difference caused him to resign in 1654.[29] However hostile they were to bishops, this church foreswore the radicalism of some, never elevating an uneducated man as their leader.

Finding a pastor for the Plymouth church suddenly became easier because of a shifting context; many reform-minded, educated men with pastoral experience came to New England with the so-called Great Migration that began in 1630. Not only the first man appointed, Ralph Smith, but all those that came after, arrived in Plymouth as a result of the deluge of clerical talent that flooded into neighboring Massachusetts and overflowed into their tiny settlement. These men had the university education that Robinson thought requisite. Although most of them had undergone episcopal ordination as clergymen in the Church of England, they all accepted that it was the Plymouth church's call to them that made them its minister. With the arrival of the first Massachusetts Bay

26 Cushman letter, January 24, 1623/4, "Of plimoth plantation," 223.

27 "Of plimoth plantation," 309.

28 "Of plimoth plantation," 329. The first minister, he stayed in the post until 1637, assisted informally by Roger Williams (1631–1634) and by John Norton (1635–1636), both of whom went on to Massachusetts churches afterward.

29 William Bradford, *Of Plymouth Plantation, 1620–1647*, ed. Samuel Eliot Morison (New York: Alfred A. Knopf, 1952; reprint edition, 1966), 293 n. 1. Rayner went on to serve the Dover, New Hampshire, church until his death in 1669. See Harold Field Worthy, *Inventories of the Records of the Particular (Congregational) Churches of Massachusetts Gathered 1620–1805*, Harvard Theological Studies XXV (Cambridge, MA: Harvard University Press, 1970), 488.

Company ships in 1629, the Plymouth church soon had candidates to fill its needs.

I have elsewhere argued that some variants of Protestantism were better suited to the Atlantic context because of their greater portability. That advantage could be thwarted, however, in the absence of the needed components. A portable faith that only requires a minister and believers to make a church cannot be transplanted without both. Had the ecclesiastical context of the English Atlantic world not undergone the unexpected transformation that resulted when crisis in England sent a flood of qualified men into the Americas, Plymouth might have continued its frustrated attempts to locate an adequate leader. Archbishop Laud, pursuing policies that drove many vigorous believers away, inadvertently benefited the Plymouth church. The leadership gap was filled only because of the effects of Laud's efforts to reshape Protestantism in England.

Membership

Although the challenges of finding a pastor were only resolved with aid inadvertently given by the much maligned archbishop, transplanting a church also posed issues of inclusion and exclusion. Those who left Leiden to journey to America agreed in advance that they constituted a church distinct from that in Leiden but that any future Leiden migrants who were in that church would be included in the Plymouth church without question. Difficulties in making the voyage meant that some of the intended migrants from Leiden stayed behind, so that the new church gathered in anticipation of leaving Europe did not travel intact to Plymouth.[30] Those who did ultimately sail included not only fewer Leiden passengers than anticipated but also numerous additional persons who had not been gathered into the new migrant church prior to their departure. While a gathered church arrived intact, it did not encompass all the passengers who might potentially want to be a part of it.

Arriving in New England as a mixed group meant that the Leiden remnant on the *Mayflower* faced in stark form one of the major issues animating the Reformation movement throughout Europe – and perhaps most pressingly in the Atlantic world: how should the church relate to the world? In Scrooby, Amsterdam (where the migrants tarried briefly), and Leiden, the answer had been clear: following Robinson's teaching, the

[30] For the gathering and the agreement governing the relationship of Leiden and Plymouth members, see "Of plimoth plantation," 73. When one ship proved unable to make the crossing, not all the Leiden passengers transferred to the *Mayflower* for the voyage.

church separated from the Church of England, gathered an independent congregation of self-selected individuals, and carved its own path. In all three settings, those who did not join Robinson's congregation enjoyed other options: first, the local Church of England parish in England; then a number of English-language Protestant churches in Amsterdam; and finally an English Reformed Church affiliated with the Dutch Reformed establishment in Leiden. Coming to a part of the North American coast heretofore unsettled by European Christians, the people in Plymouth had no options other than what they organized for themselves. The nearest alternative – the churches in Virginia – were over 600 miles away. The migrants themselves had to create their own institutions. In considering the status of the strangers who journeyed with them to America, the former members of the Leiden church directly confronted the problem of how to accommodate those that they had previously left out of their calculations.

The question of membership – how one qualified and what to do with a rising number of residents who did not – would eventually dog churches elsewhere in New England. In the first colonies (Virginia and Somers' Island) organized under the Church of England, everyone was considered a member, in accordance with the parish model. The Leiden congregation had never been a parish church – as a gathered church, its members left their parish home to form an alternative. In England and in the Netherlands, the church accepted like-minded people who sought them out but had no responsibility for the wider community's spiritual welfare. In Plymouth, no dominant ecclesiastical order existed, presenting a new situation to the migrating Leiden remnant. They had in effect become the parish church, in the sense that they were responsible for the spiritual care of all residents. If they chose to neglect that care, by restricting membership to only a select group, the unchurched residents would go without.

How Plymouth church addressed the question of membership initially cannot be fully discerned. Did they expand the limited parameters that included only some of those who had gathered a new church in Leiden to accept all residents as members? The early records, sparse and unsystematic, hint that additional individuals won formal acceptance as members.[31] Some scholars have concluded that the bar for admission to the Plymouth church was low, so that all who sought admission attained it.[32] Surviving evidence does not clarify whether the Plymouth church

[31] "Of plimoth plantation," 223. Lyford was one who was accepted into the church, which we only know as a result of the controversy that erupted around him later.

[32] This is Robert G. Pope's sense in discussing the area church's slowness to adopt the Half-Way Covenant later; *The Half-Way Covenant: Church Membership in Puritan New England* (Princeton, NJ: Princeton University Press, 1969), 200, 201, 204, 241–43, 265. Also see

instituted any particular admission requirement such as testifying to a saving grace experience in order to gain admission. The practice, which would be adopted in neighboring colonies later, may not have been part of Plymouth practice in the first years. In 1634, while in England, church member Edward Winslow described their expectations that new members be able "to render a Reason of that ffaith & hope they have in Christ . . . togeather wth a good testimony of an honest life," which suggested some ritual surrounding admission.[33] Bradford described the occasion on which one new member joined, giving "a large confession of his faith; and an acknowledgemente of his former disorderly walking." Confession of previous sins – many different sorts of which could be encompassed under the phrase "disorderly walking" – was standard both in those churches that did require such a narrative (as well as more generally in the spiritual autobiographies that lay people occasionally penned). Bradford's account gives the impression that this individual offered a particularly elaborate profession, which he reported as evidence of his hypocrisy. Given that, Bradford's recounting does not make clear if the church demanded this ritual moment of confession as the price of admission or if the prospective member volunteered it of his own accord.[34] Whether the church admitted all or left some out, they clearly welcomed all residents to their religious gatherings. Just as in Massachusetts Bay subsequently, members and non-members alike attended worship services. Those who failed to hear the word preached the Plymouth authorities sought out, although the court records give no sign that they meted out punishments in the early days in order to coerce attendance.[35]

John Demos, *A Little Commonwealth: Family Life in Plymouth Colony* (Oxford: Oxford University Press, 1970), 8. On political participation (which would be dependent on admission in Massachusetts) numerous scholars conclude that Plymouth decoupled the two. See Virginia deJohn Anderson, *New England's Generation: The Great Migration and the Formation of Society and Culture in the Seventeenth Century* (New York: Cambridge University Press, 1991), 172; Demos, *Little Commonwealth*, 7.

33 Bangs, *Pilgrim Edward Winslow*, 150. Stephen Brachlow, *The Communion of Saints: Radical Puritans and Separatist Ecclesiology, 1570–1625* (Oxford: Oxford University Press, 1988), 134, asserts that the mere act of joining the church made a statement and rendered a specific confession moot. But he described the church functioning within the European religious environment where the act of separation connoted a choice, even an act of defiance, which differed from the Plymouth context.

34 Bradford later described the confession to establish the controversial John Lyford as a hypocrite, and his account can be read as if this were an extraordinary, even unexpected, moment. "Of plimoth plantation," 237.

35 Alison Games, *Migration and the Origins of the English Atlantic World*, Harvard Historical Studies 133 (Cambridge, MA: Harvard University Press, 1999), 174, says it was only required after 1651. Yet in the confrontation over Lyford they claimed to go after those who were idle on the Lord's Day or avoided the preaching.

Gaining admission (or being denied it) would have been felt most compellingly at the various moments in the community's life when members separated themselves out to practice ordinances. When they brought their children to be baptized or they themselves approached the table for the Lord's Supper, they drew lines of inclusion and exclusion. Yet the members of the Plymouth church had no opportunity to set themselves apart in this way initially. Without a pastor – with only their ruling elder for spiritual leadership – and with a firm commitment to having the ordinances performed only by a clergyman, the church went without both baptism and communion throughout the 1620s. As a consequence, the church did not enact the ritual separation of members from non-members in the first years. The so-called Particulars (as those who paid their own way to the settlement and thus had no part in the arrangement that bound the *Mayflower* arrivals and others to the financial arrangements with the Adventurers) complained that they would have "none to live heare but themselves." This accusation, which Bradford hotly denied, suggested that Plymouth was rife with exclusionary impulses and indeed wanted to limit not only membership in the church, but also residences in the plantation to those they selected.[36]

What this situation meant in effect was that the only form of worship in existence was fully available to anyone who attended their services. Everyone gathered to hear Brewster preach and teach. It would seem then that the Plymouth church, in its first decade, looked rather like those that would be founded later in Massachusetts Bay and other "orthodox" New England churches, with members and non-members together attending services. The latter were welcomed even though they were likely to have formerly been (and even to consider themselves still) Church of England communicants (and therefore those from whom the Scooby/Leiden church had separated).[37] If nothing else, the church included them in worship gatherings, appreciating that they "might benefit from mutual admonishment."[38] In any case, Robinson had taught that limited communion with such individuals might be acceptable, and hence the church's position did not constitute a rejection of his precepts.

At the moment when the residents of Plymouth first had to confront the question of what to do when the ordinances were available and only some

[36] "Of plimoth plantation," 245.

[37] We know this in part because of the debate launched by Charles Chauncy, who was in Plymouth in the late 1630s, about whether it was sufficient for the church members to gather for the Lord's Supper at the end of regular worship services, with non-members dismissed after attending the prayer and preaching portion of the service. He thought that might constitute an insufficiently strict division, and that perhaps the members should gather at an entirely different time for this ordinance. Finch, *Dissenting Bodies*, 159.

[38] Finch, *Dissenting Bodies*, 150.

could come forward to partake, the ground under their church had begun to shift for other reasons. The new migration stream that brought in prospective pastors also vastly increased the Plymouth population, leading to the founding of new towns and new churches within its jurisdiction. Just at the moment when Robinson's followers finally had access to the full panoply of church rituals, this influx added numerous Reform-minded Protestants with their own evolving views about the proper church order. Plymouth church came into its own even as a regional religious culture was taking shape. Prior to that, Plymouth had not been in a position to establish a strictly separatist church – or even to sort out precisely what that might look like in the very different American context. Given the paucity of information, we cannot conclusively know that Plymouth had looser admission standards, but it appears likely that John Demos was correct in asserting as much in his study of early Plymouth Plantation.[39] A mixed company from the first, Plymouth church immediately compromised, under circumstances very different from those that Massachusetts churches initially faced. With a possibly undeserved reputation as the strictest local variant of Protestantism, Plymouth grew after 1630 by absorbing overflow population from its neighbor to the north. Occasionally Plymouth offered sanctuary to unconventional Christians – including Baptists and Quakers – looking for a more amenable home.[40]

If their separatist legacy might have made the former Leiden church members less inclined to compromise over questions of membership qualifications, their experience after migrating taught them different lessons. Plymouth arrived at New England's second generation dilemma at the outset: it immediately confronted the question of the status of unbelievers, the non-saints, those who would not be included in a gathered church of self-selected saints. Plymouth began with many non-members in tow, as opposed to the Massachusetts Bay Colony migrants, who generally arrived expecting to join a gathered church different than the parish churches they left behind. Over time, New England as a whole hosted more non-members, as subsequent generations failed to join (much to the religious leaders' chagrin), whereas from the outset Plymouth confronted their presence and the dilemmas they posed to a gathered church that accepted no responsibility for the wider world.

[39] Demos, *A Little Commonwealth*, 8.

[40] For instance, Harvard College President Henry Dunster left his post once he embraced antipedobaptism, and made his way to Plymouth; see Carla Gardina Pestana, *The English Atlantic in an Age of Revolution, 1640–1661* (Cambridge, MA: Harvard University Press, 2004), 145.

Given this situation, the scholarship treating Plymouth church as dedicated to separatism and laboring to uphold that tradition in the face of countervailing forces has little basis in the facts of New England's first English settlement. Taking Bradford's narrative arc of separatists fleeing England and later abandoning Leiden for Plymouth at face value, we have overlooked the facts that the first church founded in Plymouth's jurisdiction included many non-separatists and that most churches subsequently gathered in the colony had no relationship to the Leiden church or the separatist tradition. The one clear exception, Duxbury Church, looked to Brewster as its leader once he was displaced from his quasi-pastoral role in Plymouth by the advent of clergy. When in 1630 William Bradford composed his detailed history of the background to Plymouth Plantation, charting the Scrooby/Amsterdam/Leiden trajectory, he did so to promote a particular view of the church's and the community's origins. He wrote when this background seemed in danger of being forgotten. He established the common view that Plymouth represented a transplanted church, pure and simple. As the early editor of his work asserted, Bradford demonstrated "a lesson the importance of which can hardly be over-rated. The one central fact of New England history was that it was an emigration not of individuals but of churches."[41] The church-based narrative of Plymouth's origins has become the standard narrative not only for Plymouth but for all of New England.

Guided by Bradford and aware that Plymouth's enemies attacked it on the basis of its separatist connections, scholars have not looked closely at the admittedly limited information about local practice, but have simply assumed that Plymouth established its church along particular lines. Little direct evidence supports the emphasis on Plymouth's commitment to separatism, yet scholars do not linger over that question but rather proceed to analyze the extent to which it may have influenced the non-separatism of every place else. It surely matters that the first moment when Plymouth church could act on questions of inclusion and exclusion around baptism or the Lord's Supper occurred only after the arrival of the Massachusetts settlers, when Plymouth gained its first pastor, a huge influx of residents, and a series of new churches. Scholars have pointed out that migrating to a region of America without a bishop or a Church of England structure rendered moot questions of separating and non-separating – even implying that everyone became a de facto separatist in New England.[42] Yet the opposite may have been the case: that separatism

[41] John A. Doyle, "Introduction," *History of the Plimoth Plantation*, 2.

[42] Sargent, "The Best Parts of Histories," 37, decided that in America, where there was no church, the issue of a separating congregation became "virtually meaningless."

become inconsequential in an environment in which a minority separatist group first provided parish-like religious services to all and sundry and then became overwhelmed by the arrival of others, who were bent on erecting pure churches that excluded the unworthy.

Praxis

Arguably, religious practice for English Protestants in the 1620s Atlantic world was deficient. From St. Christopher through Virginia and the Somers Islands to Plymouth, a shortage of ministers, a dearth of church buildings, and other lacks meant that services never replicated precisely what worshippers had known before migrating. In Plymouth, as noted, the church appointed a minister only in 1629, nine years after the first arrivals. Well before that date, the settlers built a combined fort and meeting house, described as "a large square house with a flat roof, built of thick sawn planks stayed with oak beams, upon the top of which they have six cannon ... The lower part they use for their church, where they preach on Sundays and the usual holidays."[43] A space for worship represented one familiar English ecclesiastical practice – although including it in a fortified building departed from custom – and the Plymouth people created such a space relatively quickly. To solemnize the occasion of Sunday worship, a contingent of settlers marched, armed, from the door of the home of the militia captain (Miles Standish) – where they gathered "by beat of drum" – to the building; they processed "in order, three abreast, and are led by a sergeant without beat of drum. Behind comes the Governor, in a long robe; beside him on the right hand, comes the preacher with his cloak on, and on the left hand, the captain with his side-arms and cloak on, and with a small cane in his hand." While this ritual may have been staged to demonstrate martial readiness for the benefit of the visitor who described it, the community's ability to put on this show suggested they had practiced it prior to his arrival. Gathering for Sabbath worship represented an occasion for the community, and they used it in part to display their military prowess and possibly also to remind the residents to be prepared.

However much pomp and architecture the settlers could marshal to support their community worship, what happened inside the fortified meetinghouse revealed deficiencies. As we have seen, the services, in the absence of a clergyman, never included the baptisms or the Lord's Supper

[43] Isaack de Rasieres to Samuel Blommaert, 1628 or 1629, in *Three Visitors to Early Plymouth: Letters about the Pilgrim Settlement in New England during its first seven years, by John Pory, Emmanuel Altham and Isaack de Rasieres*, ed. Sydney V. James, Jr. ([n.p.]: Plimoth Plantation, Inc., 1963), 76.

that punctuated the community life of every Protestant in Europe. On a day-to-day level, the Leiden people would have found the services otherwise familiar, as they expected the gathering to revolve around preaching and teaching. Lacking a minister to administer sacraments, they at least received the edification and guidance that had been the mainstay of their worship life in Europe.

Others present would have marked further omissions. Those coming directly from an English parish would have missed the liturgy of the prayer book. English Protestants elsewhere in the Americas without clergy often appointed someone to read the service, receiving comfort from the familiar language contained in the Book of Common Prayer. Although Judith Maltby has gathered evidence of devotion to the prayer book in England – and I have found some elsewhere in the English Atlantic – surviving Plymouth records reveal no one articulating an attachment to its language and routines.[44] Those who criticized Plymouth praxis in the first decade did not list failure to follow the prayer book as an issue – a book that may not have been present there anyway; the lack of any reference to debates over the established church liturgy suggested no one advocated for it or else no one complaining perceived it as an issue that would garner much attention. Thomas Morton, who was eventually run out of a nearby trade outpost, cited differences over the liturgy as one area of contention, but he did so only much later, at a time when he hoped to enlist Archbishop Laud against both Plymouth and Massachusetts.[45] No contemporary evidence raised the issue.

Beside the liturgy, Church of England members would have missed other sacraments, especially church weddings. The Church of England solemnized marriages, but many reformed Protestants elsewhere relied on civil magistrates instead. Robinson's former congregants firmly opposed solemnizing marriages in church. Having found no biblical precedent for the practice, they adopted civil ceremonies from the Dutch and continued that practice in New England. Later, during the interregnum when parliament ruled the nation without king or House of Lords, marriage in England temporarily became a civil institution. Although that moment lay in the future, Church of England officials were already on the alert to object to this derivation from their approach, and Edward

[44] Judith Maltby, *Prayer Book and People in Elizabethan and Early Stuart England* (Cambridge: Cambridge University Press, 1998), 136–45.

[45] Jeremy Dupertius Bangs suggests that Lyford did not raise the point because he did not use it either; see his *Pilgrim Edward Winslow*, 110. For Morton, see Charles Francis Adams, Jr., "Introduction," in *New English Canaan of Thomas Morton, with Introductory Matter and Notes*, ed. Francis Adams (Publications of the Prince Society, XIV; Boston, 1883. Reissued, in the Research and Source Work Series, 131; American Classics in History and Social Science, 2. New York: Burt Franklin, 1967), 68–69, 94

Winslow may have been thrown in Fleet Prison at the behest of Laud in part for performing such marriages.[46] In Plymouth at that time, the only options – in the absence of a minister – were to forego marriage or to allow a magistrate to solemnize them. Whether or not they missed church marriages, everyone in Plymouth would have found the religious practice truncated. That lack was felt by Leiden separatists as well as by those who came directly from an English parish church.

Even those who were satisfied with the omission of the prayer book and found Brewster fully competent to instruct and motivate them in his role as ruling elder also noted privations. Robert Cushman worried that their presence "in a Heathen Country," would cause their countrymen to assume that "the grace of Christ" had been "quenched in us," and he assured the readers of his lay sermon that it had not.[47] Still, they lacked a teacher, leaving parents to catechize their children as best they could. More generally, they missed the vigorous spiritual life they had enjoyed in Leiden – a university town, where they were guided by a pastor who was also a renowned theologian, and where a few of their more elite members had launched a printing press that briefly produced English-language works.[48] The most tangible remnant of that history in Plymouth could be found in Brewster's enormous library (at his death its 400 books and 382 distinct titles rivaled John Harvard's bequest that helped launch the college that bears his name).[49] The people of Plymouth enjoyed the benefit of Brewster's library, which he continued to build after migrating

[46] Bangs, *Pilgrim Edward Winslow*, 152.

[47] [Robert Cushman], *A Sermon Preached at Plimmoth in New-England December 9. 1621. In an assemblie of his Majesties faithfull Subjects, there inhabiting. Wherein is shewed the danger of selfe-love, and the sweetnesse of true Friendship. Together With a prefact, shewing the state of the preface, shewing the state of the Country, and Condition of the Savages. Rom. 12.10. Be affectioned to love one another with brotherly love. Written in the yeare 1621* (London, 1622), A4. But, he went on, "we still hold, and teach the same points of faith, mortification, and sanctification, which we have heard and learned in a most ample and large maner in our owne country."

[48] The press included many items of a polemical religious nature (as opposed to devotional works) and were generally associated with the "puritan" wing of the English Protestant community. Keith L. Sprunger, "The Godly Ministry of Printing by Brewster en Brewer," in *The Pilgrim Press: A bibliographical & historical memorial of the books printed at Leyden by the Pilgrims Fathers… by Rendel Harris and Stephen K. Jones*, partial reprint with new contributions, ed. R. Breugelmans (Nieuwkoop: de Graaf Publishers, 1987), 170, 172, 176.

[49] James Deetz and Patricia E. S. Deetz, *The Times of Their Lives: Life, Love, and Death in Plymouth Colony* (New York: W. H. Freeman, 2000), 195–96. An early effort to identify the titles in his library can be found in [Henry Martyn] Dexter, "Elder Brewster's Library," *Proceedings of the Massachusetts Historical Society* 5 (1899–1900): 37–85; his work was refined in *Plymouth Colony's Private Libraries: As recorded in Wills and Inventories, 1633–1692*, trans. and ed. Jeremy Dupertius Bangs (Leiden: American Leiden Pilgrim Museum, 2016; revised edition, 2018), 38–178. The library was dispersed at his death, as neither of his two sons had their father's bookish interests.

and out of which he loaned books to his neighbors.[50] Otherwise, the Leiden people entered a backwater, where they found it difficult to recreate the religious lives they had known.

When the first contingent of Massachusetts settlers arrived in 1620, a church member from Plymouth journeyed there to aid in caring for those who had fallen ill; while there, Samuel Fuller and John Endecott agreed that they shared similar views of "ye outward formes of Gods worshipe."[51] Whatever his views of proper practice, Fuller's own recent experience had been of understaffed pulpits, a mixed population, and an incomplete recreation of the expected range of religious practices. Despite our image of this community, Plymouth's first years were entirely typical of other truncated efforts to transplant faith into the Atlantic settlements.

The Lyford Fiasco

The low point in the newly formed but not yet fully functional Plymouth church surely came in 1624. Plymouth was split over defenders of the nascent church and newly arrived individuals who wanted to undermine the power of the few Leiden men who headed both church and government. The clash prompted a transatlantic debate over the nature of the new settlement and of its church order, a clash which inadvertently captured aspects of Plymouth practice in this first decade. In a reversal of usual scholarly practice, a vignette not at the opening but offered by way of (an extended) conclusion allows a reconsideration of the issues of minister, membership, and praxis.

In 1624, controversy swirled around Plymouth's little church, revealing otherwise unarticulated details about practices as well as the tensions arising from the aim to create a gathered church on the American strand. The investors prompted the crisis when they dispatched a prospective minister early in 1624 (instead of financing Robinson's journey, as his former congregants hoped). How the unemployed Oxford graduate John Lyford came to the attention of the Adventurers is not known. He traveled with a sizeable household that included his wife, children, and servants. They arrived in New England in the *Charity*, which sailed in late April 1622 and reached Plymouth around the end of June. The terms on which Lyford went were later contested: at the time Robert Cushman assured friends there that Lyford knew he had been promised no post, but

[50] David A. Lupher, *Greeks, Romans, and Pilgrims: Classical Receptions in Early New England* (Leiden: Brill, 2017), 185, documents such a loan from Brewster to Bradford.

[51] John Endecott to William Bradford, May 11, 1629, "Of plimoth plantation," 329.

other Adventurers asserted that he was to be paid a stipend as a teacher.[52] Upon his arrival, Lyford asked to be made a member of the church. As Bradford later put it: "he made a large confession of his faith; and an acknowledgemente of his former disorderly walking, and his being Intangled with many corruptions, which had been a burthen to his conscience; and blessed God for this opportunitie, of freedom & libertie, to injoye ye ordinances of God in puritie among his people."[53] Lyford accepted that he would only serve as the church's pastor if called to do so by the other members. Disgruntled at receiving no call, he soon joined other residents, among them John Oldham (best known because his death in the next decade would contribute to the causes of the Pequot War). Oldham, Lyford, and others conspired to start their own church, with Lyford as its head – which they characterized as constituting, within the Plymouth context, "a reformation, in church and commone wealth."[54] The two men also wrote damning accounts of the infant settlement, maligning both religious and secular affairs.[55]

These transatlantic missives reverberated both in Plymouth and in England. With the cooperation of ship's captain William Pierce, the settlement's leaders retrieved the letters from his outbound ship. Making copies before sending them, they confronted the letters' authors with the evidence of their duplicity. Like Anne Hutchinson in Massachusetts in the next decade, Lyford faced punishment from both the church – which excommunicated him – and the government – which banished him as well as Oldham. Oldham soon violated his exile; upon his return, "they comitted him, till he was tamer, and then apointed a gard of musketers wch he was to pass threw, and ever one was ordered to give him a thump on ye brich, with ye but end of his musket, and then was conveied to ye water side, wher a boat was ready to carry him away."[56] Both men went to Virginia, Oldham later returning to meet his end in New England in 1636. In the meantime, their letters alerted the Adventurers about tensions in Plymouth.

The concerns of the Adventurers – besides the fact that Plymouth was proving a money pit – focused largely on the state of religious affairs. Lyford and Oldham accused the church of neglecting sacraments – an obvious accusation since they had no minister and therefore no sacraments; "familie duties on ye Lords day" – by which they meant gathering for family prayer and Bible reading; and the need to catechize children.

52 Cushman letter, January 24, 1623, "Of plimoth plantation," 223, 257.
53 Bradford, "Of plimoth plantation," 237. 54 "Of plimoth plantation," 241.
55 These letters do not survive but are extensively described in Bradford's "Of plimoth plantation"; see the discussion below.
56 "Of plimoth plantation," 263.

They also alleged that the church was guilty of "diversitie aboute religion." This phrasing, given the later uses of the Plymouth legacy as a harbinger of religious freedom, contained a peculiar irony. The accusation alleged that Plymouth departed from standard English practice, in that they embraced an alternate viewpoint to that promoted by the Church of England; in modern parlance, they were guilt of adopting a differing position. From their perspective, diversity (or difference) was deleterious, as only one way was appropriate. The criticism may have been somewhat disingenuous, as Lyford himself may not have been entirely supportive of all aspects of Church of England practice. His history of services in the Irish Protestant Church could indicate that he was opened to the currents of reform within the mainstream English church, as was often the case with clergy who opted for an Irish Protestant pulpit. Bradford and Brewster's response to this last point was classic obfuscation: they avoided the substance, merely noting that no one residing there had ever objected to any practice. "We know no such matter, for here was never any controversie or opposition, either publike, or private (to our knowledge) since we came."[57] In other words, no one had previously noted any divergences in their ways from those of the established church. An absence of such criticism did not connote lack of divergence from accepted practice, of course, but instead sidestepped the question entirely.

As for the other matters, some they admitted while laying the blame elsewhere. Such was the case with the lack of a minister (the fault, they said, of the Adventurers who failed to send Robinson).[58] His absence also explained the unavailability of baptism or the Lord's Supper, the sacraments they would have offered had they enjoyed the guidance of a clergyman. Some complaints they dismissed, such as religious weddings (which lacked biblical warrant). Still others they hotly denied: families saw to catechizing and teaching children, as Plymouth had no one to employ as a school teacher. Similarly, they never neglected the Sabbath, averring that "every lords day some are appointed, to visite suspected places, and if any be found Idling, and neglecte ye hearing ye word (through Idlnes or profanes), they are punished for ye same."[59] Those defending the settlement pressed the point that they upheld basic principles that infused reformed Protestantism more generally: they accepted the need for Sabbath observance, literacy, and religious instruction. That common ground represented the safest place for those defending Plymouth to stand.

[57] "Of plimoth plantation," 225. [58] "Of plimoth plantation," 261.
[59] "Of plimoth plantation," 259.

In the end, the confrontation persuaded some Adventurers to withdraw their support on the grounds that the Plymouth faithful remained "Brownists." The term, referencing early English separatist Robert Browne, was not a compliment. Indeed, the disgruntled Adventurers asserted that they would "sine against god in building up such a people."[60] The Leiden church, in seeking permission to go to America, had presented itself to the king and the Adventurers in a way that deemphasized its separatism. Accentuating Robinson's moderation and equating their church with the practices of French Huguenots, the Leiden community dissembled slightly. While the French Protestants did not overtly object to bishops, they were prevented from having them by their marginal status in France – so Leiden believers could equate the two church orders to give a reassuring impression, sidestepping the differences between their own practices and those of the Church of England.[61] The Adventurers who continued to abide by their obligation claimed that their irate co-investors sought any excuse to disassociate themselves from the settlement.[62] While Bradford and Winslow denied the accusations that they wanted none to live among them save separatists and that they held non-separatists in "distaste," they ultimately could not dismiss some allegations.[63] The church gave itself away when it rejected common practices for which its leaders could find no warrant in the Word of God. When they could not deny or explain away, they took the high ground and revealed their disagreements with the accepted practices within English Protestantism.

The controversy climaxed in a dramatic confrontation in England, in which the church and its accusers faced off before the Adventurers. In the "trial" which took place presumably in London in late 1624 or early 1625, moderators were appointed to represent the two sides, with Thomas Hooker (later of Connecticut fame) representing Plymouth.[64] Edward Winslow, who was in England defending Plymouth's interests, had been accused of maligning Lyford. Captain Pierce was also present and supported the plantation. In the session, which drew a sizeable crowd, accusations were aired and addressed. The highlight, however, had to be the startling revelations about Lyford's past. Winslow received a tip to investigate his time in Ireland, which revealed him to be – as one scholar

[60] "Of plimoth plantation," 271.

[61] Discussion of this issue, "Of plimoth plantation," 245, 271. Sprunger, *Dutch Puritanism*, simply notes that they acknowledged the 39 Articles of the Church of England (135). Winship suggests they misrepresented their views, *Godly Republicanism*, 159; Sergeant sees their separatism as softening, as opposed to being misrepresented; see "The Best Parts of Histories," 38.

[62] "Of plimoth plantation," 273. [63] "Of plimoth plantation," 245.

[64] "Of plimoth plantation," 267–69.

put it – "a lecherous hypocrite."[65] If anything, that characterization was too gentle: a serial rapist, Lyford left his previous post after assaulting a young woman sent to him by a prospective husband who asked him for advice about whether she appeared a worthy wife for a godly man. After raping her, Lyford then declared her acceptable as his parishioner's bride. When the woman subsequently revealed the assault, the church censured and drove him out. Lyford had already brought a bastard child into his own household, having initially denied the rumors of his past dalliance to his then prospective wife. His wife eventually confided to those in Plymouth that he routinely assailed their maids, even when these servants slept at the foot of the couple's bed (and she herself was present). Winslow, who had been chastised for characterizing Lyford as a knave, was vindicated by these revelations.[66]

Besides the long arm of English authorities unhappy with American religious practices, this incident encapsulated numerous problems with transplanting Reformation. Most obviously, Plymouth had trouble – until the deluge of clerics that began in 1629 – finding a suitable man to serve their church. The core church members wanted Robinson, but he refused to migrate without all those within the congregation who wanted to go. His position pushed up the expense of sending him, which dampened the interest of the investors in shouldering that added burden. Some of the Adventurers may have thought that Lyford – who was on hand and who only required the investment of transporting his household – was a suitable compromise. The Adventurers may have thought Lyford a suitable substitute, given his previous willingness to serve the Irish Protestant church which tended to more vigorous reform than the English church.

For his part, Lyford may have been the first scandalous English cleric to enter the wider Atlantic hoping to escape his past, but he would not be the last. He hoped to take advantage of the distance that inhibited the circulation of information about his history, and he might have succeeded if he and Oldham had not waged an attack on the Plymouth church order. His efforts called attention to himself and ultimately brought out his story. Had Plymouth not been trying to keep the office of minister open for Robinson, the church might have named Lyford before the news of the scandal broke. Even when his past and his efforts to undermine Plymouth with his transatlantic denunciations had been revealed, some church members wanted to forgive his transgression and allow him to re-enter the church. In this case, however, repentance did not earn a clergyman

[65] Gill, *Mayflower Remembered*, 111.

[66] Bangs, *Pilgrim Edward Winslow*, 109–11, for the Lyford affair from his point of view.

with a history of sexual assault reincorporation into the religious community. He was exiled for his attack on the church and what Edward Winslow called his knavery.

The controversy also revealed how an Atlantic location, although it could not entirely hide alternate religious practices, created a buffer for those pursuing illegal or unconventional options. The Plymouth church did as its leaders thought best but at the same time tried to conceal any divergences from accepted practices. The distance that made the church potential prey for Lyford also gave it room to maneuver towards its own ends. As the only church in town, the Leiden-derived Plymouth church may have accorded membership somewhat selectively, leaving some people out. Yet it objected to the seemingly obvious solution that Lyford, Oldham, and company offered when they moved to start a more broadly inclusive parish church as an alternative to the church already founded in Plymouth. The Plymouth members objected that they acted in secret and that Lyford as a member of their church had an obligation to speak to them before making such a move. It seems unlikely, however, that the Plymouth church would have accepted the formation of an alternative had it been pursued more openly. They wanted religious homogeneity, and on their own terms. They preferred a mixed community in one church rather than the proliferation of alternatives beyond. This dilemma lay at the heart of the Reformation project everywhere.

Returning to my title: "Reworking Reformation in the early English Atlantic" refers not only to what the people of early Plymouth – or some of them – tried to do. It alludes as well to our own work of reconsideration. Scholars gleefully break down national myths: religious liberty or harmonious intercultural relations make tempting targets. Yet while we overturn old verities, we persist in our own habitual thinking. We view religion as portable, picked up like luggage and carried unchanged to a new location. We treat religious identities as complete entities, likely to appear recognizably themselves in any location. When a fragment of the Leiden church boarded the *Mayflower*, did they carry a separatist alternative to America? Scholars have always assumed so, placing Plymouth's history within the Bradford narrative that drew a line from Scrooby all the way through to New England. That narrative supports the assumption that Reformation converged with mobility in order to allow refugees to move with and thereby protect their faith. Looking closely at one small religious community, we can see how easily that goal could be thwarted. Even the best-known colonies – the easily categorized places – in practice had complex and contingent relationships to their purported identities. Plymouth came into being not as a transplanted Leiden church but as a mixed community struggling to create common ground, debating anew all the issues of Reformation that we assume they had settled long before. Dubbed "pilgrims" later to capture their status as exiles, they have been made to carry the weight of religious purity and commitment. They have also been held up as "not Massachusetts" for those looking for tolerance and piety. The burden may be too great for them to bear.

2 Puritanism in a Local Context: Ministry, People, and Church in 1630s Massachusetts

David D. Hall

The English women and men who moved to newly founded Massachusetts in the 1630s were experienced travelers of a special kind. Known among themselves as "the godly" and to their countrymen as "puritans," they were accustomed to a social, cultural, and theological geography organized around the difference between places deemed "profane" and others deemed pure or "lawful" because they were furnished with "means," a code-word for evangelical preaching. Catholics, too, were travelers in early Stuart England, but of a different kind. Theirs was a geography of "safe" houses where priests were sheltered and altars secretly maintained alongside outward expressions of loyalty to a Protestant monarch and Protestant state church. Another half-hidden group, the "Familists," was also practicing a geography that mingled the covert or hidden with accommodation to the larger culture.[1]

Important though they were at certain moments in English history, the many rumors about these covert groups was not really what shaped the colonists' sense of space and its bearing on religion. Instead, they inherited a long-standing Puritan-style politics of religion and, more broadly, a politics fostered by the English Reformation. As Alexandra Walsham has shown in *Reformation of the Landscape*, one version of this politics involved iconoclastic violence aimed at the residues of Catholicism in cemeteries, churches, and other sites. Another version concerned worship, a politics that flared up during the early decades of the seventeenth century when the first two Stuart kings, James I and Charles I, began to favor a group of clergy in the state church who wanted to re-emphasize its connections with Catholicism at the expense of connections with the Reformed tradition. Known eventually as the "Laudians," after William Laud, who became bishop of London in 1626 and archbishop of Canterbury in 1633, this group wanted to reintroduce altars, insisted

[1] Alexandra Walsham, "'Yielding to the Extremity of the Time': Conformity, Orthodoxy, and the Post-Reformation Catholic Community," in *Conformity and Orthodoxy in the English Church, c. 1560–1660*, ed. Peter Lake and Michael Questier (Woodbridge: Boydell, 2000), 211–61; Christopher Marsh, *The Family of Love in English Society, 1550–1630* (Cambridge: Cambridge University Press, 1999).

that lay people kneel when they participated in the Eucharist, and reaffirmed episcopacy as apostolically sanctioned.[2]

The Laudian program was openly hostile to a "godly" version of worship and, more generally, to the anti-Catholicism and anti-clericalism of English Protestants. Ever since the middle of the sixteenth century, the godly had lobbied for a pattern of worship keyed to the forceful preaching of repentance, singing of psalms, prayer, and extensive readings from Scripture. Any alternative and, especially, the Laudian alternative of emphasizing the "ceremonies," endangered true religion. Hence the many efforts of local people to live in parishes or towns where the right kind of preaching was available and the ceremonies could be avoided or at best, intermittently observed. Another goal of the godly was community-related, a preference for local churches where strong preaching was accompanied by an ethos of "edification," or becoming like the body of Christ in practicing mutual love and support. The bitter truth about many churches in England was how few were aligned with this scriptural ideal. Instead of putting pressure on the "ungodly" to repent and accept the disciplinary weight of divine law, too many parish churches were allowing everyone to partake of the sacraments of Holy Communion and Baptism. Hence the practice – limited to towns where the godly could avoid the gaze of the authorities – of forming private associations or "conventicles" where sermons could be discussed, the Bible parsed, and purity sustained to a far greater extent than in a typical parish.[3]

The contested geography of religion in early seventeenth-century England was among the major reasons why so many of the godly joined in the founding of Massachusetts and its sister colonies in the 1630s. The organizers of the Massachusetts Bay Company (f. 1629), which oversaw the creation of Massachusetts, wanted everyone who crossed the Atlantic to inhabit the same space, a "great town" where familiar ways of living could be resumed and the Company's authority sustained.[4] Instead, the immigrants preferred to establish towns of their own, a process the Company agreed to facilitate by distributing large grants of land to

[2] A politics ably described in Anthony Milton, *Catholic and Reformed: The Roman and Protestant Churches in English Protestant Thought, 1600–1640* (Cambridge: Cambridge University Press, 2002). See also Alexandra Walsham, *The Reformation of the Landscape: Religion, Identity, and Memory in Early Modern Britain & Ireland* (Cambridge: Cambridge University Press, 2011).

[3] Ibid., chapter 4; Susan Guinn-Chipman, *Religious Space in Reformation England: Contesting the Past* (London: Pickering & Chatto, 2013); Kenneth Fincham, *Altars Restored: The Changing Form of English Religious Worship, 1547–1700* (Oxford: Oxford University Press, 2004); John S. Coolidge, *The Pauline Renaissance in England: Puritanism and the Bible* (Oxford, UK: Clarendon Press, 1970).

[4] Darrett B. Rutman, *Winthrop's Boston, 1630–1649: Portrait of a Puritan Town* (Chapel Hill: University of North Carolina Press, 1965), chapter 2.

"companies" of newcomers. Thus came into being "Newtown," the town on which this essay focuses. Its location on the Charles River a short distance upstream from Boston had been marked out for settlement as a place of safety from Spanish ships that might attack the new colony and therefore where the leadership of the Massachusetts-Bay Company would congregate. Instead, John Winthrop, the governor, stayed in seaside Boston and, in 1633, Newtown passed into the hands of the well-known Puritan minister Thomas Hooker and the people who accompanied him from England. A few years later, as this group was leaving for the region that became Connecticut, another wave of colonists arrived and founded a church of their own (February 1636), with Thomas Shepard (1605–1649) as its minister.

An unusually abundant archive survives from the early years of Shepard's ministry, an archive I exploit in this essay as a means of discerning how the Reformation in general and the Puritan version of Protestantism fared in its new-world setting.[5] From the moment the residents of Newtown (renamed Cambridge in 1638, the place name I use for the rest of this essay) set foot in Massachusetts, they knew what they wanted by way of ministry, church, and doctrine. The story I tell is therefore a story of continuity, for the worldview of these people had been deeply marked by the principles of Reformed (Calvinist) Protestantism and the politics of religion in early Stuart England. They also brought with them a more troubling baggage, the tensions that had accumulated within a movement ever on the verge of splintering into radical, moderate, and conservative factions – some willing to accept state-imposed conformity, others fashioning a half-way house that combined conformity and non-conformity, and still others pursuing the goals of lawfulness and purity to the point of separating from the state church.[6]

[5] George Selement and Bruce C. Woolley eds., *Thomas Shepard's Confessions* (Boston: Publications of the Colonial Society of Massachusetts 58 [1981]); Mary Rhinelander McCarl, "Thomas Shepard's Record of Relations of Religious Experience, 1648–49," *William and Mary Quarterly*, 3rd ser., 48 (1991): 3–41; Michael McGiffert, *God's Plot the Paradoxes of Puritan Piety Being the Autobiography & Journal of Thomas Shepard* (Amherst: University of Massachusetts Press, 1972); Thomas Shepard, *The Parable of the Ten Virgins Opened & Applied* (London,1660), reprinted in *The Works of Thomas Shepard*, ed. John Albro (3 vols., Boston, 1853). I have not drawn on the relations edited by McCarl because they date from the late 1640s and say much less about the English side of the story. I narrate the secular and ecclesiastical history of Newtown/Cambridge more fully in *A Reforming People: Puritanism and the Transformation of Public Life in New England* (New York: Knopf, 2011), chapter 5. Church records for this period have not survived.

[6] Complications sketched in part in Peter Lake, *Moderate Puritans and the Elizabethan Church* (Cambridge: Cambridge University Press, 1982).

From day one, these tensions were in play in newly founded Massachusetts and, as we will see, in the church and town of Cambridge. Like Carla Pestana in her essay for this volume on ministry, church, and community in 1620s Plymouth, I describe continuities with the broader Reformation, though the emphasis in what follows falls on local circumstances as mirrored in spiritual, communal, and ministerial practice. In some older versions of the immigrants' story, they have been described as "uprooted" in ways that set them on the path towards improvisation and adaptation. In keeping with this perspective, it is sometimes argued that the colonists hastily invented a looser, congregation-centered form of church government and a law-centered evangelism in response to what seemed like utter chaos. Often, these narratives are also accompanied by the argument that "edification," or an ethos of "charity" gave way to something approximating a future "individualism."[7]

Arguments of this kind rest on a narrow understanding of geography as empty space and emigration as profoundly disruptive Mine is different because, as we learn from listening to their reflections on what it meant to be godly, the people of new-world Cambridge were haunted by the shape of their lives in England and haunted, too, by a confusion they inherited from the Puritan movement about the church as a new "Sion," a place where corruption had been overcome and purity prevailed.

Godly and Ungodly Space in Early Stuart England

Safely on the western edge of the Atlantic, the women and men who joined the newly founded church in Cambridge in the 1630s reminded each other of what it had been like to navigate the religious and social geography of their homeland, both of them disturbing because so few towns or villages employed ministers of the right kind and because local people were accustomed to mocking anyone who seemed "precise." To attend a local church on Sundays was problematic, for the official liturgy was tainted with remnants of Catholicism. Instead of being a haven where

[7] A thesis egregiously voiced in Oscar Handlin, "The Significance of the Seventeenth Century," in *Seventeenth-century America: Essays in Colonial History*, ed. James Morton Smith (New Nork: Norton, 1959), 3–12, and reiterated in a more sociological form in Bernard Bailyn, *Education in the Forming of American Society* (Chapel Hill: University of North Carolina Press, 1960). Scholars working in the field of early American literature endorsed the same argument; cf. Patricia Caldwell, *The Puritan Conversion Narrative: The Beginnings of American Expression* (New York: Cambridge University Press, 1983). It also informs Perry Miller's *The New England Mind: The Seventeenth Century* (Cambridge, MA: Harvard University Press, 1939) and its sequel, *The New England Mind: From Colony to Province* (Cambridge, MA: Harvard University Press, 1953).

Christ was sensibly present, parish churches were compromising the substance of true religion. Hence a restlessness among the colonists during their English years, a restlessness forced upon them by a troublesome geography of religion.

So we learn from the "relations" or testimonies made by people applying for membership in Shepard's Cambridge church. Robert Holmes, who came to Massachusetts in the 1630s, recalled a phase of life in which he had been "contented" with "common prayer and homilies" (sermons printed in an officially endorsed book that no Puritan-affiliated minister would ever use). He remembered, too, living in a place where he "heard a sermon once a month" and fell asleep as he listened to them. Moving to a larger city, he finally encountered preaching that made him "terrified about my estate" (that is, whether he was among the redeemed) for having lived so long as a sinner. The pattern of John Sill's life had been similar, "brought up in an ignorant place" until he moved to a town where his identity was altered by sermons that emphasized the vast difference between being a "hearer and not a doer." "This did work sadly upon" Sill, who changed sides after encountering a community of "God's people" he learned to "love." A similar geography was deeply consequential for John Trumbull, who remembered living "in sin without contradiction in a town without means [i.e., the right kind of preaching]," a place where "the people of God" were mocked by people who thought nothing of "swearing" in God's name. Unexpectedly, a godly book came into Trumbull's hands. After reading it, he was "moved to seek after some other means [of grace]" that would help him find "a place where the sermons were twice" (meaning, presumably, twice on Sundays). Although warned by erstwhile friends "that I would go mad ... with study," he, like Still, found sustenance and support in a community of people who "love[d] Sabbaths [and] saints."[8]

Others who testified in new-world Cambridge had experienced the same recurrence of presence and absence as evidenced in powerful preaching, on the one hand and lifeless sermons borrowed from a printed book on the other. Jane Holmes did not like her stepmother and, perhaps for this reason, "thought I could not live holily in [my] father's house." Then, to her dismay, she stumbled into the household of a minister who "taught free will" (that is, bad doctrine) and was bitterly critical of "Puritans." When she tried to persuade her father to "carry" her to a place where she could become a "servant" to a worthy minister, he seems to have refused. The situation was worse in the unnamed "sinful place" where Elizabeth Cutter was born, a town where, in her terse

[8] Selement and Woolley, *Shepard's Confessions*, 142–43, 44–45, 107–9.

appraisal, "no sermon [was] preached." When she transitioned to working as a servant in another household than her own, she found it "carnal." People also remembered the contempt rained upon them in the small world of an English village or town. Testifying in Cambridge, Goodman Shepard remembered being "laughed at because I would not drink and break Sabbath" as his fellow workers did. For John Stedman, the problem was the "vain and idle companions" whose company he had enjoyed until he was aroused by a sermon to seek out "the private societies of the saints," whereupon he "resolved against ill company and hence was hated." Few were as fortunate as Henry Dunster, who, when he was about twelve years old, lived in a town where "God gave us a minister and the Lord gave me an attentive ear and heart to understand." For others, moving from one place to another could mean giving up "plenty of means [of grace]" for a region Martha Collins remembered as having "no good Sabbaths" and no "blessing under that ministry." Edward Collins had been "brought up of godly parents" until, after his father's death, he "was cast into a gentleman's house, a profane house." Richard Eccles had been "brought up in popery," from which he was rescued by "getting some light" and abandoning "ill company." Beginning to read godly books, he looked around him "for more means and so went to Yorkshire, where there were good means," that is, a "powerful ministry." In Nicholas Wyeth's testimony, he described how he "went four miles" outside his parish to hear the sermons of a certain minister and, when he found that someone well-known for his preaching was sixteen miles away, "went often to hear him" having "none at home" worth listening to. Indeed, going elsewhere to hear sermons – usually those preached at the afternoon services on Sundays – was so customary that it acquired the nickname of "gadding."[9]

These experiences bear out the picture of the Church of England painted by Puritans as early as the reign of Elizabeth I and by Parliaments then and later. The problems were two-fold. When Catholicism gave way to Protestantism in 1558 with the accession of Elizabeth, the state church inherited thousands of priests who had not been expected to preach and, for the most part, had not been educated at one of the English universities. Replacing them was hampered by a second problem, the pillaging of church properties under Henry VIII and his successors. The outcome was a state church deprived of the revenues it needed to recruit, train, and support a vigorously Protestant clergy. As a result of this and other circumstances, the Church of England was burdened with the compromises known as pluralism and non-

[9] Ibid., 76–77, 144, 173, 161, 74, 130–31, 82, 115, 193–94.

residency. Pluralists were ministers appointed in more than one parish – possibly several – and collecting income from each. Non-residents were those who did not live in the parish to which they were appointed, sometimes because they were attached to a cathedral or because they were also pluralists who hired a "reader" to provide a minimum level of services in a town or village.

The extent of these practices and the enduring presence of a semi-competent ministry were documented in Puritan-sponsored county by county "calendars" identifying parishes without regular preaching or controlled by pluralists. A project initiated in the 1570s and 1580s and its dismal tabulation of "dumb dogges" (Is. 56:10) was publicized in the surreptitious *A Parte of a Register* (1593). It was warmly supported by the more forcefully Protestant members of Parliament, notably when Job Throckmorton told the House of Commons in 1586 that, "If I were asked what is the bane of the Church and commonwealth, answer make, 'The dumb ministry, the dumb ministry'; yea, if I were asked a thousand times, I must say, 'the dumb ministry.'"[10] Men of this temperament were quick to blame the bishops of the state church for a situation that deprived so many people of the spiritual food on which their salvation depended. According to the outspoken minister John Udall, the bishops were soul-killers because they refused to eliminate pluralism and suppressed godly preaching. Little had changed by the 1630s, when people such as John Sill and John Trumbull were deciding to immigrate to Massachusetts. When the "Long" Parliament began to meet in November 1640, a moment that most historians regard as the starting point of the "English Revolution," it was deluged with petitions detailing the many ministers deemed "scandalous" and the few who were effective preachers. In response, the House of Commons empowered various committees to identify and dismiss pluralists, non-residents, and others whose moral or political behavior made them unwelcome. By the time this process ended, some 2,800 clergy had been suspended or dismissed.[11]

[10] *Proceedings in the Parliaments of Elizabeth I, 1584–1589*, ed. Terence E. Hartley (London: Leicester University Press, 1995), 315 (modernized); William Fulke, *A Brief and Plain Declaration Concerning the Desires of All Those Faithful Ministers* (1584)), repr. in Leonard J. Trinterud, Tudor Puritanism (New York: Oxford University Press, 1971), 257–59, a situation exacerbated by pluralism and non-residency (ibid., 259). According to a census carried out by 1586, of 2,537 parishes, only 472 had "preachers," some of whom may not have preached very often. Albert Peel ed., *The Seconde Part of a Register* 2 vols (Cambridge: Cambridge University Press, 2015), 2: 70–87, 88–184. In *A very fruiteful Sermon preched at Paules Crosse* (London, 1559), John Stockwood estimated (sig. A3r–v) that "scarse the twentieth parishe were provided" with an "able Teacher," that is, someone "godly, paynefull" and devoted to preaching the "worde."

[11] John Udall, *A Demonstration of the trueth of that Discipline* ([London, 1588]) sigs. A2–3; Jim Sharpe, "'Scandalous and Malignant Priests' in Essex: The Impact of Grassroots Puritanism," in *Politics and People in Revolutionary England: Essays in Honour of Ivan Roots*,

The stories told in new-world Cambridge were thus of a piece with the everyday experience of thousands of evangelical Protestants in England. As of ca. 1630, these people were also on the wrong side of the religious policies of Charles I and church leaders such as William Laud regarding worship and doctrine. In response, the godly were relying on self-devised forms of sociability and religious practice to meet their needs. As noted in the Cambridge relations, some of the godly gathered in "conventicles" (a red flag to the official Church) and, less tendentiously, in communities of the kind John Winthrop, the first governor of the new colony, had helped organize among his neighbors in Suffolk, a fellowship of a dozen people focused on praying for "every one of us each Friday ... to be mindefull one of another in desiring God to grante the petitions that were made to him that daye." As did many such groups, Winthrop's sang psalms together.[12] In some parishes, a self-selected group of the "godly" covenanted to "yield ... subjection to the gospel of Christ," a procedure John Cotton, who immigrated to Massachusetts in 1633, had introduced in the Lincolnshire town of Boston. At an extreme, lay people abandoned the state church entirely, a step that earned them the designation of "Separatist."[13]

None of the people who arrived in Cambridge in the 1630s and early 1640s had given up on the state church and become Separatists. Like many others around him, however, Edward Collins had participated in "private Christian meetings" in London where people shared notes they had taken as they listened to sermons. In his relation, John Stedman recalled being "admitted to private societies of saints where I found much sweetness." Underlying all such practices was the assumption – voiced by Nathaniel Sparrowhawk – that in England "superstitions clouded God [i.e., God's presence] in ordinances." And, although Collins, Stedman, and Sparrowhawk had not descended into Separatism, in nearby Boston (Lincolnshire), the congregation included a woman named Anne Hutchinson who believed that any minister ordained by a bishop in England was allied with the Antichrist and

ed. Colin Jones, Malyn Hewitt, and Stephen Roberts (Oxford, UK: Blackwell, 1986), 253–73, provides local details. More emerge from the sketches of ministers in A. G. Matthews, *Walker Revised Being a Revision of John Walker's Sufferings of the Clergy during the Grand Rebellion 1642–1660* (Oxford, UK: Clarendon Press, 1948). See also Ian Green, "The persecution of 'scandalous' and 'malignant' parish clergy during the English Civil War," *English Historical Review* 94 (1979): 507–51.

12 *Winthrop Papers* (Boston, 1929–), 1: 169.

13 The English radical Katherine Chidley, who eventually became a Baptist, was participating in a private "conventicle" in the 1630s. So were the people who organized the Broadmead (Bristol) gathered church in 1640, for which, see Edward Bean Underhill ed., *The Records of a Church of Christ Meeting in Broadmead, Bristol* (London, 1847).

could not be trusted. We will encounter her again, for the ways in which she drew the line between purity and danger would roil 1630s Massachusetts.[14]

Taming a Wilderness: The Making of "Virgin" Churches

Casting about for words to describe the space they had entered, the colonists turned to the stories of exodus and exile in Scripture they saw themselves re-enacting. They too were a covenanted people and divine providence was enabling them to build a new "Sion" in the corruption-free "wilderness" of Massachusetts.[15] To the north, in New France, and to the south, in New Spain and Maryland, Catholics were erecting crosses and consecrating cemeteries. Not in Massachusetts, however, for the colonists carried out a far-reaching disenchantment of space and time. No icons or relics, no sites of pilgrimage, no altars, no consecrated ground – all such markers of the sacred vanished overnight. Nor did the customary stages of the Christian Year reappear, for the colonists rejected saints' days and the traditional events associated with Christmas and Easter. When the local printer (whose printing shop was in Cambridge) began to issue almanacs in the 1640s, these had no "red-letter" days that, as was customary, indicated saints' days or other holy times. As well, the Cambridge-printed almanacs abandoned the traditional names for months and weekdays, which the colonists deemed too "pagan." Instead, purity dictated using numbers for months and words such as "seventh" for the days of the week.[16]

[14] Selement and Woolley eds., *Shepard's Confessions*, 83, 74, 64; David D. Hall ed., *The Antinomian Controversy, 1636–38: A Documentary History* (Middletown: Wesleyan University Press, 1968), 336–37.

[15] Much misunderstood, the biblical and post-biblical frameworks that informed the colonists' understanding of their place in sacred history are illuminated in Reiner Smolinski, "Israel Redivivus: The Eschatological Limits of Puritan Typology," *New England Quarterly* 63 (1990): 357–95, and Theodore Dwight Bozeman, *To Live Ancient Lives: The Primitivist Dimension in Puritanism* (Chapel Hill: University of North Carolina Press, 1988). How the colonists understood the biblical figure of "wilderness" and applied that framework to their surroundings is described in George H. Williams, *Wilderness and Paradise in Christian Thought: The Biblical Experience of the Desert in the History of Christianity & the Paradise Theme in the Theological Idea of the University* (New York: Harpers, 1962); Peter Carroll, *Puritanism and the Wilderness: the Intellectual Significance of the New England Frontier, 1629–1700* (New York: Columbia University Press, 1969).

[16] I draw here on Walsham, *Reformation of the Landscape*. What made the natural world in Massachusetts so troubling was the weather, for which see Karen Ordall Kupperman, "Climate and Mastery of the Wilderness in Seventeenth-Century New England," in *Seventeenth-Century New England*, ed. David D. Hall and David Grayson Allen (Boston: Colonial Society of Massachusetts, 1984), 3–37. The reworking of almanacs is described in David D. Hall, *Worlds of Wonder, Days of Judgment: Popular Religious Belief in Seventeenth-Century New England* (New York: Knopf, 1989), 62–63.

Barren though it must have seemed at first, and intimidating because the weather was so extreme – much hotter in summers and colder in winters – the landscape in Massachusetts would rapidly include gardens, orchards, pasture, roads, fences, houses, grist mills (the first of these in Cambridge was constructed in 1636), and meetinghouses. As well, congregations were gathering on Sundays to listen to readings from Scripture, public prayers, and preaching. Utterly bare and possibly to a modern eye, spiritually void, meetinghouses became sites where the quest for purity reached a satisfying endpoint. So we learn in particular from the rituals that unfolded when a local church was organized in Cambridge in February 1636. Accepting the advice of colleagues who were present that seven persons were needed to "make a Churche," Thomas Shepard, who would become its first minister, and six or seven men of the town "declare[d] what worke of Grace the Lord had wroughte in them" and "gave a solemne assent" to the church covenant. That the sermon text Shepard chose was Ephesians 5: 27 "That he might present it to himself a glorious church, not having a spot, or wrinkle or any such thing, but that it should be holy and without blemish" indicates how fervently he wanted the new congregation to be "a glorious church" or, as he was saying in sermons preached about the same time, a "virgin" church.[17] Not only was this a church stripped of an unlawful episcopacy and a Catholic-style liturgy, membership as territorial (the system that prevailed in the Church of England) had been replaced by the rule that it was voluntary and selective: open only to those who, to Shepard's satisfaction, were "visible saints." Hence the practice of requiring "relations" of those who wanted to become church members, relations in which prospective members described their personal encounter with Christ and the "work of grace" that lifted them out of bondage to sin.[18]

Here, at long last, the twin goals of personal purity and a fully cleansed mode of worship converged, or so it seemed to Shepard, who reminded his congregation that the requirements for church membership eliminated what the godly had found so disturbing in England, the presence

[17] Richard S. Dunn et al., *The Journal of John Winthrop 1630–1649* (Cambridge, MA: Harvard University Press, 1996), 168–70; cited hereafter as Winthrop, *Journal*.

[18] What churches expected of these testimonies and whether they were universally required has been variously described by historians of early New England. To be sure, none should be termed "conversion" narratives. See, for example, Francis Bremer, "'To Tell What God Hath Done for Thy Soul': Puritan Spiritual testimonies as Admissions Tests and Means of Edification," *New England Quarterly* 87 (2014): 625–65; Baird Tipson, "Samuel Stone's 'Discourse' Against Requiring Church Relations," *William and Mary Quarterly*, 3rd ser. 46 (1989): 786–99; and David D. Hall, *The Puritans A Transatlantic History* (Princeton, NJ: Princeton University Press, 2019), 232–35, and the relevant endnotes.

of "profane persons" at the Eucharist. Now, with access to the sacrament limited to the "saints alone," the new congregation could relish a fellowship "not polluted with the mixture of men's inventions [a code name for Catholic practice], nor defiled with the company of evil men." In the same sermons, Shepard spoke rapturously of "pure people, pure churches," evoking, as he did so, the "brightness of [Christ's] coming" prophesied in Daniel and Revelation, a spiritual event that, in his understanding of the end times, would motivate the faithful few to prepare the church for Christ's return in judgment.[19] As he pointed out, this "Middle Advent" was the moment when gathered churches would "make themselves ready" by admitting only those "virgins espoused to Christ, escaping the pollutions of idolatry and the world."[20]

Such a church was also likely to practice an ethics of mutual love, or edification. In England, this possibility had been thwarted by the everyday experiences of "hear[ing] Gods name's blasphemed" and encountering churches filled with a "mixed multitude." A tiny number of covenanted Separatist congregations of English exiles living in the Netherlands had claimed to meet this high standard. Now, in new-world Cambridge, edification seemed certain to flourish anew, with visible saints experiencing a "glorious portion" when and as they practiced "love [of] the brethren" (1 Jn. 3:14). When an economic downturn struck in the late 1630s, church members contributed money and cattle to a special fund to aid those who were slipping into poverty or in some manner had become disabled. Among themselves, they used "brother" and "sister" as terms of address. Hence the reason William Hamlet gave for crossing the Atlantic and joining the newly gathered church in Cambridge: he wanted to enjoy the fellowship of "the sweet people that came hither." And hence, in Shepard's sermon series of the late 1630s, his warm words about the unique affection among those who joined in covenant with each other and, in the context of economic crisis, his encouraging of local charity.[21]

Satisfying though it surely was to many of the colonists, this spiritual and social geography seemed incomplete to those in the new colony who craved a more forceful version of purity. To the quasi-Separatist minister Roger Williams, who arrived in early 1631, genuine purity was possible only when every minister rejected his participation in a corrupt Church of England. Repudiate your ordination at the hands of a bishop, Williams

[19] Albro, *Works of Shepard,* 2: 65, 20. [20] Ibid., 2: 24–26.

[21] Ibid., 2: 20; 126–27. The importance of this theme and its significance to church members in Cambridge is described in Abram van Engen, *Sympathetic Puritans Calvinist Fellow Feeling in Early New England* (New York: Oxford University Press, 2015). I describe the social ethos of the Cambridge church more fully in Hall, *Reforming People,* chapter 5.

demanded. George Phillips, who had been a minister in the state church, felt the same way. Shortly after arriving in 1630, he told the prospective church members in newly founded Watertown that he would renounce his ordination in the Church of England and start afresh. Casting about for other evidence of imperfection, Williams hit upon the military flag the colonists were using and urged the magistrate in Salem, where he was living, to cut out the St. George's cross. This act of iconoclasm startled the lay leaders of the colony, who knew it would displease the government in England. Enlisting Thomas Hooker to explain why the flag was not an example of idolatry, the government censured John Endicott, the magistrate in Salem. (A few years later the government went half-way towards Endicott by confining the flag to a single location, a fort in Boston harbor.) And, in 1637, most of the ministers agreed among themselves that, although mistakes had been made in England, they would not follow Phillips's example.[22]

This back-and-forth gave way to a deeper crisis. It was the doing of two ministers, the veteran John Cotton and the younger, less experienced John Wheelwright. Both could count on the support of the laymen in Cotton's Boston congregation. Their most intriguing ally was Ann Hutchinson, a charismatic woman in the same church who arrived in Massachusetts in 1634 with a reputation of being able to foresee the future. Soon, Hutchinson was openly impugning the sermons of the other ministers in the new colony. So, less bluntly, were Cotton and Wheelwright. Thus came into being an event that has become known as the "Antinomian controversy." At one level it was a dispute about the system of theology the immigrant clergy had inherited from their teachers at Cambridge and Oxford, a system that aspired to synthesize "law" and "gospel," or divine sovereignty and human effort, the witness of the Spirit and "sanctification." The back-and-forth among the ministers would generate the principal documents that survive from 1636 to 1637, when the controversy reached its climax – Cotton and Wheelwright questioning this synthesis and others, including Shepard, strongly defending it.[23]

But as other documents indicate, more was at stake than a clerical tiff about the fine points of theology. Although not directly influenced by Williams, these new-world Antinomians were dissatisfied with what

[22] *Winthrop Papers,* 3: 54, 101; Winthrop, *Journal*, 136, 140, 170, 212; Hall, *Puritans*, 226–27.

[23] The English context is described in David R. Como, *Blown by the Spirit: Puritanism and the Emergence of an Antinomian Underground in Pre-Civil War England* (Stanford, CA: Stanford University Press, 2004) and Theodore Dwight Bozeman, *The Precisionist Strain: Disciplinary Religion and Antinomian Backlash in Puritanism to 1638* (Chapel Hill: University of North Carolina Press, 2004). I describe the theological issues in 1630s New England more fully in *The Puritans*, chapter 9.

others in the new colony were willing to accept as evidence of the Holy Spirit at work in people who were seeking church membership. As this feeling spread, it reanimated a habit of the Puritan movement in England, the practice of accusing opponents of being enemies of true godliness. In 1620s England, the popular politics endorsed by the godly relied on the rhetoric of "anti-popery" – in essence, the thesis that certain bishops close to Charles I were agents of a popish plot to subvert English Protestantism.[24] This rhetoric made little sense in 1630s Massachusetts, but a rhetoric borrowed from scripture and a Spirit-edged theology was another matter. Everyone in Massachusetts recognized the sting in words or phrases that Hutchinson and her allies were beginning to hurl at their opponents. "Legal" and "covenant of works" were the most common of these epithets, alongside self-references as the party of "free grace" or the true friends of Christ.[25]

Rhetoric of this kind was intentionally divisive. As those on the receiving end pointed out, "it may trench upon the devils office in accusing the Brethren, and then it will be good ... to bite one another." And, as had quickly become evident, the authority of the ministers was being questioned – in Boston in particular, where most of the congregation tried to chastise or dismiss John Wilson, Cotton's more conservative colleague. "Now the faithfull Ministers of Christ must have dung cast on their faces, and be no better then Legall Preachers, Baals Priests, Popish Factors," was how a witness to these events remembered the turmoil of ca. 1636–1637.[26]

Hutchinson may have been a major source of this anti-clericalism. Settling in Boston with her husband and family, she became a spiritual advisor to women about to undergo childbirth, a role in which she was "much inquisitive" of "their spiritual estates, and in discovering to them the danger they were in, by trusting to common gifts and graces, without any ... witnesse of the Spirit." According to a close observer, "many were convinced that they had gone on in a Covenant of works, and were much humbled thereby." In 1638 and again in the mid-1640s, Cotton described her as "helpfull to many and to bringe them of[f] from thear unsound Grounds and Principles and from building thear good estat[sic] upon thear owne[sic] duties and performances or upon any Righteousness of the Law." By way of endorsement, he added that "all this was well ... and suited with the publike Ministery [his own], which had gone along in the same way." Almost certainly, Hutchinson had

[24] See, for example, Caroline M. Hibbard, *Charles I and the Popish Plot* (Chapel Hill: University of North Carolina Press, 1983). See also Hall, *Puritans*, chapters 7–8, on the entangled vocabularies of radicals and moderates in mid-century England.

[25] See, for example, Hall, *Antinomian Controversy*, 206, 246, 205.

[26] Ibid., 237, 209.

become critical of how most congregations were deciding who could become a church member. When her critics put together a list of "errours" they wanted to squash, one was the assertion that "The Church in admitting members is not to looke to holinesse of life, or Testimony of the same" and another, that "such as see any grace of God in themselves, before they have the assurance of God's love sealed to them are not to be received members of Churches."[27]

What made matters worse was Hutchinson's harsh words about the sermons being preached by the other ministers in the new colony. When the government intervened to quell the crisis in late 1637, it singled out her practice of "reproach[ing] ... the Ministers ... in this country saying that none of them did preach the Covenant of free Grace ... and that they have not the Seale of the Spirit, and so were not able Ministers of the New Testament."[28] Although the Separatist-like turn she had taken in 1620s England was not fully revealed until near the close of her "Examination," she had already remarked that Cotton and Wheelwright were the only two men preaching a valid theology of free grace.[29]

Hutchinson and her ally Wheelwright played another powerful card in this polemical back-and-forth – the term "hypocrite." A close cousin of anti-popery and its thesis of false Christians betraying those who were truly faithful, "hypocrite" targeted people who outwardly seemed true Christians but inwardly were not. Although not always noted in modern scholarship on Hutchinson, she was insisting that the system of the ministers enabled hypocrites to pass as "Gods children" when in fact they were false servants of Christ.[30] When Wheelwright preached a fast-day sermon in January 1637, he also heightened the meaning of the term by attaching it to the apocalyptic scenario of the faithful few contending against a multitude of enemies, a scenario central to the book of Revelation. Drawing expressly on this apocalypticism, Wheelwright told his audience that the colonists were divided between the faithful few who adhered to Christ and the many who adhered to a covenant of works. Massachusetts, he warned, had its false Christians or "hypocrites," the people who were saying that "sanctification" was reliable evidence of justification. Agreeing with Hutchinson and Cotton that those who depended on this evidence should not have become church members, he insisted that anyone who "urged" sanctification as a basis for assurance "oppresseth the poore soules of the saints of God." To this message he added the ultimate imperative of apocalypticism, the mandate to "kill" the enemies of Christ "with the word of the Lord." You may lose

[27] Ibid., 371, 412, 236, 227. See also Cotton's comments on duties, ibid., 121.
[28] Ibid., 269. [29] Ibid., 43. [30] Ibid., 223, 239, 375.

everything you own, he told those he was characterizing as true "saints," yet waging war against the Antichrist would only strengthen their relationship with the Christ who "cutteth down all hipocrites, and those that build upon anything besides Christ." Hence Wheelwright's concluding prophecy: the few may suffer now, but at the end times the many would be "burnt up."[31] "Therefore let the saints of god rejoice, that they have the Lord Jesus Christ, and their names written in the book of life."[32]

No one knew this in mid-1630s Massachusetts, but the Antinomian controversy anticipated a similar uprising in mid-1640s England when lay women and men and a handful of ministers denounced the "legal" system that kept them from encountering either the Christ who offered "free grace" or the liberating presence of the Holy Spirit. People of this temperament were not institution builders in the usual sense of that term. In England, some made their way into Baptist congregations because these communities confined church membership to adults who qualified as visible saints; no children were admitted until they reached the age when they could testify about their spiritual journeys. Others followed George Fox into Quakerism, drawn to that movement by its message that an "inner light" liberated the saints from all outward systems – church, ministry, sacraments. Anyone who tilted in this direction in 1630s Massachusetts had to leave the colony – Wheelwright and Hutchinson because they were banished, and others such as Hansard Knollys, who became a leading Baptist in England, departing voluntarily.

The Antinomian controversy came to a close in late 1637, but the quest for purity and argument about church membership did not. Until his death in 1649, Shepard was deeply involved with these issues. How he helped turn the tide in 1636–1637, and how he understood the quest for purity in the aftermath of that crisis, leads us back to his personal history as a Puritan in England and the themes of his preaching in 1630s Massachusetts.

The Spiritual Journeys of Thomas Shepard

As winds of conflict began to blow in the new colony, Thomas Shepard was initiating his ministry in Cambridge. As was true for many of his parishioners, Massachusetts was the first place where he could escape the troublesome geographies of early Stuart England. No relation of his own making survives, but in an "autobiography" dating from the early 1640s and addressed to his oldest son and namesake he remembered having grown up in places both "profane" and godly. Towchester, where he and

[31] Ibid.,166. [32] Ibid., 153–72.

another eight children were born to the same parents, was a "little poor town" with "no good ministry," a place so spiritually dissatisfying that his father purchased a house in another county where the family could "live . . . under a stirring ministry." When the plague struck the town of his birth, Thomas was sent to live with his grandparents in a "most blind town." After his parents became victims of the plague, he was taken in hand by an older brother and the course of his life changed by an unnamed minister who "stirred up . . . a love and desire of the honor of learning." Off to Cambridge he went at age fifteen. There, after alternating between "loose" behavior and "shame and confusion" in his early years, he "began to listen" to sermons preached by the famous Puritan minister John Preston, sermons that made him aware of his "hypocrisy and self and secret sins." The turning point was learning from Preston that Christ offered him "free mercy" and could truly be his if he "would come in and receive him as Lord and Savior and Husband." This he finally did, knowing that mercy was his only if he acknowledged his "own constant vileness."[33]

That he left Cambridge – "the best place for knowledge and learning" – for a post as a lecturer in Essex County was the doing of another geography, a network of godly ministers in that county who wanted to recruit Cambridge graduates to serve as parish priests or sometimes as lecturers, a position that spared a non-conforming minister the burden of practicing the ceremonies. A patron having recently donated the funds for a position of this kind, the group selected Shepard and picked Earle's Colne as the village where he would begin his career. Now, he could preach in keeping with what his mentors at Cambridge had taught him. His would be an "awakening" ministry dedicated to "show[ing] people their misery;(2) the remedy, Christ Jesus; and (3) how they should walk" afterwards, that is, righteousness according to a Puritan understanding of the moral life. Before long, he had won over the Harlakendens, the most important family in the village, converting its senior member and forming strong friendships with the son Roger as well as with other families of means.[34]

All too soon, word reached the authorities that he was a nonconformist. William Laud, in whose diocese he was preaching, turned up in person and told Shepard he was unacceptable. A haven became available in far-away Yorkshire, where Shepard entered the household of a wealthy family as its chaplain. Only after he arrived did he discover that the "house" was "profane," none of the family being "sincerely good," and the nearest town "most wicked." His response was an outburst of fervent preaching at a family wedding that silenced the merriment and

[33] McGiffert, *God's Plot*, 37–48. [34] Ibid., 47–51.

provoked a spiritual crisis in the bridegroom. A year of tending to this household was more than enough, although another reason for moving elsewhere was becoming a husband and prospectively a father. By this time, he knew that Massachusetts was emerging as a haven for like-minded Puritans. Back in the vicinity of Earle's Colne with his pregnant wife, the two of them were sheltered by various families as passage on a ship was arranged. Bad weather thwarted the first attempt at leaving and tragedy struck when his infant son died. His wife having born another son given the same name as the first-born, the Shepards finally reached Boston in October 1635.[35]

The ups and downs of his English years may have vanished – no Laud to harass ministers of his persuasion, no "profane" towns, no sacraments tainted with idolatry, no more living a life on the run – but plenty of challenges awaited Shepard in his new role as minister in Cambridge. As he would quickly realize, the message of his sermons in England did not reckon with the very different geography of religion in Massachusetts. For the first time in his professional career, he was responsible for the well-being of a town-based church – a "gathered" church limited to "visible saints," but also a church attended by every adult in the town, a rule enforced by the colony government. In Earle's Coln, his mandate had been to summon the townspeople to repent the many ways in which they defied divine law and to warn them – using the weapon of "terror" – that an angry God would cast them off unless they speedily repented. At best, one among a hundred of you may be saved, he told the villagers, a figure he sometimes stretched to a more terrifying one out of a thousand. Straight is the way, and narrow the gate, were themes Shepard employed in his homeland in order to undermine the casual piety – so casual it verged on profaneness – that seemed so endemic among English Protestants.[36]

Elements of this message reappear in a sermon series on the parable of the ten virgins (Matt.25: 1–13) that he began to preach in mid-1636, but these were eclipsed by others in which he responded to local "Antinomians" and referred to a spiritual malaise he discerned among his new parishioners. In the early going, he did his best to ensure a high

[35] Ibid., 52–53 and passim.

[36] This is how I interpret the English sermons published in the 1640s as *The Sincere Convert,: Discovering the Small Number of True Believers* (London, 1640) and *The Sound Believer* (London, 1645); for these figures, see Albro, *Works of Shepard*, I, 57, 49. Thomas Hooker, a mentor of Shepard and also not a parish minister in England, was just as scathing in the sermons he preached to the townspeople of Dorchester, England, in the mid-1620s. Baird Tipson, *Hartford Puritanism: Thomas Hooker, Samuel Stone, and Their Terrifying God* (New York: Oxford University Press, 2015), chapter 8. A more general dismay with "the people" is noted in Hall, *Puritans*, 31–33.

standard of purity when it came to church membership. After listening to lay testimonies in the nearby town of Dorchester in the spring of 1636, he told the town minister-to-be that the would-be church members were not fit to be the foundation stones; they were too "weak and simple, and unable to discern" the evidence on which churches should be relying.[37]

But in his response to Wheelwright and Hutchinson, he re-emphasized the generosity of the parable of the ten virgins. The five virgins without oil in their lamps had not been exposed until Christ returned in judgment. Beforehand, they passed as worthy, a situation intrinsic to the very being of the church on earth, which would remain imperfect until the last days. Though he hoped that the Cambridge congregation was almost spotless, the theological truth that hypocrites could pass as true believers rose up and bit him in 1638 when a man who had testified movingly about his journey from sinner to redeemed turned out to be a moral fraud. A university graduate with family connections to important colonists, Nathaniel Eaton had been selected to serve as the first head of newly founded Harvard College in 1638. All too quickly, rumors were circulating of his abusive behavior and his wife's mismanagement of the students' "commons." Ejected from his post at Harvard and fleeing the colony before he could be disciplined by the Cambridge church, Eaton was a troubling example of how a "virgin" church could be deceived.[38]

No one else in Cambridge was so thoroughly discredited in the 1630s. On the other hand, plenty of people in the congregation were describing a spiritual "deadness" that came upon them unexpectedly. As many would acknowledge, they had looked forward to exchanging a spiritual and social geography of absence for one of presence – that is, the "means" in far greater abundance and completely purified of corruption. Edward Collins was typical in reporting both sides of this story, the "great change" that "did much transport" his "heart" once he arrived, followed by the experience of being "quickly lost by distractions and thoughts and cares which deadened my spirits." Alice Stedman reported hearing from a neighbor of people who "did think they had grace but since they came here could not see it," and described herself as experiencing "much emptiness in ordinances."[39] Edward Hall said something similar. Acknowledging that God "brought him to this place," he testified to

[37] Albro, *Works of Shepard*, 1: cxxvii–xxx.

[38] Eaton's downfall is described in Samuel Eliot Morison, *The Founding of Harvard College* (Cambridge, MA: Harvard University Press, 1935), chapter 17. Shepard's reaction is indicated in Susan Drinker Moran, "Thomas Shepard and the Professor: Two Documents from the Early History of Harvard," *Early American Literature* 17 (1982): 24–42.

[39] Selement and Woolley, *Shepard's Confessions*, 104.

being overcome with "worldliness and this bred many fears whether ever any work of Christ in him was in truth." Here as in other testimonies, self-confidence or closeness to God came and went with remarkable speed. Elizabeth Olbon reported, "Since she came hither she hath found her heart more dead and dull= etc." Brother Crackbone's wife "forgot the Lord" after she arrived and, in a turn of phrase, spoke of having "a new house" but not a "new heart. And means [preaching] did not profit me and so doubted of all [the] Lord had done." Brother Jackson's maid was initially "affected" by the words a minister was speaking, "but afterward left to a dead blockish frame and knew nothing," to the point of discerning "much emptiness in ordinances" (that is, worship and especially sermons). Although Golden Moore chose to immigrate because "means [were] being taken away" in England and "did think to enjoy more of the Lord" in Massachusetts, after "coming hither" he "found his "heart in a worse frame than ever."[40] At an earlier moment (probably in England), Martha Collins "had a hungering after means which were most searching," but like so many others, found "no life in ordinances" in Massachusetts.[41]

To Hutchinson and John Cotton, the source of such deadness would have been obvious, the "legal" preaching that diverted people from the witness of the Spirit. In the Parable sermons and elsewhere, Shepard strongly disagreed with this analysis. An acute observer of immigration and its unintended consequences, he attributed the deadness described by his congregation to the geographies of religion on each side of the Atlantic. Drawing on his own life history as well as that of his church members, he reminded them of how "when you went many miles to hear, and had scarce bread at home, O, you thought, if once you had such liberties; but when they are made yours, now what fruit? Doth not plenty of means make thy soul slight means"? Another way of making this point was to cite the spiritual benefits of persecution; it kept people on their toes, but in persecution-free Massachusetts zeal was slipping away. In almost the same breath, he acknowledged the presence of "many sorrows and temptations in this wilderness; and hence no means sweet, no bed easy, your bones or broken, ... the spirits of others flat, and thine ... to, whom God sent into church fellowship to quicken them."[42]

Never, however, did Shepard abandon the stance of shepherd who encourages the weak or sorrowing to come to him. One measure of his greatness as a minister is how readily he acknowledged the spiritual consequences of coming to Massachusetts. Although the New Testament

[40] Selement and Woolley, *Shepard's Confessions*, 123.
[41] Ibid., 34, 41, 84, 104, 123, 131, 140. [42] Albro, *Works of Shepard*, 2: 257, 259.

parable he was using as his text was ultimately about five maidens exposed as hypocrites, Shepard made a point of acknowledging people who had suffered the sensation of a heart that "dries and parches away" or, as he noted a little later, to think of themselves as "castaway[s]" Christ will never embrace.[43] In a back-and-forth initiated in December 1636 when Shepard and his colleagues had solicited Cotton's answers to sixteen questions, the emphasis fell on the plight of those who were in "a poor drooping condition," or, alternatively, people "put to sad doubts of their own Estate." Shepard may have penned this part of the "Elders Reply," for he used almost the same language in chapter 9 of the sermon series, which opens with an "exhortation 1. To quicken all those doubting, drooping, yet sincere hearts that much question the love of Christ to them." Several sentences later, he blamed Satan for this situation, a Satan active "here" (that is, in Massachusetts), in a not-so-indirect allusion to Hutchinson's attempts to undermine the common wisdom about assurance of salvation. As was customary among preachers of the practical divinity in England, Shepard acknowledged that "very few living Christians have any settled comfortable evidence of God's eternal love to them in his Son, and hence many sad events follow." This may sound abstract, but Shepard was directing these words at people he addresses as a "you." Throughout this long passage, he reiterated his concern for those who "rest in uncertain hopes," characterizing theirs as "one of the most dangerous" situations a follower of Christ could tumble into.[44]

In these same pages, Shepard detailed the antidote to uncertainty in ways that would surprise the modern reader who assumes that Puritan ministers said little about Christ. The sermon series represented Christ as "tender-hearted" and loving, indeed as someone deeply sympathetic to those who suffer. Shepard's was a Christ who brushes by the doctrine of election by offering everyone the opportunity to accept the gospel promise. "Never any came to him that he cast way," Shepard avers, an assertion anchored in Matt. 8: 17 ("He bore our infirmities"). Telling, too, is that Christ is so tender-hearted in the presence of those who know the "miseries" of sin. Allusions of this kind come thick and fast – to the Christ who seeks the "lost sheep," who pities the plight of sinners and "mourn[s] for the hardness of their hearts," who will "seek out" those who "reject" the offer of grace no matter how many times this happens. As the literary historian Michael Colacurcio has pointed out, the language of the *Parable* sermons is remarkably fervent in its references to the "real love" Christ has for sinners, a phrase Shepard alternated with phrases such as "fervent, vehement, earnest" love, "constant and continual" love,

[43] Ibid., 34, 37. [44] Albro, *Works of Shepard*, 2: 77; Hall, *Antinomian Controversy*, 74.

dwelling "with thee as a man must dwell with his wife," and "rejoic[ing] in thee . . . as a bridegroom does over the bride," all of them underscoring the thesis that "the Lord draws a soul by cords of love" and craves everyone's salvation.[45]

Shepard wrote these words at a moment when John Cotton was recommending an "immediate witnesse of the Spirit" as the basis of assurance. Shepard regarded this remedy as too stringent, insecure, and parsimonious. Reaching into the theology he had absorbed in England, he drew out a remedy endorsed by dozens of ministers before him. Hypocrisy was a genuine problem, as was "security," the name for an illusory self-confidence. Yet both could be overcome or avoided if the pathway to Christ began with repentance or, as he put it in other sermons, "humiliation." Christ invited every sinner to come to him – truly, every sinner – but as Shepard insisted, only those who prepared themselves beforehand would actually be included within the gospel promise. Being prepared had everything to do with self-examination and the humility it produced, a humility tied to realizing that sinners had nothing to offer Christ – nothing meritorious, no "duties" that won Christ to their side. Repentance was the doorway to an acute sense of being wholly dependent on the Christ who died on the Cross.[46]

In the same pages, Shepard suggested that some who were listening to him had been "careless in seeking" assurance. For them, the parable of the ten virgins was instructive, for it dramatized the importance of being "prepared." From his mentors at Cambridge and the community he entered once he moved to Earle's Colne, Shepard had imbibed the lesson that the "law" remained in force for sinners – not the "ceremonial" law abolished with the coming of Christ, but the law as a manifestation of divine authority that, by definition, sinners were rejecting. Hence, for Shepard, the imperative that sinners acknowledge their alienation from God. He summed up this argument by emphasizing the great danger of "sloth" and the importance of using the "means." Do so vigorously, he urged everyone in Cambridge, in order to align your outward lives with righteousness and your inward "heart" with faith.[47]

The Christ who reaches out in tenderness to those who are of drooping spirits, the God (speaking through the minister) who demands constant self-searching and sanctions moral behavior as a valid sign of true godliness – a package of this kind may epitomize what historians such as the late Michael

[45] Albro, *Works of Shepard*, 2: 84–85; Michael J. Colarcurcio, *Godly Letters: The Literature of the American Puritans* (Notre Dame, IN: University of Notre Dame Press, 2006), 375.

[46] Albro, *Works of Shepard*, 2: 66. I describe Shepard's theology and the tradition of which he was part more fully in *The Puritans*, chapters 4 and 9.

[47] Albro, *Works of Shepard*, 2: 77–78.

McGiffert have characterized as the "paradoxes" of Puritan divinity. When we turn back to the relations, we may also want to read them as inherently paradoxical given the fits and starts that so many people seem to have experienced. Among the possibilities for illustrating the layers of lay piety, Alice Stedman's relation (already quoted on other matters) is characteristic. Stedman spoke frankly about the stress of hearing a godly minister in England describe her spiritual estate as "woeful" unless she reconciled with God. Nor, he had remarked, was she doing enough to "humble" herself. Possibly after reaching her new home, she was hearing sermons that emphasized "the freeness of His love" to those who acknowledged their sinfulness – free but also contingent, for the gospel promise was transmitted through "means" that included her willingness to repent. This intertwining of divine love, grace, repentance, and the means was reinforced by what Shepard was saying. At one moment, he encouraged her to "believe" that "the Lord" would reach out and help her. At another, something he said led her to conclude that there was "nothing for me" in the gospel promise. She also remembered another minister's message (possibly an echo of Hutchinson and Cotton's rhetoric) that some people "build upon wrong foundations to close and catch the promise and missed Christ." How long these mixed messages kept her in suspense is not known, but when she testified to the church she could report that she had received Jesus, "And so was much confirmed, and many times since the Lord hath spoken to me to help me."[48]

Situations such as this one help to explain why, as the sermon series proceeded, he did his best to specify the qualities that differentiated the real Christian from the hypocrite when, at first glance, the two seemed so alike. This was a question he inherited from his Cambridge teachers and other makers of Puritan theology, chief among them William Perkins (d. 1599). Self-deception or an outward show of godliness was a principal theme of Perkins's *A treatise Tending unto a Declaration Whether a Man be in the Estate of Damnation, or in the Estate of Grace* (1588), from which readers learned "that a reprobate might attain to as much as" the true saint. He made the same point in another of his treatises, *A Golden Chaine* (1591), where he described "men … who, outwardly professing the faith, are charitably reputed … true members" of the church, but in fact were "deceiving … themselves." For Perkins and other evangelical ministers in early Stuart England, this was a commonplace. But in 1630s Massachusetts, Hutchinson, Cotton, and Wheelwright had turned it into a weapon to use against their

[48] Selement and Woolley, *Shepard's Confessions*, 102–5.

opponents – and used in an unlimited manner, as though everyone who defended the merits of sanctification was of this ilk.[49]

Shepard told his congregation time and again that nothing was "easie" about the way to salvation. Stedman and the other men and women who testified in Cambridge took for granted that the pilgrim's road was marked by ups and downs, divine presence and divine absence, seasons of assurance and, more commonly, seasons of doubt. Yet to end the story here would be to shortchange Shepard's practice in new-world Cambridge. As already noted, he penned a catechism he used to instruct all the young people in the basic elements of doctrine. Of more significance in the long run, he embraced infant baptism, but only after this sacrament had been purged of the corruptions he discerned in the English liturgy. When he and his wife Margaret embarked for Massachusetts in late 1635, they brought with them a newborn son who had not been baptized because the Shepards did not trust the "ordinances" in England, a situation that frightened Margaret and surely frightened Shepard as well, for both of them regarded the sacrament as a means of incorporating their son into a deeply reassuring covenant. During the long delay, Margaret had "made . . . many a prayer and shed many a tear in secret" for her newborn child. Several years later, Shepard addressed young Thomas using words that may echo what was said in February 1636: "through "the ordinance of baptism . . . God is become thy God and is beforehand with thee that whenever thou shalt return to God, he will undoubtedly receive thee – and this is a most high and happy privilege and therefore bless God for it." As he remarked in his journal several years later, he remembered "what a great blessing . . . to my child" it had been that he was incorporated within the framework of the gospel promise and vowed "to desire the blessing and presence of his ordinances in this place and the continuance of his poor churches among us."[50]

As the years went by, baptism began to loom large in Shepard's ministry as a means of incorporating the next generation of colonists into a still-fragile church. Hence his intervention in an English-based debate about the sacrament in which Baptists denounced it as unbiblical, and others, like Shepard, emphasizing the covenant God entered into with Abraham, a covenant extending to a thousand generations (Gen. 17:7). As he remarked in the mid-1640s, children may have been "of wrath by nature" but, once baptized, became "sons of God by promise." The difference was not that sin had been swept away but that God had become

[49] Ian Breward, *The Work of Willliam Perkins* (Abington, UK: Sutton Courtenay Press, 1970), 227.

[50] McGiffert, *God's Plot*, 36, 121.

the child's benefactor and – in the context of recurrent illnesses of the kind little Thomas had suffered – a source of protection.

Baptism was a privilege that Shepard as parent and pastor wanted not only for his own children but also for those of church members in general. In his anti-Baptist treatise he appealed directly to parents concerned about the spiritual well-being of their children, assuring them that through the sacrament "God gives parents some comfortable hope of their children's salvation, because they be within the pale of the visible church; for as out of the visible church (where the ordinary means of grace be) there is ordinarily no salvation ... [which] is very hard, and horrible to imagine." He reiterated this point in another text, this time underscoring the long-term consequences of having – or not having – a child baptized. To withhold a child from being baptized, he declared, was to "undermine all hopes of posterity for [all time to] come." The time frame of posterity was extensive, stretching for "generations without limitation in the Lyne of Beleevers," an argument warranted by the covenant extending to a "thousand generations" God made with Abraham (Gen. 17:7).[51]

The congregation agreed with him and, in doing so, altered the meaning of religious space in Cambridge. Wanting, like Shepard, their children to be encompassed in a gathered church set apart from the profane world, they endorsed – perhaps without grasping the long-term significance of doing so – a church that sustained the connections between parent and child, one generation and another. Making their relations before the church, several people had already emphasized the connections between church membership and the welfare of their children. Mary (Angier) Sparhawk remembered feeling anxious when her husband decided to immigrate and how she reconciled herself to his decision by "thinking that [if] her children might get good it would be worth my journey." Here, the implied context was the difference between the sacraments as administered in their primitive purity in Massachusetts compared with how they were performed in England. Mrs. Crackbone (we do not know her first name) remembered the sadness she felt when one of her children died and how she worried about the others, thinking they would go "to hell ... because I had not prayed for them," a statement of self-blame followed in her relation by the sentence, "And so came to New England." There she

[51] Thomas Shepard, *The Church-Membership of Children* (1663); repr. in Albro, *Works of Shepard*, 3: 521–24, 536; Shepard, "Considerations Commended in a Brotherly way to those brethren that doe scruple ... the Seale of baptism to theyr children," Shepard Family Papers, Folder 2, American Antiquarian Society. The broader debate and its implications are sketched in Ann S. Brown and David D. Hall, "Family Strategies and Religious Practice: Baptism and the Lord's Supper in Early New England," in *Lived Religion in America: Toward a History of Practice*, ed. David D. Hall (Princeton, NJ: Princeton University Press, 1997), 41–68.

learned the comforting message that she "was under [the] wings of Christ," as (theologically) were her children once she became a church member. The same feeling of responsibility for one's children, together with a high opinion of the sacraments, was voiced by Ann Errington when she told the church that she knew of children who "would curse parents for not getting them to means" (i.e., the "means of grace").[52]

Words were matched by behavior. That people credited baptism with a distinctive significance is apparent in the promptness with which they brought their newborn children to the church to be baptized. Two examples must suffice. Within the family of the printer and land speculator Samuel Green, the interval between the birth and baptism of three of his children was two days, six days, and one day. Shepard's successor in the Cambridge pulpit, Jonathan Mitchell, had not been able to baptize a newborn son before the baby died, though he baptized another of his children seven days after it was born. Distressed that he had failed his infant son, Mitchell wrote in his journal that "to be deprived of [the sacrament] is a great frown, and a sad intimation of the Lord's anger."[53]

Religion and its Geographies

Shepard the fervent evangelical and Augustinian to his fingertips was also Shepard the purist, wanting pure churches and the pastoral, incorporating parent/pastor who spoke of his children as "innocent." The several themes that animate the *Parable* sermons and his wider ministry would have been familiar to the godly in England. On the other hand, the exultant ceremony of February 1636 could not have happened in England; there, a state church system prevailed, a church that was unwilling to allow Puritans to organize voluntary congregations of their own. Not until the coming of the English Revolution would this become possible. Simultaneously, English "Antinomians" were turning against the customary structures of ministry and doctrine.

In Shepard's Massachusetts, the revolution that unfolded in the 1630s and 1640s was of an entirely different kind: gathered congregations which limited their membership to "visible saints" but admitted children to the sacrament of baptism and therefore to the church covenant, purity in worship, orthodoxy in doctrine, a church-state alliance sustained, and Antinomianism suppressed. Only in New England did a synthesis of this kind prevail, and only in New England did it mutate by the end of the

52 Selement and Woolley, *Shepard's Confessions*, 66, 140, 185.

53 Stephen Sharpless ed., *Records of the Church of Christ at Cambridge in New England* (Boston: E Putnam, 1906), 10: Cotton Mather, *Magnalia Christi Americana* (1702; repr. Hartford, 1853–1854), 2: 111.

century into a quasi-parish system that united two or more generations in a single congregation – a parochial congregationalism singular to Puritan New England.[54]

Amid disruptions of many kinds – old world to new, parish church to gathered, the harsh words of Hutchinson and Wheelwright – the theme of incorporation acquired a fresh significance, for on it depended the future health (spiritual and otherwise) of family, child, church, and colony. Old themes thus became refreshed in the wilderness of the New World.

[54] A synthesis described in marvelous detail in Douglas L. Winiarski, *Darkness Falls on the Land of Light: Experiencing Religious Awakenings in Eighteenth-Century New England* (Chapel Hill: University of North Carolina Press, 2017), part 1.

3 Learned Reading in the Atlantic Colonies: How Humanist Practices Crossed the Atlantic

Anthony Grafton[*]

In 1613 Lancelot Andrewes and Isaac Casaubon went on holiday together. Andrewes told his Huguenot friend an engrossing story, which Casaubon recorded in detail. A Londoner, with a reputation for piety, had died of the plague on Lombard Street in 1563. He startled his wife, who had come to lay out his corpse, by asking for food, and actually ate some bread and cheese. She summoned the minister. The supposedly dead man confessed that he had escaped detection when he murdered his first wife, and then died a more permanent death. Casaubon found the story credible. Andrewes, he pointed out, had heard it directly from an eyewitness who was personally involved. A minister, he "was a man of the highest credibility and of known piety" – "fuit presbyter homo summae fidei et notae pietatis."[1] In Casaubon's world – the world of Reformed humanism in the late Renaissance – tales of Providential intervention were usually welcome, even simple ones like this, especially if the witness who described them, in writing or in speech, was credible.

Casaubon was one of the transcendent polymaths of a polymathic age. It is not surprising that he knew how to deal with stories of this kind. But what happened when men with his sort of training ventured into the Atlantic world? Casaubon and his fellows practiced a particular kind of reading. They went through the books that mattered to them pen in hand. They inscribed them with notes about their authors and the circumstances in which they had obtained them. Then they underlined and annotated their way through everything from immense folios to tiny pamphlets, leaving a record of their progress. Every now and then they broke off their ferocious concentration on the texts in front of them to record a personal experience: the place and time where they had read a related text or heard a story from a friend. That experience too could be scrutinized – really read and verified. These men

[*] Much of the material in this essay was gathered in the course of research for a collaborative enterprise, the Winthrop Project, supported by a David A. Gardner '69 Magic Project grant from Princeton University. Heartfelt thanks to Jennifer Rampling, co-director of the project, and to our original collaborators: Richard Calis, Frederic Clark and Madeline McMahon.

[1] Oxford, Bodleian Library MS Casaubon 25, 115v.

gathered knowledge in many ways: through travel, which many of them saw as an art, to be practiced in accordance with formal rules; through conversation, with colleagues, but also with artisans and others who had opportunities to gain expert knowledge of plants, animals, and other *naturalia;* and through direct examination of everything from narwhal horns to ancient coins. Through it all, though, books remained their preferred source of information, and systematic, interpretative reading their model for acquiring and judging it.[2]

Historians of the English colonies have begun to map the forms of reading that took root and flourished there. Men and women practiced many of the same forms of religious reading, from mastering the Scriptures to meditating on sermons and other pious texts. Women often took charge of teaching children, male as well as female, to read, and sometimes founded formal schools. One area, however, remained a largely male precinct: that of erudition. Male collectors – Samuel Lee, Cotton and Increase Mather, Thomas Prince and other Bostonians, for example – imported books, in Latin and other foreign languages as well as English.[3] They approached these books, as Casaubon did, equipped with languages and trained in interpretation, and read them pen in hand. Cotton Mather, incredulous at the impiety of Isaac la Peyrère's argument that men had lived before Adam, crossed out the word DIVINITY in a section title and the running heads in his copy and replaced it with HERESY.[4] Signatures, presentation inscriptions, and more elaborate notes record the ways in

[2] See for example, Lisa Jardine and Anthony Grafton, "'Studied for Action': How Gabriel Harvey Read his Livy," *Past & Present* 129 (1990): 30–78; William Sherman, *John Dee: The Politics of Reading and Writing in the English Renaissance* (Amherst: University of Massachusetts Press, 1995) and *Used Books: Marking Readers in Renaissance England* (Philadelphia: University of Pennsylvania Press, 2008); Kevin Sharpe, *Reading Revolutions: The Politics of Reading in Early Modern England* (New Haven, CT: Yale University Press, 2000); Anthony Grafton and Joanna Weinberg, *"I have always loved the holy tongue": Isaac Casaubon, the Jews, and a Forgotten Chapter in Renaissance Scholarship* (Cambridge, MA: Harvard University Press, 2011).

[3] Insightful studies and descriptions of comparably erudite libraries from the northern colonies include J. H. Tuttle, "The Libraries of the Mathers," *Proceedings of the American Antiquarian Society* 20 (1910): 269–356; Jon Butler, "Thomas Teackle's 333 Books: A Great Library on Virginia's Eastern Shore," *The William and Mary Quarterly*, 49 (1992): 449–91; Hugh Amory, "A Boston Society Library: The Old South Church and Thomas Prince," in *Bibliography and the Book Trades*, ed. David Hall (Philadelphia: University of Pennsylvania Press, 2005); "Mather Family Library," American Antiquarian Society (www.americanantiquarian.org/matherlib.htm (accessed July 30, 2018); See also Anthony Grafton, "The Republic of Letters in the American Colonies: Francis Daniel Pastorius Makes a Notebook," *American Historical Review*, 117 (2012): 1–39. For the contrasting story of how a European family library served as cultural capital for more than two centuries, see Caroline Sherman, "The Ancestral Library as Immortal Educator," *Proceedings of the Western Society for French History*, 35 (2007): 41–54.

[4] See Mark Peterson, "Theopolis Americana: The City-State of Boston, the Republic of Letters, and the Protestant International, 1689–1739," in *Soundings in Atlantic History*, ed.

which books served them, as gifts and memorials to erudite friendships as well as sources of information.

The practices of reading, as well as the books they were applied to, were passed on from generation to generation through personal contacts. Like Bible study, learned reading could be a family matter. A recent study follows the reading practices of the Winthrop family from Adam, a Suffolk lawyer educated at Cambridge, through his son John and grandson John Jr., products of Trinity College Cambridge and Trinity College Dublin respectively, who crossed the Atlantic and cast their fates with the colonies that both governed, to his great-grandson Wait, who studied at Harvard and served as magistrate in Massachusetts.[5] Adam, who kept records of important events in the margins of almanacs, taught his grandson, John Jr., to do the same – as a surviving almanac, annotated in Adam's hand but in the name of John Jr., shows.[6] His son saw his conscience as awakened, dramatically, by a theft – of books, rather than pears, which his exemplar, St. Augustine, had stolen.[7] John Jr. avidly collected books on alchemy, paying special attention to such distinguished previous owners as the Dutch engineer Cornelis Drebbel and the German Paracelsian Heinrich Nolle. He entered notes of his own, sometimes below those of the previous owners, to identify them and make clear his own role in the transmission of the book.[8] John Jr.'s son Wait shared this interest. A copy of Robert Lovell's *Enchiridion botanicum*, a herbal, now in the Massachusetts Historical Society, has

Bernard Bailyn and Patricia Denault (Cambridge, MA: Havard University Press, 2009), 329–70 at 353–54 and Fig 10.7.

[5] Richard Calis, Frederic Clark, Christian Flow, Anthony Grafton, Jennifer Rampling and Madeline McMahon, "Passing the Book: Cultures of Reading in the Winthrop Family, 1580–1730," *Past & Present* 241/1(November 2018): 69–141.

[6] Adam used Richard Allestree, *A New Almanack for 1620* ([London], 1620); Massachusetts Historical Society, Winthrop Papers, MS N-262, v. 61, verso of title page: "John Winthrop junior, est huius libri possessor. Nomine Johannes dictus, cognomine Wintrop sum: possessorem quem vocat iste liber" (in Adam's highly recognizable italic hand). These entries are printed in *Winthrop Papers*, I: 1498–1628 (Boston, 1929), 243–47.

[7] Winthrop Papers, I, 193.

[8] Examples include Drebbel's copy of Basil Valentine [pseud.], *Von den natürlichen unnd ubernatürlichen Dingen* (Leipzig, 1603), New York Society Library Win 254, and Dee's copy of Paracelsus, *Das Buch meteororum* (Cologne, 1566), New York Society Library Win 188, both owned and annotated by John Winthrop Jr. On the first flyleaf recto of the Dee, Winthrop wrote: "This above written, and the name on the top of the frontispiece of this booke, and ye writing in the middle of the fro[n]tispice, and the severall notes in the margent through the whole booke, was written by that famous Philosopher and Chimist, John Dee, with his owne hand. this J. Dee was he y^{t} wrote the philosophicall treatise called *Monas Hieroglifica*; also *Propaideumata Aphoristica*, also the learned preface before Euclides *Elementes* in English in folio. He was warden of Manchester. I have divers bookes y^{t} were his wherin he hath written his name and many notes &c: for which they are worthyly the more esteemed. John Winthrop."

a presentation inscription on its flyleaf: "Be pleased to axcepte of this from your moste oblyged faithfull servant Charles Howard." A second inscription explicates the first: "Who was then brother to t[he] [Du]ke of Norfolke and w[as] (I think) afterward [Du]ke himselfe, he gaue [thi]s book to my father in about the yeare 1662, [w]hen I was with him in London. Wait Winthrop."[9] Both men liked to signal their possession of a book by entering the *Monas hieroglyphica*, the symbolic summary of John Dee's natural philosophy.

In a very different corner of the English colonies, Quaker Philadelphia, the notary and founder of Germantown, Francis Daniel Pastorius, and his friend, the statesman and fur-trader James Logan, both took a passionate interest in books. Both men's tastes extended from erudite treatises and editions in Latin to the newest books and periodicals from London. Pastorius had learned his Latin and Greek at Gymnasium and studied at the Academy of Altdorf and the University of Strasbourg. Logan, by contrast, had no formal education. His father, a schoolmaster, probably taught him his excellent Latin and Greek. In Philadelphia, their love of books and arguments brought them together. Both men liked writing in their books. Pastorius filled every blank space in the allegorical title page of an encyclopedia of the arts and sciences by the Jesuit Michael Pexenfelder with slogans and verses indicating, as he noted in a central place, that the book "served the studies of Francis Pastorius." These inscriptions were probably what inspired Logan, in his turn, to write on the flyleaf that "This book was bought from Philip Monckton, to whom it was sold by the son of my dear friend Francis D. Pastorius of Germantown."[10]

The Winthrops, the Mathers, Pastorius, Logan, and their like were all in close contact with highly innovative circles in London and on the Continent, from the Royal Society and alchemists on the Continent, to Halley and Newton. They eagerly read the newest issues of the London periodicals, carried out their own experiments with furnaces and alembics, and compiled their own statistics about the incidence of smallpox.[11]

9 Robert Lovell, *Enchiridion botanicum, or, A Compleat Herball: Containing the Summe of what hath hitherto been published either by Ancient or moderne Authors both Galenicall and Chymicall, Touching Trees, Shrubs, Plants, Fruits, Flowers, &c.* (Oxford: Ric. Davis, 1659); Massachusetts Historical Society, Winthrop Lib.; flyleaf v.

10 James Logan, note on the flyleaf of Michael Pexenfelder, *Apparatus eruditionis tam rerum quam verborum per omnes artes et scientias* (Nuremberg: Michael & Joh. Friedrich Endter, 1670); Library Company of Philadelphia Rare | Sev Pexe Log 626.O: "Emptus hic Liber a Phillipo Munckton cui vendidit eum filius mihi Amicissimi ffr. D. Pastorij Germanopolitani. . 1720." See Grafton, "Republic of Letters."

11 For the Winthrops, see esp. Neil Kamil, *Fortress of the Soul: Violence, Metaphysics and Material Life in the Huguenots' New World* (Baltimore and London, 2005), chapters 10,11; Matthew Underwood, "Unpacking Winthrop's Boxes," *Common-Place*, vii/4 (July 2007)

But though they eagerly read the works of thinkers who were proclaiming their pursuit of new forms of knowledge, they themselves lived in cities – even Philadelphia – where the spirit had never blown through the streets for long, and the power of traditional elites and the intellectual authorities they appealed to had never been shattered, even temporarily. They had "no incentive to break away with the past" and "every reason to sustain the idea of continuity."[12]

In these conditions, books, and the traditional ways of using them, often played a special role in their intellectual, social, and personal lives. Traditional ways of reading and annotation – ways that went back to the world of Casaubon and his ilk – also remained current. Books not only illuminated the work of Providence: they embodied it. In 1640, John Winthrop recorded in his journal a discovery that his son had made. A storeroom containing his books had been entered by unwelcome visitors:

> About this time there fell out a thing worthy of observation. Mr. Winthrop the younger, one of the magistrates, having many books in a chamber where there was corn of divers sorts, had among them one wherein the Greek testament, the psalms and the common prayer were bound together. He found the common prayer eaten with mice, every leaf of it, and not any of the two other touched, nor any other of his books, though there were above a thousand.[13]

According to Winthrop, the mice who ate the Anglican Book of Common Prayer, while preserving the Word of God, had made the difference between papist nonsense and divine Revelation material – although the actual volume is not so thoroughly eaten as Winthrop's journal suggests.[14]

Here too John Winthrop followed ancient paths. His father Adam was a practical man, who succeeded at the bar where his son did not. Adam did the accounts for Trinity College, Cambridge, racked rents for St. John's and farmed prosperously as lord of Groton Manor in Suffolk. He led a busy life of work and travel, rescuing drunken neighbors from ditches, listening to sermons and holding court as a local magistrate. Like

(http://common-place.org/article/unpacking-winthrops-boxes/, accessed October 2, 2016); and Walter Woodward, *Prospero's America: John Winthrop, Jr., Alchemy, and the Creation of New England Culture, 1606–1676* (Chapel Hill: University of North Carolina Press, 2010). For the Mathers, see Peterson. For Logan, see esp. the magnificent catalogue of his library by Edwin Wolf, *The Library of James Logan of Philadelphia, 1674–1751* (Philadelphia, 1974).

[12] Peterson, 356.

[13] Richard S. Dunn, James Savage, and Laetitia Yeandle eds., *The Journal of John Winthrop, 1630–1649* (Cambridge, MA and London: Belknap Press at the University of Harvard Press, 1996), 340–41.

[14] Boston, Massachusetts Historical Society MS N-262, v. lxiv.

his son, though less decisively, he inclined to the Puritan cause. He supported a lectureship in a town near his own. He took a discriminating interest in biblical exegesis, both in written form and in the sermons that he heard in church. Adam recorded the texts of a few sermons in his extensive diary:

> August 5, 1596: my b[rother Roger] Weston preched at Boxford super 13 Marcum versu ultimo, pie & eloquenter.
>
> August 5, 1603: Mr. [Joseph] Birde preached at Boxforde vppon the 124 psalme, pie & docte.
>
> December 31, 1607: Mr. William Aymes preached at Boxford vppon the 80 psalme & first verse pie & docte.[15]

As he read, he followed the arguments in the Zurich divine Rudolf Gwalther's commentaries on the minor prophets, numbering them to keep track. As a learned reader, Adam knew that to assess a writer, one needed to know about him. He regularly looked up the authors of his books in the bibliographical compendia of John Bale and recorded what he found out about them in the books. It is all the more striking, then, that he treated sermons as comparable in weight to published exegetical texts. In his copy of Gwalther's printed homilies, Adam listed a series of written commentaries on the minor prophets. Sermons preached in his local church appear in the same list: "Mr Henry Sands preached vpon Jonas in Groton churche, divers Sermons, anno 1620. 1622."[16] John went further in the same direction. He kept a small notebook in which he recorded sermons, laying out their oral arguments as carefully as his father had analyzed Gwalther's written ones.[17]

Learned reading, for Adam, could be political. Cambridge-trained readers of history like Gabriel Harvey scrutinized the past for political lessons that they hoped Queen Elizabeth and other good and great statespeople would follow. Winthrop himself was one such reader, when he wanted to be. He owned a copy of the major work of Harvey's patron, Thomas Smith. At the start he inscribed a letter from Smith to Walter Haddon, which offered guidance on how to read the book that followed as the reconstruction of one of Aristotle's lost constitutions. In the margins of the book he entered highly secular reflections on such issues as the ways in which judges were allowed to treat juries.[18] At the end of his life,

15 *Winthrop Papers*, I, 68, 82, 96.

16 Gwalter, *Certaine godlie Homelies or Sermons,* NYSL Win 22, verso of title page.

17 "John Winthrop Sermon Notes, 1627–1628." Boston, Massachusetts Historical Society MS N-262, box lxii.

18 Thomas Smith, *De republica Anglorum* (London, 1584), New York Society Library Win 232.

disenchanted with King James's regime, he recorded his disappointment in a new edition of Machiavelli's *The Prince*, in Latin.[19]

But even for Adam reading was above all, religious. He scrutinized Foxe's *Acts and Monuments* for stories of Protestant martyrs and entered the appropriate ones in his copy of William Lambarde's *Perambulation of Kent*. He transcribed long passages from Foxe into the blank leaves in his Lambarde. And though he appreciated the erudite materials on topography, history, and English law that made Lambarde's book the model for later county histories and a favorite text for gentry readers, he also used the book to record his reading of a pamphlet on a monstrous birth and chronicle entries on beached whales and sinking trees.[20] His son John and grandson John Jr. both carried on this form of providential reading: when they read reports about the monstrous infants born to the Antinomians Mary Dyer and Anne Hutchinson, both saw the hand of God directly at work.[21]

The transmission of these forms of erudite reading – and their transformation in the Atlantic world – may help us to understand one of the lasting puzzles of early New England history. Adam's great-grandson Wait Winthrop – christened Wait Still, he preferred the shorter form of his name – studied at the new Harvard College rather than in Europe, and thereafter led a very public life. He spent almost thirty years as an elected member of the Massachusetts Council, and led the colony's militia. Over time he became known as a defender of the "ancient liberties" of his province against royal encroachment and a firm adherent of the orthodox form of Christianity as defined by Cotton Mather. Wait took part in the successful revolt against Governor Andros in 1689 and belonged to the coalition that ruled Massachusetts until 1702. He spent years trying, unsuccessfully, first to prevent Joseph Dudley from becoming governor and then to undercut his regime. Though he had no legal training, he became an associate justice and then, for two terms, the chief justice of the new Superior Court of Judicature, the highest court in Massachusetts.

Wait is most vividly remembered for one aspect of his first judicial service. In 1692 the governor appointed him to the Court of Oyer and Terminer that tried the Salem witches. He voted to condemn the nineteen who were executed in 1692. In winter and spring 1693, however, as a member of the Superior Court, he voted with the court again. This time he and his colleagues found most of the remaining suspects not guilty and dismissed charges against almost all of the rest. So far as is known,

[19] Niccolò Machiavelli, *Princeps* (Frankfurt, 1622), New York Society Library Win 151.
[20] William Lambarde, *A Perambulation of Kent* (London, 1596), Boston, Massachusetts Historical Society N-262 v. 57.
[21] See Clark et al., "Passing the Book."

Wait never publicly discussed the Salem trials – much less publicly repented his role in them, as his colleague Samuel Sewall did. Though the Salem trials have attracted talented historians for generations, Wait has remained a blank, indecipherable figure, whose failure as a politician illustrated the decline of his family, and whose understanding of the Salem crisis is lost to history.[22]

Yet evidence suggests that Wait may have come to the Salem trials with a particular view of events already set – one that came to him, in large part, from the reading traditions of his family, and shaped how he saw the ugly web of accusations that faced the judges at Salem. He was a friend and protégé of Cotton Mather, the onetime Harvard prodigy who had joined his father in a ministry at the Old North Church. Mather saw true Christianity as besieged not only by the many who failed to experience full conversion, but also and above all by the devil.[23] In summer 1688, four of the six children of a Boston mason, John Goodwin, came under what they experienced as diabolic attacks that caused them terrible physical pain. A local laundress, Goody Glover, was accused of bewitching them; she was convicted and executed.

Mather became involved with the case early on. He and his wife took thirteen-year-old Martha Goodwin into their house, where he observed her behavior with scrupulous attention to detail. Mather, who had some early medical training and later became a FRS, would eventually support the use of inoculation to combat smallpox (and to hasten the patients' conversion).[24] Appropriately enough, he designed experiments to investigate Martha's condition, and described them and their outcome in his *Late Memorable Providences, Relating to Witchcrafts and Possessions* of 1689.

While she was in her Frolicks I was willing to try, Whether she could read or no; and I found, not only That If she went to read the Bible her Eyes would be strangely twisted and blinded, and her Neck presently broken, but also that if any one else did read the Bible in the Room, tho it were wholly out of her sight, and without the least voice or noise of it, she would be cast into very terrible Agonies . . . I brought her again one that I thought was a Good Book; and presently she was handled with intolerable Torments. But when I show'd her a JestBook, as, The Oxford Jests, or the Cambridge Jests, she could read them without any Disturbance and have witty Descants upon them too . . . A popish Book also she could endure very well; but it would kill her to look into any Book, that (in my Opinion) it might have bin profitable and edifying for her to be reading of. These

[22] See Dunn, *Puritans and Yankees*, 258–85.

[23] *American National Biography*, s.v. Mather, Cotton, by Robert Middlekauff.

[24] Lucas Hardy, "'The Practice of Conveying and Suffering the Small-Pox': Inoculation as a Means of Spiritual Conversion in Cotton Mather's Angel of Bethesda," *Studies in Eighteenth-Century Culture*, xliv/1 (2015): 61–79.

Experiments were often enough repeated, and still with the same Success, before Witnesses not a few.[25]

Mather admitted that "this Girls Capacity or incapacity to read, was no Test for Truth to be determined by, and therefore I did not proceed much further in this fanciful Business, not knowing What snares the Devils might lay for us in the Tryals."[26] But he also insisted that his "Story all made up of Wonders" was true, and that he had "Writ as plainly as becomes an Historian, as truly as becomes a Christian, tho perhaps not so profitably as became a Divine. But I am resolv'd after this, never to use but just one grain of patience with any man that shall go to impose upon me a Denial of Devils, or of Witches."[27]

Mather dedicated the *Late Memorable Providences* to Wait Winthrop. Wait came from a family whose male members took a serious interest in women's reading of the Bible at least: one might expect Mather's efforts to test a bewitched girl with bibles and joke books to appeal to him. But Mather made it clear that he saw Wait as qualified in a deeper sense to judge and evaluate his account. He himself had provided only "a little History," based partly on "Ocular observation" and partly on "my undoubted Information." To explain these happenings, one would need to be an expert in the learned literature of demonology and witchcraft. Mather clearly believed that Wait was such an expert:

Your Knowledge has Qualified You to make those Reflections on the following Relations, which few can Think, and tis not fit that all should See. How far the Platonic Notions of Daemons which were, it may be, much more espoused by those primitive Christians and Scholars that we call The Fathers, than they see countenanced in the ensuing Narratives, are to be allow'd by a serious man, your Scriptural Divinity, join'd with Your most Rational Philosophy, will help You to Judge at an uncommon rate.[28]

What in particular did Mather have in mind here? Did he have some reason to see Wait as an especially appropriate judge in these matters?

Adam's books tells distinctive tales about how learned men might try to see the invisible work of devils, angels, and witches. One of the annotated books that his descendants brought with them was John Cotta's *The triall of witch-craft*, first published in 1616. Cotta, the son of the prominent Coventry physician Peter Cotta and Adam Winthrop's sister Susan or

[25] Cotton Mather, *Late memorable providences relating to witchcrafts and possessions clearly manifesting, not only that there are witches, but that good men (as well as others) may possibly have their lives shortned by such evil instruments of Satan* (London, 1691), Sect. xx, also available at http://law2.umkc.edu/faculty/projects/ftrials/salem/ASA_MATH.HTM.

[26] Ibid., sect. xxi. [27] Ibid., sect. xxxiii.

[28] Ibid., 'To the Honorable Wait Winthrop Esq; Sr.'.

Susanna, studied at Cambridge and built a prosperous medical practice in Northampton. He was one of the Puritans for whom the town was noted, and was accused of spreading malicious libels against the authorities in 1607 (1575?–1627/8).[29] But he did not despise authorities. Cotta wrote against unlicensed practitioners of medicine and empirics. *The triall* – which he dedicated to the great lawyer Edward Coke – offered a "true and right methode" for discovering witchcraft and a confutation of "erroneous ways."[30]

All diseases, Cotta argued, were detected either by the eye and "outward sense, or conceiued only by Reason and the inward understanding." Some diseases of the latter sort were detectable "by certaine notes or signes." others "by likely markes onely, which are the grounds of 'artificial coniecture.'"[31] And in some cases – like that of "a right Noble Lady" whom Cotta had treated – no conjecture could reveal the existence of "a black round gelly as bigge as a Tenice ball," next to her heart. Medicine, he argued, worked rather like the law.[32] Some offences were "apparent vnto the outward sense," some were "euident to reason," and some, though concealed, could be brought to light by "the learned, prudent, and discerning Iudge." Still others, however, "stand perpetually inscrutable vndecided and neuer determined."[33]

In the later chapters, Cotta made clear that some investigations of witchcraft fell into this final category – partly because the authorities went about them the wrong way. He rejected – for example – the idea that one could detect witches by casting them into water. "If then this experiment in the tryall of Witches, bee as a thing ordinary (as it is vulgarly esteemed) it must be found likewise naturall. If it cannot be found naturall, it cannot be ordinarie."[34] The evidence made clear that it was not natural: "It wanteth the vniversall testimonie of former ages and Writers; in this our age it is held in iealosie with the most iudicious, sage, and wise; It hath no reasonable proofe, no iustifiable tryall hath dared to avouch it vpon publike record."[35] This and other sections, such as the one in which Cotta denied that the witch's mark served as a clear sign of guilt, earned him a reputation as something of a skeptic in older literature.[36]

Actually, Cotta was anything but skeptical about either witches or the larger fact, as he saw it, that hidden causes operated everywhere in the natural and social world. An avid reader of Jean Fernel's work on secret

[29] See *Oxford Dictionary of National Biography*, s.v. Cotta, Johm, by Peter Elmer.
[30] John Cotta, *The triall of witch-craft: shewing the true and right methode of the discouery, with a confutation of erroneous wayes* (London, 1616), New York Society Library Win 78, 1.
[31] Ibid., 8. [32] Ibid., 16. [33] Ibid., 17. [34] Ibid., 105. [35] Ibid., 107.
[36] Ibid., 114–28.

causes, he summarized numerous cases from Fernel's practice. The French reformed Galenist, Cotta argued, had described his experiences in such graphic detail as to leave no doubt. Like Casaubon, Cotta believed that humans – especially trained professionals – could have certain knowledge of the invisible realm of natural wonders. The skilled doctor, he explained, "doth not easily or rashly with vulgars, erre or runne made in the confusion of vaine and idle scruples."[37] Sometimes sense evidence left no doubt. Fernel, for example, told the story of a man "who by the force of charms, would coniure into a looking glasse certaine shapes or visions." Given the testimony of witnesses, some of them learned, Fernel insisted that this story was absolutely credible.[38]

Sometimes, by contrast, rational conjecture could provide certain knowledge. Fernel described the case of a young man tormented by violent convulsions. Doctors could not agree on either the cause or the location of his disease. But two clues led Fernel to the truth – which was then supernaturally confirmed. When a man in convulsions moved with astonishing rapidity, "impossible vnto the force of man," and kept his "sense and vnderstanding," the devil, rather than natural causes, must be at work. Adam followed Cotta's arguments with every evidence of respectful attention, scattering manicules and references to Fernel's name in the margins.[39] He took an interest in other stories of Cotta's from the literature of witchcraft and natural magic as well – for example, Giambattista della Porta's famous story of the witch whom application of a salve deluded into thinking that she had flown, while in reality she slept even when she was being beaten.[40] He drew a manicule by Cotta's argument that in the time of their "puroxismes or fits, some diseased persons haue beene seene to vomit crooked iron, coales, brimstone, nailes, needles, pinnes, lumps of lead, waxe, hayre, strawe, and the like, in such quantity, figure, fashion and proportion, as could neuer possibly passe downe, or arise vp thorow the naturall narrownesse of the throat, or be contained in the vnproportionable small capacity, naturall susceptibility and position of the stomake."[41] He even added a reference of his own to Henry Cornelius Agrippa's attack on theurgy in his work *On the Vanity of the Arts and Sciences*.[42] At times, Adam – a lawyer himself – seems to have read the book, or tried to, as a guide to the best way to exercise his own authority in a witchcraft case. He certainly took care to make clear, in his special way, that he saw the whole work as both solid and important. On the verso of the title-page, Adam wrote:

[37] Ibid., 74. [38] Ibid., 83. [39] Ibid., 71–72. [40] Ibid., 35. [41] Ibid., 76.
[42] Ibid., 46.

luce licet propria clarum sit, clarius eius
fit splendore tamen, cui titulatur opus.
A.W.G.

Qui deo fidit
~~Si legis librum~~, furiosa Philtra
non sibi possunt, nec amara Circes
vasa, non atrox rabies Megerae
ulla nocere.

Though this work is distinguished by its own light,
The splendor of its dedicatee makes it brighter still.
A.W.G.

If you read this book He who trusts in God [you] cannot be harmed
By the mad love potions or the bitter vessels
Of Circe, nor by the dire madness of Megara.[43]

This was a book of great practical utility. Still, a different sort of material – one that Cotta produced in greater quantity than that of medical professionals – seems to have interested Adam even more than the details of witches' operations. As we saw, when Cotta argued that the rejection of witches was not a natural property of water, he appealed to "the vniversall testimonie of former ages and Writers." In fact, he larded page after page of his work with anecdotes drawn from ancient and modern historians. Cotta insisted that their credible testimony showed that the devil had not ceased to operate through secret causes after "the speciall ages and times" described in the Bible. The "faithfull histories and true reports of Ethnicke writers" showed that such happenings had never ceased. Not everyone would have been reassured by the first example that Cotta cited, a statement that ancient oracles had been spoken through the genitals of a young woman, which he drew from an ancient source at second hand. Nor would everyone have agreed that the legendary British history offered a reliable account of ancient events. But Adam underlined Cotta's reference to the oracles.[44] He also went through his descriptions of Merlin's prophecies and other anecdotes, point by point, checking Cotta's summaries against the original texts and duly noting his results in the margins of his book. Sometimes we can bring the actual books back together. The Winthrops had two copies of Melanchthon's world chronicle – one, which he annotated, and is now in the Massachusetts Historical Society; the other, which belonged to his wife, and is now in the

[43] Ibid., title page verso. Winthrop has adapted this from a liminary poem by Christopher Carleil, in Lodowick Lloyd, *The Pilgrimage of Princes* (London, 1573) sig. **iij^{vo}.
[44] Ibid., 28.

New York Society Library.[45] The page number he noted in Cotta shows that he compared it to the latter copy of Melanchthon. Adam, in short, collated Cotta's text with those of the sources that he had in his own possession. He was so dedicated to identifying Cotta's sources that he drew up an index of them – which is, in fact, his most elaborate response to the book. It seems likely, in other words, that Adam read *The triall of witch-craft* less as description of up-to-date medical thought or even as a how-to-manual for trying witches than as a guide to history itself, and the operation of hidden causes within it.

In reading Cotta as he did, Adam saw clearly. The great summa of the new British antiquarianism, Camden's *Britannia,* was one of Adam's favorite books. Cotta's argument came down, as he himself explained, to one simple point: if a disease proved more virulent than it normally should, or if remedies acted much more or less effectively than they normally should, then superior powers were intervening. In a central passage in his text, Cotta referred to Camden's description of Cheshire.[46] Adam noted that this appeared in the *Britannia*. The passage in question not only told a story of supernatural powers at work, but also offered an interpretation:

> A wonder it is that I shall tell you, and yet no other than I have heard verified upon the credit of many credible persons, and commonlie beleeved: that before any heire of this house of the Breretons dieth, there bee seene in a poole adjoining bodies of trees swimming for certaine daies together ... I am no Wisard to interpret such strange wonders. But these and such like things are done either by the holie tutelar Angels of men, or else by the devils who by Gods permission mightilie shew their power in this inferiour world.[47]

Cotta did more than cite Camden: he made clear that he rested his argument for the detectability of the invisible on the authority of "the learned and worthy preseruer of reverent antiquitie, Master Camden," who rightly saw that these happenings must be the work of angels or devils.[48] The physician and the lawyer were as one, it seems, in finding in history the strongest warrant for their belief in invisible powers.

The most striking feature of the stories Cotta told is the way in which he banalized them. When Fernel told the story of the man who could conjure spirits into a mirror, he set it into a Miltonic context, a description of the armies of angels and devils and their battles. The story itself was rich in

[45] Ibid., 49, where Winthrop fills out the reference to a prophecy made to Diocletian and recorded by Melanchthon with "lib: 3. p. 291." The passage in question appears on p. 291 in Philipp Melanchthon, *Chronicon Carionis* (Geneva, 1581), Winthrop 161.
[46] Cotta, *The triall of witch-craft*, 70.
[47] William Camden, *Britannia* (London, 1607) 462, trans. Philemon Holland.
[48] Cotta, *The triall of witch-craft*, 70.

scary, evocative detail, which not only demonstrated the presence of diabolic entities but depicted the practices of divination in which they took part:

I have seen a person use the power of words to divert various phantoms into a mirror, images that promptly displayed there whatever he requested, either in writing or in genuine images, so lucidly that everything was being rapidly and readily recognized by those present. Sacred words were certainly being heard, but foully corrupted with obscene names, such as powers of the element, [and] some revolting and freakish names of the princes who preside over the regions of the East, West, South and North.[49]

Cotta's version crushed this Lovecraftian poetry into dull prose:

Fernelius ... doth make mention of a man, who by the force of charms, would coniure into a looking glasse certaine shapes or visions, which there would either by writing, or by lively presentations so perfectly expresse and satisfie, whatsoeuer he did demaund or commaund vnto them, that easily and readily it might be distinguished, and knowne by standers by.[50]

Where Cotta's sources told diverse tales – of witches and diviners, of devils and angels – Cotta crunched them into a single, spuriously coherent classificatory system (which actually left the difficult cases unaccounted for). Though Adam checked Cotta's references, he made no complaint about his treatment of them.

And that was only natural. Cotta – and Adam – were using a particular tool of humanistic knowledge. From Erasmus to Bodin, humanists told their readers that there was one way to capture the richness of experience and its lessons: make excerpts from the sources and arrange them under topical headings in a notebook. Assessing and annotating these short passages would teach prudence; comparing them would yield rules. The only problem with this method – as Ann Blair has shown in *Too Much to Know* – was its potential consequences for the actual building blocks of knowledge. Wrenched from context, detached from details, smoothed and homogenized like pebbles rolled in the surf, they yielded general lessons – such as Cotta's classification of the forms of invisible action – at the price of losing any individuality and color.[51]

Adam's copy of Cotta was by no means the only book in the Winthrops' collection that suggests what might have been on Wait Winthrop's mind. He also owned a copy of George Giffard's *Dialogue Concerning Witches*

[49] Jean Fernel, *On the Hidden Causes of Things*, trans. John Forrester and Jon Henry (Leiden and Boston: Brill, 2004), 393.

[50] Cotta, *The triall of witch-craft*, 83.

[51] Ann Blair, *Too Much to Know: Managing Scholarly Information Before the Modern Age* (New Haven, CT: Yale University Press, 2010).

and Witchcraftes. This very unusual work, cast in the form of a dialogue, argued that though witches did exist, they could not and did not harm others.[52] This, however, did not mean that spells and charms wreaked no havoc in society. Unusually, Giffard condemned "cunning folk" – the men and women who found lost objects and sold love potions in every village – as the truly dangerous figures, and he called on readers to join in combating them.[53] Pen in hand, Adam went through the book with great care. One of the speakers had served on a jury that condemned a witch to die. Adam called attention to his testimony with a manicule and summarized it: "Euidence giuen to a Jury against a witche."[54] When the same character stated that "The holy scriptures doe command that witches should be put to death," Adam boldly wrote "Witches must be putt to death."[55] True, he also noted that Giffard offered a counterargument, noting that the nature of the evidence in witchcraft cases made obtaining convictions "the hardest matter of all."[56] But the book – and its notes – could have been suggestive in many ways.[57]

Even more suggestive is another book from the family collection. As we have seen, Wait's father, John Winthrop Jr., prized books annotated by John Dee, a few of which he owned. In addition to books on chemistry and mathematics, his little collection of Dee's books included a weighty collection of theological writings by an innovative sixteenth-century German scholar and teacher, Johann Rivius.[58] Characteristically, Dee annotated only one portion of the book: the one that dealt with angels and devils. Rivius explained that the Christian attacked by devils could use prayer for self-protection. Dee wrote: "This happened to me in January 1582, when I had set out to expel from my study a devil that was threatening me, because of Saul. See that history."[59] We do not know

52 George Giffard [Gifford], *A Dialogue Concerning Witches and Witchcraftes, In which is laide open how craftely the Divell deceiveth not onely the Witches but many other and so leadeth them awrie into many great errours* (London, 1593); Boston, Massachusetts Historical Society, Winthrop Lib. Pamphlets.

53 Cunning men and women were generally seen as innocent practitioners of arts that helped, rather than harmed, ordinary people. Giffard's treatment of them as the true villains was as innovative and distinctive a feature of his work, as was his deconstruction of the evidence normally used to convict witches. See Alan Macfarlane, "A Tudor Anthropologist: George Gifford's Discourse and Dialogue," in *The Damned Art: Essays in the Literature of Witchcraft*, ed. Sidney Anglo (London: Routledge, 1977).

54 Giffard, *A Dialogue Concerning Witches and Witchcraftes*, sig. L3 r. 55 Ibid., sig. H v.

56 He enters a manicule, ibid., sig. H2 r. 57 Ibid., sig. L3 r.

58 Johann Rivius, *Opera theologica omnia, in unum volumen collecta, libris constans XXVI*, ed. Georg Fabricius (Basel, 1562); New York, New York Society Library Win 210. Winthrops after Wait continued to value this book: the title page bears the signature of Wait's son, John Winthrop FRS, and the date 1697.

59 Rivius, *Opera theologica*, 719: Dee underlines Rivius as follows "Sic ergo ibi: Castra metabitur angelus Domini, in circuitu timentium eum, et eripiet eos," and then remarks

if Wait knew that "Saul" was Barnabas Saul, one of the scryers who gave Dee messages from the angels who visited him. Saul, who was "strangely trubled by a spirituall creature about midnight" on October 9, 1581, was still in Dee's household in 1582.[60] Wait almost certainly did not recognize the devil in question, one Lundrumguffa, whose appearances Dee described in what he called "that history," his angel diaries.[61] Still, from this note, and from others now lost, he could have drawn a very powerful moral. A predecessor in the realms of alchemy and physic, a man whom his erudite father had revered, had experienced the presence of devils in the everyday world.

It is notoriously hard to generalize about the history of reading. For the Winthrops, books seem to have been both a treasure and a burden: more likely to control their responses to the new situations, however dramatic, that they encountered in the New England colonies than to give them tools with which to make open-ended inquiries. In other cases, though, European books and learned reading functioned very differently. On February 12, 1688, Francis Daniel Pastorius and three friends examined the custom of slaveholding that many Quakers accepted and practiced. They took joint responsibility for the document. But parts of it strongly suggest that the cosmopolitan Pastorius was the main author – the one who criticized Christian slavers as resembling the Turks who enslaved Christians.[62] He never stopped worrying about the issue, as is clear from the fact that he took notes on "Negroes" in his massive commonplace book, the *Bee-Hive*.

These notes, moreover, suggest that learned reading played a major role in determining Horn's view of people of color and of slavery. He had a special interest in the synthetic works of the Leiden scholar Georg Horn on history and natural history. This was natural: they included the *Arca Noae* (Noah's Ark), the first textbook of world history that folded the Americas and China into a general account for students.[63] In 1666 Horn

in the margin "A[nn]o 1582 Januario hoc mihi accidit dum Diabolum minitantem mihi, propter Saulum ex Musaeo meo exterminare aggressus eram. vide historiam illam."

60 Harkness, *John Dee's Conversations with Angels*, 19.

61 Warm thanks to Stephen Clucas for this identification.

62 The original text of the 1688 petition is held in the Quaker and Special Collections, Haverford College. A digitized text is available at http://en.wikipedia.org/wiki/File:The_1688_germantown_quaker_petition_against_slavery.jpg (accessed on December 5, 2011). For Pastorius's part in the 1688 Germantown Protest see Hildegard Binder-Johnson, "The Germantown Protest of 1688 against Negro Slavery," *The Pennsylvania Magazine of History and Biography* 65 (1941): 145–56, and Katharine Gerbner, "Antislavery in Print: The Germantown Protest, the 'Exhortation,' and the Seventeenth-Century Quaker Debate on Slavery," *Early American Studies: An Interdisciplinary Journal* 9 (2011): 552–75, who warns against hagiographical interpretations.

63 Georg Horn, *Arca Noae* (Leiden and Rotterdam, 1666).

had brought out another synthetic textbook, *Arca Mosis, sive Historia mundi* (Moses's Ark, or the History of the World). It surveyed the history of nature and God's relation to it. In it Horn noted that "the skin of the Ethiopians is soft and porous, because the sun has consumed its stiff grains."[64] A firm traditionalist believes that all humans, from Europe to Asia and Africa, descended from Adam and Eve, Horn drew on natural philosophy to explain differences in skin color. Pastorius put a line beside the passage, and later copied it into the entry entitled "Negro" in the *Bee-Hive.*[65] It is clear that as someone who lived in a slave society and could have examined black men and women directly, he still found information that he saw as useful in a Latin compendium written decades before his time. And it seems likely that Horn's now antiquated book, with its effort to save biblical history even as Europeans' global travel and settlement called it into question, opened Pastorius's eyes to the fact that African slaves were as human as he was. The collections of evidence for learned reading in the colonies still await exploration, and it seems likely that they will turn up a good many more stories with surprising conclusions.

[64] Georg Horn, *Arca Mosis* (Leiden and Rotterdam, 1669), Library Company of Philadelphia Rare Am 1668 Hor Log 798.D, 47: "Aethiopia cutis mollis & porosa, quia sol absumsit particulas rigidas."

[65] Brooke Palmieri, "'What the Bees Have Taken Pains For': Francis Daniel Pastorius, The Beehive, and Commonplacing in Colonial Pennsylvania" (BA Thesis, University of Pennsylvania, 2009); available via the University of Pennsylvania Scholarly Commons at www.google.com/search?q=pastorius%20bee-hive%20digitization&ie=utf-8&oe=utf-8 (accessed August 21, 2011), 18–19 and Fig 4.

4 Portable Lives: Reformed Artisans and Refined Materials in the Refugee Atlantic

Neil Kamil

> It consisted of two large rollers, and the piece was wound gently, off the one, and upon the other, and the fire applied during its passage; when both sides were singed it was washed in the river, then pressed, and it really had much the appearance of true Cal[a]manco; the strength of coarse worsted gave it substance and the fineness of the warp gave it luster.[1]

How to write a history of global Reformation? In the 1780 edition of his epic study of global empire, *Histoire philosophique des établissements et du commerce des Européens dans les deux Indes*, the Abbé Raynal announced his intention to answer that question by focusing his next project on the Huguenots. Raynal's "History of the Revocation of the Edict of Nantes," aspired to trace the movement of French refugees "over the entire globe." He sent questionnaires to as many expatriates and their mostly foreign-born families as possible because he hoped to combine the mountain of data into a total history of 200,000 individuals and their progeny over the course of three generations. Yet every refugee had a different story of their portable lives.[2]

Carolyn Lougee Chappell, in her transnational history of the Champagné family of Aunis-Saintonge, embraced the pursuit of difference by training the lens of Raynal's totalizing project narrowly on the singular story of an individual family network that in fact predated the Revocation and was limited to the diaspora's "nobles' plane." "The Huguenot diaspora," Chappell writes,

[1] Ann Maury, trans. *Memoirs of a Huguenot Family: Translated and Compiled from the Original Autobiography of the Rev. James Fontaine* (New York: George P. Putnam & Co., 1853), 161–62.

[2] Bertrand Van Ruymbeke, "Le Refuge: History and Memory From the 1770s to the Present," in *A Companion to the Huguenots*, ed. Raymond A. Mentzer and Bertrand Van Ruymbeke (Leiden: Brill, 2016), 422–23; Gilles Bancarel, *Raynal ou le devoir de vérité* (Paris: Honoré Champion, 2004), 187; and Patrick Cabanel, *Histoire des protestants en France XVIe–XXIe* (Paris: Fayard, 2012), 781–82. Raynal's Huguenot project never appeared in print, although a number of questionnaires were completed and returned.

needs to be conceptualized – not as a mere dispersion – but as layers of superimposed networks that cut across local and national boundaries to lend cohesion to the Refuge ... networks ran from congregation to congregation, between pastors, among intellectuals, through the readership of publications – and, among the nobility, between kin and from client to patron. This last, the nobles' 'plane' of the diaspora, rested upon long-standing cosmopolitan patronage networks that predated the Revocation, having long circulated military men and marriageable women through ... national frontiers ... The Champagné used that preexisting patronage network – now infused with newly arrived Huguenot expatriates in both client and patron roles – to resettle their first and second generations in diaspora.[3]

This essay seeks to explore the artisans' plane of one Huguenot family diaspora and so to consider ostensibly very different types of material lives. In a surprising twist, however, this particular family history conflates artisanry with nobility in order to muddle the diasporic "planes" and to reinvent themselves outside France as noble artisans. This was achieved by reaching back in time to combine patterns derived from an undocumented noble bloodline purportedly lost through Counter-Reformation violence with methods of material refinement originating in Renaissance Saintonge during the French Civil Wars of Religion. It illuminates a more changeable, expansive, and mobile experience of human geography than undertaken by the Champagnés – including the prospect of New World migration – among artisans' families in the Refuge. It centers on Jacques Fontaine (1658–1728), one of the most resourceful figures of French Calvinism, who fled his homeland and ministerial career when the Revocation of the Edict of Nantes outlawed Protestantism in France in 1685, and moved to England and Ireland where he transformed himself into the patriarchal "re-founder" of a family diaspora in the dispersion; a pious artisan-entrepreneur who continued to evangelize the French refugee community while proclaiming himself an "inventive genius."[4] It reveals how reformed religious, regional, and material histories were embodied in a refugee family's choices and emerged in mobile artisans' working lives.

[3] Carolyn Chappell, "Family Bonds across the Refuge," in *Memory and Identity: The Huguenots in France and the Atlantic Diaspora*, ed. Bertrand Van Ruymbeke and Randy J. Sparks (Columbia: The University of South Carolina Press, 2003), 183. For her nuanced study of the Champagné family set in a larger context, including branches that chose to stay in France while others chose diaspora, see Carolyn Chappell, *Facing the Revocation: Huguenot Families, Faith, and the King's Will* (New York: Oxford University Press, 2017). The cited author changed her surname on later publications.

[4] "Re-founder" is the useful term Chappell uses to describe the matriarchal role – analogous to the patriarchal role played by Jacques Fontaine for his artisan family – assumed by the noble Marie de La Rochfoucauld, dame de Champagné, see Chappell, "Family Bonds across the Refuge," 175.

What are the telling differences when comparing choices available to a noble network in the Refuge with those considered by the Fontaine family of artisans? To begin, these choices were deeply implicated with transgenerational New World entanglements. Unlike the Champagnés, who depended on preexisting patronage networks to resettle for the long term in Holland, Ireland, and Germany, where they stayed in place for generations, the Fontaine family suffered from the absence of such established connections and were always on the move in search of more promising patronage relationships. Instead of remaining in Britain and Ireland to rebuild the family patrimony of rural Reformed Church pulpits and the modest lineage lands that were lost in Saintonge, France, Jacques sent his son John, a first-generation English-born Huguenot, to purchase new land in Virginia, to extend and diversify family holdings and search for new patronage in America.

That the Fontaines sent a member of the first exiled generation born in England to America to purchase land from the relatively modest cash proceeds of Jacques's British textile manufactory is a fascinating contradiction to the Champagné family practice in diaspora. The artisan clan produced and consumed movables in the form of textiles, sundries for retail clients, books for personal libraries, and valuable household furniture for high-status display and resale in times of dearth, but the Fontaines also sought real property in America as a lynchpin of family security and upward mobility. On the other hand, while in France, if the rural nobility tended to plow liquid assets back into land, the Champagné matriarch and family re-founder, Marie de La Rochfoucauld, did the opposite and collected movables in exile. Controlling the family portfolio of investments from Holland and following the Saintongeais tradition of partible inheritance for the equal benefit of her children and grandchildren, Marie invested exclusively in "intangibles," including bonds, pensions, English financial instruments, investments in the Dutch and English East India Companies, petty banking, and the occasional lottery. Real property was not part of Marie's investment strategy, in part because easily liquidated movables were more attractive to refugees who were unable to send proceeds from the sale of lineage lands outside of France after 1685. Unlike Jacques Fontaine, moreover, the dame de Champagné's worldview never expanded west beyond northern Europe and across the Atlantic to include cheap and abundant land for resettlement in America. If anything, the geography of her economic imagination pointed east. Her preexisting, long-term financial and patronage assets meant that she and her family would stay closer to home.

What Marie de la Rochfoucauld did share with Jacques Fontaine and many other re-founders in diaspora was an active and urgent desire to instruct and discipline succeeding generations in the proper means to consolidate family assets across borders. In pursuit of this goal, both wrote family memoirs to demonstrate their experience with the best (and worst) practices in their respective economic domains. "For my purpose," Marie wrote in the investment ledger she kept in Holland between 1690 and 1717, "is to leave to my children all the instruction I can and that I believe necessary for their property and to make them see the use I shall make of it." While their intentions were similar, the movable resources at stake and the borders in question varied substantially. Jacques's transgenerational and transatlantic instructions concerned his knowledge-based assets: primarily the deployment of artisanal skill, improvisation with newfound local materials to create niche markets potentially anywhere in the world, knowledge of the old alchemical artisanry of Aunis-Saintonge at the dawn of the British industrial revolution, charismatic stories celebrating the ingeniousness with materials and refined nobility of Fontaine family history, and the inventive artisan's practice of opportunistic mobility.[5]

Much has been written about Fontaine's family history, a classic of the genre in French Reformation and diasporic studies. Yet despite more than 150 years of historiography, virtually nothing has been written about Fontaine's granular focus in the history on his working life as an artisan. This includes the overlooked alchemical narrative from England's early industrial period in which this "inventive genius" tied his family's claims to what he called "noble" artisanry and the earliest histories of Huguenot martyrdom from his natal region to his creation of the portable fire machine, which transmuted local woolens into calamanco, a cheap "import substitute" for silk.[6] This essay will show how the rhetoric and workshop practices of sixteenth- and seventeenth-century regional French Huguenot alchemical artisanry re-emerged in Fontaine's family

[5] Ibid., 176–77; Chappell connects Marie's noble (and, as I will argue in this essay, Jacques Fontaine's artisanal) "orientation toward future generations," with Natalie Zemon Davis's important claim in a now classic article that a new historical consciousness arose in early modern France that supported different Catholic and Protestant family strategies towards an upwardly mobile future for succeeding generations, a process that included violently dispossessed refugees with hopes for resettlement in America, see Natalie Zemon Davis, "Ghosts, Kin, and Progeny: Some Features of Family Life in Early Modern France," *Daedalus* 106 (Spring, 1977): 87–114.

[6] On the centrality of import substitution and the process of imitation of forms and materials in the pre-modern English trades, see John Styles, "Product Innovation in Early Modern London," *Past and Present* 168 (August 2000): 128–29; and Helen Gifford, "Invention, Identity and Imitation in the London and Provincial Metal-Working Trades, 1750–1800," *Journal of Design History* 12/3, Eighteenth-Century Markets and Manufactures in England and France (1999): 241–55.

history, written as a stranger in Ireland during the first quarter of the eighteenth century.

Jacques Fontaine's historical claims to noble artisanry and the production of the material culture of politeness were at the core of his refounder's project to rebuild an ostensibly humble family's lost patrimony in diaspora, with links across the Atlantic to America. Lacking noble assets or patronage to arrange advantageous marriages, military commissions, or lucrative investment portfolios for succeeding generations of Fontaines – as Maria was able to accomplish for the first and second foreign-born generations of her dispersed family – Jacques was the impresario of an alternative route to upward mobility for his kinship network in exile. The family mythology of the noble artisan emerged from Jacques's substitution of his alchemical narrative of the "inventive genius" to produce import substitutes, whereby everyday local materials replace intrinsically valuable imports by substituting surface gloss for noble refinement based on mastery of fire in the production process. For Jacques Fontaine, this was not merely a process of commodification, but simultaneously an act of piety and the skillful basis of a portable reformation to redefine the fixed values associated with the landed aristocracy downward. Here was the noble asset Jacques Fontaine bequeathed through oral and written instructions to future generations of his line. The Fontaines harnessed their portable reinvention of nobility as a manual skill and a spiritual calling to the production of politeness out of the found materials of everyday life that were available anywhere in the world. The historical, filial, and material aspects of this bequest were fundamental to John Fontaine's choices in Virginia. There he tried unsuccessfully to complete a land transaction with the colony's historian Robert Beverley, Jr. (ca. 1667–1722) to fulfill his father's vision to extend the refuge to the New World by "recovering" lineage lands for the prestige of succeeding generations with money accumulated through the "noble" production of polite materials.

The recovery of Fontaine's artisanal biography is thus particularly relevant to the global themes of this volume. The artisan-preacher associated himself, his bloodline of noble artisans, and his portable skills with a materio-centric process of global Reformation – albeit local in origin – that by its very nature spread quietly and incrementally throughout the early modern Atlantic world. Fontaine tells us that the everyday craft practice that succeeding generations carried to America was based on mobile skills "imitate[d]" from Pauline models of itinerant, evangelical, primitive-church religiosity that the first-century apostle blended seamlessly with his working life as a tentmaker – skills that were inextricably entwined with his spiritual and material forbears: the first Reformed artisan-preachers in his home region of Saintonge. Portability, pious artisanry, and boundary-crossing were crucial components of the light-footed Fontaine's toolkit and at the nexus of his historical worldview, inseparable from religious, material, family, and textual concerns.[7]

Weaver and Manufacturer

Jacques Fontaine was born in the family house of his agricultural and salt-producing hometown of Genouillé, in Gallo-Roman Saintonge on France's southwest Atlantic coast, close to where the Charente River empties into the Bay of Biscay. An early regional stronghold of the French Reformation, Genouillé is known today for the remnants of its thirteenth-century stone church, one of several remarkably similar fortified churches with carved three-tier towers that survive from medieval Saintonge. Damaged extensively by centuries of armed conflict and Protestant iconoclasm, this impressive shell of a building was ultimately put to the torch during the sixteenth-century Wars of Religion.[8]

Genouillé was thus a frequent target of confessional violence. It stood directly between the Huguenot fortresses of La Rochelle and St. Jean d'Angély, both beseiged during the Civil Wars of Religion and Thirty Years War.[9] Proximity meant that Genouillé was prey to marauding armies. The town changed confessional allegiance out of necessity during a century and a half of warfare, becoming a steady source of Huguenot refugees to La Rochelle and its connections to the Atlantic centers of international Protestantism.

Jacques's great-grandfather and grandmother, Protestants from Le Mans in the province of Maine, were killed in 1563, during the first of eight Religious Wars fought between 1562 and 1598. The orphaned male survivors escaped death and found refuge in La Rochelle, approximately

[7] Christopher Hill, *A Tinker and a Poor Man: John Bunyan and His Church, 1628–1688* (New York: Knopf, 1989), 362; for Hill's groundbreaking views on animate-materialism in England with implications for Quakerism and the British Atlantic, see Hill, *The Religion of Gerrard Winstanley* (Oxford, UK: Past and Present Society, 1978); and his influential civil-war history, *The World Turned Upside Down, Radical Ideas During the English Revolution* (New York: Viking Press, 1972); for thoughts on Hill's work and the Atlantic tradition, see Neil Kamil, "The Refiner's Fire's Atlantic," *Journal of Mormon History* 41/4 (October 2015): 223–25; for a remarkable study of the depth and pervasiveness of such ideas and their connection to millennial thought, albeit limited controversially to a "radical" community of Puritan artisans, scientists, and physicians, see Charles Webster, *The Great Instauration: Science, Medicine, and Reform, 1626–1660* (London: Duckworth, 1975).

[8] It is easy to confuse the Fontaines' hometown of Genouillé, in the present-day department of Charente-Maritime, with another small town called Genouillé, which is located in the department of Vienne, in the Nouvelle-Aquitaine region, 70 miles due east.

[9] The two fortresses were situated only about 40 miles apart, a journey of two days or less on horseback.

175 miles to the southwest. "They found their way to Rochelle," Jacques wrote, "which was then a safe place, and, indeed, for many years a stronghold of Protestantism in France, containing within its walls many devout and faithful servants of the living God." Thereafter, the family maintained strong religious and domestic ties to La Rochelle, where Jacques's father, the minister Jacques de la Fontaine, began his theological training as a youngster before completing his studies at the college of Saumur. Once ordained, de la Fontaine traveled to London where he met a "lady named Thompson," his first wife of twelve years, thus initiating the family's links to England. Upon his return to Saintonge, de la Fontaine was named minister of the United Churches of Vaux and Royan, situated within two miles of one another on the Atlantic coast, where the Gironde River meets the Bay of Biscay. He remained there to preach at both churches for the rest of his life. "When the great persecution [of 1685] came on, eighteen years after his [father's] death," the younger Fontaine wrote in his history, "a most unusual proportion of the Protestant population of Vaux and Royan fled the kingdom for the sake of truth. There were few parishes in which so small a number of persons abjured their religion under the terrors of the dragonade, and of those who were terrified into doing so with their lips, I believe there are many who still worship God in sincerity around their family altars."

Fontaine's assessment of Vaux and Royan conforms to archival evidence drawn from the resettlement of French refugees in British North America. For example, after 1685, a cohort of skilled woodworking artisans from coastal Huguenot towns clustered closely around the United Churches who specialized in the shipbuilding, luxury furniture, and cooperage trades found their way to New York City.[10] Given the Fontaines' long association with these towns, it seems reasonable to ask whether the younger Jacques's facility with intricate woodworking, a skill later used to construct his textile machines, may have been acquired there?

Once in Britain, together with his wife and sister-in-law, Jacques Fontaine claimed he invented his small portable fire machine to produce calamanco (Fig 4.1). Hence, Fontaine's assertion of innovation, what he

[10] **Maury, Memoirs of a Huguenot Family**, 21, 25, 35–37; see, for example, my craftsman's biography of the Huguenot chairmaker, upholsterer, and cobbler Jean Suire (naturalized in New York City's West Ward in 1701–d. March 1715), in Neil D. Kamil, "Hidden in Plain Sight: Disappearance and Material Life in Colonial New York," in *American Furniture 1995*, ed. Luke Beckerdite and William N. Hosley (Hanover, NH; London: The University Press of New England, 1995): 219, 220–22, 224–25, 231, 237, 246–47(n. 17).

Fig 4.1 *Eighteenth-century American room setting.* The Anne H. and Frederick Vogel III Collection of Early American Furniture and Decorative Art; photo: Jim Wildeman. The bed cover is made of indigo-dyed calamanco quilted in the "tree of life" pattern, 96 x 90 inches, Britain or America, ca. 1790–1810

called his "inventive genius." And yet, Fontaine's process of calendaring wool had already been in use elsewhere since the early seventeenth century, especially in Holland and Norwich, the center of calamanco production in England. Both places had large French refugee artisan communities and were hubs of émigré Huguenot commercial networks with which Fontaine likely communicated to buy shop goods. In this regard, Fontaine's *mobility*, born of flight from religious violence, not necessarily his engineering acumen, made him an inventive genius. He set up shop in isolated Taunton, where his small fire machine for calendaring wool was as yet unknown; his inventive genius in many ways lay in his ability to adapt old technology from contacts in the Atlantic Huguenot craft network to a new local niche economy. Still, there is evidence to suggest that inspiration may also have come closer to home, making Taunton a specific target for migration. The Devonshire-Somerset region, where Taunton is located, was an early center of experimentation with the steam engines invented around 1710 in Devon by another artisan-minister: the hardware manufacturer and Baptist lay preacher Thomas Newcomen (1664–1729), arguably under the theoretical influence of the Huguenot émigré engineer Denis Papin.[11]

If so, Fontaine was among the first textile entrepreneurs to benefit from the new fire technologies that became available during his early sojourn in Taunton. Possibly for the same reason, however, his strategy for taking advantage of a niche economy was imitated locally to his own disadvantage, for soon enough he was stigmatized, copied, and undersold by local native artisans who used his method to produce a glut of shiny "polite" material. What did Fontaine, this inventive genius, do as a result of being outmaneuvered within the local economy? He did what he had done before so successfully: he moved. Consequently, following the habit of religious refugees as well as the habit of the preacher-artisan apostle Paul after whom he self-consciously modelled himself, Fontaine transported his family to Ireland where he worked as a minister to supplement other mechanical enterprises before finally opening his French and Latin school offering lessons in the culture of politeness for young Dublin elites. There, in Ireland, the charismatic Fontaine showed that the pedagogy of pious politeness was a winning family strategy. Politeness promised to mitigate bloodletting from religious warfare by substituting non-violent rituals of multilingual conversation and the material culture of polished deportment for force of arms. Indeed, divisive class, national, confessional, linguistic, and ethnic distinctions were softened, at least in theory, by the mutual adherence of traveling strangers and economic competitors to the culture of politeness. As we shall see, the unexpected absence of otherwise ubiquitous Atlantic implements of polite material culture at Beverley Park in Virginia short-circuited commerce and curtailed John Fontaine's quest to find common ground and complete his mission. Politeness was thus essential to the process of New World entanglement.

[11] On Norwich and the renown of its textile workers who specialized in dying calamanco in a variety of colors and patterns, see Florence M. Montgomery, *Textiles in America, 1650–1870* (New York: W. W. Norton, 1984), 185. Newcomen's eldest son, also Thomas, born around the time his father invented his steam engine, was a cloth maker in Taunton, specializing in the production of serge (a woolen also produced by Fontaine). Fontaine left for Ireland long before the younger Newcomen set up shop in Taunton, but perhaps Newcomen chose Taunton because it was a center for fire technology in serge manufacture as early as Fontaine's time; see "Thomas Newcomen," *Oxford Dictionary of National Biography* <https://doi.org/10.1093/ref:odnb/19997>; and Brian Corfield, "Thomas Newcomen the Man," *International Journal of the History of Engineering and Technology* (2013), 83: 209–21. I am grateful to my colleague Professor Bruce Hunt of the University of Texas at Austin for bringing these regional connections to steam engines and the accompanying citations to my attention.

To control this process and to profit by it was value-added to the Fontaines' manual skills, to which their singular expertise as artisans of politeness was harnessed. The pedagogy of politeness that Jacques sold was an extension of his transactions with portable machines producing "polite" materials for a public that was heavily invested in politeness in all its cultural and social ramifications in the early modern period.[12]

Palissy and Fontaine

The old alchemical dream of finding the philosopher's stone to create infinite production converged with Fontaine's claims of nobility and inventive genius in the manufacture of the polite woolen textile calamanco. Historians of alchemy and the artisanal trades have argued that the sixteenth and seventeenth centuries constituted a period of global reform in thinking about and debating affinities between the two and of the philosophical control of fire to refine and regenerate half-dead earthly materials infused with hidden remnants of translucent prelapsarian matter.[13] The two were entwined in the influential work of the Germanic physician and alchemist Paracelsus (1493–1541). Paracelsus's books, medical recipes, and experiments in translation and by oral tradition became a focal point and frame of reference for all Protestant (and indeed, Catholic) alchemists, experimental natural philosophers, and artisans during the Reformation, even though Paracelsus himself did not convert from his natal Catholicism and received the sacrament of Extreme Unction on his deathbed. At the same time, the alchemist's heterodox publications were on the Vatican Index of Prohibited Books.

Bernard Palissy was a first-generation French reformed Paracelsian and Calvinist lay minister who, like Fontaine, spent his formative years in the crucible of wartime Saintonge, before being summoned to Paris by Catherine de Médicis to produce ceramic gift medallions for the courtly economy and build a Renaissance grotto at the Tuileries Palace. Palissy's "rustic" legend as an inventive genius who innovated to replace his

[12] For another artisan who was deeply immersed in the available printed materials of politeness and wrote about it, although less as an artisan "of" than "in" polite culture, see Lawrence E. Klein, "An Artisan in Polite Culture: Thomas Parsons, Stone Carver, of Bath, 1744–1813," *Huntington Library Quarterly* 75/1 (March 2012): 27–51.

[13] See, for one representative example in a growing literature, Pamela H. Smith, Amy R. W. Meyers, and Harold J. Cook eds., *Ways of Making and Knowing: The Material Culture of Empirical Knowledge* (Ann Arbor: The University of Michigan Press, 2014); for the classic text on this subject see Owen Hannaway, *The Chemists and the Word: The Didactic Origins of Chemistry* (Baltimore, MD: The Johns Hopkins University Press, 1975); on artisanry and the alchemical regeneration of "half-dead" materials, see Kamil, "The Refiner's Fire's Atlantic," 225–26.

original idolatrized trade as a stained-glass painter for Catholic churches with reformed artisanry, was at the core of the religious and material life of Fontaine's home region. His "Petit Narré" [little relation] (1563), on the origins of the primitive church of Saintonge, was fundamental to Fontaine's pastoral and artisanal life and those of his ministerial forebears. Violently harried from France after the Revocation, Fontaine constructed active links between his late seventeenth-century experience, innovating with new materials in exile and Palissy's alchemical artisanry during his Civil-War past. As Saintes devolved in bloodshed, corruption, and chaos, he focused on the potter's description of laborious and frustratingly unsuccessful experiments with new varieties of ceramic glazes produced in a hybrid glass-ceramic kiln of his own making. Palissy represented the cruel violence of the 1562 war and his status as a religious refugee in besieged Saintes, as taking place in an alchemical crucible during the end of time. The ordeal was essential to the development of his persona of the Reformed inventive genius. It was the matrix for postlapsarian material perfection and proof of election: the material-holiness synthesis in the form of a pure white glaze on a ceramic body.[14]

Palissy's ceramic medallions, which substituted common glazed earthenware for expensive bronze, were early Huguenot variants of the economy of import substitution and product imitation that the Saintongeais potter developed as a natural extension of his alchemical paradigm. Just as Palissy openly acknowledged Paracelsus's role, after only the Scriptures, in the formation of his artisanal practice and worldview, so too Fontaine reached back to Palissy, also a (lay) preacher, artisan, and local historian, to appropriate the potter as his spiritual and material predecessor, regional inspiration, and textual guide. Palissy, inspired by his mentor – the martyred Calvinist colporteur and itinerant minister Philibert Hamelin – was also a follower of the peripatetic artisanal and evangelical traditions of the apostle Paul as he tramped through the remote Atlantic province of Aunis-Saintonge. Fontaine and his descendants were thus a multigenerational link to Palissy, the first Reformed artisan from the "primitive church" of

[14] For the larger context of the converted Palissy's innovations in his crucial spiritual and artisanal shift from stained-glass painting to ceramics, see the brilliant consideration of German artists and artisans in the midst of change from pre-Reformation to Reformation production, by Jeffrey Chipps Smith, *German Sculpture of the Late Renaissance, c. 1520–1580: Art in an Age of Uncertainty* (Princeton, NJ: Princeton University Press, 1994), 3–126; for a brief discussion of the history of the Fontaine family of ministers in Saintonge, see Elisabeth Forlacroix and Olga de Saint-Affique, *Les Pasteurs d'Aunis, Saintonge, et Angoumois devant la Révocation: Dictionnaire* (Paris: Rivages des Xantons, 2010), 71–74; on the relation between religious war, labor pain, and the alchemical process in Palissy's pottery workshop, see Neil Kamil, *Fortress of the Soul: Violence, Metaphysics, and Material Life in the Huguenots' New World, 1517–1751* (Baltimore, MD: Johns Hopkins University Press, 2005), 125–70, 316–88.

Saintonge to represent alchemical death and rebirth as the pious artisan's way to achieve material and spiritual translucency in refuge. Palissy famously achieved this material-holiness synthesis with the invention of his personal holy grail: a regenerate earth material in the form of a sparkling white ceramic glaze. Here was yet another import substitute, in this case for both Italian majolica and Asian porcelain.

Palissy's well-known story of the alchemical invention of his glazes while secreted in his laboratory in Saintes during the Civil Wars of religion was developed in his widely read essay, "On the Art of the Earth, its Usefulness, On Enamels and Fire," which first appeared in his *Discours admirables* (1580), a regional paradigm Fontaine followed for wool over a century later in diaspora in Taunton. Like Palissy, Fontaine perceived that his post-Revocation narrative occurred in end times as prophesied in *Revelation*, which infused sacred violence with the alchemical work of regeneration in his fire machine, just as did Palissy's enamel kiln during the Civil Wars. Fontaine's favorite eschatological convention included the phrase, "until the end of the world." To wit, he hoped his children and grandchildren stayed together "until the end of the world," the family credo at the heart of John Fontaine's mission to purchase land for resettlement in America.[15]

Like Palissy, Fontaine represented himself as a spiritual refugee engaged in the pious but physically laborious transformation of elemental materials by fire in pursuit of survival through innovation and commerce. The invention and mass production of cheap and fashionable textile materials were central to the Fontaine family program for transatlantic relocation with personal and financial security. Secrecy about processes by which raw materials were transformed prevented "drugs" (alchemical recipes) or inventions from falling into the hands of competitors. Profiting from secrecy harnessed artisanal "art and mystery" to the natural philosophical traditions of alchemical "Arcanum," interests the Fontaines shared with Palissy.[16]

[15] Kamil, *Fortress of the Soul*, 49–51, 107–12, 320–86; Bernard Palissy, *Discours Admirables, de la Nature des Eaux et Fonteines, tant naturelles qu'artificielles, des metaux, des sels & salines, des pierres, des terres, du feu & des emaux. Avec plusieurs autres excellens secrets des choses naturelles … Le Tout dressé par Dialogues, lesquels sont introduits la theorique & la practique* (Paris: Martin le Jeune, 1580); Bernard Cottret, "Postface: Jacques Fontaine ou la Providence dans le Texte," in *Persécutés Pour Leur Foi: Mémoires d'une Famille Huguenote*, ed. Bernard Cottret and Jacques Fontaine (Paris, France: Les Éditions de Paris, 2003), 231.

[16] On the positive early modern rhetoric, understanding and practice of the "knowledge economy," "economy of secrets," and "arcanization," see Daniel Jütte, *The Age of Secrecy: Jews, Christians, and the Economy of Secrets, 1400–1800* (New Haven, CT: Yale University Press, 2015), 1–36. It is noteworthy that Jütte places Jews at the center of this trade and rhetoric of secrecy, a religious group and history to which Huguenots harnessed

Fontaine despised guilds as exclusionary in the economy of secrets and fought them in court. Absent guild protections for his family's trade secrets, Fontaine instructed descendants to keep their own counsel, while passing proprietary skills and practices down the line to male heirs exclusively. Although female family members had significant manual and retail roles in his textile manufactory and boutique, the patriarchal Fontaine made clear his disdain for women in his history, particularly those he represented coarsely as poisonous, parasitic, or self-interested in-laws. They were often his sons' wives, who vied with Fontaine for influence in their own households. If the Revocation tore his family apart from the outside, Fontaine made clear, women relations were historically the miscreants who did so from within. Alternatively, in her history, Marie de La Rochfoucault provided a powerfully positive account of her active role as matriarch of the Champagné, and of other women family members with whom she interacted.[17] In the end, however, Fontaine's program of secrecy was a failure. Despite his best efforts, the fire machine was imitated and exploited by local competitors who undercut his business.

Import Substitution

At the end of the seventeenth century, portable devices were manufactured with customer mobility in mind. On April 20, 1697, a pocket globe, readymade for travelers at two inches in diameter, was advertised in the *Amsterdam Current Newspaper*. Dutch mapmakers recommended the little novelty to clients who also "customarily carry a pocket watch with them." Unfortunately, the pocket globe never really caught on, especially by comparison with the commercial success of the pocket watch. Pocket watches were crafted not only for the rich but fit every economic bracket. They were purchased by the affluent from the start, but by 1770, pocket watches appear in 38 percent of British pauper inventories. When pocket watches were introduced, they were manufactured in the tens of thousands per year; a century later, 400,000 were produced annually.[18]

themselves frequently, particularly during the sixteenth-century Wars of Religion and the Thirty Years' War. In Anthony Grafton and Joanna Weinberg with Alistair Hamilton, *"I have always loved the Holy Tongue": Isaac Casaubon, the Jews, and a Forgotten Chapter in Renaissance Scholarship* (Cambridge, MA: Belknap Press of the Harvard University Press, 2011), Professor Grafton and colleagues explore Casaubon's commitment to Hebraic language and textual studies and his complex fascination with Jews and Judaism.

17 For one early example in Jacques Fontaine's history of his polemical attitudes towards women family members, see *Memoirs of a Huguenot Family*, 22–23; on Marie's very different perspective, see Chappell, "Family Bonds across the Refuge," 175.

18 Jan de Vries, *The Industrious Revolution: Consumer Behavior and the Household Economy, 1650 to the Present* (Cambridge: Cambridge University Press, 2008), 1–3.

During the Reformation, French clockmakers converted to Protestantism. Blois and La Rochelle became centers of pocket watchmaking. During the Revocation era, more than ninety refugee watchmakers registered with Huguenot congregations in London. English dominance in watchmaking emerged from such refugee innovations as jeweled movements, augmented by guild laws that required native apprenticeship to immigrant artisans. As Tessa Murdoch writes, "by the early eighteenth century," after France was emptied of exiled horologists, "the French authorities had to invite an English clockmaker to revitalize the French clock making industry at Versailles."[19]

While every story was different, necessity and opportunity allowed sixteenth- and seventeenth-century refugee tradesmen who lacked formal training to find apprenticeships and employment in London when demand was high. After 1685, when the labor markets were glutted with foreigners, guild-trained tradesmen like those ninety watchmakers were more likely to settle close to home in Britain and Germany, where mercantilist and cameralist recruiters offered privileges to refugee artisans with documented skills. Only 10,000 risked Atlantic or Indian Ocean voyages to settle in such faraway places as British North America. Available land was certainly a major inducement for the Fontaine family and most others in this group, as colonial recruiters made clear in French-language pamphlets circulated throughout refugee communities in Europe. Yet second and third generation Fontaines arguably joined the American contingent because they lacked provable guild-training, which restricted opportunity and invited local hostility. They were also less attractive to recruiters in Europe, who were expected to employ strangers registered with local guilds. In 1716, in one iteration of many, a certain John Chevallier, "[was] adm[itted] for [a] m[aster]" in the weavers' company of London, "upon his affid[avi]t of service in France."[20] Unlike Chevallier, the Fontaines' lack of guild membership in France contributed to the family's move to America in much the same way that Marie's solid investment portfolio improved the Champagné family's odds of remaining in northern Europe. New York Colony had

[19] Tessa Murdoch, *The Quiet Conquest: The Huguenots 1685–1985* (London: Museum of London in association with the Huguenot Society of London, 1985), 243–54; William Herbert, *The History of the Twelve Great Livery Companies of London* (New York: Augustus M. Kelley, [1837], 1968).

[20] William Chapman Waller ed., "Extracts from the Court Books of the Weavers' Company of London, 1610–1730," in *The Publications of the Huguenot Society of London* (Frome, UK: Butler and Tanner LTD, 1931), 33:76; for a thoughtful study of the complex realities of economic and social life for skilled refugee tradesmen in the early industries of early modern London, see Lien Bich Luu, *Immigrants and the Industries of London, 1500–1700* (Aldershot, UK: Ashgate, 2005).

a Huguenot minority of just 11 percent; few if any were guild-trained in Europe (there were no guilds in colonial British America), although as elsewhere New York Huguenot artisans dominated the luxury trades.[21] Many reformed Atlantic artisans including the Fontaines re-embarked, sometimes repeatedly, after finding their initial choice inhospitable due to a variety of circumstances, including a glut of guild-trained refugee artisans already in place.

Macroeconomic study of the immigration of Huguenot craftsmen to Brandenburg-Prussia from 1640 to 1802, provides evidence that "Huguenot influence [was] positively correlated with technology use."[22] Of the 20,000 Huguenot immigrants who received privileges in cameralist Prussia during the seventeenth century, the artisanal and manufacturing sectors predominated; 45 percent were artisans and craftsmen, 20 percent workers and apprentices, and 8 percent in trade and manufacture as entrepreneurs or factory owners. These immigrants were from the most well-educated and highly skilled artisanal and manufacturing occupations in France. Fifty-eight percent of the population was engaged in textile manufacture.[23] Cameralists directed Huguenots to produce goods to counteract imports, especially from France. Huguenot success in import substitution increased Prussian textile manufacture markedly over the long term. Transfer of technological knowledge, innovation of multi-shuttle engine looms, and the re-use of domestic materials, in combination with the reorganization of both large and small-scale textile manufactories through division of labor, were essential to this process. Growth and productivity among refugees in Prussia were neither simply local or linear. Improvements were imported continuously through networks of Atlantic coreligionists.[24]

Huguenots excelled at the creative re-use of cheap local materials to substitute for exotic imports or more expensive "noble" materials. This became central to the new luxury market in Europe and America. Not predicated on the unique art object made of intrinsically valuable materials that were melted down later and transformed into some other form of value, rather, the new luxuries were reproduced in multiples and sold in a range of prices. Durability and intrinsic value were less important than short-term fashion and price, with silver plate representing the most dramatic example. "Plate" was sold readymade with rapidly changing

[21] Kamil, *Fortress of the Soul*, xvii, 711–66.
[22] Erik Hornung, "Immigration and the Diffusion of Technology: The Huguenot Diaspora in Prussia," *American Economic Review* 104/ 1(2014): 117.
[23] Ibid., 90.
[24] Ibid., 91–117; Alfred Plummer, *The London Weaver's Company, 1600–1970* (London and Boston: Routledge and Kegan Paul, 1972), 162–72.

designs that emphasized dazzling surface polish, challenging the depth and quality of solid silver.[25]

The word "ingenious" was harnessed to artisanal innovation in general but in particular to the transformation of commonplace materials into polished import substitutes. This meaning migrated to the cheap raw materials from America and Asia that were flooding English port cities during the seventeenth century. Ingenious use of "little" materials invited religious as well as commercial analogies. This included the Christian preoccupation with small things, spiritual "duty," and the power of weakness. In 1693, the archdeacon of Norwich and the Cambridge Platonist John Jeffery (1647–1720) preached to the weavers' guild of his town that "there are many things in nature, which are little, or not at all useful, which are by Art, made very profitable to men."[26] Jeffery knew these ideas reached sympathetic ears in the pews, as "Norwich calamanco" was in demand globally as the most colorful produced by English weavers.[27] He also knew the most innovative Norwich weavers were French Calvinists who carried their trade secrets to England.

Still, there is new evidence that the use of polite materials by outsiders exacerbated religious animosity in England rather than the opposite, the long-accepted historical commonplace. Despite the Toleration Act of 1689, which allowed Reformed dissenters from the Church of England to worship openly in their own meeting houses for the first time, opponents remained powerful. As a result, the discourse of politeness was used as a weapon of exclusivity rather than unity against religious dissenters. Similar to the claims of inauthenticity raised against Huguenot makers of import substitutes, if dissenters used polite idioms, fashions, and deportment to interactively promote religious coexistence despite accusations of hidden differences, they were stigmatized by opponents of the act with dangerous accusations of hypocrisy.[28]

[25] Jan de Vries, *The Industrious Revolution*, 44–65; and Helen Clifford, "Concepts of Invention, Identity and Imitation in the London and Provincial Metal-Working Trades, 1750–1800," 241–55.

[26] John Jeffrey, *The Duty and Encouragement of Religious Artificers Described in a Sermon Preached in the Cathedral Church of Norwich at the Weavers Guild, On Munday in Whitsun Week, June 5, 1693* (Cambridge: Printed by John Hayes for Samuel Oliver Bookseller in Norwich, 1693), 4, 7, 19; see "John Jeffery" by Gordon Goodwin, in *Dictionary of National Biography*, ed. Leslie Stephen and Sidney Lee (New York: Macmillan, 1885–1906), 29: 268; and *The Cambridge Platonist Research Group: A Research Portal for Scholarship on Cambridge Platonism* at https://cprg.hypothesis.org/bibliography/whichcote.

[27] Florence M. Montgomery, *Textiles in America*, 185.

[28] Carys Brown, "Politeness, Hypocrisy and Protestant Dissent in England after the Toleration Act, c. 1689–1750," *Journal for Eighteenth-Century Studies* 41/1 (2018): 61–76.

The Fontaine Family Publication History

The Fontaine Family history is among the best-known French refugee narratives for the British Atlantic. A massive document, it is a composite of multiple family texts. Jacques Fontaine was the original narrator, beginning with a genealogy of improvably noble ancestors and the deracinated fate of his family stemming from the Civil Wars. "I ... commenced writing this history for the use of all my children," Jacques wrote on the first page. He took up the pen after "I have related my own adventures to you, or given you details of the incidents that befell your ancestors." The oral history with its operatic set pieces was a family catechism committed to memory by the children long before the summer of 1722, when John Fontaine (1693–1767) received the gift of his father's handwritten manuscript. John used the narrative as a template while writing his journal of travels to Virginia and New York (1715–1719). Jacques's manuscript remained in private hands until translated for publication by an American descendent in 1838. A 512-page edition appeared in 1853, this time including John's diary and correspondence from various family members scattered around the Atlantic rim during the eighteenth century.[29]

The 1853 compendium represents a multigenerational Calvinist Atlantic *livre de raison* (commonplace book), an early modern French variant of the Florentine Renaissance *ricordi* (memory book) tradition. Like the *livre de raison* and *ricordi*, the Fontaine texts encouraged consideration of current situations enmeshed within a non-linear web of family experience and advice that scrolled backward and forward in time. Didactic though they may be, such texts projected forceful authorial voices "of my old grandfathers" that echoed powerfully through centuries of family history, what Isabelle Luciani calls a continual process of locating and "ordering the self."[30]

[29] Maury, *Memoirs of a Huguenot Family*, 14–15; a modern French edition from the original document is now available in Bernard Cottret ed., *Jacques Fontaine, Mémoires d'une famille huguenote, victim de la revocation de l'édit de Nantes* (Paris: Les Éditions de Paris / Paroles Saingulières, 2003); Edward Porter Alexander ed., *The Journal of John Fontaine: An Irish Huguenot Son in Spain and Virginia 1710–1719* (Charlottesville: The University Press of Virginia, 1972).

[30] On the *livre de raison*, see Isabelle Luciani, "Ordering Words, Ordering the Self: Keeping a Livre de Raison in Early Modern Provence, Sixteenth through Eighteenth Centuries," *French Historical Studies* 38/4 (2015): 529–48; and Martine Barilly-Leguy, *"Livre de Mes Anciens Grand Pères": Le Livre de Raison d'une famille Mancelle du Grand Siècle, 1567–1675* (Rennes: Presses universitaires de Rennes, 2015). On the *ricordi* tradition, see L. Polizzotto and C. Kovesi eds., *Memorie di casa Valori* (Florence: Nerbini, 2007), the introduction sums up and critiques earlier scholarship; and Mark Jurdjevic, *Guardians of Republicanism: The Valori Family in the Florentine Renaissance* (Oxford: Oxford University Press, 2008). I am most grateful to my colleague Professor Alison Frasier for sharing the

Piety was thus part of an overall process of self-identification established through shop practice or vocation in personal service to the fragmented and vulnerable refugee family. Fontaine's text was recognizable as a well-known refugee genre, which functioned simultaneously as a reformed craftsman's narrative; providing readymade stories for family members in the mobile trades to enact theatrically in various verbal contexts and to different live audiences. It also extends the benefit of experience in business transactions and answers the question of how to play the cards refugee craftsmen were dealt in competitive contexts on the road: from workshop to church, to street corner, to guild hall, to courtroom.[31]

Four Mobile Traditions

Fontaine harnessed manual work to religiosity in four mobile religious traditions; all added intellectual respectability to a sketchy reality. The first of these, again, was his spiritual and material foundation as a preacher-artisan following the primitive-church example of the Apostle Paul: Pharisee, tentmaker, and evangelist among the hostile Corinthians (Acts 18:1–4). Modeling himself after Paul was "imitation," a word he used to describe import substitution. "It was a very great pleasure for me to imitate St. Paul," he wrote on arriving in Cork, where he manufactured textiles while preaching to French refugees; "preaching the Gospel and at the same time earning my living by the labor of my hands."[32] Palissy learned Paul's practice through the Geneva-trained itinerant preacher and colporteur Philibert Hamelin, who preached on the road in Saintonge while working alongside the artisans he evangelized, and where he was executed by the *Parlement* of Bordeaux.

Paul was similarly essential to the transatlantic Quaker cosmos. Traveling preachers for the Friends refused support, accepting work as

latter two citations as well as her knowledge of the *ricordi* tradition and its possible relation to Huguenot narrative.

[31] For a pioneering analysis of Huguenot escape accounts as genre, see Carolyn Lougee Chappell, "'The Pains I took to Save My / His Family': Escape Accounts by a Huguenot Mother and Daughter after the Revocation of the Edict of Nantes," *French Historical Studies* 22/1 (Winter 1999): 1–64.

[32] Jacques Fontaine, *A Tale of the Huguenots, or Memoirs of a French Refugee Family: Translated and Compiled from the Original Manuscripts of James [Jacques] Fontaine, by one of his Descendants*, trans. Ann Maury (New York: J. S. Taylor, 1838), and Jacques Fontaine, *Memoirs of a Huguenot Family: Translated and Complied from the Original Autobiography of the Rev. James [Jacques] Fontaine, and other Family Manuscripts; Comprising an Original Journal of Travels in Virginia, New-York, etc., in 1715 and 1716*, trans. Ann Maury (New York: George P. Putnam, 1853). The quotation is from the 1853 edition, p. 170. I will cite the 1853 edition hereafter.

tradesmen. Lay journeymen also found Quakers appealing. Unlike John Chevallier, who, as we have seen, was appointed a master in the guild in 1716, on June 2, 1684, "Hugh Marnue, a French Quaker, who served but one year [as an apprentice] in Germany," was warned by London's Weavers' Company Court "to desist" work, "or be indicted."[33] Heterodox Calvinists and Quakers intermarried in early New York, where they formed prosperous artisanal networks. Paul's first *Epistle to the Corinthians* stressed the inward holy spirit over the babel of human speech and was central to Calvinist exegesis and Quaker quietism. Palissy's "art of the earth" compares productively with the English leveler Gerrard Winstanley (1609–1676), also fascinated by manifestations of spirit in earthly matter, and the Germanic pietist Jacob Boehme (1575–1624). Boehme extolled early Luther as the second savior of humankind. Twelve years earlier, he envisioned the "sudden appearance of a pewter vase," wherein the divine light danced politely like "brilliant and jovial" signatures.[34]

Boehme's translations and those of the Behemists were preached to simple folk everywhere.[35] Paracelsus discouraged university scholasticism and traveled the world. God's hidden knowledge was meant to be discovered in everyday materials by the side of the road. How much Fontaine absorbed is unclear, but Palissy, the heterodox Calvinist who "taught myself alchemy," is foundational to this material-holiness tradition.

The second mobile religious tradition drawn on by Fontaine was the artisanal and material adaptation of the Christian power of weakness: the small and weak prevail over strong competitors through either agile or incremental mobility, ingeniousness, and the manifestation through spiritual labor of the light of grace in everyday materials.[36] This framework supports the potential of humble materials to supersede noble ones. It is defined by refugees who bide their time working industriously yet imperceptibly in the interstices made available by dominant hosts. Fontaine

[33] William Chapman Waller ed., "Extracts From the Court Books of the Weavers' Company of London, 1610–1730," 33: 51.

[34] Kamil, *Fortress of the Soul*, 325–26; and Kamil, "The Refiner's Fire's Atlantic," 223–27; on Paul and Quaker theology, see Richard Bauman, *Let Your Words Be Few: Symbolism of Speaking and Silence Among Seventeenth-Century Quakers* (Prospect Heights, IL: Waveland Press, 1983), 1–2.

[35] On Boehme, Paracelsus, and the French Prophets in England, see Hillel Schwartz, *The French Prophets: The History of a Millenarian Group in Eighteenth-Century England* (Berkeley: University of California Press, 1980), 8, 46–8, 155–246; on Boehme, behemism, and Quakers, see Bauman, *Let Your Words Be Few*, 3–4, 32.

[36] Elegantly elucidated for the Middle Ages in Carolyn Walker Bynum, *Fragmentation and Redemption: Essays on Gender and the Human Body in Medieval Religion* (New York: Zone Books, 1991).

extends sixteenth-century regional tactics into the age of manufacture through family ties that combine the old *noblesse d'épée* or fortress culture of urban La Rochelle with the dissimulating artisanal culture of rural Saintonge.[37] Fontaine's patriarchal identity is an ambiguous hybrid, incorporating aggressiveness, violence, and pride in his noble and martial history with dissimulation. Centered on the noble artisan, his history narrates this synthesis.

The third of these religious traditions was the continuity of alchemical rhetoric and practice in the Fontaine history. This reflects enduring rhetorical conventions from the book of secret's tradition, combined with regional connections between France and England through the enduring influence of Bernard Palissy. These continuities were ramified by the new centrality of fire machines. Palissy pioneered fire manufactures with ceramic glazes by combining alchemical strategies of material substitution with reformed religious experience.[38]

Fourth, was the noble artisan with uncertain documentation. Fontaine changed the trajectory of his family history to encompass a new category of nobility forged by religious violence and martyrdom. Fontaine built security from "inventive genius" with materials naturalized by claims of decent from La Rochelle's "ancient" Huguenot nobility, impoverished by the Civil Wars. These claims were proved by "lost" documents signed "De la Fontaine" by his grandfather and father following the noble formula. Fontaine's history assured his children that "you might find the original name on record in Rochelle" and on a deed to "my sister Gachot['s]" confiscated house in the city. Then there were six silver spoons Jacques inherited from his father and carried to exile, "one of them a very handsome silver gilt, with the initials I. D. L. F. engraved upon it." Unfortunately, the spoon engraved "D.L." was sold in England out of desperation.[39]

Here was evidence of greater nobility than Jacques's tenuous genealogies, forged by violence and recorded in martyrologies. "I have insinuated that our family was of noble origin, and it is true," he wrote, redefining Huguenot nobility by a different kind of blood: "But I would not have you glory in that knowledge, but rather in the much greater and more glorious nobility which I am going to lay before you – the suffering and martyrdom for the cause of true religion of those from whom we are descended ... Oh, my children ... never forget that the blood of martyrs flows in our veins! And may God ... grant that the remembrance of it may enliven our faith, so that we may prove not unworthy scions from so noble a stock ...

[37] Kamil, *Fortress of the Soul*, 52–124. [38] Ibid., 49–51.
[39] Maury, Memoirs, 15–16, 124.

[for] ... his providential care guard[s] the children of those whose blood has been shed in his service."[40] Hence, the history itself, which "lay before you" the experience of ancestors' ordeals by sacred violence was authentic proof of nobility that superseded mere repetitive documentation of lineage.

Artisanry was the bridge between past and present in Fontaine's noble history. After escaping the religious wars in Le Mans to the safety of La Rochelle in 1563, Jacques's young orphaned grandfather and great uncle, like the refugees of 1685, were "deprived of parents and property, and from ease and affluence plunged into poverty." Having nothing left to signify nobility but his "prepossessing exterior ... evident marks of belonging to a good family," Jacques grandfather was taken in by a pious shoemaker and taught the trade "without binding him to it as an apprentice." He is thus represented as having inaugurated the nebulous family tradition of independent skills harnessed to the subtext of a lost but unforgotten noble history. After all, the chaotic violence and deracination of the Refuge left "no time for pride of birth or titles of nobility," only being "thankful to God for putting it in his power to earn his daily bread by honest labor."[41]

This was a new kind of artisan, with clear links to old regional histories and practices. Artisanal skill for this new nobility was acquired independently in the permeable refuge and was unbound by guild definitions of mastery which forbid crossover into protected trades. Like kings, boundaries were ignored by natural philosophers and alchemists whose noble artisanry, Fontaine claimed, was universal and driven by invisible impulses to release spirit from matter.

Fontaine's conception of religious martyrdom transmuting lost nobility in France into noble artisanry in the diaspora is entwined with his reactivation of Palissy's violent regional paradigm in peaceful Taunton. What higher status might an alchemist hope to achieve than that of noble artisan? "I shall be the monarch of physicians [*monarcha medicorum*]," Paracelsus proclaimed, "and mine will be the monarchy." Like most Paracelsians, when Palissy singled Paracelsus out in the *Discours*, he recognized him as "a king among physicians." In so doing, as a follower of Paracelsus, Palissy also assumed the throne; as, in turn, did Fontaine, a follower of Palissy. Thus, Fontaine's noble artisan was forged in blood and fire.[42]

40 Fontaine, *Memoir*, 16, 21. 41 Ibid., 21–22.

42 Bernard Palissy, *The Admirable Discourses of Bernard Palissy*, trans. Aurele La Rocque (Urbana: University of Illinois Press, 1957), 113–14; *Paracelsus: Selected Writings*, ed. Jolande Jacobi, trans. Norbert Guterman, Bollingen, ser. 28 (New York: Pantheon Books, 1958). lv, 5.

The Noble Artisan and Calamanco

To place the grandiose alchemical subject of himself as inventive genius at the center of the history, Fontaine patterned this representation after the rhetoric of the noble artisan as manual philosopher, extending beyond the court, laboratory, and workshop into the expanding world of refugee manufacturers. He situated himself above ordinary categories of artisans, an essential attribute of the alchemist. The fire machine was made available as coded evidence to further document the extraordinary spiritual, material, and heredity gifts of the Fontaine family artisanal network.

Fontaine performed the fire-machine story at every stop as *bona fides* of skillful independence, to allay fears that he needed charity. Fontaine insists on his terror of charity and debt. He celebrated his remarkable ability to retire loans rapidly and move beyond credit to finance his own shop. Debt was a capital offence in seventeenth-century France. The first legal rights for bankrupts passed by the English Parliament in 1706 and 1707 made fundamental changes in the law but hanging remained an option if bankrupts "wilfully" stole from creditors.[43] So, Fontaine documented transparency in the acquisition of credit and repayment of debt. Poverty afflicted refugee communities throughout Britain. The glut of migrating French refugee craftsmen on the labor market in the 1680s, forced stranger churches in London to redirect exiles elsewhere at the earliest opportunity. The success or failure of the noble artisan's fire-machine narrative to convince creditors and coreligionists (often one in the same) that the family's suffering would soon turn to financial independence had life or death consequences.

The alchemical narrative provided a charismatic way to separate philosophical artisans from commonplace *ouvriers* wandering homeless in the street. Vulgar manual workers had no access to the material-holiness synthesis of microcosm and macrocosm that connected the pious labor of a chosen few Calvinists elected to the artisan-God in *Genesis* (1:1–31).[44] Yet despite his conventional aversion to revealing sources, Fontaine's history suggests a specific narrative. Fontaine clearly and self-consciously harnessed himself to the natural philosophical tradition of his influential regional predecessor: Bernard Palissy, the alchemist, potter, lay-minister, and historian of Saintes.

[43] Ann M. Carlos, "Conformity and Certificate of Discharge: Bankruptcy in Eighteenth-Century England," Paper delivered at the 2010 Economic History Association Meetings, Evanston, Illinois, 2–3; the laws were registered as 4 & 5 Anne 1 c 4 (1706) and 6 Anne 1 c 22 (1707).

[44] Charles Webster, *From Paracelsus to Newton: Magic and the Making of Modern Science* (Cambridge: Cambridge University Press, 1982), 22–23.

Palissy's books, material experimentation, and "rustique *figulines,*" were as well known in England as Saintonge. Palissy's claim to "inventive genius" derived from "ingenious" manipulation of alchemical fire to "invent" translucent ceramic glazes. From these successes, he secured royal protection during the violent Civil War years. He recorded the physical and spiritual dangers of the alchemical process in *Recepte Veritable* (La Rochelle, 1564) and particularly in "On the Art of the Earth, its Usefulness, On Enamels and Fire," from *Discours admirables* (Paris, 1580).

Fontaine's chapter on calamanco deployed strikingly similar narrative conventions, particularly Palissy's coded alchemical rhetoric. Fontaine revives venerable Palissien plot variations, including the invention and mastery of fire-producing technological devices to achieve a "translucent" glaze that migrates to the surface of calamanco. Like Palissy's enamels, glaze is the attribute that gave calamanco its polish and value.[45] Glaze also obscured the inherent cheapness of earthenware and wool. Calamanco's market price lay in surface gloss rather than material value. However, superficiality was also harnessed to alchemical counterfeits made by shadowy foreigners.[46]

Understanding his family's regional history to be a generational extension to the potter's, it is certain that Fontaine read Palissy's famous books on Huguenot artisans, Saintonge's beginnings in the Reformation, and its earliest Civil War religious history. Fontaine coveted his technical library as his primary source of artisanal knowledge. He was keenly aware of Palissy's rustic pottery and experimental glazes. Examples were available in La Rochelle and Saintonge and coveted by collectors in eighteenth-century Britain. Anyone with Fontaine's education, religious background, and artisanal aspirations venerated the potter from Saintes. His name was synonymous with Reformed and refined materials. Fontaine also observed consumer interest in "Palissy dishes," crude copies made by seventeenth-century English and French refugee potters. Consumers of calamanco were drawn to Palissy dishes for similar reasons. If Palissy's alchemical paradigms reinvented Reformed artisanry in Civil-War Saintonge, then it is unsurprising that a native son obsessed with continuity implemented a post-Revocation mechanized variant in the refuge.

What, exactly, is calamanco (Fig 4.1)? The *OED* finds multiple foreign origins for the word confirming sixteenth-century importation. "Glossy on the surface and woven with . . . satin twill and chequered in the warp,"

45 For Palissy's "On the Art of the Earth," see Kamil, *Fortress of the Soul*, 316–45.

46 Ibid., 544–61. "Country Party" Tories who opposed Whig views on manufacturing and immigration or native artisans displaced by foreigners played the counterfeit card with increasing frequency in the 1680s.

calamanco was woven satin side up, "so that the checks are seen on one side only." Like earthenware, calamanco had a glazed show-surface and a durable coarse underside. Malachy Postlethwayt's translation of Jacques Savary des Bruslons's *Dictionnaire universel de commerce* (Geneva, 1723–1765) describes calamanco as . . . worsted "stuff . . . [with] a fine gloss upon it. There are calimancoes of all colours, and diversely wrought; some are quite plain; others have broad stripes, adorned with flowers; and others watered [having a wavy shimmer, like silk]."[47] Because of this silk-like luster, calamanco was sold as the poor-man's silk. Alchemical artisans specialized in making dull natural materials sparkle politely. Palissy called this effect *étincelles*, analogous to the "sparkling signatures" that appeared in a pewter pitcher's bottom in Boehme's youthful alchemical vision. Calamanco was thus a perfect import substitute.

The need for faux-silk woolens was recognized by the Weavers' Company as early as 1669, when Charles II received petitions by London's French and Dutch Churches to allow more refugee silk weavers to immigrate, over the strong objections of "the ancient woolmanufacturers of this Kingdom."[48] By the eighteenth century, calamanco garments cost half the price of similar ones in silk, but they were commonly sold side by side. On April 20, 1757, Robert Brasil was sentenced to death at London's Old Bailey for shoplifting. Brasil stole five gowns from the shop of Archibald Marr, clambering on one knee onto a countertop to take the garments down from a seven-foot-high shelf, before running to the pawn shop. A calamanco gown from Brasil's takings was valued at 5 shillings (a skilled craftsman's daily wage) and a silk gown at 10 shillings, but both were displayed and stolen together.[49]

Luster made silk and calamanco polite but calamanco's gloss manufactured on dull wool was not intrinsic. That was acceptable at half price. Politeness was thus a key word in early English manufacturing discourse by the second half of the seventeenth century. Philological inquiry merged early with "polite" material culture and was originally reserved for things made distinctive by shining surfaces. The word came into common usage in England by the fifteenth century when it "was close in meaning to 'polished' and often applied, literally, to physical

[47] Malachy Postlethwayt, *The Universal Dictionary of Trade and Commerce Translated, form the French of the Celebrated Monsieur Savary . . . with Large Additions*, 2 vols (London, 1751–1755), quoted in Montgomery, *Textiles in America*, 185.

[48] "Extracts From the Court Books of the Weavers' Company of London, 1610–1730," 33: 101–02.

[49] *The Proceedings of the Old Bailey*, Robert Brasil. Theft: shoplifting. April 20, 1757. Reference Number t17570420-4. www.oldbaileyonline.org/browse.jsp?id=t17570420-4-off17&div=t17570420-4#highlight. I am grateful to Professor Julie Hardwick for bringing this reference to my attention.

objects."[50] "Polite" thus dwelled in materiality and artificial optical effects, which endured powerfully as a preoccupation in overlapping civil, domestic, and ecclesiastical contexts. Polish created by spiritual artificers in the textile trades was virtuous and hence perfectly polite, preached John Jeffery in his 1693 sermon to Norwich weavers. "For as both our Faculties and our Arts are from God," he said, "so they ought to be used for him: and Vertue is the perfection of Politeness."[51] Virtuous textiles such as calamanco manufactured in imitation of silk were marketed specifically with reference to polish. In Ephraim Chamber's *Cyclopaedia* (London, 1741), for example, satin was described as "a kind of silken stuff, very smooth, and shining, the warp whereof is very fine, and stands out . . . on which depends that gloss, and beauty, which is its price."[52]

The semantic field accompanying "politeness" underwent extensive elaboration.[53] Like satin or calamanco among textiles, fashionable objects in England were made with smooth components to take a high polish in every media. The word was derived in part from the French *poli*, which meant both polish and polite (*polir*, was "to polish"), and was often associated with the materiality of cleanliness. "The literal meaning of *polir*," writes Peter France, "suggests an aesthetic view of the subject." In Palissy, any ostensibly crude natural material had polite *potential*, if a godly artisan and regenerative process intervened to advance its growth prematurely towards millennial perfection. Fire was the alchemical solution, but there were others. "One starts with a rough, untreated material, and by rubbing and similar processes one transforms it into something smooth and agreeable to the touch and sight. A common dictionary example is that of marble ... Polish is thus opposed to roughness." Fashion cultures created a demand for production of both prestige and commonplace items such as calamanco among the expanding numbers of adherents of the material culture of refinement in the Atlantic and Mediterranean worlds during the later Middle Ages and early modern times.[54]

[50] Lawrence Klein, "The Third Earl of Shaftesbury and the Progress of Politeness," *Eighteenth-Century Studies* 18/2 (December 1984): 186.

[51] John Jeffery, *The Duty and Encouragement of Religious Artificers*, 2.

[52] Quoted in Montgomery, *Textiles in America*, 339–40.

[53] The *OED*'s earliest listing under "polish" comes from Sir Isaac Newton's *Optics* (1704), regarding the clarity and "polish" of a prism.

[54] On cleanliness, see Douglas Biow, *The Culture of Cleanliness in Renaissance Italy* (Ithaca, NY: Cornell University Press, 2006); Norbert Elias, *The Civilizing Process,* op. cit., 57, 64–65, 156–57; Peter France, *Politeness and its Discontents: Problems in French Classical Culture* (Cambridge: Cambridge University Press, 1992), 55; for an analysis of prestige materials associated with polish, cleanliness, civility and comportment, beginning in the late fourteenth century, see Richard A. Goldthwaite, "The Economic and Social World

Calamanco was produced in Britain and America through the early nineteenth century and had a substantial export market to the colonies. It was used in everything from furniture upholstery to the lining of women's skirts. While popular in Europe and the Atlantic world for its polite and attractive polish, the glossy side was often stigmatized as exceedingly fragile, a common rhetoric leveled against all import substitutes. Yet the American experience with colorful calamanco shoes made for middling-market women in England and America from 1730–1780, was just the opposite. Calamanco shoes proved to be more durable, warmer, and egalitarian than expensive silk shoes. In the 1750s, England's shift to Arkwright water-frame and spindle-mule technology enabled factories to meet expanding transatlantic demand while lowering labor costs. So American shoemakers throughout the colonies bought their calamanco cheaply from Huguenot weavers in Norwich. This changed in the pre-Revolutionary period of the 1760s and 1770s, when American artisans dramatically increased production of locally made calamanco to meet consumer-demand to restrict British imports. Thus, American-made calamanco shoes became the everyday footwear of patriotic women. The materiality of politeness was fashioned into a nonviolent response to the imposition of British political economy on the eve of revolution.[55]

The Trial of a Noble Artisan

The story of the fire machine begins when Fontaine encountered two impoverished refugees who "applied to me for assistance." After finding a charity for the funds "which I could not furnish myself," Fontaine admonished the men to follow his family's tradition: become self-reliant artisans and "learn a trade at once, [so] you will never be obliged to ask for charity again but will become independent. There are in Bristol French manufacturers of light stuffs [woolens], to whom I would recommend you to bind [apprentice] yourselves."[56]

of Italian Renaissance Majolica," *Renaissance Quarterly* 17/1 (Spring 1989): 1–32; and France, "Polish, Police, Polis," in *Politeness and its Discontents*, 53–73.

55 Kimberly Alexander, "The Woolen Shoes that Made Revolutionary-Era Women Feel Patriotic: Calamanco Footwear was Sturdy, Egalitarian, and Made in the U.S.A.," *Zócalo Public Square* (accessed November 7, 2019) www.zocalopublicsquare.org/2019/11/07/the-woolen-shoes-that-made-revolutionary-era-women-feel-patriotic/ideas/essay/?fbclid=IwAR2dGMYdBrNGT0tJDeA9bvQfCLSkRkKANxHuKquJPs-hp1AInrC0sghhmGc. I am grateful to Julie Hardwick for this reference; J. R. Harris, *Industrial Espionage and Technology Transfer*, 361–422; for "strategies of consumer resistance" and the American revolution, see Timothy H. Breen, *The Marketplace of Revolution: How Consumer Politics Shaped American Independence* (Oxford: Oxford University Press, 2004), 195–234.

56 Maury, *Memoirs*, 143–44.

The men followed his advice and after Fontaine "established myself at Taunton, they called on me for the express purpose of returning their thanks." Also, they offered the new skills they learned from Bristol Huguenots on a profit-sharing basis. Fontaine found their terms of employment irresistible and convinced a local English investor to lend twenty pounds sterling for "worsted, yarn and dyes" to get started. The workers were responsible for their own tools. "Behold me now," the status-conscious émigré boasted, "not only a ... shopkeeper, but a manufacturer also." Fontaine had risen to the top 8 percent of all refugees in the Atlantic textile trades.[57]

The skillful workmen were Fontaine's source of specific manual knowledge drawn from Bristol's urban Huguenot network. "At the end of three months," Fontaine claimed with an adept's conventional immodesty, "I knew much more than the workmen did." Gifted with his unique inventive genius, student soon became teacher: "I invented new patterns for the stuffs, which I showed them how to execute." Fontaine paid off his investor quickly, proving a good credit risk. This enabled him to put the workmen on low fixed wages, pocket all the profits, and quadruple his initial investment by pouring his remaining capital back into the growing manufactory. The once penniless Huguenot no longer operated exclusively on credit. Injecting personal capital allowed flexibility, so Fontaine seized attractive price opportunities on the Continent. He purchased shop goods at reduced prices from refugees in Holland to undercut local competitors in Taunton. Profits allowed him to attract new customers away from local competitors by selling for "light gains." "Everything now seemed to prosper with me," and Fontaine presided over "the handsomest shop in Taunton." He "manufactured stuffs in the upper part of the house," which his wife, "sold, at a profit, in the lower part."[58]

"Other shopkeepers were very angry" at the success of this cosmopolitan strategy. Charges were brought before Taunton's Mayor and Alderman's Court. At trial, Fontaine denigrated the mayor and aldermen as mere woolen workers, poorly educated and beneath him in intellectual and spiritual status. Fontaine represented himself as a philosophical and theological subject; a rare self-made artisan-manufacturer with Neoplatonic knowledge of intellectual and spiritual unities. An adept who excavated profound connections to the artisan-God beneath the dross of postlapsarian matter. Yet this knowledge was at the crux of deepening problems with neighbors. Fontaine felt entitled to undercut

57 Ibid., 144; Hornung, "Immigration and the Diffusion of Technology: The Huguenot Diaspora in Prussia," 117.

58 Ibid., 144–46.

the value of Taunton's free tradesmen by crossing boundaries protected by law and custom, as did his "noble" grandfather when he first arrived as a refugee in La Rochelle. Fontaine was brought before the court to hear the damaging charge that he "was a sharper, a Jack-of-all-trades."[59]

"One word would describe him as well as a thousand," Fontaine accusers complained; "he was a French dog, taking ... bread out of the mouths of the English." Migrant labor was valuable and proven itinerant masters had been courted, accommodated, feted, and gifted by local guilds for hundreds of years. Yet strict rules were put in place against sharpers without credentials to avoid collisions with natives. If strangers abided by the rules there were few problems, but the charge against Fontaine and the inability of authorities to prevent transgressions were not atypical.[60] In sixteenth-century London, the influx of stranger weavers and "the settling down of Weavers as the new, small masters of the domestic system," forced the Weavers' Company to "[cease] in any vital sense to control the London trade." Simultaneously, "the prosperity of the Company increased," due to the strangers' skill and innovation.[61]

Fontaine's trial story instructed family members to exploit loopholes and circumvent guild laws. His narrative centers on artful strategies of non-compliance with local restrictions on the noble artisan's freedom anywhere in the world. The trial turned on the mayor's question: "Have you served an apprenticeship to all these trades?" "This question was quite to the purpose," Fontaine admitted, "for by law no man can carry on a trade to which he has not served an apprenticeship." Fontaine then defined his place in the new independent order of noble refugee artisans. For a select few pious "men of letters," the "prepossessing exterior" of learned cosmopolitanism, physical beauty, and polite comportment combined to create the foundations for a limited meritocracy of adepts. Such artisans demolished legal or social barriers and transcended apprenticeship protections in every locality of the old world:

Gentlemen, in France a man is esteemed according to his qualifications; and men of letters and study are especially honored by everybody, if they conduct themselves with propriety even though they should not be worth a penny. All the nobility of the land, the lords, the marquises, and dukes take pleasure in the society of such persons. In fact, there, a man is thought fit for any honorable employment, if he be but learned; therefore, my father, who was a worthy minister

[59] Ibid., 146–49.

[60] Josef Ehmer, "Perceptions of Mobile Labour and Migratory Practices in Early Modern Europe," in *The Idea of Work in Europe from Antiquity to Modern Times*, ed. Joseph Ehmer and Catharina Lis (Aldershot, UK: Ashgate, 2009), 307–20.

[61] Frances Consitt, *The London Weavers' Company, Volume I: From the Twelfth Century to the Close of the Sixteenth Century* (Oxford, UK: Clarendon Press, 1933), 114.

of the Gospel, brought up four boys, of whom I was the youngest, in good manners and the liberal arts, hoping that wherever fortune might transport us, our education would serve instead of riches, and gain us honor among persons of honor. All the apprenticeship I have ever served, from the age of four years, has been to turn over the leaves of a book. I took the degree of Master of Arts at the age of twenty-two, and then devoted myself to the study of the Holy Scriptures. Hitherto, I had been thought worthy of the best company wherever I had been; but when I came to this town, I found that science without riches ... So much so, that if a poor ignorant wool-comber, or a hawker, amassed money, he was honored by all, and looked up to as the first in the place. I have, therefore ... renounced all speculative science; I have become a wool comber, a dealer in pins and laces, hoping that I may one day attain wealth, and be also one of the first men in the town.[62]

Fontaine's condescending definition of "nobility of letters" was accurate. Individual genius was a noble quality in *ancien régime* France. "Among the 'men of talent' there was a 'nobility of letters,' a sort of social nobility of the mind ... expected to receive letters of ennoblement from the king." Every person of genius did not meet these high expectations. One group that received ennoblement consistently "were technicians whose inventions were recognized as useful," and had "outstanding talent to which the country [was] indebted." This natural talent grew from lifelong devotion "to the study of mechanics." Fontaine's declaration that he "renounced all speculative science" was rhetoric associated with the stigmatized nobility of letters. Laboratory research was rarely ennobled. Inventions with short-term practical applications were rewarded more frequently than long-term scientific achievements.[63]

Fontaine was ambivalent about the trial's outcome, despite his masterful courtroom performance. Only a similarly well-educated court recorder spoke in his defense. Charles II gave Huguenots the right of refuge in England, his advocate reminded the court, so "they are fully entitled to every privilege that we enjoy." The defendant's exceptional social status as a noble artisan was key to the scribe's argument:

Although Mr. Fontaine was brought up to nothing but study, yet in the desire he has to live independently, without being burdensome to anyone, he humbles himself so far as to become a mechanic, a thing very rarely seen among the learned men ... Are you, his accusers, disposed to raise a fund, and settle an annuity upon him and his family for life? Strangers are as much entitled to justice at our hands, as our neighbors are ... if you secure him a moderate income, he will leave mechanical occupations, and gladly return to intellectual labor.[64]

62 Maury, Memoirs, 149–50.
63 Roland E. Mousnier, *The Institutions of France under the Absolute Monarchy, 1598–1789* (Chicago, IL: University of Chicago Press, 1979), 226–28.
64 Maury, Memoirs, 150–51.

Christian humility harnessed spiritual gravitas onto Fontaine's evolving persona. Yet no one came forward and Fontaine's case was dismissed. To which the court recorder proclaimed, in recognition of Fontaine's Pauline mission and sense of Calvinist election, "God bless you and your labor!" But victory was costly. The Mayor's faction "hated me all the more." Fontaine continued his noble and pious labor, but "they exaggerated my profits very much . . . and I was taxed to the utmost."[65]

The best option for a "Jack-of-all-trades" was reinvention. He kept a low profile and honored his debt by "dispos[ing] of my shop, and stock and trade." Left with the fundamentals of a noble artisan's enterprise – his books, ingenuity, and noble comportment: "I was [also] the sole owner of the tools and utensils required in manufacturing the stuffs, [and] I was the proprietor of good, comfortable household furniture." Polite furniture was an indispensable prop for commerce. "And [he] had fourteen pounds in cash." Fontaine opened his first Latin school and taught French, but this provided insufficient income. So, he picked up his tools, reread Palissy, and invoked the conventions of the inventive genius.[66]

The Fire Machine

"There was a sort of stuff manufactured at Norwich at that time, called Calimanco," Fontaine remembered, "which was very substantial, and also fashionable, and I determined upon making the attempt to imitate it." Fontaine admitted buoyantly, "I had never, you know, served any apprenticeship." But of course, this was a positive, for two reasons: First, without training in a specific trade, the refugee labored as a universal artisan outside guild restrictions, for "it was all the same to me what I undertook to make." Second, "I must call upon the ingenuity of my own brain to aid me." This invokes the Reformation critique of received wisdom in Latin Church and medieval scholasticism, common to Palissien natural philosophy and Calvinism. Reformed artisans added value to the light of grace with manual experience:

> I therefore thought it would be better, when I began again, to try something new instead of going on in the old beaten track. The stuff called serge, which we had made before, was now out of fashion, and those who manufactured it barely earned salt to their porridge; but then they had served an apprenticeship to it, and as they worked together mechanically, and not with the understanding, they were really incapable of putting their hands to anything else. I was possessed of a large share of that sort of perseverance which some people call obstinacy, and

[65] Ibid., 151–52; on the evidence Fontaine perceived of his Calvinist election, see Bernard Cottret, "Postface: Jacques Fontaine ou la Providence dans le Texte," 231–34.
[66] Ibid., 153–58.

without which I certainly could not have overcome the almost insurmountable difficulty, which met me at the outset . . . I had not long been at work before the profitable nature of my new trade became known, and the old-fashioned manufacturers of serge were envious of it. Their astonishment at my inventive genius was very great; they almost looked upon it as sorcery.[67]

The "insurmountable difficulty" of physical labor to bring the embryonic artisanal work to fruition and the final product "almost looked upon as sorcery" by the uninitiated was fundamental to the coded language of alchemical narrative. This rhetoric was available to unlearned readers from the Renaissance, with important variations grafted on during the Reformation, including Palissy's Huguenot narratives from Saintonge on his experimental glazes in the Paracelsian tradition. Other venerable tropes central to Palissy's essay on glazes were activated pointedly here, as physical "distress," reproductive, and obstetric themes conflated male with female labor. For example, one weaver applied for work just as Fontaine's "experimental attempts" began. "He was in extreme distress, absolutely penniless, and his wife in hourly expectation of confinement:

He entreated me to give him some employment, and that he would spare no pains to give me satisfaction . . . his urgent need would be a spur to his assiduity in laboring for one who should help him at this pinch. I took him and his wife into my house, I fed the two, and soon three of them. I fitted up a loom for him, to try what he could do; and he kept his word, for he worked day and night . . . if he was successful, he would certainly be able to earn a comfortable subsistence.

In the end, not only did the weaver's wife give birth, but "my wife had not been less fruitful than my brain." Fontaine's family grew to six children by conjoined male and female labor.[68]

Fontaine's initial collaborations with the industrious weaver to imitate calamanco were "fruitless attempts," despite his "fruitful . . . brain," with only "small proceeds resulting from the sale of the first piece." The second piece, several yards long, was more promising, however; "taken out of the frame it appeared really handsome and was as strong and substantial as the Norwich Calimanco." Unfortunately, after sending it out for treading and tentering at the local fuller, he lost control of the material: "it looked no better than a coarse coverlet, for it had great strong hairs sticking out in all directions."[69] At this critical juncture between success and failure, fire was introduced as the transformative element. Fontaine's inventive genius converged with the narrative conventions of

[67] Ibid., 158, 162. [68] Ibid., 158–59, 167.

[69] Ibid., 160; fulling consisted of pounding, stamping, scouring, soaking, and stretching newly made wool fabric on hooks using a tenter frame.

the alchemist, his fire machine a crucible for wool, the most "ancient" and politicized of all British homegrown materials.[70]

While labor pain of "almost insurmountable difficulty" beset his potential triumph, exorbitant rhetorical expressions of obstetric pain were a paradigmatic requirement of the genre. Fontaine recalls a hatter's shop from his Saintonge childhood, harnessing risk of pain and humiliation to working with fire:

> I recollected that when I was at school I had often gone to warm myself in the hatter's shop opposite to the school, and I used to watch the process of burning off the long hairs from the hats with a wisp of straw, so I thought that a similar plan might be adopted for remedying the defect in my Calimanco.

Using fire to remedy a "defect" signified purification of corrupted material, bringing the calamanco to perfection. Fontaine's universal artisan moved easily between trades and countries. So too, Palissy began his career as a stained-glass painter in Agen, before becoming a mapmaker for the *gabelle* in the Saintonge salt marshes where he converted to Calvinism and learned informally to make ceramics from local potters. But difficulties remained; to perfect the stuff, hand craftsmanship must first relinquish its age-old dominance to the "certainty" of a machine:

> A hat can easily be turned round in the hand to apply the flame to all sides, not so a long piece of stuff. A machine would be required to apply it with certainty and regularity. I was too impatient to wait for the production of a machine and determined to singe this first piece as well as I could by hand.[71]

Repetition is privileged as the aspiration of inventive genius while alchemical frameworks link the experimental manufacturer's early eighteenth-century move from the workmanship of risk to the mechanized efficiency of the workmanship of certainty.[72]

Impatience precipitated failure to repeat the process with certainty. An unsalable product resulted. Failure was marked by dishonor, leveled by the women of childbearing age in Fontaine's workshop (Fig 4.2). "I had to call in the aid of my wife and her sister Jane Boursiquot," Fontaine admitted, "who laughed so much at my dilemma that I almost felt discouraged." Just as Palissy's hermaphrodite *Conjunctio sive coitus* conjoined macrocosm and microcosm in the crucible, so too triumphant alchemists internalized male and female attributes to manipulate fire and achieve metamorphosis. The alchemist transcends the stigma of vulgar handwork by learning the female-gendered virtue of patience

[70] Maury, Memoirs, 160. [71] Ibid., 160–61.

[72] On workmanship of risk and certainty, see David Pye, *The Nature and Art of Workmanship* (London and New York: Studio Vista / Van Nostrand Reinhold, 1971), 5–24, 57–66.

Fig 4.2 *Unattributed oil-painting, ca. 1760*, 30 x 21 inches, E & H Manners, London. Nicolas Sprimont (1716–1771), a Franco-Flemish porcelain manufacturer, seated in his Chelsea, London, manufactory, with porcelain made as import substitutes – mainly by workmen from Huguenot backgrounds – for French Vincennes and Sèvres ceramics. The ailing émigré is attended by wife Ann and sister-in-law, Susanna Protin, who, like Anne Elizabeth Fontaine and Jane Boursiquot, participated in both production and retailing

(*patientia*). Success came to those who patiently endured the pain of labor to refine imperfect materials, like pregnant women, laboring *au lit.*

"On the Art of the Earth" represented a similar failure of patience during Palissy's innovative glaze experiments at his hybrid glass and ceramic kiln outside Saintes. Reimagined against the background of religious persecution, the shamed potter endured sexual "persecution" from his disappointed wife ("[I] wonder now that I did not die of sadness"). Only after relinquishing carnality's transient passion (after his wife spurned him in bed) in exchange for eternal spiritual union through feminine reception of the holy spirit, did Palissy perfect earth materials. The occluded "drugs" mixed into his new recipes were reborn sparkling and translucent in the fire. Following this narrative formula, Fontaine adapted an analogous castration scenario. Frustration with his wife and *belle soeur* initiated a process of metamorphosis that opened an interior space for autonomous creation. Following the alchemical standard, Fontaine's self-representation internalized the hermaphrodite's double nature and exchanged idiosyncratic singularity of human reproductive labor for the fire machine's repetitive "certainty and regularity." Interior ambiguity conformed to exterior mastery. The evidence was material. As with Palissy's glazed earthenware, Fontaine manipulated fire to combine matter with spirit in calamanco; harvested without light from fallen earth creatures yet made distinctive in its signature sparkling glaze by art. Containing the potential for infinite repetition and profits, Fontaine discovered his philosopher's stone.[73]

And like the philosopher's stone, the fire machine's inner workings were secret, and portable, known fully only to Fontaine. Interchangeable parts disempowered his base workmen, none of whom mastered the philosophy of the work like the noble artisan. "When I planned a machine to singe off the hairs," he wrote, "I employed a different mechanic to make each part, so that not one of them knew the use of that which he was making, and when I got the various parts ready I put the machine together myself." Division of labor was nothing new to Huguenots. Since the time of the Waldensians, refugee artisans devised covert ways to disassemble sacred objects for transport or to hide in plain sight.

Fontaine thus described himself as a manufacturing entrepreneur; a noble artisan and impresario directing work of inventive genius without getting his hands dirty. One distasteful moment of physical labor was acknowledged apologetically, but the exception proved the rule: "for it was absolutely necessary to keep the secret by which we removed the

[73] Maury, Memoirs, 160–61 and Kamil, *Fortress of the Soul*, 306–07, 333–35, for an image of *Conjunctio* in the alchemical process of becoming the hermaphrodite, see 306, Fig 7.2.

course hairs, and therefore I was obliged to do that part of the work myself. My wife or my sister-in-law turned the spit while I roasted the joint."[74]

Mechanization for producers brought long-term liabilities along with short-term windfall profits. Fontaine's Taunton competitors learned the secret of his fire machine and set up their own calamanco manufactories. Predictably, "the market became overstocked with calamancos, and the price fell to two shillings, then to eighteen pence, and at last to fifteen pence per yard." This was the price cycle that fed the great maw of the consumer revolution, ramified by Fontaine's unending quest for novelty to meet the challenge of changing fashion for the middling orders on the cheap: "I contrived fresh variations in the patterns," he wrote, "which sold at three times the price of the old-fashioned kind. I spent the whole of the year 1694 in this most vexatious occupation; all the time racking my brains to invent something new and as soon as I succeeded, I had the mortification of finding myself imitated and undersold."

In the end, Fontaine's farfetched claim that he invented the fire machine was insupportable. He supplied no evidence of precedence, only heroic assertions. In the epigraph for this essay, Fontaine describes a common mechanism for "calendering" worsteds by thinning and smoothing the surface with heat and rollers, a process brought to England in the early sixteenth century.[75] The origin of this machine itself is unclear, although calendering machines are mentioned in the seventeenth century. Perhaps Fontaine learned to make one from books in his library; or he inspected, adapted, purchased, or copied a calendering machine in Norwich from fellow refugees, where this process of making calamanco was probably in use by the 1680s. To copy was to own, especially if Fontaine made substantial improvements or, in fact, "invented" the machine locally. It is not impossible that he was the first to introduce the device to Taunton, with knowledge gained from contacts in the Huguenot textile network then spread throughout Britain and the Netherlands.

[74] On the entrepreneur in later eighteenth-century France, see Valérie Nègre, *L'art et la Matière: les Artisans, les Architects et la Technique: 1770–1830* (Histoire des Techniques, 11; Recherche, 7. Paris: Classiques Garnier, 2016). There is substantial evidence of women weavers in the refugee Huguenot woolen trades, especially wives and sisters-in-law in family shops like Fontaine's, but less evidence of women master weavers. Sometimes women master weavers were widows who took over their husband's shops, as with "Rachel, widow of Peter Mercier, for m[aster]" of London, in 1729. Widowhood was not always a clear predictor of female mastery, however; as in the unqualified record of Mary Willis [or Willet], as a master weaver of London, in 1725; see "Extracts from the Court Books of the Weavers' Company of London, 1610–1730," 93, 96.

[75] For two eighteenth-century descriptions of calendaring machines and processes similar to Fontaine's, see Montgomery, *Textiles in America: 1650–1870*, 184.

Fontaine is an unreliable narrator. Rather than "inventive genius," Bernard Cottret calls him "the evil genius" of the text.[76] Yet the force of these stories was less veracity than craft, in the double sense of teaching succeeding generations experience with the art and mystery of skilled work using available materials alongside devious tactics of self-presentation and survival. Fontaine's real genius was his invention of the noble artisan. In so doing, he reimagined family and regional histories to reassemble and animate the shattered fragments of an old, undocumented genealogy in British America. There, after all, was a vast, labor-starved country with unlimited natural resources and no guild restrictions – a portable paradise for the noble artisan with universal skills to migrate from trade to trade while prospecting for available materials. Peter Fontaine (born Taunton, 1691), the fourth of Jacques and Anne Elizabeth Boursiquot Fontaine's eight children, was a first-generation refugee who migrated to Virginia. Peter was minister of Westover Parish, so he continued one of his father's trades in America. In a letter dated November 4, 1749 to his younger brother Moses in England, he reported the death in America of their youngest brother Francis. He also wrote approvingly that Francis's two sons followed the other family business: they were skilled artisans who selected their trade in diaspora as their ancestors had instructed, by adapting to available materials. "Both Frank and John are carpenters," he wrote, "as good trades as any in this wooden country."[77]

Calamanco and Cane: John Fontaine in America (1715–1719)

What is known about the Fontaine migration to Virginia? Peter was married in 1714, and Jacques Fontaine decided to send Peter, his young wife, and John (his fifth child) to lead the next generation of noble artisans across the Atlantic. "It was about this time," Jacques wrote in the history, "that we began to turn our eyes towards America, as a country that would be most suitable for the future residence of the family. John ... was without employment ... it was therefore determined ... [he would] purchase a plantation, in such situation as ... would prove ... the most advantageous." John visited New York as well as Virginia on his American sojourn, but Jacques wrote, John "came to the conclusion that Virginia presented the most desirable circumstances."[78]

[76] Bernard Cottret, "Postface: Jacques Fontaine ou La Providence dans Le Texte," 235.
[77] Maury, Memoirs, 335. [78] Ibid., 238.

Hence, the most notable transatlantic inheritor of Jacques's history was his son John Fontaine (b. Taunton, 1693 – d. Wales, 1767), who wrote a remarkable first-generation journal in the family tradition while traveling in America from 1715 to 1719. John, a British soldier in Spain during his youth, did indeed sail to Virginia at the behest of his father to buy land to relocate Fontaine family members on a plantation in the New World. Once he settled Peter's family in Virginia, he returned to England, and John continued to put the family's craft paradigms to use throughout his later career as an artisan. Trained initially by his father as a wool weaver, the younger Fontaine followed Jacques's example by circumventing guild restrictions, rising in disparate trades to master watchmaker and silk manufacturer before dying a wealthy gentleman-landowner and Whig political operator in Wales. John did not succeed in the first land transaction that Jacques tasked him to complete, although he was successful on his second try, with a different seller. John's initial failure is more interesting for our purposes here than his eventual success. This aspect of his American story was, in two critical instances, a self-conscious extension of his father's history.[79]

First, the initial focal point of John's Virginia sojourn was a prospective land deal with the influential creole historian, politician, and plantation owner, Robert Beverley (ca. 1667/8–1722), author of *The History and Present State of Virginia* (1705). John tacitly predicted the transaction's failure in his traveler's diary for reasons that resonate with the history. On November 14, 1715, John wrote, "We were very kindly received" at Beverley Park, a fortified plantation house on the Virginia near frontier. "This man lives well, but has nothing in or about his house but just what is necessary, tho' rich. He hath good beds in his house but no curtains and instead of cane chairs hath stools made of wood, and lives upon the product of his land."[80]

Fontaine's close reading of Beverley's worldview through his household furnishings considered a potential business partner as his father would; by using things at hand to quickly size up transactional possibilities. We have seen that Jacques Fontaine was proud of his furniture; it provided appropriate props for doing business. Yet what John perceived

[79] Edward Porter Alexander ed., *The Journal of John Fontaine: An Irish Huguenot Son in Spain and Virginia, 1710–1719* (Charlottesville: The University Press of Virginia, 1972); for John Fontaine's unsuccessful land transaction in the context of his role as a first-generation artisan of Huguenot heritage and family history writer, see Neil Kamil, "Mark of Disgrace or Matter of Politeness? Materiality, Trust, and Expectation in Early Eighteenth-Century Virginia," in *Crafting Artisanal Praxis: Networks of Power in the Long Eighteenth Century*, ed. Lauren Cannaday and Jennifer Ferng (Liverpool: Liverpool University Press, forthcoming in 2021).

[80] Alexander ed., *The Journal of John Fontaine*, 86.

at Beverley Park did not engender trust in his prospects. Beverley's enclaved self-containment advertised no need for outsiders. He notices immediately and records the specific absence of polite materials, textiles, and London caned chairs. Textiles were the center of life for father and son. So were caned chairs. Imported from London, which, precisely like calamanco, were upholstered with tightly woven cane, another cheap and glossy substitute for silk made by refugee Huguenot chairmakers to market throughout the Atlantic. Virginia was a particularly large consumer of caned chairs relative to the other colonies in British America. Virtually identical in cultural logic, modes of production, markets, and consumers, such as cheap and popular pseudo-silks, calamanco and cane were kindred Atlantic materials.

Caned chairs were cosmopolitan signifiers of politeness, but the stools offered in their place were particularly disturbing. Central to Jacques's history was the story of his trials in Saintes and Bordeaux for preaching to illegal reformed assemblies. The courtroom drama turned on Jacques's refusal to sit on the "stool of disgrace," offered with "great civility" to Huguenot defendants. Jacques's refusal of the offer was key to his survival. He demanded that his children follow this example by remaining upright, never lowering themselves physically at an adversary's request.

Finally, the conditions and language of the transaction are striking. "I would have agreed for this tract of land but that Mr. Beverl[e]y would not dispose of it as commonly land is disposed of, but would have the deeds made to me for nine hundred and ninety nine years, which I would not, but insisted on having it for me and my heirs for ever. So I did not buy the land of him."[81] Beverley signaled his desire to maintain ownership, assuming the role of rentier, a hated figure in southwestern France. The Fontaines wanted an independent freehold, "as commonly land is disposed of" in America, which befitted a noble family. Only documented title in fee simple to Beverley's land would do, to replace the lost homestead in Genouillé and end the family's wandering. To accept Beverley's terms displaced that intention – and continued the diaspora – for a millennium. Hence, the striking millennial language of John's refusal, which approximated a favorite eschatological construction that restated Jacques's quest for a secure place where "his children and grandchildren stayed together until the end of the world." Absent that, like his father before him, he moved on.

Ultimately, John Fontaine found and purchased a plantation in King William County, Virginia, the original Fontaine lineage land in America. Land records have been destroyed so the seller is uncertain, as are

[81] Ibid., 87.

particulars of the transaction. At the same time, John found Peter a suitable parish at Weyanoke in Charles City County. Thus, in 1715, Peter and his wife embarked for Virginia where John awaited them. Westover Parish came into being in 1720, when Peter was called to the pulpit and where he stayed most of his life. John had left the colony by that time. By 1719, "Fontaine had finished his work in Virginia as advance man for the family." By 1721, the migration of first and second generation Fontaines to their new Virginia lands was well underway, as three more brothers and their families arrived to take up residence.[82] In Reformed Virginia, two of Jacques's sons returned openly to the pulpit their father relinquished as his primary occupation when he became a weaver after the Revocation. The other two went into commerce. Over the generations, however, long after Frank and John, Peter's carpenter-nephews, had come and gone, many American Fontaines repeated the cycle, becoming highly skilled artisans, engineers, and inventors, who read closely Jacques Fontaine's history of calamanco as the foundational family narrative, were challenged by it, and self-consciously added their names to the genealogy of inventive genius as living proof that noble artisanry was in the blood.[83]

[82] Ibid., 19–21. Unlike John, none of these brothers was known to be an artisan. Two (one of whom was a brother-in-law from the Maury family) engaged in transatlantic commerce as well as settling on part of the plantation, the third, like Peter, was a minister, and also professor of Hebrew at William and Mary for two decades.

[83] The most well-known of these family artisans and "manual philosophers" of the later generations who understood Jacques Fontaine's history of calamanco to be the foundational family narrative, was Matthew Fontaine Maury (1806–1873) of Spotsylvania, Virginia. Maury was first superintendent of the U.S. Naval Observatory and Hydrographical Office, where he charted the winds and currents of the sea and famously made the deep-sea soundings that led to the discovery of the Atlantic's "telegraphic plateau," essential to laying the Atlantic cable. Maury submitted his resignation as superintendent to Abraham Lincoln in 1861 and joined the confederacy where he built up Virginia's navy and worked on development of underwater torpedoes and electronically detonated mines. To quote an early Maury biographer: "What particular ability and quality were met in Matthew Fontaine Maury to open his eyes to that which others had not perceived? From what source did he gain the mind and energy needed to investigate and systematize knowledge of the sea until a science was born? Environment played a part, but Maury was to a marked degree the product of his heritage," and the story of Jacques Fontaine in particular, see Frances Leigh Williams, *Matthew Fontaine Maury: Scientist of the Sea* (New Brunswick, NJ: Rutgers University Press, 1963), quote on 2, also "A Challenging Heritage," 1–25, and 365–98. Maury's decision to join the confederacy and his support for slavery begs the question of the relationship between his "heritage" of noble artisanry with its focus on bloodlines and the presumed "fair" and "handsome" physical attributes of the family's nobility, and slavery. Generations of Fontaines in Virginia were slaveowners. He was also a proponent of manifest destiny. For Maury's forceful views on slavery and states' rights, see Williams, 103–04, 348–49, 357, 425. For more recent biographies, see Chester G. Hearn, *Tracks in the Sea: Matthew Fontaine Maury and the Mapping of the Oceans* (Camden, ME: International Marine / McGraw Hill, 2003); and John Grady, *Matthew Fontaine*

The Genius of Distance

To maintain public credit for authorship of the fire machine, Fontaine employed for as long as possible a combination of secrecy and manipulation of the contingencies of geographical distance in all his transactions with coreligionists, creditors, consumers, guild courts, and other artisans. Geography and timing mattered enormously in the early modern Atlantic, as did Fontaine's access to Huguenot networks. Distance from centers of mechanical innovation in textile production was essential to Fontaine's claims as an inventive genius of what elsewhere may have been commonplace machinery. Distance is essential to historical questions concerning change over time and distinctions between local and nonlocal knowledge. We might think of "distance," says historian of science Mario Biagioli, "neither as a problem nor as a resource, but rather as part of the conditions of the possibility of knowledge." For a while, distance was Fontaine's ally. Lack of local knowledge of innovations elsewhere allowed him to claim unique expertise and helped the mobile Fontaine maintain his status as a genius. This status was always temporary wherever he went, contingent on timing when local conditions relative to distance changed. In this instance, the agent of change was Fontaine himself.[84]

Too small to scale up his operation and unable to maintain a pace of invention to profit from the cycle of glut and novelty, Fontaine collected 1,000 pounds made from his success with calamanco during the early 1690s and took his wandering family on the road again. Here was the essence of the mobile niche economy. The refugees revived old patterns from southwestern France and traveled north, for "I thought I would leave the place and try whether I could not find a church in want of a minister. I knew that there were many French Protestant Refugees in Ireland, so I went to Dublin to make inquiries." He eventually opened a successful French and Latin school while preaching the gospel at the same time. Young elites learned piety along with politeness and appropriate comportment, especially in the proper staging and use of the glossy "new luxuries" that Fontaine and his coreligionists manufactured and sold. Like the new luxuries, schools such as Fontaine's were a Huguenot brand in the Atlantic world and represented another part of the transactional economy.

Maury, Father of Oceanography: A Biography, 1806–1873 (Jefferson, NC: McFarland and Company, 2015). I am indebted to Professor Bruce Hunt for bringing these citations to my attention.

84 Mario Biagioli, *Galileo's Instruments of Credit: Telescopes, Images, Secrecy* (Chicago, IL: University of Chicago Press, 2006), 3.

When one aspect of Fontaine's Pauline strategy faltered, he shifted seamlessly to another, his inventive genius tied inextricably to new opportunities afforded by distance, improvisation, and alchemical stories from his family's violent past. While he looked forward to the possibility of assuming his first official pulpit in Ireland, a country like France with a small Protestant population surrounded by a seething majority of Catholics, his hoped-for ministry was only one part of a wide-ranging, transgenerational, indeed global material-holiness synthesis that informed Fontaine's strategic and practical cosmology.[85] His history of one family's quest for noble artisanry in the late seventeenth-century Atlantic set in motion the sixteenth-century textual and material innovations of Bernard Palissy, the rustic potter of Saintonge. Palissy was there at the beginning of his region's transatlantic Reformation history, and Fontaine at the end. Because of their shared martyred bloodlines in that painful but newly constructed noble history, Fontaine's text on calamanco taught his heirs that the material and spiritual practice at the heart of southwestern French Huguenot alchemy continued to labor towards the future in the DNA of the industrial revolution.

[85] On Fontaine's church project and Irish-Catholic hostility, see Maury, Memoirs, 189; on the global material-holiness synthesis, see Kamil, *Fortress of the Soul*, 167–214, 294, 325, 355, 369, 381, 477–98, 922–23; and for its transatlantic and cosmopolitan pathways, see William R. Newman, *Gehennical Fire: The Lives of George Starkey: An American Alchemist in the Scientific Revolution* (Chicago, IL: University of Chicago Press, 2013); Lawrence M. Principe, *Alchemy Tried in the Fire: Starkey, Boyle, and the Fate of Helmontian Chymistry* (Chicago, IL: University of Chicago Press, 2002); Margaret C. Jacob, *Strangers Nowhere in the World: The Rise of Cosmopolitanism in Early Modern Europe* (Philadelphia: University of Pennsylvania Press, 2017); *The Radical Enlightenment: Pantheists, Freemasons, and Republicans* (London and Boston: Allen & Unwin, 1981); and *Practical Matter: Newton's Science in the Service of Industry and Empire, 1687–1851* (Cambridge, MA: Harvard University Press, 2004).

5 Idolatry, Markets, and Confession: The Global Project of the de Bry Family*

Susanna Burghartz

In the spring of 1590, a splendid and lavishly illustrated book was published in Frankfurt am Main. It appeared almost simultaneously in four separate editions in French, English, Latin and German, and became a veritable European bestseller.[1] The *Briefe and True Report of the New Found Land of Virginia*, whose longer German title refers to "the customs of the savages," was the first book that the publishing neophyte Theodore de Bry produced together with his two sons (Fig 5.1).

Printed by Johann Wechel, the books were sold on commission by the renowned Frankfurt publisher Sigmund Feyerabend. In 1588, at the age of sixty, the Liège-born Calvinist, economic migrant, and religious refugee de Bry settled in Frankfurt with his family, becoming a member of the Calvinist community active in the city. Despite the rather late start, with this work he laid the cornerstone for a highly successful, large-scale publishing enterprise. This collection of travelogues would eventually become the pictorial archive of European expansion and its new worlds *par excellence*, shaping the imagery of early globalization to the present day.

As Calvinist publishers with European ambitions, the de Bry family managed to create a new place for the northwestern European Protestant nations on the globalizing visual map of the world, which had heretofore been dominated by the Spanish and the Portuguese. In their two series, the *India occidentalis* and the *India orientalis*, published from 1590 to 1630, they documented and accompanied, with prescriptive intent, the global range of the emerging Protestant colonial enterprise, marked as it was by dynamism but also by precariousness and setbacks (Fig 5.2).

In 1609 the most important Dutch publisher and bookseller at the time, Cornelis Claesz, advertised "a very fine collection of copper plates,

* English translation by Pamela Selwyn.

1 Peter Stallybrass, "Admiranda narratio. A European bestseller," in *A briefe and true report of the new found land of Virginia / Thomas Hariot* (Charlottesville & London: University of Virginia Press, 2007), 9–30.

Wunderbarliche / doch Warhafftige
Erklärung / Von der Gelegenheit
vnd Sitten der Wilden in Virginia / welche newlich von den Engelländern / so im Jar 1585.
vom Herrn Reichard Greinuile / einem von der
Ritterschafft / in gemeldte Landschafft die zu be-
wohnen geführt waren / ist erfunden worden / In
verlegung H. Walter Raleigh / Ritter vnd Obersten deß Zinbergwercks / auß vergünstigung der
Durchleuchtigsten vnnd Vnvberwind-
lichsten / Elisabeth / Königin in
Engelland ꝛc.

Erstlich in Engelländischer Sprach beschrieben
durch Thomam Hariot / vnd newlich durch Christ.
P. in Teutsch gebracht.

Mit Römischer Keys. Maiest. Frey-
heit auff vier Jar nicht nach-
zudrucken.

Gedruckt zu Franckfort am Mäyn / bey Johann
Wechel / in verlegung Dieterich Bry.
Anno 1590.
Werden verkaufft in H. Sigmund Feyerabends Laden.

Fig 5.1 Theodore de Bry, *Indiae occidentalis*, Germ., vol. 1, Frankfurt/M., 1590, title-page

by the finest masters in Europe," among them Theodore de Bry, as well as Hendrick Goltzius and several others.[2] By that time, the Calvinist engraver de Bry had become famous throughout Europe for his widely

[2] Cornelis Claesz, *Constende Caert-Register*, 1609.

Fig 5.2 Johan Theodore de Bry, *Self-portrait*, in Jean-Jacques Boissard, *Tractatus posthumus*, Oppenheim ca. 1615, showing Johan Theodore de Bry presenting the two series of the Voyages to the West and to the East

circulated prints. Later, with the 1598 publication of Las Casas's *Narratio regionum indicarum per Hispanos quosdam devastatarum verissima*, which appeared outside the framework of the two travel series, and, starting in 1594, with the inclusion in the *India occidentalis* of anti-Spanish texts, including Girolamo Benzoni's *Historia del mondo nuovo*, for which de Bry used the highly ideological translation of the French Calvinist Urban Chauveton, the de Brys were touted as the initiators of the so-called *leyenda negra* or Black Legend, which would cement the image of the especially brutal Spanish conquest of America for centuries to come.[3] Recent research has juxtaposed this narrative of the confessionally defined collection of Protestant polemics with the image of market-oriented publishers active throughout Europe who softened the ideological exaggerations of their sources in their collections with an eye to their Catholic readership.[4] Accordingly, scholars no longer regard the de Bry travel collections as an "instrument of Protestant propaganda" but instead as a collection whose choice of texts, engravings, and paratexts was clearly Protestant in orientation but not necessarily anti-Catholic or anti-Spanish.[5] This is where the present chapter begins. It aims to present the de Bry voyages as part of a Protestant, northwestern European "visual economy."[6] This visual economy facilitated the emergence of European information and image markets (and their corresponding networks) that functioned across confessional lines. It linked the question of the significance of visual culture for understanding divine creation in post-Reformation Europe with national-confessional rivalries, and it did so within the framework of European expansion in the late sixteenth century and the growing interest in proto-ethnographic information about the New Worlds and their religious practices.

Given that the de Brys published the first, lavishly illustrated Protestant pan-European travel collection, which was marked by an intricate combination of confessional and market-oriented features, their West and East Indian Voyages may be read first as a Calvinist image collection of

[3] Patricia Gravatt, "Rereading Theodore de Bry's black legend," in *Rereading the Black Legend: The Discourses of Racial and Religious Difference in the Renaissance Empires*, ed. Margaret R. Greer, Walter D. Mignolo, and Maureen Quilligan (Chicago, IL: University of Chicago Press, 2007), 225–43.

[4] Michiel van Groesen, *The Representations of the Overseas World in the de Bry Collection of Voyages (1590–1634)* (Leiden: Brill, 2008).

[5] Helge Perplies, *Inventio et repraesentatio Americae. Die India occidentalis-Sammlung aus der Werkstatt de Bry* (Heidelberg: Universitätsverlag Winter, 2017), 55.

[6] In his *Antwerp Art after Iconoclasm. Experiments in Decorum 1566–1585* (New Haven, CT and London: Yale University Press, 2012), 267–68, Koenraed Jonckheere even speaks of "pictorial ecumenicism" for the Antwerp case.

topical interest for the period around 1600; second as a Protestant visual archive on European expansion that retains its huge impact to this day; and finally as a timely contribution to one of the most heated intellectual and religious debates around 1600 over the meaning of images and idols. In this way, the de Bry travel collections contributed to a global Protestantism. Confessional as well as national propaganda, circulation in markets, and a prominent contribution to the topical discourse on idolatry – all of these features were significant elements of an emerging Protestant awareness of the global.

Networks, Markets, and the Emerging Protestant Nations

Theodore de Bry settled in Antwerp, the global hub of Europe at the time, in or before 1578.[7] The city on the River Schelde, which by this time had recovered from the so-called Spanish Fury, was a vibrant center of art, printing, and commerce. Goods and objects from all over the world arrived here every day.[8] New forms of knowledge production in the fields of cosmology and geography were also booming here, and copperplate engraving developed new forms of book illustration, which appear to have held great attraction for Theodore de Bry, just as they aroused interest across Europe well beyond Antwerp, and even in the Mogul Empire.[9] In Antwerp, the status of images was debated with greater intensity than perhaps anywhere else in Europe at this time. Since the first wave of Reformation iconoclasm in 1566, there had been a rather paradoxical explosion of imagery, especially in the area of prints.[10] It was here that "Dierik" or "Thiery" de Bry, as the Antwerp sources refer to him, transformed himself from a goldsmith into an engraver. As a member of the Guild of St. Luke, he very likely built up important relationships, among others probably with Christophe Plantin, Phillip Galle, Jan Sadeler, or Joris Hoefnagel, the families van der Heijden and Soreau, scholars like Franciscus Raphelengius the bookseller, and perhaps even with members of the court of the House of Orange, as some of de Bry's drawings seem to

[7] Michiel van Groesen, "De Bry and Antwerp: A Formative Period," in *Staging New Worlds*, ed. Susanna Burghartz (Basel: Schwabe Verlag, 2004), 19–45.

[8] Herman van der Wee and Jan Materné, *Antwerp: Story of a Metropolis*, ed. Jan van der Stock (Ghent: Snoeck-Ducaju & Zoon, 1993), 19–31.

[9] Karen L. Bowen and Dirk Imhof, *Christopher Plantin and Engraved Book Illustrations in Sixteenth-Century Europe* (Cambridge: Cambridge University Press, 2008).

[10] David Freedberg, "Art after Iconoclasm. Painting in the Netherlands between 1566 and 1585," in *Art after Iconoclasm. Painting in the Netherlands between 1566 and 1585*, ed. Koenraad Jonckheere and Ruben Suykerbuyk (Turnhout: Brepols Publishers, 2012), 21–49, here 43. The author speaks of "one of the greatest expansions of image-making before the age of the computer."

suggest.[11] More generally, as an emporium for all manner of objects from the New Worlds, and as a center for collectors, scholars, and savants, Antwerp certainly promoted de Bry's access to all kinds of trade, markets, and knowledge exchange.

Having moved to London even before the fall of Antwerp in 1584 or 1585, Theodore de Bry could rely on Calvinist as well as artistic networks. He left Antwerp, the northwestern European centre for the production of visual information and especially engraving, and arrived at the beginning of the "English moment" (Joan Pau Rubiés) in London, where Richard Hakluyt had become the mastermind of a group of English intellectuals and politicians who were active in colonial policy. At this specific historical moment, following the defeat of the Armada, Hakluyt's interest in travel literature functioned "as an integral part in the development of a proto-colonial vision that was both national and Protestant."[12] In London, de Bry soon connected with Protestants committed to the new colonial projects in America devoted to the memory of Sir Philip Sidney. Thus, as a labour migrant and perhaps also a religious refugee, he engaged in two projects of eminent national significance for the English. One brought him into contact with courtly circles not only in England, but also on the continent; the other, brought him into contact with seafarers. The concrete turning point was doubtless his work as engraver for Thomas Lant's sensational publication on the funeral procession of Sir Philip Sidney[13] (Fig 5.3). This was a sequence of extraordinary and sumptuous memorial pictures paying homage to Sidney, the youthful heroic martyr of the Protestant cause in the Netherlands who had fallen in October 1586.[14]

The model for the unusually luxurious publication of Sidney's funeral procession was Hendrik Goltzius's series of engravings for the 1584 funeral cortege of William of Orange in Delft. Both Goltzius and de Bry borrowed from representations of the funeral

[11] Van Groesen, "De Bry and Antwerp," 35 ff.; van Groesen does not mention any direct relationship to the Orange court, however. The question of whether the de Brys became members of the Family of Love also remains a subject of speculation.

[12] Joan Pau Rubiés, "From the 'History of Travayle' to the History of Travel Collections: The Rise of an Early Modern Genre," in *Richard Hakluyt and Travel Writing in Early Modern Europe*, ed. Daniel Carey and Claire Jowitt (Abingdon, UK: Ashgate, 2012), 25–41, here 30–33.

[13] Thomas Lant, *Sequitur celebritas et pompa funebris* (London, 1588).

[14] As Elizabeth Goldring shows in "The funeral of Sir Philip Sidney and the Politics of Elizabethan Festival," in *Court Festivals of the European Renaissance: Art, Politics and Performance*, ed. J. R. Mulryne and Elizabeth Goldring (Aldershot, UK: Ashgate, 2002), 199–224.

Fig 5.3 Thomas Lant and Theodore de Bry, *Sequitur celebritas et pompa funebris*, London 1588 – The coffin of Sir Philip Sidney, plate 16 (Shelf Mark: C.20.f.12)

procession of Charles V, which had been published by Plantin in Antwerp in 1559. When Theodore de Bry began working as an engraver on Thomas Lant's *Sequitur celebritas & pompa funebris* he had to interrupt his collaboration on the English edition of Lucas Waghenaer's *Mariner's Mirror,* which was being prepared by Sir Anthony Ashley, clerk of the Privy Council in London (Fig 5.4). This publication, too, would attract great attention, since it was the first maritime handbook printed in England, which was on the verge of becoming an important seafaring nation.

Around the same time, Richard Hakluyt was working on the first edition of his famous *Principal Navigations.* He encouraged de Bry to undertake a publication project of his own that would lend visual form, on a scale never seen before, to the still precarious new English and French colonial projects, as well as to the established Spanish and Portuguese colonial worlds. As a result, de Bry left London with the texts and drawings for the first two volumes of his new series of travel accounts on the Americas. The visual and ethnographic quality of the drawings and watercolours by Jacques Le Moyne and John White, two painters who had documented as eyewitnesses the early French and English attempts to found colonies in Florida and

Fig 5.4 Lucas Janszoon Waghenaer, *The Mariners Mirrour*, London 1588 – Title-page engraved by Theodor de Bry

Virginia, was key to the lasting success of de Bry's travel collection, which has shaped the visual archive of early European expansion to this day.

In September 1588, just a few months after the defeat of the Armada, de Bry and his family settled in Frankfurt, his wife's hometown.[15] Probably because of his family connections, he was soon able to become a citizen. By electing to establish his new publishing enterprise in Frankfurt, Theodore de Bry also allied himself with the site of the most important German book fair, which was influential beyond the region and also beyond Germany. Publishers and booksellers like Jan Moretus of Antwerp and Cornelis Claesz of Amsterdam, who sold their products throughout Europe, were also present at the fairs.[16] In the ten years before de Bry's arrival, Frankfurt had also emerged as the most important centre of printing in the German-speaking world, thanks to the entrepreneurial acumen of Sigmund Feyerabend.[17] Furthermore, Frankfurt already possessed a relatively large, active community of Calvinist exiles in this period.[18] Once there, de Bry clearly wasted no time establishing business connections with Sigmund Feyerabend, one of the most important German-speaking publishers of his day, who was already involved in the business of colonial travel literature. When Theodore de Bry arrived in Frankfurt, he had already built up key competencies over several decades that would make his extraordinary success as a publisher possible: He already had connections in Frankfurt from his time in Strasbourg and he was integrated into a super-regional Protestant Calvinist network. His sojourn in Antwerp had acquainted him with the latest book illustration technology and helped him to make contacts in Flemish-Dutch learned, artistic, printing and publishing circles. He had already been working in court circles since at least his time in London,[19] and had built up

[15] Perplies, *Inventio et repraesentatio*, 50.

[16] For more precise information on the business activities of Plantin's son-in-law Moretus vis-à-vis the de Bry publishing company at the Frankfurt book fairs, see Michiel van Groesen, "Entrepreneurs of Translation: Latin and the Vernacular in the Editorial Strategy of the de Bry Publishing House," in *Translating Knowledge in the Early Modern Low Countries*, ed. Harold J. Cook and Sven Dupré (Berlin: LIT, 2013), 107–28, 113; on Cornelis Claesz, see Andrew Pettegree and Arthur der Weduwen, *The Bookshop of the World: Making and Trading Books in the Dutch Golden Age* (New Haven, CT and London: Yale University Press, 2019), 40.

[17] Tina Terrahe, "Frankfurts Aufstieg zur Druckmetropole des 16. Jahrhunderts. Christian Egenolff, Sigmund Feyerabend und die Frankfurter Buchmesse," in *Frankfurt im Schnittpunkt der Diskurse. Strategien und Institutionen literarischer Kommunikation im späten Mittelalter und in der frühen Neuzeit*, ed. Robert Seidel und Regina Töpfer, Zeitsprünge 14/1-2 (2010): 183.

[18] Heinz Schilling, *Niederländische Exulanten im 16. Jahrhundert. Ihre Stellung im Sozialgefüge und im religiösen Leben deutscher und englischer Städte* (Gütersloh: Mohn, 1972), 52; Roman Fischer, "Glaube. Churches," in *Glaube Macht Kunst. Antwerpen – Frankfurt um 1600. Faith Power(s) Art. Antwerp – Frankfurt around 1600*, ed. Frank Berger, exhibition catalog (Frankfurt am Main: Historisches Museum, 2005), 51–67.

[19] Theodore de Bry was later the first to publish a corresponding album of emblems, *Emblemata nobilitati, Stam- und Wappenbuch* (Frankfurt am Main, 1592). See Carsten-

relationships with the intellectual promoters of the northwestern European Protestant colonial movement.

"Écriture protestante" and the "Black Legend"

De Bry's selection of texts and images for the first seven volumes of the America series, which appeared in the years between 1590 and 1597, had its origins on the one hand in his contacts with Hakluyt's circle, and on the other in the early production of German-speaking, anti-Spanish and Calvinist so-called colonial texts, which he had gained access to in Frankfurt. In this way, he inscribed himself into a discourse on America that has been characterized as *écriture protestante*.[20] Until quite recently, scholars have treated Theodore de Bry as a proponent of a vehemently Protestant, anti-Spanish position, indeed as a founding figure of the so-called Black Legend. Michèle Duchet has referred to his work as "a massive piece of anti-Spanish, anti-Catholic propaganda, a 'machine à guerre' in the struggle for religious and political dominance in both the New World and the Old."[21] This view has recently changed.

If we read the first volumes of the de Bry travel collections, we find a fascinating mixture: With the aid of engravings after drawings by John White, the first volume, on Virginia, transforms Hariot's promotional colonial text into a proto-ethnographic one, which informs us about the country's natural resources, social organization, religion, and manners. Volume two, on Florida, integrates this proto-ethnographic interest into the images, reports on the promise of the new continent for French Protestants, which the Spanish massacre brought to an abrupt end, and depicts the French as potential allies for individual indigenous groups, despite the natives' "outlandish" religious notions, rituals, and manners. The third volume takes up the Protestant Hans Staden's account of his sojourn among cannibals, based on a German bestseller that had described the culture of the Tupinambá in fascinating detail for German readers. This is combined with the Calvinist pastor Lery's account of the same culture, which is considered one of the founding texts of ethnology. The next three volumes integrate the representation of the cruel Spanish conquest of America taken from the account of the

Peter Warncke, *Symbol, Emblem, Allegorie. Die zweite Sprache der Bilder* (Cologne: Deubner, 2005), 104.

20 Cf. Kirsten Mahlke, *Offenbarung im Westen. Frühe Berichte aus der Neuen Welt* (Frankfurt am Main: Fischer, 2005).

21 Cited from Michael Gaudio, "The Space of Idolatry: Reformation, Incarnation, and the Ethnographic Image," *RES Anthropology and Aesthetics* 41 (Spring, 2002): 72–91, here 75.

Milanese Girolamo Benzoni, thereby accentuating the collection as an ideological battleground on Iberian atrocities, while the first volume of the East Indian voyages published shortly thereafter incorporates Africa in the form of Pigafetta's account of missionaries in the Congo. The next three volumes in the series use the founding text of the Dutch colonial enterprise, Linschoten's travels in the service of the Portuguese, to combine the ambitions of the Dutch, who were just beginning to establish themselves as players in the East, with a nearly encyclopedic description of the treasures of India and Southeast Asia, their kingdoms, manners, and natural regional potentials. The opening of the Voyages to the East cast a spotlight on emerging Dutch expansion. With each new volume, the collection of the West and East Indian Voyages became ever more clearly a place in which God's new world of wonders was revealed as a site of astonishing natural, ethnological, and religious features.

The Creation of a European Collection by Calvinists

The selection of the texts for the first seven or eight volumes of the America series undoubtedly had some Protestant bias. Nevertheless, in their recent research, Michiel van Groesen and Helge Perplies have argued convincingly against any clear ideological labelling of de Bry and his travel series, focusing instead on the publisher's strong orientation towards a transnational European book market. Given this orientation, an all-too obvious anti-Catholic and anti-Spanish bias would have been inopportune, with respect to book censorship as well.[22] The de Bry publishing family successfully exploited a specific northwestern "global moment" in which the global and colonial projects of the northwestern European newcomers (England and the Netherlands) intersected with the establishment of a European-orientated print and information market in the Netherlands and a clear intensification in the formation of confessional orthodoxy. With their concrete approach, they demonstrated an excellent feel for the specific business, social, and political situation that existed around 1590. The linguistic program of the series – quadrilingual in volume one and bilingual in Latin and German in all further volumes – already demonstrated the publisher's deliberate marketing strategies through market differentiation and expansion. The Latin edition addressed the European market across confessional lines. The vernacular editions in German, English, and French, in

[22] Van Groesen, *Representations*, chapters 8–10, see also Perplies, *Inventio et repraesentatio*, passim.

contrast, more clearly targeted a northwestern European, but by no means exclusively Protestant, audience.[23] Theodore de Bry and his sons nonetheless maintained extensive contacts in the quite cosmopolitan Protestant milieu. This is also evident from the collaborators they managed to attract for their large-scale project. They included, for instance, Charles de l'Écluse (Clusius), who had come to Frankfurt as a Protestant in 1587, the engraver Joost van Winghe, and the Calvinist scholar Jean-Jacques Boissard. These people represented an international, northwestern European scholarly network closely linked via printing centers such as Frankfurt, Basel, Antwerp, and also Leiden, which published for the republic of letters. From the outset, however, as capable businessmen, the de Brys also had their eye on other markets.

Apart from urban elites, who were probably the main audience for their German editions, the de Brys also deliberately appealed to an aristocratic and courtly public, thus opening up an additional Europe-wide market. This is already evident in the dedications of their first volumes, which were mainly to young princes and dukes:[24] Prince Maximilian, elected king of Poland and later archduke of the Tyrol, a fervent supporter of the Counter-Reformation; Duke Christian of Saxony with his crypto-Calvinist leanings; and the Protestant Elector Palatine Frederick IV. The de Brys' business model of addressing their publications not only to an audience of humanist scholars, or at least interested citizens, but also to a noble public becomes even more evident if we look at their publishing program beyond the great travel series.[25] In 1592, for marketing and financial reasons, Theodore de Bry published the *Emblemata Secularia*, which very clearly targeted European high society and, in various editions and versions, contributed significantly to the company's financial success (a multilingual edition of 1596 in Latin, German, French, and Dutch was perhaps the most successful title on the de Bry list).[26] As in the dedications, here, too, the represented members of the European high nobility crossed confessional lines. This publishing strategy, which was always orientated towards the market and by no means towards membership in a confessional camp, became even more evident in subsequent years, anticipating a practice that would make Dutch

[23] Cf. van Groesen, *Representations*, 259.

[24] Anna Greve, *Die Konstruktion Amerikas. Bilderpolitik in den Grands Voyages aus der Werkstatt de Bry* (Cologne: Böhlau, 2004), 77–78.

[25] See esp. van Groesen, *Representations*, which provides all the details of the de Brys' publishing activities.

[26] Cornelia Kemp, "Nachwort," in *Johann Theodor de Bry Emblemata secularia*, ed. Wolfgang Harms and Michael Schilling (Hildesheim: Olms, 1994), 206.

printers so very successful in the seventeenth century: they printed what they could sell. This approach did not go unchallenged within the family, however, with disagreements between father and sons. In the years 1594–1596, the de Brys published Girolamo Benzoni's *Historia del Mondo Nuovo*, the history of the Spanish conquest of South America, with a commentary by the Calvinist Chauveton. In his close reading and intertextual analysis, Helge Perplies has shown that in these volumes too, which "are often cited in the literature as evidence of a confessional anti-Spanish agenda" pursued by the Calvinist publishers, the de Brys "continued their strategy of softening the confessional or political attacks in the originals or countering them, with the help of paratexts and illustrations, with other, particularly moral, interpretations."[27] That same year, in 1596, when Theodore de Bry published the final volume by Benzoni in the America series, his two sons, on the intercession of Jean Jacques Boissard, published in Montbéliard the *Opera misericordiae ad corpus penitentia* by the Catholic Julius Roscius, canon of Santa Maria in Trastevere,[28] after the Frankfurt censors had branded the work papist in 1595 and banned its publication there. This must have greatly dismayed their father, as we learn from a letter from Theodore de Bry to Raphelengius. As a Calvinist immigrant, de Bry "had always taken care not to aggrieve the Frankfurt magistrates."[29] After the death of Theodore de Bry two years later in 1598, his sons brought out Bartolomé de Las Casas's *Narratio regionum indicorarum per Hispanos quosdam devastattarum verissima* with the illustrations that would establish their reputation as co-initiators of the so-called Black Legend.[30] Maríaluz López-Terrada and José Pardo-Tomás have recently emphasised the dense circulation of books about the New World and its natural history "published and exchanged between the Iberian Peninsula and the Low Countries."[31] Las Casas's *Brevísima relación* is a highly pertinent example: first published in Spanish in 1552, it appeared in Flemish translation under the title *Spieghel der Spaenscher tirannije* in 1578. The next year saw an equally

[27] Perplies, *Inventio et repraesentatio*, 73.

[28] Warncke, *Symbol, Emblem, Allegorie*, 74 and Anne-Kathrin Sors, *Religiöse Druckgraphik in Antwerpen um 1600 – Jan Davids Andachtsbücher und Theodor Galles Illustrationen* (Göttingen: Universitätsverlag, 2015), 189.

[29] Van Groesen, *Representations*, 71.

[30] The "Black Legend" refers to the idea that there was an ongoing trend of biased reporting on Spanish atrocities in the New World in historical writing, with an anti-Spanish tendency. See Ricardo Garcia Carcel, *La Leyenda negra: Historia y opinion* (Madrid: Alianza Editorial, 1992).

[31] Maríaluz López-Terrada and José Pardo-Tomás, "Reading about New World Nature in the Low Countries: The Editions of Crónicas de Indias, 1493–1600," in *Translating Knowledge in the Early Modern Low Countries*, ed. Harold John Cook and Sven Dupré (Zurich: Lit-Verlag, 2012), 53–78.

successful version in French printed in Antwerp by Franciscus Raphelengius, the son-in-law of Christophe Plantin, a correspondent of Carolus Clusius and later one of Theodore de Bry's collaborators.[32] In Dutch it was Cornelis Claesz, another immigrant from the southern Low Countries and by that time one of the most successful booksellers and printers in Amsterdam, who started a new wave of reception, publishing Las Casas again in 1596. In the years that followed, it was Cornelis Claesz's travel publications that were to provide the most important input for the de Brys' travel series. For their 1598 Latin edition of Las Casas's *Brevissima relacion*, however, the de Bry brothers resorted to the 1578 French edition of Raphelengius. Remarkably enough, this work was not published within the framework of the travel series. This again clearly shows how anxious the de Brys were "to keep their *India occidentalis* collection free of confessional and political controversies."[33]

The previous year, the de Bry brothers had already supplemented the America series with a second series, the *India orientalis*. In this way, they took up one of the most current political developments: the departure of the Dutch for Asia and their attack on the Portuguese-Spanish monopoly. Two series from one publishing company, which together encompassed the entire world, responded to the latest developments in the field of (national) voyages of discovery, and formulated veritable global aspirations. It was a new concept in the travel literature market.

In this project, the de Brys pursued neither the older geographical-cosmological principle of the four corners of the earth or continents, nor a national principle, as did Hakluyt, who had published his own collection of travel accounts just one year before. Their division relied instead on the direction of departure for the two hemispheres, with their different patterns, conditions, and circumstances (commercial colonization, highly developed empires, wind systems etc.), thereby primarily pursuing the northwestern European nations' claim to, or even assault upon, the Spanish and Portuguese spheres of influence. Their Flemish-Dutch networks and business connections, and their interest in the newly emergent Dutch expeditions to the New Worlds, increasingly determined the information market from where they acquired texts that had generally already been illustrated and printed, for example, Jan Huygen Linschoten's *Itinerario*, originally published in Amsterdam in 1596, or José Acosta's

[32] Ibid., 68–69. It was this version that served as the basis for the de Brys' Latin edition of 1598.

[33] Perplies, *Inventio et repraesentatio*, 183; van Groesen, *Representations*, 250–53, 287–307; Sven Trakulhun, "Three Tales of the New World: Nation, Religion and Colonialism in Hakluyt, de Bry, and Hulsius," in *Richard Hakluyt and Travel Writing in Early Modern Europe*, 57–66, esp. 63.

The Natural and Moral History of the Indies, translated from the Dutch version printed in Enckhuizen in 1598, which appeared, respectively, as volumes two to four of the *Indiae orientalis* in 1597–1599 and as volume nine of the *Indiae occidentalis* in 1601. The global perspective of this concept became especially clear in the accounts of English and Dutch circumnavigations of the globe that the de Bry brothers included in their America series. It was, however, also communicated by individual protagonists who arrived in the two hemispheres on their various voyages. In this way, they made significant contributions to a discourse that, before the eyes of a European public, deployed texts and above all images to carve out room for the future Protestant colonial powers in a global space that was apparently already assigned and occupied. This project was dedicated to the mental re-occupation of a world that had been previously divided up between Spain and Portugal. At the same time, as astute businessmen, the de Brys were always eager to entertain their readers with interesting news and information from the New Worlds and thus to place and sell their books successfully on the market. And finally, the pious Calvinists and humanist-orientated de Brys also aimed to provide edifying reading that would lead to an understanding of the marvellous New Worlds as divine creation. The market, religion, and politics could indeed be combined in the new culture of "pictorial ecumenicism."[34]

Reading the Book of Creation: The New Worlds as Divine Miracles

Over a period of forty years and three generations, parallel to the rise of the Dutch, the de Brys published a text corpus that also included Spanish or Portuguese texts and gave European elites the opportunity to see and purchase the whole world from the comfort of home, all from the perspective of the northwestern European Protestant nations. This was an economic as well as a religious or at least morally edifying enterprise. Accordingly, the de Brys did not conduct their critique of the Spanish and their cruelty primarily as anti-Catholic propaganda, but instead as an admonition to repentance directed at Protestant audiences as well. This is made evident in exemplary fashion in the preface to volume one of Benzoni's *Historia del Mondo Nuovo*, which appeared as volume four of the *Indiae occidentalis* or *America* series. In this preface, de Bry urgently warned readers not to judge the Spanish hunger for gold too harshly and to ignore the beam in their own eye. Instead, recognizing the sins of

[34] Cf. n. 6.

others – indigenous people as well as (Spanish) Catholics – should also lead "us" Calvinists to contrition and repentance:

Our hearts feel terror when we hear/ that those blind folk worship the Devil. But why do we see the mote in their eyes/ while often failing to note the beam in our own? Read this tract and thou shalt see/ that the blind Indians remarked our frailties and avarice better than we did ourselves/ and also chided us once / pointing at a piece of gold and saying / See the God of the Christians. It is a disgrace to be sure / that the Christians require such schoolmasters: Thou shalt / see in this book / how an insatiable greed among the Spanish / led to terrible disgrace and vice driven by avarice / how cruelly and tyrannically they treated the poor Indians / how shamefully they slaughtered one another, spurred on by senseless greed. Which matter is always to be criticized and lamented of Christian folk. But so that no one may accuse the Spanish people of dishonor and disgrace/ let each look to himself / and ask whether we do not do daily what other people in other nations do . . .[35]

The de Brys, father and sons alike, repeatedly emphasized that their travel series aspired to allow those reading at home to experience the world as God's wondrous creation without danger to life and limb. Thus, reading their books as *contemplatio* combined entertainment with edification, without having to assign the travel collection itself or its concrete readers to one or the other confessional camps exclusively. Instead, it could be considered the obligation of all Christians to understand the world as universal divine creation, an awareness of which was perceived as a religious duty. Levinus Hulsius, with whom the de Brys co-operated, wrote the following in the preface to Ulrich Schmidel's *Warhafftigen Historien*, which appeared as a volume of his *Schiffahrten*:

The histories and accounts of the new lands and peoples/ are in my opinion / not simply entertaining / but also necessary reading for Christians: For in this way we wish to observe God's boundless marvellous work / and his ineffable mercy /which he has shown in many ways to us poor unworthy Christians / granting us not just

[35] Theodore de Bry, *Indiae occidentalis*, vol. 4, preface to the reader. "Unser hertz erschrickt wenn wir hören / daß jene blinde Leuth den Teuffel anbetten. Aber was sehen wir den Splitter in ihren Augen / aber unter dessen werden wir deß Balckens in unsern Augen nit gewar? Liese diesen Tractat so wirstu sehen / daß die blinde Indianer unser schwächen und Geitz besser als wir selber gemercket haben / und auch einmal auffgerupffet / da sie ein stück Goldts zeigende sprachen / Siehe der Christen Gott. Es ist zwar ein schendlicher Handel / daß die Christen solche Lehrmeister haben müssen: Uber das / wirstu in diesem Buch sehen / was und wie ein unersättiger Geitz bey den Spaniern gewesen / zu was und wie grosse schand und Laster die der Geitz getrieben hat / wie grewlich und tyrannisch sie mit den armen Indianern umbgegangen / wie schändlich sie durch unsinnige Begierligkeit erhitzet sich selber under einander gemetziget haben. Welche ding allzumal an Christenleuthen sehr zu schelten unnd zu beweinen seyn. Aber doch damit nit jemand dieses dem Spanischen Volck zur unehr und schmacheit uffhebe / betrachte ein jeder bey jm selbs / was ander Leut in andern Nationen thun und Begehen wir nit täglich dergleichen stücke. . ." All English translations by Pamela Selwyn, unless otherwise noted.

His knowledge / but also such precious ransom / that we were lost in Adam / and were redeemed again: In contrast, however / how many hundreds of thousands of poor folk / never knew anything of God and His Commandments / of honorability / matrimony / discipline / law / reason nor counsel / But instead were reared and lived in idolatry/ obscenity / lasciviousness / gluttony / cannibalism and uncleanness.[36]

Reading travel accounts thus benefited Christian readers in two ways: as worldly books, they led directly to a knowledge of God's creation and merciful redemption, and thereby also implicitly assured readers of their own predestination. The de Brys argued quite similarly in the preface to the fourth volume of the *Indiae orientalis*:

For that reason the Lord God then /awakened us from our slumbers / now and again leading us by the nose through the world / and opening our eyes/ so that we might see and recognize his great wonders / and be moved by them / and call His holy and mighty name all the more / and consider and recognize him as Almighty God.[37]

Reading the de Bry travel series was thus stylized as a form of religious awakening, which would arouse the unconscious sleeper to the knowledge of the world as divine creation and to a veneration of the divine name. In this way, reading travel literature was transformed into a form of worship.

The Omnipresence of Idols in the New Worlds

As the de Bry collection made abundantly clear, travel accounts did not simply demonstrate God's miracles; they also consistently treated the subjects of idolatry and Devil worship. Theologians had always been concerned with the biblical prohibition of graven images. Accounts of the veneration of idols written in the course of European expansion, and

[36] Levinus Hulisus, *Schiffahrten*, vol. 4 (2nd ed., Nuremberg, 1602), dedication to Johann Philip, bishop of Bamberg. "Die Historien und Relation der newen Länder und Völcker / seind meines Erachtens / nit allein lustig / Sondern auch den Christen zu lesen nötig: Dann so wir wöllen die unermessliche wunderbare Werck Gottes betrachten / vnd seine unaussprechliche Bamherzigkeit /die er vns armen vnwürdigen Christen vielfältig bewiesen / zugemüht führen / indem er vns nicht allein seine Erkenntnuß gegeben / sonder auch mit so köstlichen Rantzion / da wir in Adam verlohren waren / vns wider erlöset hat." See also Dorothee Schmidt, *Reisen in das Orientalische Indien: Wissen über fremde Welten um 1600* (Cologne: Böhlau, 2016), 187.

[37] Johan Theodore and Johan Israel de Bry, *Indiae orientalis*, vol. 4. Vorrede: "derhalben vns dann Gott der Herr /gleichsam auß dem Schlaff aufwecken / mit der Nasen hin vnnd wider durch die welt führen / vnd unsere Augen vns aufthun muß / seine grosse Wunderwerck zusehen vnnd zuerkennen / auf daß wir durch dieselben bewegt werden / seinen heiligen Großmechtigen namen so viel dest mehr anzuruffen / vnnd jhn für den Allmechtigen Gott zuhalten vnd zu erkennen."

Reformation discussions of the power of images in the early sixteenth century, lent new urgency to the problem of idolatry, especially because the destruction of the Mexican idols by the Spanish invaders occurred almost simultaneously with the first acts of iconoclasm in the Reformation.[38] The topic remained highly controversial throughout the sixteenth century. In his *De vera et false religione,* the Zurich Reformer Zwingli, for example, used heathen idolatry as an argument with which to criticize the Latin Church and its practices of piety.[39] In the years that followed, the accounts and discussions of Peter Martyr of Anghiera and his successors on Mexican idolatry and human sacrifice gradually shifted the emphasis from a rather neutral description of the alien practices to a condemnation of indigenous rites as the work of the Devil.[40] In the first half of the century, Protestant theologians firmly condemned the use of images in sacred contexts. A counter movement began with the Council of Trent. The Catholic Church now declared the legitimacy of venerating images and developed clear distinctions between the permissible (Catholic) veneration of images and the practices of (heathen) idolatry, which were to be condemned. Thus "idolatry" remained a hotly contested terrain between the Christian confessions in subsequent years as well. And the false, superstitious veneration of images in the non-European (pagan or Muslim) worlds proved a suitable medium for self-positioning and disassociation via the allegedly proper and improper use of images attributed to the various religions and confessions.[41] The lavishly illustrated de Bry travel series thus became a privileged site of

[38] Joan-Pau Rubiés, "Theology, ethnography, and the historicization of idolatry," *Journal of the History of Ideas* 67/4 (October 2006): 571–96, esp. 582.

[39] Carina L. Johnson, "Idolatrous Cultures and the Practice of Religion," *Journal of the History of Ideas*, 67/4 (October 2006): 597–621, here 607.

[40] Ibid., 611–13.

[41] Carina L. Johnson, *Cultural hierarchy in Sixteenth-Century Europe: The Ottomans and Mexicans* (Cambridge: Cambridge University Press, 2011), esp. chapter 6 on "Collecting idolatry and the emergence of the exotic"; Jonathan Sheehan, "Introduction: Thinking about idols in early modern Europe," *Journal of the History of Ideas* 67/4 (October 2006): 561–69; art history in particular has made important contributions in this area in recent years. See, for example, Michael W. Cole and Rebecca Zorach eds., *The Idol in the Age of Art. Objects, Devotions and the Early Modern World* (Farnham, Surrey and Burlington, VT: Ashgate, 2009), esp. 1–10; Christine Göttler, "Extraordinary things: 'Idols from India' and the visual discernment of space and time, circa 1600," in *The Nomadic Object: The Challenge of World for Early Modern Religious Art*, ed. Christine Göttler and Mia M. Mochizuki, Intersections, vol. 53 (Leiden: Brill, 2017), 37–73; Maria Effinger, Cornelia Logemann, and Ulrich Pfisterer eds., *Götterbilder und Götzendiener in der Frühen Neuzeit. Europas Blick auf fremde Religionen* (Heidelberg: Universitätsverlag, 2012); Jonckheere, *Antwerp Art after Iconoclasm*; see also David Freedberg's now classic study *Iconoclasm and painting in the revolt of the Netherlands 1566–1609* (2nd ed., New York and London: Garland, 1988). Heartfelt thanks to Christine Göttler for all her information and inspiration.

conflict over the improper use of images by pagans and Catholics, which was clearly an important issue to the Calvinist engravers and publishers from Frankfurt with their multifarious connections in Antwerp and Amsterdam.

Religion and idolatry, accordingly, play an important and topical role in the collection. Their significance is already evident from the first title pages of the two series, which depict pagan gods, idols, priests, and shamans. The series' various travel accounts show that pagans all over the world worshiped idols. The title page of the first volume on Virginia, for example, depicts the idol Kiwasa (shown in a "Tympanum").[42] Plate xxi presents a kind of Algonquin ossuary, after a painting by John White that would gain prominence in the eighteenth century[43] (Fig 5.5). On a bench to the right of the desiccated corpses we see "the idol Kiwasa" as a guardian, while in the foreground squats a shaman or priest, who lived under the tomb scaffold and prayed for the dead.

De Bry preceded this plate with another image of Kiwasa borrowed from Le Moyne's volume on Florida. The picture caption tells us that this is a painted wooden idol "in the temple of the Towne of Secota," the burial ground of the kings, erected to serve as a guardian and terrible to behold because wooden figures like these were set up in dark places. Laced with pity, the caption patronizingly explains that these poor people had no other understanding of God, but clearly were eager "to gain knowledge of the true God." For this reason, they could be easily converted (Fig 5.6).

False religious practices, muttering prayers for the dead, and venerating painted blocks of wood are presented here as "superstition" in need of conversion and correction. While the picture of Kiwasa seemed exotically disconcerting, the description of the ritual in the caption carries clear reminders of Catholic funerary rites and practices of veneration.[44] The Florida volume heightens the impression of disturbing exoticism with images of a stag idol as part of a spring ritual and a human sacrifice, more specifically, the sacrifice of a first-born child, which also readily evokes the Old Testament.[45]

The world revealed to us by the collection is full of idolatry. This is also true of Africa and Asia. Thus, the title page of the first volume of the *Indiae orientalis* already depicts the animist worship of the celestial bodies. And the title page of the second volume shows a three-headed idol which the Chinese in Bantam used as an oracle before important undertakings,

[42] See Ill. 5.1. above. [43] Gaudio, "Space of idolatry," 74.

[44] Theodore de Bry, *Indiae occidentalis*, German, vol. 1 (Frankfurt, 1590), plate xxi, caption.

[45] Theodore de Bry, *Indiae occidentalis*, German, vol. 2 (Frankfurt, 1591), plates xxxiv, xxxv.

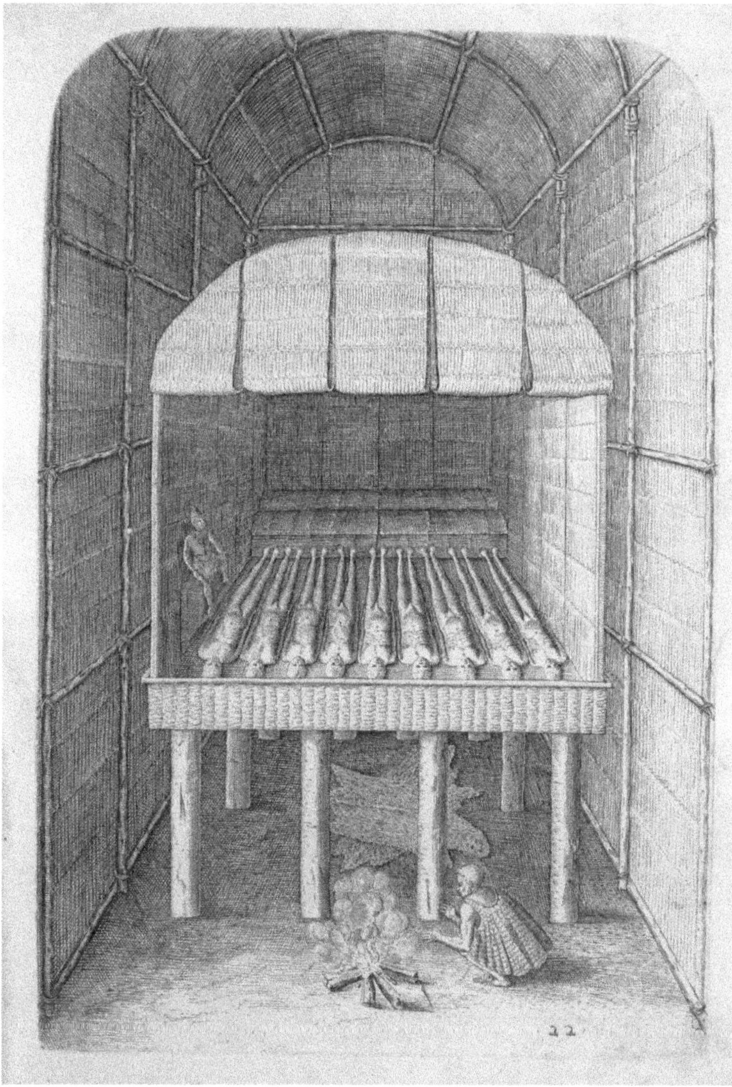

Fig 5.5 Theodore de Bry, *Indiae occidentalis*, Germ., vol. 1, Frankfurt am Main 1600[2], plate XXI

in order to fathom the future with magic rituals, as plate xxviii explains under the title “Wondrous ceremonies of the Chinese for their false god” (Fig 5.7).

XX.

Von einem Götzen/ den diß Volck ehret/vnd Kiwasa nennet.

DJeser Landschafft Innwohner haben einen Abgott/ deß Name ist Kiwasa/auß einem höltzern Klotz gemacht/welcher vier Schuh hoch ist/ vnd der Kopff den Häuptern der Leute/ so in Florida wohnen/ gleichförmig. Sein Antlitz ist mit Fleischfarb angestrichen/ die Brust ist weiß/ das vbrige theil deß Leibs ist schwartz/ die Schenckel sind mit verschiedener weisser Farbe bemahlet. Von seinem Halse herab hangen Ketten von weisen ronden Knäufflein/ vnter welche etzliche andere rondelichte in die lenge auß Kupffer gemacht/ vermenget werden. Dann sie halten bey jhnen von Kupffer viel mehr als von Golt oder Silber. Derselbige Abgott ist im Tempel der Statt Secota gestellt/ zu einem Hüter jhrer Könige/ so darinn begraben ligen. Sie haben in gemein in jren Tempeln je zween derselbigē Götzen/ bißweilen auch drey/ mehr aber nit/ welche/ dieweil sie an tunckele örter gestellt sind/ schrecklichen außsehen. Keine andere erkañtnusse Gottes haben die armen Leute. Wiewol ichs darfür halte/ daß sie sehr begierig seyn/ deß waren Gottes erkañtnusse zu haben. Dann als wir niderknieten/ vnser Gebett zu dem lieben Gott zu thun/ folgten sie vns in dem nach/ vnd als sie vermerckten/ daß wir vnsere Lefftzen regeten/ thaten sie auch dasselbige. Darumb ist es wol gläublich/ daß sie leicht zur erkañtnuß Gottes zu bringen weren. Darzu jhnen Gott gnad verleyhen wölle.

K ij

Fig 5.6 Theodore de Bry, *Indiae occidentalis*, Germ., vol. 1, Frankfurt am Main 1600², plate XX

In a separate chapter on “Moors and Jews in India,” Linschoten expressly addressed their right to practice their religions outside the Portuguese cities, “as often occurs outside the city of Cochin / where

XXVIII.

Wunderbarliche Ceremonien der Chiner für jhrem Abgott.

VIel Affenwercks treiben die Chinischen vor jhren Abgöttern/ deren sie viel haben / denn so sie etwas wichtiges/ zu Wasser oder Landt/ zuverrichten vorhaben / kommen sie für allhie vorgemaltes dreyköpffiges Bildt/ binden zwey Höltzlein/ so auff einer Seitten flach/auff der andern rundt/ zusammen / werffen dieselbe in die höhe/ fallen sie beyde auff die flache/ so bedeut es glücklichen vortgang/ fellt aber eins flach/das ander rundt / so halten sie es für vnglücklich/ bitten derowegen das Bildt mit vielen Verheissungen jhnen ein glückliches Zeichen zugeben / fallen dann vo-der beschehenes bitten die Höltzlein noch vngleich/ schelten vnd schmehen sie den Abgott / geben jhme doch widerumben gu-te Wort/ vnd werffen die Höltzlein / so aber das begerte Glücks Zeichen nicht fallen will / tretten sie das Bild mit Füssen/ werffen es ins Meer/ oder Feuwr / lassens ein wenig brennen / oder schlagen es so lang biß die Höltzlein recht fallen / als-dann setzen sie es wider zu recht/ entschuldigen sich gegen jhme / vnd bringen jhm mit grossen Freuden reichliche Opffer.

Es pflegen auch diese Völcker den bösen Geist anzuruffen vnd zubeschweren / auff nachfolgende weiß. Einer auß jhnen legt sich mit dem Angesicht auff die Erde/ein anderer lißt in einem Buch/ welchem die vbrige mit Gesang vñ Schel-lenklang antworten / Alsbaldt fehret der böß Geist in den auff der Erden ligenden/ welcher sich mit dem Angesicht vnnd seltzamen Geberden grausamlich verstellt / dieser besessene so er gefragt wirdt / gibt jhnen eine vom Teuffel empfangene Antwort. Im fall aber sie keine Antwort auff diese weiß bekommen / streuwen sie eine rote Decke auff die Erde/streuwen Reiß darauff / vnnd geben einem so nicht schreiben kan/ ein Höltzlein in die Handt/ fangen ahn zu singen vnd klingen/ nach solchem fangt dieser ahn mit dem Höltzlein in den Reiß zuschreiben/ wie die Charactern einer auß den Vmbstenden abmahlet vnd zusammen setzet / darauß sie ein Antwort jhrer Frag schöpffen.

Fig 5.7 Johan Theodore and Johan Israel de Bry, *Indiae orientalis*, Germ., vol. 2, Frankfurt am Main 1598, plate XXVIII

the king was holding court / and where the Jews and Moors are free to practice their superstition openly." The Dutch author seemed especially struck by the regulations concerning visits to the "Messkytas" (mosque, from the Spanish *mezquita*). He noted with appreciation: "In their churches they have no pictures or figures whatsoever / but only several upright stones or tombs with carved Chaldean letters on their Alcoran." In contrast, he found the regulations concerning purification and the requirement that shoes be removed before entering the mosque highly questionable. He reported going for a walk one day with a Portuguese man and desiring "to inspect the Mohammedan churches / and see what manner they had of praying." The Muslim doorkeeper stopped them and asked them to remove their shoes before entering. When the two Christians refused, they at least received permission to view the building's modest interior through the window. What they saw inspired Linschoten's Portuguese companion to ask "where the God and saints were / whom they venerate / for it looked very empty in their churches / as it is said." This immediately led to a heated argument about idolatry, because the Muslim responded that "they did not pray to stocks or stones / only to the living God / who is in heaven / and also said / you people / namely you Portuguese Christians and heathens are much the same / for you pray to made images / granting them the honour due to eternal and almighty God alone." According to Linschoten, this assertion made the Portuguese man so angry that he began to shout loudly "so that a crowd of Moors and Indians gathered / and a great quarrel would have arisen / had I not been there / and got the Portuguese to step back."[46] Thus in India, too, with its various religions and confessions, the question of images also had the potential to escalate. Despite their orientation towards the (overall) European market, the Calvinist brothers de Bry did not dispense with this story, which Linschoten (as a Catholic) in India, formerly in the service of the Catholic archbishop of Goa, clearly found attractive for his own book. First published in Amsterdam for a Dutch readership by the Protestant publisher and religious exile Cornelisz Claesz, it was published shortly thereafter by the de Brys for a "transnational,"

[46] Johan Theodore and Johan Israel de Bry, *Indiae orientalis*, vol. 2, German (Frankfurt, 1598), 128–29. "wie denn sich solches offtmals begibt ausserhalb der Statt Cochin / alda der König hoff helt / unnd da die Juden und Mohren jhren freyen Willen haben jhre Superstititon offenbarlich zu uben. [...] In jren Kirchen haben sie durchauß kein Bilder noch Figuren / nur allein etliche auffgerichte Stein oder Begräbnussen mit ausgehawenen Chaldeischen Buchstaben auß jhrem Alcoran [...] die Mahometischen Kirchen zu besehen / unnd was sie für ein Art zu beten hetten. [...] wo ihr Gott und jre Heiligen weren / welch: sie anbeten / dieweil er es in der Kirchen / wie gesagt ist / gantz lehr sahe. [...] sie betteten kein Holtz noch Stein an / nur allein den lebendigen Gott / welcher im Himmel ist / sagt auch / jhr Leut / nemlich jhr Portugisische Christen unnd Heyden seyt durch auß gleich / denn jhr betet die gemachte Bilder an / unnd gebet jhnen die Ehre welche allein dem ewigen allmechtigen Gott gebühret. [...] also daß die Mohren unnd Indianer hauffen weiß zusammen lieffen / unnd es were ein grosser Rumor darauß entstanden / wo ich nicht were darfür gewesen / und hette den Portugesen auff eine Seiten gezogen."

European audience. In fact, according to this tale, the Muslim worshippers were closer to the Calvinists than the Portuguese in matters of imagery. The corresponding chapter is accompanied by a laterally inverted illustration based on Johannes van Doetecum's picture for Linschoten's *Itinerario*, which showed a mosque in the Indian city of Malabar on one side, and a Hindu pagoda with a fountain of youth-like cleansing pool, a statue, and a holy cow on the other[47] (Fig 5.8).

While van Doetecum, following the text, had depicted the Indian idol with a mitre-like head covering similar to the papal triple tiara, de Bry dispensed with this detail and showed the idol instead wearing a headdress more reminiscent of a feather cap or a lotus blossom.[48]

As various stories from the *Indiae orientalis* suggest, in their treatment of religious images, the Catholics/Portuguese seem to have resembled Hindus or Buddhists, all of which drew (generally critical) comparisons to the papal church. The visit of a Dutch delegation under General Joris Spilbergen to the court of Kandy in 1602 offered them a very specific opportunity to adopt an explicitly anti-Catholic position in the matter of venerating images. The kingdom of Kandy, which contemporary Dutch sources described as decidedly cosmopolitan, was at that time embroiled in an intense defensive battle against the Portuguese. King Vimaladharmasūriya I had been forced to flee to Portuguese Goa because of the internal Sri Lankan power struggles to which his father had fallen victim and had converted to Christianity. Despite the conflict with the Portuguese, as king of Kandy he also adhered to a policy of religious tolerance and cultural cosmopolitanism.[49] Without any sensitivity to this complex religious situation, Spilbergen used his honourable reception at

[47] Johan Theodore and Johan Israel de Bry, *Indiae orientalis*, vol. 2, German (Frankfurt, 1598), plate xxi. See Anna C. Knaap, "Sculpture in pieces: Peter Paul Ruben's 'Miracles of Francis Xavier' and the visual tradition of broken idols," in *Idols and Museum Pieces: The Nature of Sculpture, Its Historiography and Exhibition History 1640–1880*, ed. Caroline van Eck (Berlin and Boston: De Gruyter, 2017), 65–84, esp. 79–81, which also locates Linschoten's illustration as the model for the toppling of the idol in Rubens's *Miracles of Francis Xavier*, without, however, pointing out the different head covering, which corresponds precisely to that in the de Bry version.

[48] Dorothee Schmidt stresses the reticent portrayal by Linschoten/Doetecum and de Bry in comparison to Jörg Breus's illustration of Varthema. See Dorothee Schmidt, *Reisen in das Orientalische Indien: Wissen uber fremde Welten um 1600* (Vienna: Bohlau, 2016), 205. See also Partha Mitter, *Much Maligned Monsters: A History of European Reactions to Indian Art* (Chicago, IL: University of Chicago Press, 1977), 21–22.

[49] For a discussion of the cosmopolitan nature of the Kandyan Kingdom, see Gananath Obeyesekere, "Between the Portuguese and the Nayakas: The many faces of the Kandyan Kingdom, 1591–1765," in *Sri Lanka at the Crossroads of History*, ed. Zoltan Biedermann and Alan Strathern (London: UCL Press, 2017), 161–77, 322, esp. 162–64. A short while later the Dutch introduced strongly anti-Catholic policies in Sri Lanka, which, however, did not really succeed in the long term. Ibid., 165–66.

XXI.

Indianischer Abgott Pagodes/ sampt der Mahometisten Tempel.

Allhie wirt vor augen gestellt die Blindheit der armen Teufelsdiener/ welche bey allẽ Wegen vñ Stegen solche Götzen/ von jhnen Pagodes genennet/ in Felsen gehauwen stehen haben/ vor denen sie jhr Gebett verrichten/ bringen jnen auch mit sonderer andacht/ Opffer/ welche jhre Priester die Brachmanes zu sich ziehen/ vnd als ob dieselbe von den Pagoden verzehrt würden/ vorgeben. Auch ist allhie zusehen ein Indianischer Mahometisten Tempel/ von jhnen Mesquita genañt/ deren es in Indien viel zu viel hat. Bey diesem Tempel steht ein groß Wasserbad/ zu welchem man etliche Staffel hinab gehen muß/ darinnen sie sich/ so offt sie für den Pagode jhr Gebet zuthun kom̃en/ waschen müssen. Weitteren Bescheidt findestu im 43. vnd 44. Capitel dieser Historien.

f ij

Fig 5.8 Johan Theodore and Johan Israel de Bry, *Indiae orientalis*, Germ., vol. 2, Frankfurt am Main, 1598, plate XXI

court to adopt an extremely clear position on the idolatry question. During their visit he and his entourage were shown not only weapons and armour, but also all of the many local pagodas, which were quite lavishly built / with more than four or five thousand carved figures and images / many as high as ship's masts / with special doors of their own, most sumptuously and artfully made of beautiful stones / quite curved / and gilded / that they verily surpass the papist churches / with their fine and handsome construction. After the General had seen all of this / the King asked him what he thought of the churches / and how he liked them /to which he replied / that he greatly preferred living people to the dead images / whom no one could offer any service or friendship / the King asked him whether their churches or pagodas were not / like the Portuguese churches adorned with all manner of pictures / and mentioned many saints such as *Mariam, Petrum, Paulum*, and others as well / and asked whether they believed in Christ? The General replied that they were true Christians / but not papist Roman Christians / like the Portuguese / / and because he wished to know / what they had in their churches / the General showed him a bare wall / but also showed / that they had the true God in their hearts / who had created Heaven and Earth / and all men. The King asked further / whether their God could not die / upon which he was given splendid proof / that no mortal man could be a god / and the General expressly said to him / that his idols and images were vain and useless / since they were all mere portraits of dead people / for which reason the General also admonished him / not to rely on his *pagodas* / but instead upon GOD who had created everything / which the King seemed to understand / and therefore pointed at his palace / and said / God has given me all of this.[50]

[50] Johan Theodore and Johan Israel de Bry, *Indiae orientalis*, vol. 7 (Frankfurt, 1603), 27 under the marginal gloss: "Conversation with the King about the worship service" and "Conversation about God and the idols or images." "deren viel waren fast köstlich gebawet / mit außgehawenen Figuren und Bildern mehr als in die vier oder fünfftausendt / etlich so hoch wie Mastbäume / zuwelchen besondere oder eygene Türne bereytet waren sehr köstlich unnd künstlich von schönen Steinen / gantz gewelbt / unnd vergült / daß sie schier die Bäbstliche Kirchen ubertreffen / wegen ihrer schönen und lustigen Gebäw. Als nuhn der General dieß alles gesehen hatte / fraget ihn der König was er von den Kirchen hielte / unnd wie jhm dieselben gefielen /drauff antwortet er / daß er viel lieber lebendige Luthe sehe als die todte Bilder / so niemandt einigen Dienst und Freundtschafft thun könnten / der König fraget jhn ob jhre Kirchen oder Pagoden nicht auch / wie die Portugesische Kirchen mit allerley Bildern gezieret weren / nannte etlich Heyligen als nemlich Mariam, Petrum, Paulum, unnd andere mehr / fraget auch ob sie an Christum glaubeten? Der General antwortet daß sie Christen weren wahrhafftig / nicht aber bäpstliche Römische Christen / wie die Portugesen / / und weil er wissen wollte / was sie in jhren Kirchen hetten / zeiget ihm der General ein blosse Mawer / zeiget aber darneben an / daß sie in jhren Hertzen heten den warhafftigen Gott / der himmel und Erden / unnd alle Menschen erschaffen hat. Der König fraget weiter / ob jhr Gott nicht sterben könnte / drauff jhm ein herrlicher Beweiß gethan wardt / daß kein sterblicher Mensch ein Gott syn könnte / auch saget jhm der General außtrücklich / daß seine Götzen unnd Bilder umbsonst und vergeblich werden / sintemal so alle nur der verstorbenen Leuthe bildtnüssen weren / derhalben jhn denn der General auch vermahnet / daß er sich nicht auff seine Pagoden solte verlassen / sondern auff GOtt der alles geschaffen hätte / welches denn der König wohl verstanden / zeiget derhalben unnd deutet auff seinen Palast / unnd sagt / dieß hat mir Gott alles gegeben."

Spilbergen's message was that "bare walls," that is walls without images, guaranteed the true form of worship. The worship of "idols and images," in contrast, was worthless, since they were merely "portraits of dead people." If we are to believe the Dutch general, the king of Kandy understood this Calvinist message quite well and understood his palace and with it his success in the struggle for power as a sign of divine predestination. This interpretation by Spilbergen is surprising, however, since King Vimaladharmasūriya fought intensely for the return of the holy tooth relic and its appropriate installation near his palace. The theft of this relic and its destruction by the Portuguese as well as its fraudulent and superstitious restoration by an enterprising "Banian" had already been the subject of another story by Linschoten in the second volume of the *Indiae orientalis* under the heading "On Picoadam mountain there was a temple for a monkey tooth / to which people made pilgrimages."[51]

The example of Spilbergen's real or invented conversation with the king of Kandy neatly underlines the possibilities that accounts of very different cultures offered those who wished to take a position on the highly topical question of the proper or improper veneration of images.

Calvinists Dealing with Idols – A Paradox?

It has become evident thus far that, with their "conscious approach to religious terminology and labelling,"[52] the de Brys contributed quite concretely to the debate on idolatry in their engravings, captions, and paratexts, and thus took a position on the image question that had become so important for Protestants and Catholics in the course of the sixteenth century.

In her analysis of cabinets of curiosities in the second half of the sixteenth century, Carina L. Johnson thoroughly explores the question of the redefinition of idols. Following Trent, she argues, there was a protracted debate on the proper use of images, in which participants such as the Jesuit Bellarmine took a firm Roman stand and attacked the Protestants – chief among them the Calvinists and the iconoclasts they inspired in France and the Netherlands – as merely the most recent group in a 600-year history of diabolically-inspired heresies.[53] Around the same time, in 1587, the Lutheran Gabriel Kaltermarckt argued that God had given the visual arts to humankind together with music because they were especially suited for use in worship, but also particularly susceptible to idolatry. According to Johnson, "Kaltermarckt illustrated this point by

[51] Johan Theodore and Johan Israel de Bry, *Indiae orientalis*, vol. 2, 131–32.
[52] Van Groesen, *Representations*, 258. [53] Johnson, *Cultural Hierarchy*, 241–42.

detailing the errors of others. Catholics and heathen Romans and Greeks produced idols, and Muslims and radical reformers refused any role for the visual arts and thus ignored their divinely supported purposes."[54] The proper use of images was closely linked to the true Lutheran church.[55] Accordingly, cabinets of curiosities associated idolatry more and more with non-European cultures and strictly distinguished the corresponding objects from Christian relics. Thus, in the second half of the sixteenth century, ethnographic texts increasingly emphasized the presence of idolatry as a central aspect of non-European cultures "in the Indies."

In the *Historia Natural y Moral de las Indias*, which the de Brys brought out in 1601 as volume nine in their America series, the Jesuit José de Acosta explicitly addressed the use of man-made images and idols by the indigenous people of America, which he differentiated from animist practices, animal cults, and ancestor worship. Thus he distinguished clearly between the various qualities of representationality, and explained the idolatry of human artifacts as follows: "one of them consists of art and human invention / such as idols of wood / stone, or gold / which are called Mercurius, Pallas, and many other names / which never / existed in Nature / but only in images."[56] The condemnation of this form of veneration of man-made objects was thus rooted in the fact that it did not refer to another, real entity. He then went on to discuss extensively the various forms of indigenous idolatry. He saw the Devil at work everywhere: "When one looks at this all in the proper light/ one finds/ that the Devil has deceived these Indians in the same way / that he led the Greeks / Latins, and ancient pagans astray."[57] To be sure, this comparison between America and classical antiquity allowed him to integrate the New World into his notion of continuously evolving human history in this respect as well. At the same time, however, as he elaborated in a further chapter on "Idolatry" among the Indios of Central and South America, the veneration of images created by human hands should be considered particularly reprehensible:

Idolatry / [is] when pictures, / figures, and such things / made by men of stone, wood, or metal / having no likeness to anything / are worshipped and venerated.....

[54] Ibid., 242.

[55] On the significance of images in Lutheranism, see Bridget Heal, *A Magnificent Faith: Art and Identity in Lutheran Germany* (Oxford: Oxford University Press, 2017).

[56] Theodore de Bry, *Indiae occidentalis*, vol. 9, 187. "eine bestehet in Kunst und Menschlicher Erfindung / als Götzen von Holtz / Stein oder Gold / die da Mercurius, Pallas und dergleichen Namen mehr haben / welche niemals / ohn allein gemahlt / in der Natur gewesen sind."

[57] Theodore de Bry, *Indiae occidentalis*, vol. 9, 190. "Wann einer diß alles recht betrachtet und zu Gemüht führet / befindet er / daß der Teuffel diese Indianer eben auff diese Weise betrogen / wie er die Griechen / Latiner unnd alte Heyden verführet hat."

The Indians have put much effort into making idols and paintings / and in different manners / and from different materials / which they worshipped as God / and called *guacas*: The idols were usually hideous and malformed / at least those we have seen.[58]

He continued: "We also have true accounts / of the Devil speaking from these *guacas* or idols and responding to questions."

This unambiguously branded the improper veneration of things and images as the work of the Devil. Thus, from a Christian viewpoint, the spiritual power of the *huacas* – local gods but also sites and objects possessed of magical demonic powers – was understood as negative and in need of suppressing. Like many other scholars, Acosta elaborated with increasing precision the line between demonically inspired idolatry in the old and new pagan cultures on the one hand, and the proper veneration of images in the Catholic Church on the other.[59] Princely collections like that of Philip II in the Escorial or the Wittelsbachs in Munich, both of which listed idols from the New World in their inventories, played an important role here. In this culture of cabinets of art and curiosities, idols were treated and collected as exotic objects, as Christine Göttler has shown with the example of a Javanese kris that Levinus Hulsius prominently portrayed in the first volume of his travel account.[60] Such exotic artifacts were ever more clearly associated with heathen idolatry and at the same time admired for their artistic quality and excellent craftsmanship.[61] Various art brokers were involved in this trade, including, for example, the Lutheran Philipp Hainhofer, who reported that during his 1603 visit to Munich he had seen "different idols and simulacra of earth and other materials through which (God keep us from him) the Devil had spoken and revealed oracles to the heathen."[62] We know from Hainhofer's correspondence with Wilhelm of Bavaria that the de Bry brothers were also involved in this trade. After the autumn book fair of 1609, he recounted having purchased from the de Brys and other dealers from the Netherlands exotic items such as a "very long snake skin … a little box

[58] Ibid., 198. "Abgötterey / da man Bilder /Figuren und dergleichen Ding / so von Stein Holtz oder Ertz durch Menschen gemacht worden/ und nichts anders alß ein Contrafeyt haben / anbetet und verehrt. …. Die Indier haben sich sehr befliessen Götzen und Gemählte zu machen / unnd solches auff underschiedliche Weise / auch auß underschiedlichen Materien / welches sie für Gott anbetteten / unnd Guacas nenneten: Diese Götzen waren gemeinlich abschewlich und ungestalt / so viel wir deren gesehen haben."

[59] Johnson, *Cultural Hierarchy*, 247.

[60] Christine Göttler, "'Indian Daggers with Idols' in the Early Modern *Constcamer*. Collecting, Picturing, and Imagining 'Exotic' Weaponry in the Netherlands and Beyond," in *Netherlandish Art in Its Global Context*, ed. Eric Jorink, Frits Scholten, and Thijs Weststeijn, *Netherlands Yearbook for History of Art* 66 (2016): 78–109, esp. 100.

[61] See Göttler, "Extraordinary things," esp. 53.

[62] Quoted in Göttler, "Extraordinary things," 49.

with Indian inks" and "fine Indian feathers." Apart from an Indio headdress made of lynx claws, "which they place upon their heads when they wish to engage in a brawl," the unusually long list also included an Indio idol:

An Indian earthen idol with a hole from which they sometimes received answers # all of which several items I bought from the de Brj Hans Heinrich and Israel de Brj, similarly from Jacques de Loufler[??] to whom Clusio and Mr Maggionibus sent it from Holland via the Indian voyages, so that they might engrave it in copper and insert it with the descriptions of the Indian sea voyages. Otherwise there was nothing else of this nature on sale at this fair in Fr[ankfurt], just as de Bry and Loufler did not offer them [at the fair], but let me have them at their houses as a great favour upon my strong urging and for a suitable payment.[63]

The de Brys thus knew of at least a few indigenous artifacts from personal experience. After all, they had received from Clusius and a "mister Maggionibus"[64] in the Netherlands not just an Indian headdress, slippers, and numerous other objects, but also an earthen idol as illustrative material for their engravings. Whether this was an object that the de Brys used to illustrate an indigenous ritual, for example, the veneration of an "idol" by means of a procession complete with a battue and animal sacrifice in South America – which the de Brys presented as the sixth engraving to accompany Acosta's account – remains in question.[65] In any case, the letter from Hainhofer shows that the de Bry brothers were familiar with statues and pictures of indigenous gods not only from books or through hearsay, and were at least occasionally able to use such (collectable) objects as the basis for their engravings.

In a remarkable engraving from volume six of the *Indiae occidentalis*, which deals with the Spanish conquest and pillaging of Peru, Theodore de Bry showed "How splendidly the princes and their courtiers were

[63] HAB, "Copierbuch Copiae der von Philippus Hainhofer an underschiedliche Orth und Personen geschriebenen Briefe," vol II: 1604–1609 (Cod. Guelf. 17.22 Aug. 4°), fol. 226r; "Ain Indianischer Irdiner Itolo mit aim loch aus welchem sie bisweilen responsa gehabt.# welches alles vast mehrerteils Ich von den de Brj Hans Heinrich und Israel de Brj Item von Jacques de Loufler[??] Erkaufft denen es vom Clusio und der Hr. Maggionibus über die indianische schiffarten aus Hollandt zugeschückt worden dz sies solden in kupfer stechen und den indianischen schiffarten beschribungen inserieren lassen. Ist sonsten zu Fr. diese mäs von dergleichen sachen gar nichts feil gewest, wie es dann auch dise de Bry und Loufler nit feil bieten sondern mirs in ihren heusern zu grosem gefallen auf mein starkhes anhalten und gegen gebürliche bezahlung überlassen haben." http://diglib.hab.de/mss/17-22-aug-4f/start.htm?image=00453. I would like to thank Ulinka Rublack for bringing this letter to my attention.

[64] The reading is uncertain.

[65] Hainhofer's concrete description of the clay idol may well awaken associations with the *huacas* and other images of idols that Acosta presented as instruments of the devil in his *Historia natural y moral* and the de Brys included in their illustrations.

buried in the western Indies" (Fig 5.9). Impressively depicting the "golden and silver dishes and whatever other precious gold and silver jewellery he possessed," this image joins the concrete funerary objects for the dead ruler with the longing for the legendary gold treasures of Peru, a false practice of worshiping the dead inspired by the Devil, and the Spanish hope of discovering more such lavish burial objects, which the European collectors of exotica would doubtless have appreciated. The next engraving makes this even clearer: in this image, the de Brys depicted an indigenous goldsmith's workshop, which vividly illustrated, and commented in detail upon the artfulness of the native gold workers in the Inca kingdom (Fig 5.10).

In this engraving that has been compared to craft manuals of the time,[66] we see "artful gold-workers" using an anvil and hammers to produce various objects whose form and size clearly identify them as the Devil's handiwork, destined for idolatrous use.

It is written that King Guaynacapae has in his treasury gigantic images in gold / but hollow inside. / Similarly, four-legged animals cast in gold and silver / birds / trees and plants / and all types of fish / which are found either in the sea / on which his kingdom borders / or in the running waters / that are in his realm. It is written furthermore of a pleasure garden of the Incas, located on an island not far from Puna / to which this same great prince often had himself rowed/ for example to hold banquets and amuse himself / in which the plants / flowers / [and] trees / are all made of gold and silver. And let it be known that the gold-workers have made such things / as columns / pictures / dishes / jewellery / clothing / in short / anything that was asked of them / all to honour the worship of idols /and to adorn their temples with them.[67]

According to the chronicler Pedro Cieza de León, whom de Bry mentions as a source of information in the caption, these indigenous artists could produce fine vessels, small fountains, candlesticks, and the like so artfully with their primitive tools that "our gold workers,

[66] Greve, *Die Konstruktion Amerikas*, 186–89.

[67] Theodore de Bry, *Indiae occidentalis*, vol. 6, German (Frankfurt, 1597), plate xxvii. "Mann schreibet daß der König Guaynacapae in seiner Schatzkammer habe Bilder von Goldt so groß als grosse Risen gehabt / jedoch inwendig hol. / Item von Goldt und Silber abgegossene vierfüssige Thier / Vögel / Bäum und gewächß / deßgleichen aller art Fisch / wie die entweder im selbigen Meer / daran sein Königreich grentzet / oder in den fliessenden wassern / so in seinem Reich sind / gefunden werden. Ferners so schreibt man auch von einem Lustgarten der Ingen, in einer Insel nicht weit von Puna gelegen / dahin sich dieselbige Großfürsten etwan Pancket zu halten unnd zu erlustieren / offtermals uberführen liessen / darinnen die Gewächs / Blummen / Bäume / alle auß Goldt und Silber gmacht gewesen. Unnd ist zu wissen daß die goldtarbeiter dergleichen ding / als Seulen / Bilder / Geschirr / Geschmid / Kleyder / unnd kurtz darvon zu reden / alles was man von jhnen begeret hat / gemacht haben / allein dem Gottesdienst zu ehren / unnd jhre Tempel darmit zu zieren."

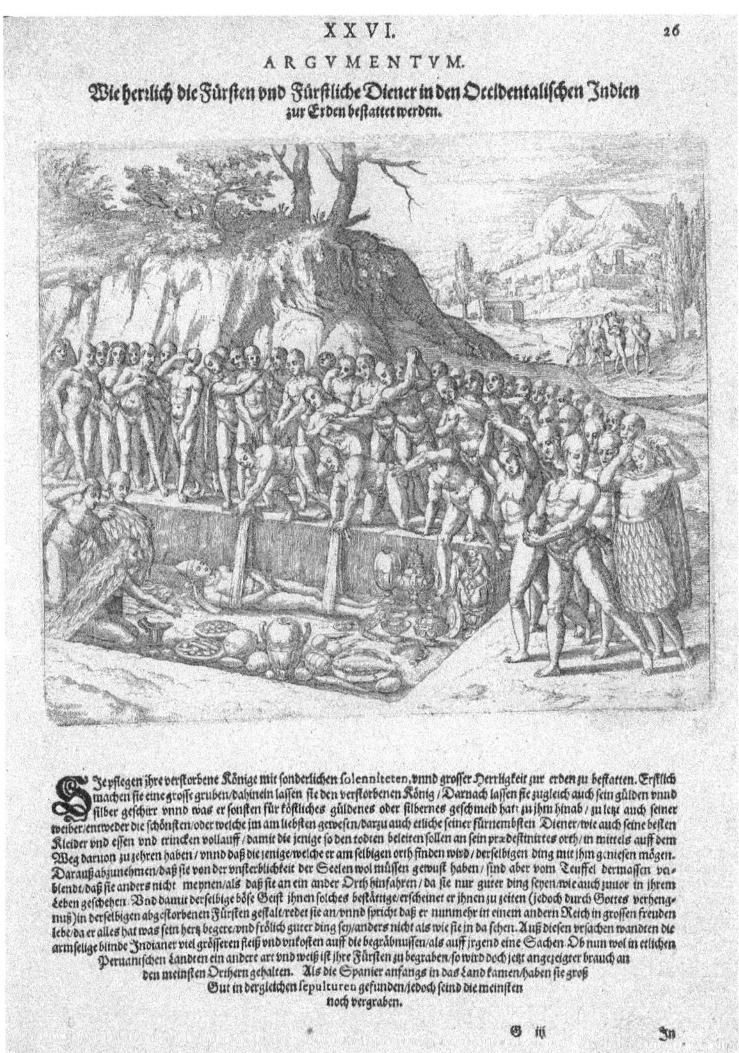

XXVI. 26

ARGVMENTVM.

Wie herrlich die Fürsten vnd Fürstliche Diener in den Occidentalischen Indien zur Erden bestattet werden.

Sie pflegen jhre verstorbene Könige mit sonderlichen solenniteten, vnnd grosser Herrligkeit zur erden zu bestatten. Erstlich machen sie eine grosse gruben/dahinein lassen sie den verstorbenen König / Darnach lassen sie zugleich auch sein gülden vnnd silber geschirr vnnd was er sonsten für köstliches güldenes oder silbernes geschmeid hat: zu jhm hinab / zu letzt auch seiner weiber/entweder die schönsten/oder welche jm am liebsten gewesen/darzu auch etliche seiner fürnembsten Diener/wie auch seine besten Kleider vnd essen vnd trincken vollauff / damit die jenige so den todten beleiten sollen an sein prædestinirtes orth/ in mittels auff dem Weg daruon zu zehren haben / vnnd daß die jenige/welche er am selbigen orth finden wird / derselbigen ding mit jhm geniesen mögen. Darauß abzunehmen/daß sie von der vnsterblichkeit der Seelen wol müssen gewust haben / sind aber vom Teuffel dermassen verblendt/daß sie anders nicht meynen/als daß sie an ein ander Orth hinfahren / da sie nur guter ding seyen/wie auch zuuor in jhrem Leben geschehen. Vnd damit derselbige böse Geist jhnen solches bestättige/erscheinet er jhnen zu zeiten (jedoch durch Gottes verhengnuß)in derselbigen abgestorbenen Fürsten gestalt/redet sie an/vnnd spricht daß er nunmehr in einem andern Reich in grossen freuden lebe/da er alles hat was sein hertz begere/vnd frölich guter ding sey/anders nicht als wie sie jn da sehen. Auß diesen vrsachen wandten die armselige blinde Indianer viel grösseren fleiß vnd vnkosten auff die begräbnussen/als auff jrgend eine Sachen. Ob nun wol in etlichen Peruanischen Landen ein andere art vnd weiß ist jhre Fürsten zu begraben/so wird doch jetzt angezeigter brauch an den meinsten Orthern gehalten. Als die Spanier anfangs in das Land kamen/haben sie groß Gut in dergleichen sepulturen gefunden/jedoch seind die meinsten noch vergraben.

G iij In

Fig 5.9 Theodore de Bry, *Indiae occidentalis*, Germ., vol. 6, Frankfurt am Main 1597, plate XXVI

with all their instruments, could not make more beautiful pieces."[68] European goldsmiths, the Spanish chronicler's somewhat ambivalent statement implies, produced treasures every bit as fabulous as the

[68] Ibid.

XXVII. 27

ARGVMENTVM.

In Peru findet man gar kunstreiche Goldtarbeiter.

EHe dann die Peruaner den Ingis underworffen waren/sind sie bey weitem nicht so kunstreich vnnd zierlich gewesen/Wie wir denn vom Landtvolck selbsten verstanden haben. Demnach aber die Ingæ das ist die Großfürsten vber sie zu gebieten hatten/ seind sie viel kunstreicher vnd Leutseliger worden/denn dieselbige Großfürsten hatten lust zu schönem Haußrath/Monumenten/Seulen vnnd künstlichen Geschirren. Darumb liessen sie hin vnnd wider in jhrem Königreich den Goldtschmiden Werckstette auffrichten/daß sie auß Goldt vnd Silber allerley Geschirr vnd Geschmeidt machten/vnd zwar man hat bey jhnen so kunstreiche vnd meisterliche Geschirr gefunden/daß alle die sie gesehen/sich höchlich darüber haben verwundern müssen/vnnd vmb so viel desto mehr/ weil sie so schlechte vnnd wenig Instrument vnd werckzeug darzu brauchen/vnd alles mit so gar geringer mühe vnnd arbeit zugehet. Wie die Spanier anfangs dasselbige Landt einnamen/hat man so außerlesenes vnd wunderkünstliches Geschirr gesehen/daß Petrus Cieca am hundert vnd viertzehenden Capitel deß ersten theils seiner Peruanischen Chronica nicht darvon schreiben will/weil er sie selbst nicht gesehen hatte. Doch spricht er/darff ich das für eine warheit sagen/wie daß sie nur mit zweyen stücken von Ertz/vnnd auff zweyen oder dreyen schwartzen Steinen haben schöne Gefäß/Brünnlein/Leuchter/ꝛc. so artlich wissen zumachẽ/daß die vnsere Goldtarbeiter mit allen jhren Instrumenten nicht schöner stück köndten zu wegen bringen. Zum schmeltzen brauchen sie nichts anders als einen Ofen von Leimen gemacht/darumbher stehen etliche Mannsperson/so die Kolen im Ofen brennend machen/vnd das Fewer mit holen Rohren/an statt der Blaßbälge anblasen/so lang biß die Materia in dem Hafen zergehet: Dieselbige nemen sie alsdenn herauß/giessen sie in ein Ingoß/biß sie erkaltet/liefern sie alsdann dem Obersten der Goldtschmiden. Mann schreibet daß der König Guaynacapæ in seiner Schatzkammer habe Bilder von Goldt so groß als grosse Risen gehabt/jedoch innwendig hol. Item von Goldt vnd Silber abgegossene vierfüssige Thier/Vögel/Bäum vnd gewächß/deßgleichen aller art Fisch/wie die entweder im selbigen Meer/daran sein Königreich grentzet/oder in den fliessenden wassern/so in seinem Reich sind/gefundẽ werden. Ferners so schreibt man auch von einem Lustgarten der Ingen, in einer Insel nicht weit von Puna gelegen/dahin sich dieselbige Großfürsten etwan Pancket zu halten vnnd zu erlustieren/offtermals vberführen liessen/darinnen die Gewächß/ Blummen/Bäume/alle auß Goldt vnd Silber gemacht gewesen. Vnnd ist zu wissen daß die Goldtarbeiter dergleichen ding/als Seulen/Bilder/Geschirr/Geschmeid/Kleyder/vnnd kurtz darvon zu reden/alles was man von jhnen begeret hat/gemacht haben/allein dem Gottesdienst zu ehren/vnnd jhre Tempel darmit zu zieren.

Fig 5.10 Theodore de Bry, *Indiae occidentalis*, Germ., vol. 6, Frankfurt am Main 1597, plate XXVII

legendary gold workers of Peru, who dedicated their skills to creating objects of idolatrous religious veneration. On an island not far from Puna, these same gold workers had created for the Inca rulers a marvelous and artful world in a pleasure garden, where all the plants, flowers, and trees were made of gold; an El Dorado as it were, dedicated to the worship of idols, as the final sentence of the picture caption does not fail to mention. Artisanal skill and idolatry were thus by no means mutually exclusive in the New World any more than the artful representation of the world as the worship of God was in the Old World. What counted was the proper form, which needed to be maintained in a process of constant effort.

Goldsmiths Creating the Marvelous

In the world of the Calvinist goldsmiths, engravers, and publishers de Bry, the Catholic Church had already relinquished its post-Reformation defensive in image theory and was pursuing an offensive, and increasingly also globally orientated, (Baroque) strategy of visualization. In this new media world, the Protestant de Brys positioned themselves quite confidently on the market as the producers of two richly illustrated travel series that spanned the globe. Much like the indigenous gold workers who artfully emulated flora and fauna in a paradisiacal pleasure garden for their rulers, they saw the particular value of their own work as vividly presenting the miracles of divine Creation to their readers, as they never tired of emphasizing. The world was to be understood as God's wonder. The de Brys accordingly believed that people had the duty to contemplate these wonders and to praise "the wisest Creator." It should be in the interest of each individual "to spread God's wonders / and to make them known far and wide"; a task that, as formulated here, was aimed less at formal proselytizing than at disseminating knowledge (and awareness), as the de Bry travel series sought to do. Accordingly, God had also endowed humans with gifts and "revealed to him, among others, the arts of painting/ engraving / etching / and the kindred arts in order to render his wonders / the more glorious and impressive."[69] And it was precisely in that vein that de Bry's sons saw their specific task as draftsmen and engravers, as they explained in the preface to volume four of the *Indiae orientalis*, which contains the final part of Linschoten's journey together with an account of the first successful

[69] "To the reader," in Johan Theodore and Johan Israel de Bry, *Indiae orientalis*, vol. 4, German (Frankfurt, 1600).

Dutch voyage to the East Indies in 1598. There they elaborated further on the significance of their art:

> The LORD GOD, however, has revealed to Man / the art of painting among others / also engraving, etching, and their allied arts / to render his wonders more sightly / because things can be placed before our eyes thereby / that occurred many thousands of miles away / which would otherwise likely remain hidden from us / for although they /can be revealed to us many times in print / they nevertheless remain dead or obscure / if they are not illuminated and brought to life through this art / especially since figurative depiction can place everything before our eyes / as if we were present in these places ourselves and saw everything personally with our own eyes.[70]

This was a remarkable address to the "benevolent reader." This statement about the significance that the de Brys accorded the quality of the images they produced was at once complex and ambiguous. The de Brys, both father and sons, repeatedly stressed the special visual quality of their travel collections, which were distinguished from other travel accounts precisely because of their unusual illustrations. In the above-cited preface to volume four of the *Indiae orientalis* series, the brothers de Bry, even went one step further and declared the superiority of images in general, which they believed were more capable than words of bringing places and events to life. This potential of pictures turned readers into eyewitnesses, and at the same time transformed artists/engravers into the creators of living beings, or at least into those who brought them to life. Accordingly, it was the particular skill of the engravers that lent their pictures an almost magical quality as media, while at the same time placing them in notable proximity to the idolatrous practices of other peoples.

This is quite remarkable, since the veneration of images has doubly negative connotations in these texts: as several key scenes show, idolatry separates pagans from Christians. But it is also the object of the Protestant critique of false Catholic practices. The above-cited preface to volume

[70] Ibid. "Es hat GOTT der HERR den Menschen unter andern / auch die Kunst des Malens / Kunststechens Reyssens und deren verwanten Künsten geoffenbaret dadurch seine Wunderwerck / ansehenlicher zu machen sintemahl hiedurch können für Augen gestellt werden solche dinge die uber viel tausent Meilen zusehen / sich zugetragen und geschehen seynd / welche uns sonst wol verborgen blieben / dann ob wol dieselben / etlicher massen auch durch den Truck der Schrifft können offenbar gemacht werden / so bleiben sie doch gleichsam Tod oder verfinstert / wann sie nicht durch diese Kunst illuminiret und gleichsam lebendig gmacht werden / sintemahlen durch die figürliche Abbildung uns alles dermassen für Augen gestellt werden kann / als wann wir an den Orten selbst zugegen weren und alles Persönlich mit unsern Augen selber sehen." See also Schmidt, *Reisen in das Orientalische Indien*, 186.

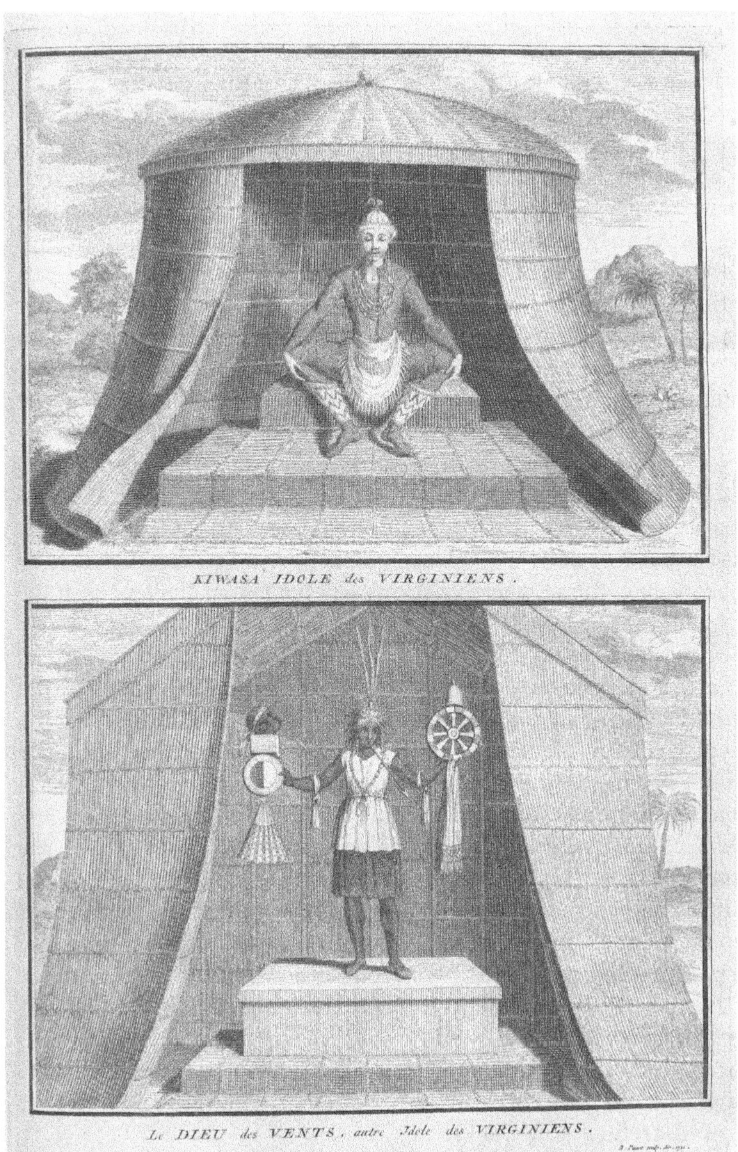

Fig 5.11 Bernard Picart, *Cérémonies et coutumes religieuses de tous les peuples du monde*, 1723

four of the *Indiae orientalis* appears to bring the de Brys quite close to the Catholic artists of the post-Tridentine *Ecclesia triumphans* with their new image offensive.[71] The aforementioned critique of the Christian veneration of images in the preface to the second volume of the *Indiae orientalis* gains particular significance against this backdrop. There, an Indian Muslim confronted Linschoten and his Portuguese companion about the actually pagan nature of venerating religious images, which are thereby granted an honour reserved for Almighty God alone. The biblical injunction against graven images appears to bring Muslims and Calvinists remarkably close together here. If we follow the de Bry brothers' further comments on the edifying religious significance of pictures, it would seem that by publishing the story of the Indian Muslim's critique, the enterprising Protestant publishers managed the double feat of criticizing the Catholic practice of venerating images while simultaneously distancing themselves from a rigid Calvinist contempt for pictures, which all too easily led its proponents into a false proximity to the Muslim prohibition of images. In this way, the de Brys positioned their pictorial policy, which they characterized as edifying, at least indirectly within a complex field of tension between confessional restrictions and the global challenges of the theory of images.

This brings me to my conclusion: If they wished to be successful on the European market, Calvinist goldsmiths and publishers like the de Brys had to adopt a rather paradoxical stance, at once positioning themselves critically towards idolatry and emphasizing the particular significance of the skillful artistic portrayal of God's wonders. With these two operations, the de Brys made room for a more or less explicitly Calvinist coding of the European pictorial archive of early globalization – one that would prove extraordinarily successful in the long term. Thus it is not surprising that even in the eighteenth century, the French Jesuit Joseph-François Lafitau in his *Customs of the American Indians compared with customs of primitive times* and the French Protestant and religious refugee Bernard Picart in *The religious ceremonies and customs of all the peoples of the world*, both producing ethnographic texts fundamental for the development of the study of comparative religions in Europe,[72] cited extensively from the de Bry pictorial archive (Fig 5.11).

[71] Johnson, *Cultural Hierarchy*, 256–57.

[72] Philippe Borgeaud and Sara Petrella, *Le signe de l'autre. Du sauvage américain à l'histoire comparée des religions* (Paris: Les éditions des Cendres, 2016); Lynn Hunt, Margaret C. Jacob, and Wijnand Mijnhardt, *The Book that changed Europe. Picart & Bernard's Religious ceremonies of the world* (Cambridge, MA: Belknap Press at the University of Harvard Press, 2010).

6 "Better the Turk than the Pope": Calvinist Engagement with Islam in Southeast Asia

Charles H. Parker

The historical convergence of the Protestant Reformation in Europe with the increased tempo of long-distance trade and empire building in Asia, Africa, and America globalized religious struggles in the sixteenth and seventeenth centuries. Ottoman expansion in eastern Europe and north Africa presented Protestants with geopolitical opportunities to gain military leverage against their Habsburg enemies. Ottoman sultans offered alliances and support to European states and dynasties, Protestant or not, to counter Habsburg attempts at political and religious hegemony. Francis I, most Catholic king of France, allied with Sultan Sulieman I in 1536 to dilute Habsburg forces in northern Italy, Naples, and Navarre. Almost seventy years later, Calvinist (Reformed Protestant) nobles in Hungary and Transylvania found the Ottomans a useful countervailing force against Emperor Rudolph II's centralizing campaigns. The Dutch and English also sought out military and commercial ties with the Sublime Port in wars resisting Spanish sovereignty.[1]

Political maneuvers such as these necessarily inserted the religion of "the Turk" into Reformation debates. Coining the term "Turco-Calvinism," Catholic critics implicated Calvinist religious teachings in the agreeable relations that Hungarian, Dutch, and English diplomats forged with the Ottoman Empire.[2] Just as Catholic writers painted Protestants with a Muslim brush, Martin Luther lumped "papists" together with Turks and Jews as unreformed people of the book; John

[1] Graeme Murdock, *Calvinism on the Frontier 1600–1660: International Calvinism and the Reformed Church in Hungary and Transylvania* (Oxford: Oxford University Press, 2000), 27; Mehmet Bulut, *Ottoman-Dutch Economic Relations in the Early Modern Period, 1571–1699* (Hilversum: Verloren, 2001), 108–109.

[2] Frédérique Guerin, "Re-Orienting the Reformation? Prolegomena to a History of the Reformation's Connection to the Islamic World," in *The Role of the Arab-Islamic World in the Rise of the West: Implications for Contemporary Trans-Cultural Relations*, ed. Nayef R. F. Al-Rodhan (New York: Palgrave Macmillan, 2012), 46.

Calvin categorized them all as blasphemers.[3] Dutch Calvinists contrasted the tyranny of Catholic powers with the religious tolerance of the Ottomans. With this polemical point in mind, the Sea Beggars that spearheaded the naval campaigns against Spain in the 1560s made the phrase "better the Turk than the Pope" a rallying cry against their Catholic enemies.[4]

Not only did Islam figure into the Reformation in Europe, but Protestant merchants, missionaries, and travelers also encountered Muslims, along with Hindus and Buddhists, across the global sea lanes. These interactions compelled Protestants not only to articulate a conception of Christianity that explained the permanence of Roman Catholicism, but they also had to construct a global vision that accounted for the prevalence of Islam and other religious traditions. Susanna Burghartz's essay in this volume illustrates quite vividly how the de Bry family in *India occidentalis* and *India orientalis* sought to insert Calvinism into the newly imagined global spaces.[5] This wider world presented both opportunities and threats. Calvinists in the Netherlands, as other religious leaders, recognized that Islam appealed to many Christians, which raised anxieties about conversions to Islam, styled as "Turning Turk."[6] This concern prompted the humanist and jurist Hugo Grotius to compose a treatise (*On the Truth of the Christian Religion*, 1627) to help Dutch seafarers defend their faith. Engaging Islam emerged as a formidable task for Calvinist theologians in the Netherlands and missionary pastors in the Dutch East India Company (VOC) in the seventeenth and eighteenth centuries.[7]

Recent scholarship has captured the ambiguous and shifting attitudes by Protestant writers about Islam and the Ottoman Empire. Anxieties about an impending apocalypse and divine wrath directed against wayward Christians dominated writings on the Turk among Protestants from Martin Luther to Menno Simons. At the same time, Adam Francisco has argued that Luther took a "subtly-nuanced approach towards the Muslim

[3] Ina Baghdiantz McCabe, *Orientalism in Early Modern France: Eurasian Trade, Exoticism, and the Ancien Regime* (New York: Bloomsbury Academic, 2008), 34; Carina L. Johnson, *Cultural Hierarchy in Sixteenth-Century Europe: The Ottomans and Mexicans* (Cambridge: Cambridge University Press, 2011), 66, 185.

[4] Alexander H. de Groot, *The Ottoman Empire and the Dutch Republic: A History of the Earliest Diplomatic Relations, 1610–1630* (Leiden: Brill, 1978), 85.

[5] See Susanna Burghartz's contribution in Chapter 5 of this volume.

[6] Nabil Matar, *Islam in Britain, 1558–1685* (Cambridge: Cambridge University Press, 1998), 19, 21–50; Maartje van Gelder, "The Republic's Renegades: Dutch Converts to Islam in Seventeenth-Century Diplomatic Relations with North Africa," *Journal of Early Modern History* 19/2(2015): 186–88; Karel A. Steenbrink, *De Islam bekeken door koloniale Nederlanders* (Utrecht: IIMO, 1991),125–42.

[7] Hugo Grotius, *De veritate religionis Christianae*, 2nd ed. (Leiden, 1629).

world": refuting its errors but praising the morals of Muslims over and above Christian piety. Over the course of the sixteenth century, the increasingly rigid and violent religious differences in Europe also produced hostile and exclusionary attitudes towards Ottomans. Susan Boettcher has characterized the sermons of the Lutheran pastor, Jacob Andreae, in 1568 as an orientalist construction of Islam drawn from a Christian medieval tradition. Nevertheless, the literary scholars Daniel Vitkus and Nabil Matar have provided ample evidence of positive appraisals of Turkish discipline and moral order in English literature of the period.[8]

The sustained engagement of Dutch Calvinists with Islam provides a means with which to analyze Protestant perceptions by those who actually traveled and resided in Muslim lands for extended periods. Embedded within the VOC, hundreds of Calvinist missionary pastors engaged in direct and sustained contact with Muslims in Southeast Asia during the period of company rule. These pastors, and even more chaplains, went to the East Indies to establish Protestant communities not altogether unlike the English ones David Hall examines in Chapter 2.[9] Dutch pastors also attempted to spread Protestant Christianity into the region by trying to convert Muslims and to establish a Christian republic in colonial territories. These church figures and company employees kept records, sometimes reported on their experiences, and corresponded with colleagues in the Netherlands about the problems they faced.[10] Pastors and theologians back home responded by writing treatises against Islam, retooling training for prospective missionaries, and advising overseas ministers about pastoral problems. These sources indeed point to the fluidity of Calvinist attitudes about Islam and Muslims during the tenure of company rule.

My research suggests that Calvinists in Southeast Asia and the Netherlands went through several phases in their attitudes about Islam and in their religious encounters with Muslims. In the period of initial encounter, roughly from the 1610s to the 1640s, Calvinists went into the

[8] Adam S. Francisco, *Martin Luther and Islam: A Study in Sixteenth-Century Polemics and Apologetics* (Leiden: Brill, 2007), 3; Susan R. Boettcher, "German Orientalism in the Age of Confessional Consolidation: Jacob Andreae's Thirteen Sermons on the Turk," *Comparative Studies of South Asia, Africa and the Middle East* 24 (2004): 101–15; Carina L. Johnson, *Cultural Hierarchy in Sixteenth-Century Europe: The Ottomans and Mexicans* (Cambridge: Cambridge University Press, 2011), 15–16; Daniel J. Vitkus, "Early Modern Orientalism: Representations of Islam in Sixteenth-and Seventeenth-Century Europe," in *Western Views of Islam in Medieval and Early Modern Europe*, ed. David Blanks and Michael Frassetto (New York: Palgrave Macmillan, 1999), 207–30.

[9] See David D. Hall's contribution in Chapter 2 of in this volume.

[10] Correspondence between overseas and Dutch churches can be found in Stadsarchief Amsterdam, 379 Archief van de Classis Amsterdam (hereafter SA 379), nrs. 157–240; Zeeuws Archief, 28.1 Classis Walcheren, nrs. 65–70, 73.

mission field with a dismissive attitude towards Islam, expecting large-scale conversions upon preaching the Word of God. The failure to convert large numbers of Muslims in the second half of the seventeenth century prompted serious historical and theological considerations of Islam in the Netherlands. This examination led to a translation movement in the mission field, focusing on biblical texts and culminating in a Malay Bible in the early 1700s. Ongoing missionary activity and detailed linguistic study of Islamic texts by Adriaan Reland, a Dutch orientalist, and others ultimately produced a more informed and less hostile view of the religion. These changes in outlook suggest the importance of global interactions in the development of Calvinist ideas and reinforce this volume's call to contextualize Protestantism in a world historical framework.

Mission and Empire in Asia

Long distance trade and empire formed the most important contexts in which Calvinists from the Netherlands encountered and interacted with Muslim peoples. At the end of the sixteenth century, merchant groups in Amsterdam financed voyages to the East Indies (today Indonesia) in order to acquire fine spices (cloves, nutmeg, and mace) at their points of production. These syndicates joined forces in 1602 to create the Dutch East India Company, which the States General awarded exclusive rights to commerce in Asia. Shortly thereafter, VOC admirals forced their way into the Moluccan Islands and Java, displacing their Portuguese and English rivals. In May 1619, the VOC Governor-General Jan Pieterszoon Coen defeated the prince of Jayawikarta and made the factory at Jakarta on the island of Java the headquarters of VOC operations in Asia. During the course of the seventeenth century, the Dutch commercial empire comprised territorial holdings across the East Indies, Formosa, Ceylon, and the Cape of Good Hope.[11]

Though trading companies enabled Calvinism to go global, they also constrained the extent of Christian mission to Muslims and other groups. The unequivocal purpose of the VOC was trade, thus the pursuit of profit ordered the priorities of all Dutch activities overseas. This overriding rationale for empire, combined with the small number of clergy available for overseas service, kept the scope of Calvinist missions much leaner and

[11] Luc Nagtegaal, *Riding the Dutch Tiger: the Dutch East Indies Company and the Northeast Coast of Java, 1680–1743*, trans. Beverley Jackson (Leiden: Koninklijk Instituut Voor Taal en Volkenkunde Land, 1996), 142–70; Leonard Blussé, *Rivalry and Conflict: European Traders and Asian Trading Networks in the 16th and 17th Centuries* (Leiden: Leiden University Press, 2005), 78–82, 95–102.

more uneven than the massive efforts of the Catholic religious orders in the Portuguese, Spanish, and French empires.[12] Missionary pastors regularly complained that the company needed to recruit more extensively, quoting the gospel passage, "the harvest is abundant, but the laborers are few."[13]

These constraints and the complaints of pastors about corporate miserliness have led many historians to conclude that the Dutch in general and the VOC in particular cared little for missionary activity.[14] Yet also across the Moluccan Islands, Banda, and Java, many local village elders formed alliances with the VOC and permitted churches and schools designed to spread the Calvinist faith. Company objectives aligned perfectly with Calvinist conversion efforts with one sizeable category of peoples in the East Indies: those who had been baptized by Catholic priests. Jesuits in territories claimed previously by the Portuguese baptized large numbers of adults and children. The VOC feared these baptized Catholics would remain loyal to the Portuguese, so company officials encouraged missionary pastors to proselytize among Catholics in the East Indies.[15]

Calvinist pastors in Amsterdam and Middleburg (Zeeland) were among the most enthusiastic promoters of a mercantile empire; a number of them invested heavily in the VOC and later in the Dutch West India Company (WIC). Pieter Plancius, Werner Helmichius, Jacob Arminius, and others saw a providential hand in the formation of the trade companies to carry "true" biblical Christianity to the ends of the earth. The directors of the VOC, the *Heren Zeventien*, consented to sponsor and send pastors and chaplains to their overseas outposts.[16] The primary purpose of these ministers was to serve in a pastoral role for company employees.

[12] L. J. Joosse, "De Kerk onder de Compagnie," in *Het Indisch Sion: De Gereformeerde Kerk onder de Verenigde Oost Indische Compagnie*, ed. G. J. Schutte (Hilversum: Verloren, 2002), 51–56.

[13] For examples, see SA 379, nr. 185, Oost-Indien, December 22, 1643, nr. 164, Amsterdam, October 26, 1652; nr. 169, Amsterdam, December 23, 1714; Hendrik E. Niemeijer and Th. Van den End eds., *Bronnen betreffende Kerk en School in de gouvernementen Ambon, Ternate en Banda ten tijde van de Verenigde Oost-Indische Compagnie 1605–1791* (hereafter *ATB*) 4 vols. (The Hague: Sidestone Press, 2015), 1: 290 (September 20, 1656); Nationaal Archief (The Hague), 11160 Minuut-missiven van de Classis Walcheren aan de kerkeraden in Indie, 1690–1722, folio 115r, 1691.

[14] Charles R. Boxer, *The Dutch Seaborne Empire 1600–1800* (London: Knopf 1965), 156–66; Jean Gelman Taylor, *The Social World of Batavia: European and Eurasian in Dutch Asia* (Madison: University of Wisconsin Press, 1983), 22–23.

[15] Carel Wessel Theodorus Baron van Boetzelaer van Asperen en Dubbledam, *De Protestantsche Kerk in Nederlandsch- Indië: Haar Ontwikkeling van 1620–1939* (The Hague: Nijhoff, 1947), 31.

[16] Rudolf Barteld Evenhuis, *Ook Dat was Amsterdam*, 2 vols. (Amsterdam: Ten Have, 1967), 2: 322–23; Boetzelaer, *Protestantsche Kerk*, 12.

Yet the pastors who went overseas also served as missionaries with a self-proclaimed divine mandate to convert pagans, Catholics, Moors, and Jews to Protestant Christianity. Over the course of the seventeenth and eighteenth centuries, close to 1,000 missionary pastors and many more lay chaplains in the pay of the East and West India companies went into the territories that comprised the Dutch commercial empire.[17] These ministers, most of whom were trained in Dutch universities, set up churches, organized and oversaw schools, preached, catechized, and translated religious materials into native languages. As a result of these efforts, thousands of non-Europeans became members of the Dutch Reformed Church. These efforts suggest that Dutch political and religious figures saw no inherent conflict between trading, empire building, and Christianizing. A more historical approach needs to understand a Calvinist sense of mission to Muslims, pagans, Jews, and Catholics within the contexts of trade and empire.

Islam in Southeast Asia

Muslim traders and Sufi divines had set down firm religious roots in the East Indies long before the arrival of Europeans, though Islamic observances varied significantly across the cultural landscape of Southeast Asia. The arrival of Islam into the region occurred intermittently and randomly between the thirteenth and sixteenth centuries. Muslim merchants from India, China, and Arabic-speaking lands traded at commercial sites along the coast of Sumatra, Malaya, East Java, and the straits of Melaka. Many of them settled locally, married, and spread their influence and religion among the inhabitants. Thus, international trade was a critical factor in the introduction and diffusion of Islam across the East Indies. A number of these foreign merchants belonged to mystical and eclectic Sufi orders that incorporated local shrines, holy figures, and observances into Islam. By the time of Tomé Pires, the Portuguese apothecary who wrote *Suma Oriental* based on his experiences in Melaka between 1512 and 1515, most of the rulers of Sumatra and Aceh were Muslim. Islamization proceeded apace throughout the sixteenth century, so that by the arrival of the Dutch, West Java (including

[17] Boxer placed the number of overseas pastors at "nearly 1,000" without specifying the evidence for his estimate. F. A. van Lieburg explicitly identified 650 who worked for the VOC. If we include pastors in the Atlantic and allow for a number not specifically mentioned in the sources, it seems that somewhere between 700 and 1,000 is a judicious approximation. Boxer, *Seaborne Empire*, 149; Frederik A. van Lieburg, "Het personeel van de Indische Kerk: een kwantitatieve benadering," in *Het Indisch Sion*, 65–101.

Jakarta), the Moluccan Islands, Banda, Ternate, and Tidore all had either Muslim rulers and/or sizeable Muslim populations.[18]

Acceptance of Islam facilitated trade in Southeast Asia, yet conversion did not usually entail a transformative displacement of one's previous religious and cultural practices. Michael Pearson has observed that "Muslim proselytizers succeeded in part because they did not press too hard, but rather were prepared to tolerate 'deviations,' and a rather syncretic form of Islam."[19] Sufis and practitioners of Sufiism embraced many local aspects of folklore and observance, which alleviated the demands and perplexities of adopting an exclusive religious creed. Theorists studying conversion in Asia and Africa have defined a "two-tier" cosmology envisaged by converts that historians have utilized to describe the mystic synthesis between Islam and traditional practices. The lower tier apprehended the realm of local mediating spirits and forces, while the higher tier acknowledged a transcendent supreme being.[20] And to complicate the situation further, a number of these people, as we have seen, had been baptized by Portuguese Jesuits. Dutch missionary pastors certainly had their work cut out for them.

Initial Engagements

For the first thirty years or so that Dutch missionaries operated in Southeast Asia, they demonstrated a heady optimism that large numbers of Muslims (as well as pagans and Jews) would convert to Christianity. This confidence stemmed from a millenarian reading of recent history within Dutch Calvinism in the 1600s. According to this view, the Reformation had reestablished the practice of true, biblical Christianity in Europe. And with the launching of the East and West India companies, the gospel would be proclaimed in the four corners of the world. In March 1622, for example, the missionary Adriaan Hulsebos proclaimed that "the Lord by one means or the other and at some time will be pleased to call many moors and heathens into belief and eternal salvation ..."[21]

[18] Merle Calvin Ricklefs, *A History of Modern Indonesia c. 1200 to the Present* (Bloomington: Indiana University Press, 1981), 6–11; *Mystic Synthesis in Java: A History of Islamization from the Fourteenth to the Early Nineteenth Centuries* (Norwalk, CT: EastBridge, 2006), 17–22; Anthony Reid, "The Islamization of Southeast Asia," in *Historia: Essays in Commemoration of the 25th Anniversary of the Department of History, University of Malaya*, ed. Muhammad Abu Bakar et al. (Kuala Lumpur: University of Malaya, 1984), 14–17, 23.

[19] Michael N. Pearson, "Conversions in South-east Asia: Evidence from the Portuguese Records," *Portuguese Studies* 6(1990): 54.

[20] Ricklefs, *Mystic Synthesis*, 21–22; Pearson, "Conversions," 54.

[21] SA 379, nr. 184, Oost-Indien, March 17, 1622; see also SA 379, nr. 184, Oost-Indien, August 20, 1624.

Thirty years later, another Reformed pastor even predicted that "God has not been pleased until this time to reveal the saving knowledge of his Son to China and the many lands of the East and West Indies. So now God will … . accomplish the final conversion of the heathens, in order to make the Jews jealous" and turn to God.[22] Throughout the first half of the seventeenth century, Calvinists involved in overseas missions continued to use buoyant expressions predicting an ample harvest of souls.[23]

Dutch Calvinists in the early period of missions exhibited a rudimentary understanding of Islam, but gave little attention to its theological concepts. In fact, the soon-to-be missionary Justus Heurnius wrote in a 1618 missionary manifesto that effective evangelism did not require knowledge in letters or philosophy, but only faith in God's power to save. Heurnius even dismissed the linguistic difficulty of mission, citing the presence of the Holy Spirit who gave the apostles the power to speak in many languages at Pentecost.[24] Grotius advocated strongly for missions and wrote *On the Truth of Christianity* (mentioned in the introduction) to support the "propagation of the gospel." His treatment of Islam made no mention of Islamic theology, but simply repeated the polemical tropes of medieval and contemporary writers. Grotius attacked Muhammad as a thoroughly evil and insatiably lustful figure and assailed Islam as a coercive and bellicose religion. The precepts that Grotius identified were revenge, divorce, polygamy, circumcision, prohibition of alcohol. For Grotius and other Calvinists, the only theological aspect of Islam worth stating was that it was "contrary to the law of Moses and the disciples of Jesus."[25] Likewise, the Reformed theologian Johannes Cocceius composed an *Oration on the Religion of the Turks* in 1625, in which he regarded Islam as the scourge of God to call Christians to repentance. The central premise underlying Islam, according to Cocceius, was lust and sensuality. He believed that once the Word of God went forth into the world, converts would stream into Christianity one hundred-fold.[26]

22 Abrahamus Rogerius, *Het Open-deur tot het Verborgen Heydendom* (Leiden, 1651), 2 (unpaginated preface). Jacob Sceperus, a pastor in Gouda, wrote the preface.

23 For examples, see SA 379, nr. 163, Amsterdam, July 6, 1637; December 12, 1641; November 26, 1647; SA 379, nr. 185, Oost-Indien, October 7, 1650; June 9, 1651; SA 379, nr. 186, Oost-Indien, January 20, 1662; September 8, 1663; SA 379, nr. 168, Amsterdam, May 12, 1682; SA 379, nr. 201 Ceylon, January 19, 1689, August 6, 1690; SA 379, nr. 167, Amsterdam, October 2, 1786.

24 Justus Heurnius, *De Legatione Evangelica ad Indos Capessenda Admonitio* (Leiden, 1618), 39–46.

25 Grotius, *Veritate*, 215–17, 220–27.

26 Johannes Cocceius, *Rede over de Godsdienst der Turken*, in *Liever Turks dan Paaps? De visies van Johannes Cocceejus, Gisbertus Voetius en Adrianus Relandus op de Islam*, ed. Jacobus van Amersfoort and Willem J. van Asselt (Zoetermeer: Boekencentrum, 1997) 37, 39, 46–47, 52.

Though Calvinists anticipated a bountiful harvest of souls, they did not seem to think it necessary to contest Muslims theologically. In a revealing conversation with a group of Muslim political leaders, the Calvinist pastor Melchior Meinertszoon tended to avoid discussing Muslim teachings and their relationship to Christian beliefs. In December 1622, he described in detail his attempt to convert Muslim elders on the island of Rosengein (Banda Islands). At one point in the dialogue, an elder asked him what he knew about Islam. Meinertszoon answered that Muslims believed in Muhammad rather than Christ and the Qur'an rather than the Bible. He added that Muslims practiced circumcision and polygamy and abstained from pork and alcohol. Finally, Meinertszoon noted that he "found it advisable to speak no longer of this religion and of all the foul deeds … of Mohammed."[27]

The meager crop of souls gave rise to steady complaints among Calvinists that Muslims were among the most obstinate opponents (along with Jews) of the Christian faith. In August 1625, Anthony Dircksen in Banda wrote to Jakarta that "Moors had little in interest in Christendom."[28] Around the same time, Adriaan Hulsebos in Amboina claimed that many heathens were coming to the Christian faith, but there had been hardly any Moors who had converted to Christianity. Though it is true that few Muslims converted to Calvinism in Southeast Asia, Hulsebos certainly exaggerated the situation, for adults and children from Islamic backgrounds did undergo baptism and affiliate with the Reformed Church in varying degrees.[29]

The conversions that did take place originated usually over the need to legitimize a partnered sexual relationship. Very few European women migrated to VOC territories and company employees sought sexual relationships among local women with widespread reports of prostitution and concubinage; in many circumstances men purchased enslaved women for sex and employed them as prostitutes. In addition, Asian Christians, baptized by Jesuits, engaged in sexual relations with non Christians, many of whom were Muslim. In this environment, Dutch churches struggled to impose Christian norms on marriage and sexuality, requiring Muslims to convert, ideally before they married Christians. There are numerous church records referring to Muslim men seeking to marry

[27] SA379, nr. 184, Oost-Indien, December 27, 1622.

[28] Jakob Mooij ed., *Bouwstoffen voor de geschiedenis der protestantsche kerk in Nederlandsche Indië*, 3 vols. (Batavia: Weltevreden, 1927), 1: 221 (September 25, 1625).

[29] See for example, Mooij, *Bouwstoffen*, 1:149 (February 3, 1621), 222 (October 9, 1625).

Christian women and of church officers requiring a cohabitating couple to marry and the non-Christian partner to convert.[30]

Frustration and Resilience on the Mission Field

It had become apparent to Dutch Calvinists around midcentury that converting heathens and Moors was going to be a long, hard slog. Reformed congregations remained small, company officers and pastors clashed over the mission, and converts often seemed equivocal about the new faith. Over 5,000 Formosans had undergone baptism in the first decades of the mission there, though by the 1650s ministers were complaining consistently about backsliding converts. The Reformed faith was advancing more slowly and unevenly in Ceylon, the Cape of Good Hope, and Brazil than missionaries had hoped.[31] At this point of transition in Dutch expectations, a number of theologians in the Netherlands and missionaries in Asia began to compose accounts of Asian religions to equip pastors in the field more ably and to explain the nature of false worship more comprehensively. Leiden University had boasted renowned orientalists since the late sixteenth century, including Joseph Scaliger, Thomas Erpenius, and Jacob Golius; it also owned an extensive collection of Arabic manuscripts. Yet they labored in the service of linguistics rather than mission.[32] Gisbert Voetius and Johannes Hoornbeeck were the first Calvinist theologians in the Netherlands to take up academic study of Islam to prepare pastors for the mission field. Their efforts and their writings provide insight into an important transition in Calvinism's engagement with and understanding of Islam.

The most influential Dutch Calvinist theologian in the seventeenth century, Gisbert Voetius taught and wrote in the theology faculty at the University of Utrecht from 1634 to just before his death in 1676. He was an unswerving orthodox Calvinist, and one of the most prolific theological writers of his day. Voetius championed Calvinist missions and produced the first comprehensive theology of missions among Reformed

[30] For a few examples, see *ATB* 1:1, 84–86 (September 5, 1625), 248 (May 28, 1645), 267 (May 1, 1649), 328 (September 26, 1667), 408 (April 28, 1673); SA379, nr. 184, Oost-Indien, May 1, 1622; August 10, 1622; June 6, 1623, August 21, 1623; Mooij, *Bouwstoffen*, 1: 222 (October 9, 1622), 277 (February 4, 1627).

[31] "Formosa Consistory to Amsterdam Classis, November 3, 1648," in *Formosa under the Dutch: From Contemporary Records*, ed. William Campbell (London: SMC, 1903), 236–44; Hendrik E. Niemeijer, *Calvinisme en koloniale stadscultuur: Batavia, 1619–1725* (Amsterdam: Vrije Universiteit te Amsterdam, 1996), 174; SA 379, nr. 212, Brasilia, November 23, 1649; S. D. Franciscus, *Faith of Our Fathers: History of the Dutch Reformed Church in Sri Lanka (Ceylon)* (Colombo: Pragna, 1982), 4–7.

[32] Alastair Hamilton, "The Study of Islam in Early Modern Europe," *Archiv für Religionsgeschichte* 3(2001): 174–76.

Protestants.[33] A student of Voetius and a like-minded theologian, Johannes Hoornbeeck matriculated into the University of Utrecht in 1633 and taught on the faculty alongside Voetius from 1644 to 1654, after which he took a position at the University of Leiden. Hoornbeeck also developed a strong interest in missions, composing a number of works tracing the history of what he believed was a universal pagan lineage and offering a theological analysis of it.[34]

Both Voetius and Hoornbeeck took up a comprehensive examination and refutation of Islam in the 1650s. Voetius had studied Arabic and the Qur'an even before coming to Utrecht and once there he lectured regularly on Islam. Voetius wrote *On Muhammedanism* at the request of his students because they "would come into contact" with Muslims in Hungary, Transylvania, and the East Indies. He noted that missionaries going out into Asia needed advanced preparation to confront the Islamic challenge and to convert Muslims.[35] His text was based on a disputation he held for students on March 25, 1648, which he edited in 1653 and eventually published in 1655 as part of a theological compendium, *Select Disputations*. Hoornbeeck devoted a very long chapter (roughly 135 pages) to Islam in a 1653 work, *Summa on Controversies with Infidels, Heretics, and Schismatics*, that critiqued Catholicism, "paganism," Anabaptism, Socinianism, and other manifestations of religious error. Thus, Voetius and Hoornbeeck were writing refutations of Islam at the same time. Though they did not cite one another, their arguments against Islam bore strong similarities and shaped a generation of students.

These writings taken together signified a transition in Dutch Calvinism's response to Islam. From the mid-1600s on, Reformed clergy took a less certain attitude about converting Muslims and, following the lead of Voetius and Hoornbeeck, began to engage with Muslim theology seriously. Voetius argued that in order to defeat Islam, Protestant Christendom needed the equivalent of a Collegium Romanum devoted to the study of the Qur'an in Arabic and to train Calvinist missionaries and pastors. Lamenting the lack of study of eastern languages in Europe, he called for building a library of Muslim writings in their original languages. Voetius recommended that students study Arabic, philosophy,

33 Jan A. B. Jongeneel, "Voetius' zendingstheologie, de eerste comprehensieve protestantse zendingstheologie," in *De onbekende Voetius*, ed. Johannes van Oort et al. (Kampen: Kok, 1989), 119–20.

34 Charles H. Parker, "The Seduction of Idols: Dutch Calvinist Readings of Worship and Society in Asia," in *Semper Reformanda: John Calvin, Worship, and Reformed Traditions*, ed. Barbara Pitkin (Göttingen: Vandenhoeck & Ruprecht, 2018), 166–67.

35 Gisbert Voetius, "De Muhammedismo," in *Liever Turks dan Paaps? De visies van Johannes Cocceejus, Gisbertus Voetius en Adrianus Relandus op de Islam*, ed. Jacobus van Amersfoort and Willem J. van Asselt (Zoetermeer: Boekencentrum, 1997),140.

and theology to prepare themselves for battle with Muslims.[36] In so doing, Voetius and Hoornbeeck placed the Calvinist engagement with Islam on an academic footing, having faith that theological debate would win the day.

Voetius believed that it was difficult to convert Muslims because of their adherence to the Qur'an, on which hung a "steadfast faith." He went on to observe that the Qur'an ascribed an important role for Christ in Islam, effectively camouflaging the truth of Christianity.[37] In essence, Voetius thought that Christians had trouble converting Muslims because Islam had an answer for Christianity. Likewise, Hoornbeeck also gave priority to the corrosive influence of the Qur'an. He maintained that it adulterated the Old and New Testament in many places, which miscast scripture and inoculated Muslims from the truth of Christianity.[38] Thus, both theologians advocated an apologetic strategy focused on championing the Bible to undermine the authority of the Qur'an. To attack the Qur'an, Voetius urged his students to show how it derived from scripture and thus corrupted teachings about the Trinitarian nature of God and the atoning work of Christ. He also enjoined pastors to study the Qur'an themselves to identify passages that ran counter to the Bible, natural law, and right reason.[39]

As Voetius narrated early Islam historically and unpacked its theology, he cast the religion as an apostasy that combined elements of many heresies, from Arianism to Nestorianism, and paralleled Socinianism and spiritualist Anabaptist sects in Europe. Like all heretics, Muslims took portions of scripture and twisted into corrupted forms of beliefs and practices.[40] Yet Voetius also read Islam through the lens of Calvinist polemics against Catholic theology. As Voetius saw it, Muslims practiced works righteousness, a common accusation against Catholics, so Muslims could merit their way into an "eternal life of carnal pleasures like a foul animal."[41] Charging Islam with idolatry, Voetius claimed that Muslims followed pagan practices of worshipping the moon and turning towards a fixed point (Mecca) to pray. According to Voetius, the set aside day of prayer fell on Friday because Muslims followed pagan customs of venerating Venus on her special day. And similar to the Catholic Church, Muslims followed a "religious order through popes, which are called muftis, and other leaders of a religious life, namely bishops, priests,

[36] Voetius, "De Muhammedismo," 83–87, 91. [37] Voetius, "De Muhammedismo," 145.
[38] Johannes Hoornbeeck, *Summa Controversarium Religionis cum Infidelibus, Haereticis, Schismaticis* (Utrecht, 1653), 167.
[39] Voetius, "De Muhammedismo," 142–43, 151–52.
[40] Voetius, "De Muhammedismo," 141–42, 148; Hoornbeeck, *Summa*, 135–44.
[41] Voetius, "De Muhammedismo," 142.

learned doctors, and lawyers."[42] Both Voetius and Hoornbeeck agreed that Catholicism made it much more complicated to convert Muslims, who equated the Roman church's use of religious images with idolatry among all Christians.[43] Voetius and Hoornbeeck hoped that a deeper theological understanding of Islam would equip missionary pastors in Asia to defend their faith and make more converts from Moors and Turks. In this way, the theology faculties in Utrecht and Leiden became participants in the global struggle with Islam.

The Bible vs. the Qur'an

The nature of the church sources from Dutch congregations in the East Indies make it very difficult to gauge how the increased attention to Islamic theology affected regular interactions with Muslims on the mission field. Calvinist missionary pastors did continue to proselytize, reporting from their circuits around islands located near Java, Ambon, Banda, and Ternate. Muslims did convert, though generally the immediate circumstances mentioned in the sources continued to be marriage and baptism of children.[44]

The most significant identifiable effect of theological study on Islam in the mission field was an increased attention to translating large portions of scripture into the language of people in the East Indies. Since arriving in Southeast Asia, Dutch missionaries learned local dialects in which they preached, taught, and translated religious materials such as catechisms. Missionaries had rendered portions of scripture into vernacular languages, yet the theological approach by scholars at Utrecht led to a greater emphasis on translating larger sections of the Bible in the second half of the 1600s. As early as the 1630s, Heurnius worked on portions of the New Testament, but he redoubled his efforts in the 1640s and 1650s producing Malay versions of the book of Acts and the gospels. A decade later in 1662, Daniel Brouwerius completed the book of Genesis and the New Testament, also in Malay. A number of other missionary pastors and chaplains, such as Francis Valentijn, Nikolaas Hodenpijl, and Simon de Lange produced unpublished versions of the New Testament from the 1650s to the 1690s.[45] At the end of the seventeenth century, Melchior Leidekker, a missionary pastor in Jakarta, translated the entire Bible into a Malay vernacular. He completed his

[42] Voetius, "De Muhammedismo," 144.
[43] Voetius, "De Muhammedismo," 145; Hoornbeeck, *Summa*, 176.
[44] See for example, *ATB*, 1:1, 267 (May 1, 1649), 328 (September 26, 1667), 358 (December 23, 1671), 408 (April 28, 1673), 415 (July 13, 1673), 443 (May 1674), 518 (April 3, 1678); Mooij, *Bouwstoffen*, 3: 197 (February 5, 1674), 206 (April 9, 1674).
[45] Boetzelaer, *Protestantsche Kerk*, 121–22.

translation in 1700, but it was not published until 1733. The dialect he chose, referred to as "High Malay" by the Dutch, derived from Muslim intellectual circles at the court of Johor, adjacent to the city of Melaka, held by the VOC on the southern tip of the Malaysia peninsula. This vernacular was heavily influenced by Arabic, and Dutch missionaries hoped that a copy of the Bible in the language of the Qur'an would enable them to convince Muslim elites through a comparison of the texts that the Christian scripture was the true Word of God. Thus, the strategy championed by Voetius and Hoornbeeck to show the Qur'an as a corrupted and false derivation from the Old and New Testaments played out in themselves out in Bible translation projects.

Informed Engagement with Islam

The focus on scriptural texts and the continued attention to missions in both Southeast Asia and the Netherlands yielded a more informed engagement with Islam by the early 1700s. Missionaries in the East Indies and South Asia persisted in bringing the Christian message to Muslims, as well as others, through schooling, catechetical instruction, and informal interaction. In 1698 Francois Valentijn, a missionary in Amboina, resounded the triumphalist refrain that the time was now ripe for God to "touch their hearts through the working of his spirit."[46] A gritty perseverance among Dutch consistories informed his optimism, as pastors and elders visited outlying areas, oversaw schools, sought to make inroads among village leaders, and reported on the state of Protestant Christianity in the far reaches of the Indian Ocean. Though the harvest of souls remained small, pastors noted baptisms and marriages of converted Muslims throughout the eighteenth century. Consistories in Banda, Amboina, Ternate, and Batavia reported regularly that Moors and heathens sought baptism, and annual pastoral reports quantified new converts, members, and school children.[47] The accounts give ample quantitative evidence of ongoing engagement through mission, but they do not provide a qualitative basis on which to evaluate Calvinists' attitudes towards Islam. The most extensive description of Muslim belief and observance came from Valentijn in his multi-volume description of the East Indies, *Old and New East Indies* (1724–1726).

Valentijn possessed an adept understanding of the history of Islam in the region, an extensive knowledge of its teachings, and a perceptive awareness of local practice. He recounted the arrival and spread of the

[46] Francois Valentijn, "Deure der Waarheid," in *ATB*, I, 2: 156.
[47] See for example, pastoral and visitation reports in *ATB*, I: 2; II:2: II:1 passim.

religion, which he dated in the 1400s, from Sunni Arab traders into the Moluccas, Java, and Ternate. Across regions, he noted the varying levels of commitment to Islam among ruling dynasties and their outlook towards other religions, especially Christianity. Occasionally citing Voetius and Hoornbeeck, Valentijn described the central tenets of Islam in generally neutral terms, though making no disguise of his contempt for the religion, calling it "a cancer and a pest." He belittled the Qur'an as a "work of deceit" and Muhammad as a "foul adulterer."[48] His most trenchant criticisms, however, grew out of missionary frustration at the resistance of local Muslims to the Christian message. He disparaged Muslims for their rote and thoughtless conformity to religious observance and for their obstinate refusal to reconsider their traditions. Explaining why few Muslims converted to Christianity, Valentijn contended that adherence to Islam required little effort. He did credit Islam for introducing greater literacy in Malay, though not Arabic, and for doing away with idols and superstitions follow by heathens. Noting their industry, he spoke respectfully of Muslim practice of praying five times during the day and of ritual washing.[49] Valentijn told a personal story that in 1687 he was allowed to observe prayers at a "temple" in Hila (Amboina). He conversed extensively with a Muslim "priest" he knew well, Hassan Soeleyman, about his religion and the service.[50] Valentijn described an earlier episode in 1706 when as chaplain in the army he befriended a "Makassar Captain" Daeng Matàra, "one of the most sensible Mohammedans." In one conversation, Matàra located the origins of Islam in Makassar from a certain merchant Dato Bendang who introduced the religion in 1605.[51]

The abiding effort to comprehend Islam in order to convert Muslims reached its apex in the Netherlands in the early eighteenth century with the work of Adriaan Reland, a professor of oriental languages at the University of Utrecht. A brilliant linguist with a wide reach, Reland possessed outstanding facility in a range of Asian languages including Arabic, Persian, Hebrew, and Malay; he also excelled in the cartography of Palestine, Persia, and Southeast Asia. The son of a pastor, Reland grew

[48] Valentijn, *Godsdienst Zaaken Java*, in *Oude en Nieuw Oost-Indien*, vol. 4 (Amsterdam, 1726), 3.

[49] Valentijn, *Oost-Indien*, 3/1: 25.

[50] Valentijn, *Oost-Indien*, 3/1: 23–24; Karel Steenbrink, *Dutch Colonialism and Indonesian Islam: Conflicts and Contacts, 1596–1950*, trans. Jan Steenbrink and Henry Jansen (New York and Amsterdam: Rodopi, 2006), 39–40.

[51] Valentijn doubted this account, noting that Portuguese sources attributed the arrival of Islam into Makassar at the hands of the king of Ternate in 1580. Francois Valentijn, *Beschryvinge van Macassar* in *Oost-Indien*, 3/2: 233. This episode is recounted in Steenbrink, *Dutch Colonialism*, 38–39.

up in a solidly Calvinist milieu and he remained loyal to the orthodox version of Reformed Protestantism throughout his life. He received his education and held a faculty appointment from 1701 to 1718 at Utrecht, the intellectual bastion of orthodox Calvinism in the Netherlands. Utrecht had also developed a robust missionary outlook under Voetius and Hoornbeeck that Reland inherited in the early 1700s. Because of his interest in Islam, he published in 1705 *On the Mohammedan Religion*, a highly influential work that reflected a decisive pivot to a more balanced view of Islam among European intellectuals. It was translated into Dutch, English, French, German, and Spanish. Perhaps because it exposed Catholic misreadings and took a relatively neutral stance towards Islam, the work made the Index of Prohibited Books in 1722.[52] Reland represents one case explored by Anthony Grafton in Chapter 3 in which close reading of texts – Islamic ones here – inculcated greater appreciation for a competing religious tradition.[53]

Though historians often cast Reland as an early enlightenment figure, the primary influence on his resolve to undertake a treatment of Islam was the global Calvinist mission. In the preface, he explained "my labors shall make way for others for the triumph of the truth and the evangelical faith and the ultimate aim of our actions, the glory of the only and one god, father, son, and holy spirit."[54] The unfulfilled opportunities that Dutch overseas enterprises offered for spreading the gospel and converting Muslims frustrated Reland, just as it had tantalized Grotius, Voetius, Hoornbeeck and others before him. It was his awareness of Dutch entanglements in these lands and his sense of urgency about the Calvinist mission to Muslims that prompted his study of Arabic and Persian literature focusing on the Qur'an. Like many Calvinist church leaders in the Netherlands, he charged that the trading companies were not doing enough to convert Muslims. He contended that many Netherlanders went overseas to make money, not to save souls.[55] He asked "Do we not have much contact with Mohammedans in Constantinople, along the borders of Hungary and Turkish lands, on the coasts of Africa, in Syria, Persia, and the East Indies, where our in our colonies and in places where we seek to make money, many Mohammedans live?" For Reland, the fact that Islam is in "the mouths of so many, demands a call to arms for the study of the entire body of

[52] Alastair Hamilton, "From a 'Closet at Utrecht' Adriaan Reland and Islam," *Nederlandsch Archief voor Kerkgeschiedenis* 78/2(1998): 243–44.

[53] See Anthony Grafton's contribution in Chapter 3 of this volume.

[54] Adriaan Reland, *De Religione Mohammedica libri duo* (Utrecht, 1705) (unpaginated preface) **** 3v.

[55] Reland, *De Religione Mohammedica*, unpaginated preface **** 4.

literature."[56] His study of that literature and the Qur'an actually was informed by the Dutch presence in Southeast Asia. Alexander Bevilacqua has shown that Reland utilized Malay manuscripts brought to Holland by merchants and missionaries from the East Indies to parse uncertain linguistic expressions in the Qur'an.[57]

Reland summarized Islamic teaching in Latin and Arabic in the first book and corrected thirty-nine views wrongly ascribed to Muslims.[58] The premise underlying *On the Mohammedan Religion* was that Christians had to understand and even appreciate Islam before they could engage Muslims successfully. He criticized and refuted many combatted portrayals of Islam by Christian apologists who relied uncritically on Latin texts and medieval commentators. Like Voetius, Reland argued that it was essential for Christian theologians to study the Qur'an in Arabic.[59] Furthermore, he pointed out to readers that they should not judge any religion based on the writings of its detractors. Roman Catholics, he reminded Calvinists, wrongly accused Protestants of despising good works, of making God the author of sin, and disparaging Mary, the mother of Christ, and the saints.[60] Likewise, Christians should not take criticisms of Islam at face value, especially by those works not based on Arabic. He even included Hoornbeeck's *Summa Controversarium* in a list of books not rooted in Arabic sources and thus "fantasized" about Islam.[61] Working from Arabic sources, Reland refuted erroneous charges that Muslims, for example, taught that God existed in bodily form, that hell and providence did not exist, and God was the author of sin.[62]

Reland argued that the problem with many Christian polemicists was that they did not take seriously the similarities between Christianity and Islam that they themselves recognized. Rather, he advised that Christians should appreciate what Islam and Christianity shared in common and begin disputations from that standpoint.[63] The conversion strategy advocated by Voetius followed logically from Reland's emphasis on

56 Reland, *Religione Mohammedica* (unpaginated preface) ****4–5. See also a Dutch version in *Liever Turks dan Paaps?*, 113.

57 Alexander Bevilacqua, *The Republic of Arabic Letters: Islam and the European Enlightenment* (Cambridge, MA: Harvard University Press, 2018), 84. See also, J. T. P de Bruijn, "Iranian Studies in the Netherlands," *Iranian Studies* 20/2(1987): 170–71; Arnoud Vrolijk, "Arabic Studies in the Netherlands and the Prerequisites of Social Impact-a Survey," in *The Teaching and Learning of Arabic in Early Modern Europe*, ed. Jan Loop et al. (Leiden: Brill, 2017), 28.

58 Reland, *De Religione Mohammedica*, 124–25.

59 Reland, *De Religione Mohammedia*, unpaginated preface ******* 1–2.

60 Reland, *De Religione Mohammedica*, unpaginated preface ** 6–7.

61 Reland, *De Religione Mohammedica*, unpaginated preface ****.

62 Reland, *De Religione Mohammedica*, 142–54, 166–77.

63 Reland, *De Religione Mohammedica*, unpaginated preface *** 4–7.

recognizing commonalities. Missionaries could highlight the points that the Qur'an departed from in the teachings of the Old and New Testament. Moreover, he declared that Muslims were not as crazy as Christians had characterized them. Islam could not, Reland continued, have spread so widely across Asia, Africa, and Europe had it not enticed many as an appealing and genuine religion.[64] He quoted Louis Marracci, a contemporary Catholic orientalist, that Islam seems on first glance to accord with the law of nature, whereas the Christian mysteries of the Trinity, Incarnation, and Resurrection seem farfetched.[65]

Reland placed his linguistic preoccupations and talents in service for the global Calvinist mission. *On the Mohammedan Religion* sought to convey a comprehensive accurate understanding of Islam, shorn of long-held misconceptions and caricatures that had plagued Christian missionaries. He remained fully within the Calvinist orbit in the University of Utrecht throughout his life and his work seems to have escaped controversy among Reformed church authorities. Calvinists in the Netherlands continued to concern themselves with theological orthodoxy. Only fourteen years prior to the publication of Reland's manifesto, Balthasar Bekker, a pastor in Amsterdam wrote a skeptical treatment of witchcraft, *The World Bewitched*, for which he was censured and expelled from the church. Reland continued to work uninterrupted on orientalist scholarship at the university until his death in 1718.

Even though Reland's work belonged to global Calvinism, he also participated in a broad reappraisal of Islam that was taking hold among other orientalists in Europe in the late 1600s and early 1700s. Steeped in Arabic, Persian, and other European languages, they translated texts and engaged in comparative study of languages, literatures, and cultures. Reland esteemed the work of other contemporary orientalists, such as Edward Pococke, Eusebius Renaudot, Louis Marracci, and others.[66] Reland's work became instrumental among European intellectuals engaged in resituating the place of religion in society in the early Enlightenment. To cite just one example, Bernard Picart and Jean Bernard leaned heavily on Reland for their depiction of Islam in the widely influential *Religious Ceremonies of the World* (1723–1737).[67] This multivolume work represented a critical transition in European attitudes about religious difference, namely "that all religions could be compared

[64] Reland, *De Religione Mohammedica*, unpaginated preface **** 2.
[65] Reland, *De Religione Mohammedica*, unpaginated preface **** 2–3.
[66] Van Amersfoort and van Asselt, *Liever Turks dan Paaps?*, 115, 116, 122.
[67] Lynn Hunt, Margaret C. Jacob, Wijnand Mijnhardt, *The Book that Changed Europe: Picart & Bernard's Religious Ceremonies of the World* (Cambridge, MA: Harvard University Press, 2010), 249, 254, 261–64.

on equal terms."[68] They marshalled his appeal to persuasion and rejection of coercion in religious matters with a long quote from the French edition of *On the Religion of the Mohammedans* : [we must allow] full and complete liberty for each to follow his own lights and to believe true that which appears to him to be such. For there is nothing more absurd that to want to oblige people to receive as truth that which they do not regard as true."[69]

Conclusion

By the early 1700s, Calvinists had come a long way in their understanding of Islam. Before the launch of the Dutch mercantile empire, Muslims existed largely in the imaginations of Calvinists, based on medieval polemical treatises and poorly translated texts of the Qur'an. In the employ of the VOC, hundreds of missionary pastors interacted with Muslims face to face, trying to bring them to a Reformed faith. That engagement, especially the failure to reap an abundant harvest of souls, provoked an intellectual response in the Netherlands, as Dutch theological faculties ramped up their study of Arabic and of Muslim texts, chiefly the Qur'an. Gisbert Voetius and Johannes Hoornbeeck wrote academic treatises to steep missionaries in Islamic theology and to devise strategies for attacking Islam in the field. The chief manifestation of this effort was Bible translation projects, culminating in Melchior Leidekker's translation in 1700. Ongoing linguistic study of oriental languages and comparative study of texts to somehow infuse the mission with new life led Adriaan Reland and others to a new understanding of Islam. His work placed Islam on a new intellectual footing in Europe, depicting the religion as flawed, but reasonable. Enlightenment thinkers, such as Bernard and Picart, appropriated Reland's work to promote a secular perspective on religious belief and practice. Thus, as Protestantism went global in the service of empire, trade, and mission, it played a significant role in transforming European approaches to Islam over the course of the seventeenth and eighteenth centuries.

[68] Hunt, Jacob, Mijnhardt, *Changed Europe*, 1–2.
[69] Hunt, Jacobs, and Mijnhardt, *Changed Europe*, 262.

7 Inventing a Lutheran Ritual: Baptisms of Muslims and Africans in Early Modern Germany*

Renate Dürr

Lutheran Germany does not usually come to mind when thinking about globalism in early modern European history. After all, it is common knowledge that neither Luther nor his fellow Reformers took much interest in the discovery of the Americas.[1] A Lutheran mission was only developed in the eighteenth century – two centuries following the establishment of the Catholic mission and several decades after other Protestant initiatives.[2] Moreover, the idea that the Holy Roman Empire languished in the backwaters of history and scarcely participated in European expansion, global trade, and slavery is hard to eradicate.

Yet some large merchant houses extended feelers towards the Americas or Asia, and quite a few Germans signed up for journeys on Dutch, English, or French ships to work in different parts of the world.[3] Recent statistics collected by Jelle van Lottum at the Dutch Huygens ING Institute show, for instance, that one in five VOC employees was from the Holy Roman Empire while more than half of the numerous non-Dutch inhabitants of seventeenth-century Amsterdam were Germans.[4] Nevertheless, state-funded commercial schemes were rare and without

* I would like to thank Judith Pollmann for inviting me to the "Research Seminar Europe 1000–1800" at Leiden University in June 2018, and Meta Henneke, Michiel van Groesen, Lionel Laborie, and Jos Platenkamp for pointing me towards the relevant research literature. I would also like to thank Rutger Kramer and Diarmuid Ó Riain for their careful translation.

1 For a multi-layered discussion on Luther's reflections on life outside Germany, see Susan Karant-Nunn, "Martin Luther, Homeboy, Looks Outward," *Archive of Reformation History* 108 (2017): 82–90; see also, Renate Dürr, "Found in Translation – the Search for Similarities between Cultures at the Time of Reformations," in ibid., 191–201, here 195–96.

2 See, for instance, Charles H. Parker's contribution in Chapter 6 of this volume.

3 Mark Häberlein, *Aufbruch ins globale Zeitalter. Die Handelswelt der Fugger und Welser* (Darmstadt: Theiss, 2016).

4 Jelle van Lottum, "Labour migration, skills and the maritime labor market in late seventeenth- and eighteenth-century Europe," paper given at the World Economic History Congress, July 29–August 3, 2018.

exception failed in their early stages.[5] With the recent "global turn" in historical studies, the Holy Roman Empire has been further relinquished to the margins of history.[6] This is also demonstrated by the renewed interest in Mack Walker's influential 1971 study *German Home Towns.*[7] The theory inherent in his concept of provinciality – the idea of the Old Reich's decline amidst stuffy *Gemütlichkeit* – has already been put into perspective numerous times, most recently by Joachim Whaley in his impressive history, *Germany and the Holy Roman Empire.*[8] This approach no longer deems the Old Reich, with its over 100 territories, deficient in comparison to France and England; rather, it is seen as just a different model of nation-building. For instance, the constant dualism between the Habsburg emperor and the estates is now considered less a constitutional weakness and more a factor of dynamics and change. Nevertheless, the image of the Old Reich's (purported) isolation remains quite prevalent among historians. The territorial disintegration of the Holy Roman Empire, its perpetual internal religious conflicts, and the simple fact that most German regions were situated hundreds of kilometers from the coast severely impeded any attempts at globalization and expansion. As a result, we still regard early modern German Lutheranism as "provincial" in two ways: it was based on small towns and territories and it was exceedingly self-centred.[9]

In this essay, I attempt to deconstruct this image by closely examining the baptisms of Muslims and so-called heathens as practised by Lutheran churches, predominantly in the seventeenth and eighteenth centuries. I argue that the baptismal sermons written especially for these occasions

[5] Roberto Zaugg, "Grossfriedrichsburg, the first German Colony in Africa? Brandenburg-Prussia, Atlantic entanglements and national memory," in *Shadows of Empire in West Africa: New Perspectives on European Fortifications*, ed. John Kwadwo Osei-Tutu and Victoria Ellen Smith (New York: Palgrave Macmillan, 2018), 33–73; Felicia Gottmann, "Fraud, malfeasance, and transnational networks: The Prussian Bengal-Company and the challenges of commercial cosmopolitanism," in *Commercial Cosmopolitanism? Policing Contact Zones and Governing 'Multinationals' in the Early Modern World*, ed. Felicia Gottmann and James Livesey (forthcoming).

[6] Renate Dürr, Ronnie Hsia, Carina Johnson, Ulrike Strasser, and Merry Wiesner-Hanks, "Forum: Globalizing Early Modern History," *German History* 31/3 (2013): 366–38.

[7] Mack Walker, *German Home Towns: Community, State, and General Estate: 1648–1871*, 2nd ed. (Ithaca, NY/ London: Cornell University Press, 1998); see also the special issue of Central European History on "German Home Towns, Forty Years Later," *Central European History* 47/3 (2014).

[8] Joachim Whaley, *Germany and the Holy Roman Empire*, 2 vols. (Oxford: Oxford University Press, 2012); see also the special issue on "Rewriting the History of the Holy Roman Empire" in *German History* 36/3 (2018); for a different new view on the history of the Holy Roman Empire, see Barbara Stollberg-Rilinger, *Des Kaisers alte Kleider. Verfassungsgeschichte und Symbolsprache des Alten Reiches* (Munich: Beck, 2008).

[9] See also: Renate Dürr, "The World in the German Hinterlands: Early Modern German History Entangled," *Sixteenth Century Journal* 50 (2019): 148–55.

were typically Lutheran in their manner of self-assertion. Baptisms of Muslims or "Africans" were usually lavish ceremonies, every detail perfectly orchestrated to reflect the self-concept of the Lutheran parish and its local rulers as well as the tenets of Lutheran belief. Dukes and duchesses of the relevant territories typically participated as godparents. Indeed, there were often dozens of them, as everybody sought to partake in the glory of the occasion by publicly displaying their involvement in these successful conversions. Like the Lutheran burial sermons of the time, the baptismal sermons were often printed and distributed, further enhancing the prestige of both the noble family and the Lutheran Church. For seventeenth- and eighteenth-century Lutherans, these baptismal ceremonies were a divine symbol of an explicitly Lutheran universalism – a global Lutheranism that did not need to embark on missions. Whereas most contributions to this anthology assess the global impact of Protestant Reformations through the experiences of Protestants outside of Europe, my contribution focuses on the effects of transcultural encounters within the very heart of the continent. I argue that our view of early modern Lutheranism in the Old Reich changes considerably once we understand wartime abduction, forced migration, and slavery as part of German early modern history.

Introduction

In the early modern period, the term *Türkentaufe* (baptism of Turks) was applied to the baptism of Muslims, mostly prisoners of war who came from all over the Ottoman Empire.[10] The baptism of these so-called heathens was usually referred to as *Mohrentaufe* (baptism of Moors) and usually referred to slaves from sub-Saharan Africa. I will use the German words *Türkentaufe* and *Mohrentaufe* in keeping with primary source terminology. Lutheran ministers employed these words to construct boundaries between the histories of Christian Europe and the non-European world – even if many of these 'Turks' actually came from Hungary or Slovenia. The word *Mohr* (Moor) was similarly applied to people from very different backgrounds, including slaves from India, for example.[11] Finally, there were people of darker skin color from the Ottoman Empire, alternately referred to as Turks and Moors such as Fatma and Mustapha,

[10] Ibrahim Metin Kunt ed., *The Cambridge History of Turkey*, vol. 2/3, ed. Suraiya Faroqhi (Cambridge: Cambridge University Press, 2006/2012).

[11] Monika Firla, "Kirchenbücher, Kirchenakten und Taufpredigten als Quellen der afrikanischen Diaspora im 17. bis 19. Jahrhundert," *Zeitschrift der morgenländischen Gesellschaft* (1995): 611–18, here: 612.

both Africans living in the Peloponnese.[12] I will attempt to avoid an excessively Eurocentric interpretation of these strategies of distinction by specifying individuals' places of origin as precisely as possible, referring to them as Turks or Moors only when discussing their global impact on Lutheran Germany.

Recent research on the importance of Luther's anti-Semitism and his contemporaries' anti-Turkish sentiment shows that we cannot simply dismiss them as disagreeable instances of the darker side of Lutheran theology.[13] Rather, this rhetoric heavily affected the self-conception of Lutheran parishes through sermons, prayers, and the liturgy. Furthermore, research on Muslims and non-Europeans in the Holy Roman Empire is still just beginning. A number of overview articles concerning Ottoman prisoners of war in the Holy Roman Empire have appeared in recent years, and these often contain reference to the so-called Turkish baptismal sermons.[14] Baptismal sermons printed for *Türkentaufen* and *Mohrentaufen*, as well as baptisms recorded in local church registers, most enduringly document this forced immigration into the Old Reich. Yet to date, the sermons themselves have been scarcely investigated. Some years ago, Markus Friedrich undertook a comprehensive analysis of the theology of Lutheran "Turkish baptismal sermons" and questioned their potential repercussions for Protestant teachings about predestination.[15] Other studies have assembled and discussed the many examples of Africans present at German courts from the seventeenth century onwards.[16]

[12] Peter Martin, *Schwarze Teufel, edle Mohren. Afrikaner in Geschichte und Bewusstsein der Deutschen* (Hamburg: Hamburger Edition, 2001), 82.

[13] Susan Karant-Nunn, *The Reformation of Feeling: Shaping the Religious Emotions in Early Modern Germany* (Oxford: Oxford University Press, 2010), 133–58; Thomas Kaufmann, *Luthers Juden* (Stuttgart: Reclam, 2014); Lyndal Roper, *Martin Luther. Renegade and Prophet* (London: Vintage, 2017), chapter 18.

[14] Markus Friedrich, "'Türken' im Alten Reich. Zur Aufnahme und Konversion von Muslimen im deutschen Sprachraum (16.-18. Jahrhundert)," *Historische Zeitschrift* 294 (2012): 329–60; Manja Quakatz, "'Gebürtig aus der Türckey': Zur Konversion und Zwangstaufe osmanischer Muslime im Alten Reich um 1700," in *Europa und die Türkei im 18. Jahrhundert*, ed. Barbara Schmidt-Haberkamp (Göttingen: V&R Unipress, 2011), 417–30; Manja Quakatz, "'Conversio Turci.' Konvertierte und zwangsgetaufte Osmanen. Religiöse und kulturelle Grenzgänger im Alten Reich (1683–1710)," in *Raum im Wandel. Die osmanisch-habsburgische Grenzregion vom 16. bis 18. Jahrhundert*, ed. Norbert Spannenberger and Varga Szabolcs (Stuttgart: Franz Steiner, 2014), 214–31.

[15] Markus Friedrich, "Türkentaufen. Zur theologischen Problematik und geistlichen Deutung der Konversion von Muslimen im Alten Reich," in *Orientbegegnungen deutscher Protestanten in der Frühen Neuzeit*, ed. Markus Friedrich and Alexander Schunka (Frankfurt am Main: Klostermann, 2012), 47–74.

[16] Monika Firla, Hermann Forkl, "Afrikaner und Africana am württembergischen Herzogshof im 17. Jahrhundert," *Tribus* 44 (1995): 149–93; Mark Häberlein, "Mohren, ständische Gesellschaft und atlantische Welt. Minderheiten und

Although the exoticizing function of so-called court Moors has generally been highlighted in this research, decidedly postcolonial enquiries into the status of Africans at the courts of the Old Reich are still rare.[17] Nonetheless, some recent studies have examined the relationship between the science of man, the emergence of theories of race in the second half of the eighteenth century, and the widespread presence of "court Moors."[18] Research on the legal status of displaced prisoners of war and Africans in the German territories has also been limited up to now. Rebekka von Mallinckrodt underlines the fact that these forced migrations often produced instances of slavery within Germany[19] while Walter Sauer und Andrea Wiesbeck have shown that baptism did not automatically guarantee a slave's freedom in the Viennese context.[20] However, most other historians contradict these findings by refusing to acknowledge that slavery existed in Germany.[21] I hope to productively contribute to this discussion with the analysis of baptismal sermons that follows. What is already clear is that non-Christians migrated to the Holy Roman Empire in significant numbers in the early modern period, especially during the

Kulturkontakte in der Frühen Neuzeit," in *Atlantic Understandings: Essays on European and American History in Honor of Hermann Wellenreuther*, ed. Claudia Schnurrmann and Hartmut Lehmann (Münster: LIT Verlag, 2006), 77–102; Stephan Theilig, *Türken, Mohren und Tartaren. Muslimische (Lebens-) Welten in Brandenburg-Preußen im 18. Jahrhundert* (Berlin: Frank & Timme, 2013); Anne Kuhlmann-Smirnov, *Schwarze Europäer im Alten Reich. Handel, Migration, Hof* (Göttingen: V&R unipress, 2013).

17 Viktoria Schmidt-Linsenhoff, *Ästhetik der Differenz. Postkoloniale Perspektiven vom 16. bis 21. Jahrhundert. 15 Fallstudien* (Marburg: Jonas, 2010), 1: 249–66.

18 Vera Lind, "Privileged dependency on the edge of the Atlantic world: Africans and Germans in the eighteenth century," in *Interpreting Colonialism*, ed. Byron R. Wells and Philip Stewart (Oxford: Voltaire Foundation, 2004), 369–91; Sünne Juterczenka, "'Chamber Moors' and Court Physicians. On the Convergence of Aesthetic Consumption and Racial Anthropology at Eighteenth-Century Courts in Germany," in *Entangled Knowledge. Scientific Discourses and Cultural Difference*, ed. Klaus Hock and Gesa Mackenthum (Münster: Waxmann, 2012), 165–82.

19 Rebekka von Mallinckrodt, "There are no Slaves in Prussia?" in *Slavery Hinterland. Transatlantic Slavery and Continental Europe, 1680–1850*, ed. Felix Brahm and Eve Rosenhaft (Woodbridge, UK: The Boydell Press, 2016), 109–31; "Verhandelte (Un-)Freiheit. Sklaverei, Leibeigenschaft und innereuropäischer Wissenstransfer am Ausgang des 18. Jahrhunderts," *Geschichte und Gesellschaft* 43 (2017): 347–80; see also: www.frueheneuzeit.uni-bremen.de/index.php/de/forschung/german-slavery (accessed February 18, 2019).

20 Mallinckrodt, "There are no Slaves in Prussia?," 112–13; Walter Sauer, Andrea Wiesböck, "Sklaven, Freie, Fremde. Wiener 'Mohren' des 17. und 18. Jahrhunderts," in *Von Soliman zu Omofuma. Afrikanische Diaspora in Österreich 17. bis 20. Jahrhundert*, ed. Walter Sauer (Innsbruck: Studienverlag, 2007), 232–56, here 47–48.

21 See, for example, Jürgen Osterhammel, *Sklaverei und die Zivilisation des Westens*, 2nd ed. (Munich: Carl Friedrich von Siemens Stiftung, 2009), 7; Becker, *Preußens schwarze Untertanen*, 13–16; Anne Kuhlmann-Smirnov, *Schwarze Europäer*, 68–77.

decades before and after 1700.[22] In his research on Brandenburg-Prussia, Stephan Theilig has concluded that few Muslim prisoners even acceded to baptism.[23] Further case studies are required to test his observations elsewhere, but the fact that we only know about those who were actually baptised presents an obvious problem.

My research on printed baptismal sermons has uncovered more than fifty such baptisms in thirty different cities and villages during the seventeenth and eighteenth centuries, and there are surely many more to be found. They are spread across Germany, from Rostock in the north to Memmingen and Lindau in the south. Some baptisms were carried out in cities like Stuttgart, Nuremberg, and Berlin, but, importantly, most of them occurred in provincial towns, if not tiny villages. One minister even specified on the title page of his sermon that the small village of Thann where Ayşe, a young woman from Buda, was baptized, is situated on the banks of the Altmühl River, two hours' travel from Onolzbach. Such details would have been of little help to anybody, even at that time.[24] Around 1800 Thann consisted of only thirty households.[25]

Most prisoners of war were taken in the 1680s, when Holy League generals and soldiers captured over 2,000 prisoners in Buda alone. They were subsequently transported to the Holy Roman Empire to be given away or sold.[26] Following the Ottoman army's Siege of Vienna in 1683, Christian European countries formed the Holy League against the Turks, hoping to reconquer Hungary as a first initiative. Whereas the siege of Buda in 1684 ended with great losses for the Holy League after more than one hundred days of besiegement, the second attempt in 1686 was successful partly because the Christian army outnumbered the Ottoman army by at least ten to one. In any event, the 1684 and 1686 sieges of Buda became prominent symbols of the cruelty of war, with thousands of casualties on both sides; this may explain why exact numbers of the dead and captured were recorded after the September 1686 siege.

22 Alexander Schunka, "Migration in the German Lands: An Introduction," in *Migrations in the German Lands, 1500–2000*, ed. Jason Coy, Jared Poley, and Alexander Schunka (New York/Oxford: Berghahn, 2016), 1–34.

23 Theilig, *Türken*, 40 n. 30; similar: Friedrich, "Türkentaufen," 345.

24 Andreas Geret, *Das Neue Leben Einer Neuen Creatur in Christo/ Aus dem 2. Cap. der Epistl. an die Galat. v. 20. Bey der Heiligen Tauff Einer von der Königlichen Haupt=Stadt Ofen aus Nieder=Ungarn bürtigen Türckin/ in der Gemeinschafftlichen Crailßheimischen Pfarr=Kirch zu Thann/ an der Altmühl 2. Stund von Onolzbach liegend [...] erkläret [...]* (Nürnberg 1691), 26–27(about the name and the former life of Aişe).

25 Johann Kaspar Bundschuh, "Thann," in *Geographisches Statistisch-Topographisches Lexikon von Franken*, vol. 5 (Ulm: Verlag der Stettinschen Buchhandlung, 1802), 518–19.

26 Thomas Winkelbauer, *Ständefreiheit und Fürstenmacht. Länder und Untertanen des Hauses Habsburg im konfessionellen Zeitalter*, vol. 1 (Vienna: Carl Ueberreuter, 2003), 166.

These records show that Holy League soldiers murdered more than 3,000 people, nearly extinguished the flourishing Jewish community in Buda, and enslaved 2,325 captives, among them 80 Ottoman generals and 546 women and children.[27] Soldiers, especially generals, were often captured in order to exchange them for Christians imprisoned by the Ottoman army.[28] These prisoner swaps might explain why the percentage of women and children captives in Germany was so much higher than the above data would suggest. Although exact figures cannot be established, most historians estimate that about half of the prisoners taken to the Holy Roman Empire were children, while men and women each made up about 25 percent.[29] The sample from my case study matches these general estimates for war captives brought to the Holy Roman Empire, where men and women are represented in roughly equal measure. More than half of the converts were still children when they were abducted from their native land while overall one-fifth of all baptisms were *Mohrentaufen.*

In contrast to most baptisms of converts in missions outside Europe, those discussed here reflect unique stories and individual conversions in specific parishes. The authors of the sermons told these stories in detail because they were important in portraying the ritual of baptism as a rite of passage. Sometimes ministers even insisted that all of the information they provided was supported by documents.[30] In what follows, I will first use the Lutheran narratives of the converts' lives before and after baptism, as illustrated by printed sermons, to reconstruct the encounters and insofar as possible the agency of these individuals. Secondly, I will interpret the ritual of baptism as a Lutheran rite of passage. Since the ministers did not have ancient traditions to fall back on, especially when it came to adult baptisms, they had to invent new rituals and explain them to their parishes. In conclusion, I will discuss the impact of these baptisms on early modern Lutheranism in provincial Germany.

[27] Joseph Maurer, *Cardinal Leopold Graf Kollonitsch, Primas von Ungarn. Sein Leben und sein Wirken. Zumeist nach archivalischen Quellen geschildert* (Innsbruck: Fel. Rauch, 1887), 199.

[28] Maurer, *Cardinal Leopold Graf Kollonitsch*, 206.

[29] Hartmut Heller, "Um 1700: seltsame Dorfgenossen aus der Türkei. Minderheitenbeobachtungen in Franken, Kurbayern und Schwaben," in *Fremde auf dem Land*, ed. Hermann Heidrich et al. (Bad Windsheim: Fränkisches Freilandmuseum, 2000), 13–44, here: 16; Anne Kuhlmann-Smirnov, *Schwarze Europäer*, 175; Rebekka von Mallinckrodt, "Verschleppte Kinder im Heiligen Römischen Reich deutscher Nation und die Grenzen der Mehrfachzugehörigkeit," in *Transkulturelle Mehrfachzugehörigkeit als kulturhistorisches Phänomen. Räume – Materialitäten – Erinnerungen*, ed. Dagmar Freist et al. (Bielefeld: transcript, 2019), 15–38, here: 27.

[30] Tobias Gabriel Ruprecht, *Eigentlicher Verlauff einer zu Rückersdorff verrichteten Türken-Tauff [. . .]* (Nürnberg 1694), 15.

Baptisms of Muslims and Africans: Encounters, Agency, and Historical Contexts

The Protestant duchy Schleswig-Holstein-Gottorp in northern Germany had important connections to Lutheran Denmark (and, later, Sweden), as well as to Saxony, which was one of the Holy Roman Empire's principal Lutheran Electorate. In many ways, it exemplifies an early modern German territory.[31] This small duchy was created in 1544, when Christian III of Denmark divided the Schleswig-Holstein duchy into three parts to share with his brothers. More divisions were implemented during the sixteenth century, resulting in two lines of Schleswig and Holstein in the seventeenth century: one connected to the Danish kingdom and the other to the small but growing line of Gottorp dukes. This already small duchy consisted of numerous, even smaller, territories situated in the area between the Baltic and North Seas. Its only larger port was tucked away at the end of a 15 km-long inlet of the Baltic. Thus, it was quite the opposite of what one would describe as a settled unified land with expansionist ambitions. The duchy did not seem to have the makings of a global player, especially not in the middle of the Thirty Years' War. However, Schleswig-Holstein had been an important player in Baltic trades for centuries and the Thirty Years' War endangered trade routes in the Baltic Sea.[32] So it may have been a response to changes in power and trade relations in this area that the Duke of Schleswig-Holstein-Gottorp decided to set up a trade route from Isfahan to Kiel via Moscow and the Baltic Sea.[33] From Kiel, it was hoped, the trade would continue on to Hamburg, Amsterdam, and London. A delegation of over 100 representatives traveled to Sweden, Russia, and Persia to negotiate trade contracts.[34] People from all over the Holy Roman Empire

[31] Walter Göbell et al., *Schleswig-Holsteinische Kirchengeschichte*, vol. 3, Reformation (Neumünster: Wachholtz, 1982); Gottfried Ernst Hoffmann, Klauspeter Reumann, Hermann Kellenbenz, *Die Herzogtümer von der Landesteilung 1544 bis zur Wiedervereinigung Schleswigs 1721*, Geschichte Schleswig-Holsteins vol. 5 (Neumünster: Wachholtz, 1986); Martin Schwarz Lausten, *Die Reformation in Dänemark* (Gütersloh: Gütersloher Verlagshaus, 2008); Oliver Auge, "Der Herzog des Hofgelehrten Adam Olearius. Friedrich III. von Schleswig-Holstein-Gottorf (1597–1659)," in *Adam Olearius. Neugier als Methode*, ed. Kirsten Baumann et al. (Petersberg: Michael Imhof, 2017), 26–31, here: 29.

[32] Michael North, *Geschichte der Ostsee: Handel und Kulturen* (Munich: Beck, 2011).

[33] Dieter Lohmeier, Kleiner Staat ganz groß: Schleswig-Holstein-Gottorf (Heide: Westholsteinische Anstalt, 1997), 38, 42ff; Hamid Tafazoli, *Der deutsche Persien-Diskurs. Zur Verwissenschaftlichung und Literarisierung des Persien-Bildes im deutschen Schrifttum. Von der frühen Neuzeit bis in das 19. Jahrhundert* (Bielefeld: Aisthesis, 2007), 159–66.

[34] Lea Kõiv, "Die holsteinischen Gesandtschaften in Reval (Tallinn). Begegnungen und Begebenheiten am Rande der Mission," in *Adam Olearius. Neugier als Methode*, ed. Kirsten Baumann et al. (Petersberg: Michael Imhof, 2017), 58–68, here: 58.

and other parts of Europe, especially the Netherlands, Scotland, Denmark, Sweden, and Finland, joined the delegation, illustrating its significance on a broad European scale.[35]

In Moscow, the tsar increased expected customs duties while in Isfahan reactions were very cautious. Nevertheless, Shah Safi did send a return delegation to Schleswig-Holstein, which arrived in Gottorp in August 1639. However, the Isfahan representatives soon realized that the Gottorp delegation had been bluffing about a potential European coalition against the Ottoman Empire although their attempt to establish global trading networks had been serious. Ultimately the initiative failed, and the Hamburg merchant who had led the delegation was executed in public.[36] All that remained of this adventure were the six members of the Persian party who asked to be admitted into the Gottorp community.

We know about all this from a member of the Gottorp delegation, the scholar and orientalist Adam Olearius (1599–1671).[37] Through the incidental details he describes, we also learn about the diverse social and ethnic mix of the Persian party, which included an Armenian and a Greek Christian among others. At first, the Armenian opted to remain in Gottorp but reconsidered and hurried home after the Persian delegation.[38] The names of some of the remaining five are recorded in the Gottorp duke's ledgers.[39] We know that two of the delegates were eventually baptized but not until a good ten years after their arrival in the north.[40] This particular story demonstrates that there was a Muslim population in early modern Germany – and that at least some of them arrived and stayed there voluntarily.

The two Persians baptized were a father and son. Haq Virdī, the father, had been the first secretary of the Persian delegation, making him its highest-ranking member. He may have had a Turkish background, as Sonja Brentjes argues, which might explain his desire to leave Persia.[41]

35 The list of the participants can be found in Adam Olearius, *Ausführliche Beschreibung Der Kundbaren Reyse Nach Muscow und Persien* [...], 3rd ed. (Schleswig: Johan Holwein, 1663), 56–60.

36 Olearius, *Ausführliche Beschreibung*, 766.

37 Elio Brancaforte, *Visions of Persia. Mapping the Travels of Adam Olearius* (Cambridge, MA: Harvard University Press, 2003); Kirsten Baumann et al. eds., *Adam Olearius. Neugier als Methode* (Petersberg: Michael Imhof, 2017).

38 Olearius, *Ausführliche Beschreibung*, 764–65.

39 Kai H. Schwahn, "Patronage, Hofgesellschaft und Gelehrtenkorrespondenz. Zum sozialen Kontext von Adam Olearius," in *Adam Olearius. Neugier als Methode*, ed. Kirsten Baumann et al. (Petersberg: Michael Imhof, 2017), 40–49, here: 48 n. 24.

40 Adam Olearius, *Holsteinische Chronica [...]* (without placename, 1674), 109–10.

41 Sonja Brentjes, "MS. or. fol. 100. Adam Olearius' and Haq Virdī's (c. 1584–1650) Persian-Latin Dictionary," in *Adam Olearius. Neugier als Methode*, ed. Kirsten Baumann et al. (Petersberg: Michael Imhof, 2017), 144–51, here: 148.

He was fifty-six years old when he arrived in Germany and after serving the duke for some years, he became a member of the Olearius household, where he lived for five years until his death in 1650.[42] Together they compiled a dictionary of words in Persian, Arabic, Turkish, German, and Latin, showing that the former Persian secretary had studied both German and Latin in Gottorp.[43] This dictionary was certainly used for their joint translation of Persian texts, chief among them a famous collection of poems entitled Persianischer Rosenthal (Persian Rose Valley) published in 1654.[44] Meanwhile, Virdī's twenty-year-old son became an armourer's apprentice before being sent to Saxony to learn the science and craft of artillery and fireworks. During all these years, he remained a Muslim.

Because these Persians were clearly well assimilated prior to their baptisms, we should not interpret the ceremonies as markers of successful integration; rather, they were intended to help celebrate the marriage of the duke's daughter, Sophia Augusta, to Prince Johann von Anhalt on September 16, 1649.[45] The festivities lasted a full ten days and included multiple forms of entertainment such as fireworks, tournaments, ballets, and comedies, as well as the baptism of two Persians. The Schleswig-Holstein-Gottorp dynasty utilized this ceremony to demonstrate both their cosmopolitan attitudes and Christian and Lutheran sensibilities. Thus, the story of the Persians in Gottorp also shows that baptizing Muslims or "heathens" served a political and representative function for the ruling families. The voices of the actual individuals who were baptized are not documented in the primary sources.

Contexts of Abduction and Enslavement

Current research tends to emphasize the speed with which Turks and people with darker skin were integrated into German courts.[46] This understanding usually stems from individual cases involving people who

[42] Adam Olearius, *Ausführliche Beschreibung*, 763.

[43] Sonja Brentjes, "Adam Olearius' and Haq Virdī's Persian-Latin Dictionary," 146 (the evidence results from the different handwritings: the Latin words are written by an untrained hand in Latin characters).

[44] Mirelle Schnyder, "Übersetzung als Gespräch. Der Persianische Rosenthal," in *Adam Olearius. Neugier als Methode*, ed. Kirsten Baumann et al. (Petersberg: Michael Imhof, 2017), 152–58.

[45] Adam Olearius, *Holsteinische Chronica [...]* (without placename, 1674), 109–10.

[46] Häberlein, "Mohren," 85, 89–90 (see the literature cited for further references); Andreas Hammer, "Türken(taufen) in Stadt und Landkreis Fürth," *Fürther Geschichtsblätter* 86 (2014): 111–22, here: 115; for a more pessimistic view, see, for instance Manja Quakatz, "Die Sesselträger des Kurfürsten: Muslimisch-osmanische Gefangene aus dem Osmanischen Reich als religiöse Minderheit im München des späten 17. Jahrhunderts,"

managed to build careers for themselves, such as the converted Muslim Joseph Borgk, ordained as a Lutheran pastor in 1717.[47] Scholars also point out that the so-called *Hofmohren* were usually financially well off and occupied positions such as court trumpeter or drummer, both of which required a formal education.[48] Clearly the fates of such individuals cannot be compared to those of slaves working on plantations or in Mediterranean galleys. Nevertheless, "court Moors" were also slaves as long as they could still be sold or given as a gift.[49] This issue is further complicated by the fact that slaves had no official legal status in Germany – or in any other European state – during the early modern period.[50] Yet the term slave does appear in some of the baptismal sermons. The Lutheran minister Johann Samuel Adami uses it explicitly when complaining that there were too many Turkish prisoners in the Holy Roman Empire and that jobs and food should be provided to poor Christians instead.[51] Benjamin Textor also refers to a woman whose newborn baby he is about to baptize as a *Sclavin* (female slave).[52] He writes that "the mother was forfeited *jure belli* to her captor, from whom she was purchased legally as a slave by another for a certain amount of money," her new owner, in turn, gifting the young woman to his duchess. Textor emphasizes that the woman "therefore became, as a slave, the inheritance and property of her Most Serene Highness."[53] Other ministers preferred the term *Leibeigener* (serf): Tobias Gabriel Ruprecht used it

in *Gottlosigkeit und Eigensinn. Religiöse Devianz im Konfessionellen Zeitalter*, ed. Eric Piltz and Gerd Schwerhoff (Berlin: Duncker & Humblot, 2015), 387–411.

47 Friedrich, "Türkentaufen," S. 347; Heller, "Um 1700," 22.

48 Anne Kuhlmann, "Ambiguous Duty. Black Servants at German Ancien Régime Courts," in *Germany and the Black Diaspora. Points of Contact, 1250–1914*, ed. Mischa Honeck et al. (New York: Berghahn, 2013), 57–73.

49 See the definition of slavery in Michael Zeuske, *Handbuch Geschichte der Sklaverei. Eine Globalgeschichte von den Anfängen bis zur Gegenwart* (Göttingen: De Gruyter, 2013), 105; Mallinckrodt, "There are no Slaves in Prussia?," 111.

50 Sue Peabody, *There are no Slaves in France: The Political Culture of Race and Slavery in the Ancien Régime* (New York: Oxford University Press, 1996); Rebekka von Mallinckrodt, "Verhandelte (Un-)Freiheit. Sklaverei Leibeigenschaft und innereuropäischer Wissentransferam Ausgang des 18. Jahrhunderts," *Geschichte und Gesellschaft* 43 (2017): 347–80.

51 Johann Samuel Adami, *Sonst Misanders Horae Succisicae [. . .]* (Dresden/Leipzig 1710), 353; regarding the difficulties in interpreting this compilation, see, Manja Quakatz, "Conversio Turci," 218.

52 Benjamin Textor, *Tauff-Sermon, Bey der Tauffe eines Heidnisches Kindes / Welches Gottlieb genennet/und von einer Türckischen Sclavin der [. . .] Frauen Eleonoren Charlotten, Gebohrnen und Vermähleten Hertzogin zu Würtenberg Teck und Chastillon [. . .] Verehret worden [. . .]* (Öls 1686), preface.

53 Textor, *Tauff-Sermon*: "Demnach nun so haben wir hier den Casum in terminis: Gegenwärtiges Kind ist ein heydnisches Kind/ von türckischen Eltern gezeuget und gebohren/ der Vater ist im Streite wieder die Christen geblieben/ die Mutter ist Jure belli an ihrem gefangennehmer verfallen/ von dehme ist sie durch einen andern/ umb ein

to describe Hussin, another prisoner of war,[54] who had been sold to the noble Friedrich Christoph von Wiesenthal for 45 *Reichstaler*. Overall, the baptismal sermons reveal countless stories about the sale, resale, or donation of Turkish and African captives at the courts and within the trading societies of early modern Europe, including German courts and cities. For example, Johann Georg Zeitz writes about a man named Ebnu, who was owned by the council treasurer Georg Neumeister and would be baptized in Cölln (near Berlin) in 1681. Neumeister had acquired Ebnu from the Hamburg merchant Andreas Schachten, who had purchased him from Dutchmen.[55] A particularly well-known account is that of Christian Real from western Africa, already sold nine times and gifted once by the time he was baptized in Lindau in 1657 at age fourteen. Following his baptism, he was gifted once again, this time to the duchess of Württemberg, who allowed him to train for the position of court trumpeter in Stuttgart.[56] Thus, the idea of owning human beings seems to have been quite normal in early modern Germany, even in the absence of slavery's legal recognition. This would explain why a Lutheran minister in Fürth could write "Miss Susanna Johanna of Crailsheim, the daughter of the owner of the Turk" in a letter from 1689 and why Ottoman prisoners were sometimes even mentioned as items of property in inventories.[57] Clearly, slaves were an intrinsic part of early modern Germany. The clergy spoke freely about donations of slaves – both male and female – destined for baptism. They discussed the legal possibilities of acquiring slaves during wartime and debated about what should be done with the children of unconverted slaves. Even though they emphasized time and again that baptism should be voluntary, some, like the

gewiß Stücke Geld/ alß eine Sclavin rechtmäßig erkauffet worden/ dieser Erkauffer hernach hat selbige an unsere Durchlauchteste hertzogin verehret und verschencket/ und ist also Ihrer Hoch=Fürstl. Durchlauchtigkeit alß eine Sclavin Erb und Eigen worden/ hat auch wie man von ihr vernimmet/ Belieben nach genugsamer Information getauffet zu werden/ und also den Christl. Glauben anzunehmen [. . .]" (no pagination).

54 Tobias Gabriel Ruprecht, *Eigentlicher Verlauff einer zu Rückersdorff verrichteten Türcken-Tauff* [. . .] (Nürnberg, 1694), 16.

55 Johann G. Zeitz, *Der Aussätzige und wieder gereinigte Maeman [. . .]* (Cölln an der Spree, 1681), 32.

56 Jakob Fussenegger, *Die Mohren Tauff/ Das ist Christliche Tauffpredigt [. . .] Bey der Tauff eines bekehrten Mohrens/ Welcher vom Herrn Joß Kramer aus dem Königreich Guinea in Africâ gelegen/ in des Heiligen Röm. Reichs Stadt Lindau im Bodensee gebracht/ und daselbst in der Pfarrkirchen zu St. Stephan/ am Abend des Heiligen Pfingstfestes getauffet worden. Mit angehengtem Bericht/ wie der Tauffactus verrichtet worden. Gehalten den 17. Maji dieses 1657. Jahrs [. . .]* (Nürnberg, 1658); Monika Firla/ Hermann Forkl, "Afrikaner," 157.

57 "Fräulein Susanna Johanna von Crailsheim, Tochter des Türkenbesitzers," quoted in Andreas Hammer, "Türken(taufen) in Stadt und Landkreis Fürth,"*Fürther Geschichtsblätter* 86 (2014): 111–22, here: 118, 121 n. 11.

Silesian pastor Benjamin Textor, argued that children of slaves could be baptized against their parents' wishes.[58]

However, not every prisoner of war was a slave in the Holy Roman Empire. This is especially true of young children, who were often treated similarly to adopted children, as the Lutheran minister Johann Samuel Adami pointed out.[59] Sometimes former Muslims were granted official citizenship upon baptism. This was the case of a woman in Memmingen; she later even received a widow's sinecure in one of the hospitals of this imperial city.[60] Some were freed from their "chains of slavery" by their masters, as was the case of a young Turk from Istanbul who subsequently worked as a groom in a noble household in Mecklenburg.[61] Others worked as house servants in cities or as day laborers, only acquiring historical significance because they were baptized. For example, we know of a Turkish woman whose father was said to have been a celebrated officer commanding over 100 Janissaries. However, after being abducted to the small city of Amberg in southern Germany, she worked as a "lowly servant" at the time of her baptism in 1599.[62] Another representative case of the lives of Turkish prisoners of war in the Old Reich was the fate of a small girl who had left her hometown of Istanbul together with her parents.[63] Her father was also a high-ranking officer in the Ottoman Army. In 1739 at age seven, she and her mother were kidnapped by Habsburg soldiers near Timişoara, Romania. They were brought to Vienna, where they scraped together a living as seamstresses for years before seeking greener pastures in Regensburg and then Bamberg, where the mother passed away. The daughter tried her luck one more time in

[58] Benjamin Textor, *Tauff-Sermon, Bey der Tauffe eines Heidnisches Kindes / Welches Gottlieb genennet/und von einer Türckischen Sclavin der [...] Frauen Eleonoren Charlotten, Gebohrnen und Vermähleten Hertzogin zu Würtenberg Teck und Chastillon [...] Verehret worden [...]* (Öls, 1686), preface.

[59] Johann Samuel Adami, *Sonst Misanders Horae Succisicae [...]* (Dresden/ Leipzig, 1710), 353.

[60] Christoph Engelhard, "Agenda für die Taufe einer Türkin zu St. Martin in Memmingen," in *Geld und Glaube. Leben in evangelischen Reichsstädten*, ed. Wolfgang Jahn et al. (Augsburg: Haus der Bayerischen Geschichte, 1998), 237.

[61] Hermann Müller, *Turca de Longe Ad-Vocatus, Eine Christliche Predigt/ Als Ein gebohrner Türck/ Seines Alters ohngefähr dreissig Jahr/ Durch die H. Tauffe dem HERRN Christo in der Grabowischen Schloß=Kapelle/ in vieler hohen und niedrigen Stadens=Manns und Weibes=Persohnen Gegenwart zugeführet wurde den 11. Julii des 1665. Jahrs/ Neben Außführlichem Bericht/ was bey dem Taufflinge/ vor/ bey und nach der Tauffe fürgenommen/ [...]* (Rostock, 1666), 57.

[62] Johann Salmuth, *Bericht von der Christlichen Tauffe einer gebornen Türckin/ Wie dieselbe in öffentlicher Versammlung Zu Amberg ihres Glaubens Bekäntniß gethan/ unnd darauff getaufft worden* [...] (Lich, 1600), 62.

[63] Andreas Seyboth, *Drey Heilige Reden bey der [...] 1756. Christ-Jahrs geschehenen Tauf-Handlung einer gebornen Türckin [...]* (Windsheim, 1756), summarized in *Nova acta historico-ecclesiastica*, vol. 1, part I–VIII (Weimar 1760), 845–49.

Schweinfurt. Having lived in the Holy Roman Empire for seventeen years, she finally asked to be baptized. Another example of a prisoner of war is Salomon Bugali, abducted and taken to the Saxon town of Halle when he was eleven years old. He was forced to wear shackles for four years before finally being allowed to take them off.[64]

The Captives' Agency

Integration is all about communication. So how did these abducted prisoners and slaves communicate? Because candidates for baptism needed to become acquainted with the most important tenets of Christianity before engaging in this ritual, the sermons often describe this part of the process quite carefully with incidental information about the candidate's ability to communicate with others. One sermon explains how the Turkish boy mentioned above came into contact with other young people from Halle who wanted to learn Arabic from him.[65] In other sermons we learn about communication between new abductees and older prisoners or slaves. A soldier from Istanbul, for example, learned German from a Croatian prisoner in Rostock.[66] As in so many cases, mutual understanding began in a third language that both parties knew, however haltingly. Polish and other Slavic languages are often mentioned in these contexts along with Italian or some versions of pidgin Latin, as Stephan Theilig has observed.[67]

Such conversations between prisoners or immigrants are often part of the stories told in sermons. Every now and then, the authors of these sermons even assert that these dialogues catalyzed the decision to convert to Christianity. For example, a woman named Ravis from Belgrade decided that she and her three-year-old son should be baptized after conversing with another Turkish woman. She had apparently been impressed by the joyful and contented disposition of her compatriot.[68]

[64] Philipp Hahn, *Consilia Sive Judicia Theologica, & Requisita Ministerii totius Ecclesiae, Neu verbessert- und vollständiges Kirchen=Buch [. . .]* (Magdeburg/ Zerbst, 1692), 64–65.

[65] Hahn, *Consilia*, 65. [66] Müller, *Turca*, 57.

[67] Textor, *Tauff-Sermon* with reference to Polish (no pagination); [Reinhart], *Möhrin-Tauf/ so geschehen in Altorf am Tag Eucharii den 20. Febr. A. 1688* ([Altdorf], 1688), 6 with reference to Italian; see also: Theilig, *Türken*, 54.

[68] Christoph Klesch, *Christianorum Pikroglykytēs. Der Bitter=Süsse ChristenOrden/ Darein wir durch die H. Tauffe treten/ Als Drey Türcken/ Ein verwittibtes Weib/ Nahmens Ravis, mit ihrem dritthalbjährigen Söhnlein/ Omer, und ein Jünglichn von 18. Jahren/ Nahmens Soliman, Zu Erffurdt In der Evangelischen Kirchen S. Gregorii, sonst zum Kauffmann genannt/ Bey Volckreicher Versammlung und in Gegenwart etlicher 1000. Personen hohes und niedriges Standes am 30. Julii nach Mittag lauffenden 1690sten Jahrs getaufft wurden. [. . .]* (Erfurt, 1690), §2: "Nun hatte zwar in Anfang das Weib keine Lust zum Christenthumb/ wolte auch durchaus nicht daß ihr Kind/ nach dem Vorsatz des Herrn Obristen Wacht-

In the end, she requested an emergency baptism after repeated bouts of serious illness.[69] Her knowledge of German was so rudimentary that the minister felt compelled to apologize on her behalf in his sermon.[70] She was certainly not the only convert to understand German only sparingly at the time of baptism.[71] Sometimes, this was because prisoners or slaves were baptized rather soon after their arrival in Germany; at other times Muslim prisoners of war met so many others from the Ottoman Empire that there was simply no need to learn German. The forty-one-year-old Mehmet from Istanbul, for example, was able to read German texts quite well, according to his baptismal minister, but still barely spoke the language despite having lived in Wolfenbüttel for ten years.[72]

Not many captives were able to read and write and certainly few of them would have read the Old Testament once and the New Testament twice in German before deciding to be baptized, as one particular Ottoman soldier had claimed to do.[73] This soldier also kept a journal of everything that happened to him during his captivity because he hoped to be able to give an accurate account of it upon release.[74] Generally, however, the agency of the baptismal candidates is barely recorded: baptismal sermons were delivered, transcribed, and printed in order to celebrate the victory of the Christian, if not Protestant, church rather than discuss difficulties, ambiguities, or rejections. Nevertheless, the last few examples show that we do sometimes have glimpses of captives' perspectives, especially when things did not run so smoothly. Initially, Ravis

Meisters/ getaufft werden solte/ wormit sie ihren harten Sinn gnugsam verrathen/ auch sonsten auff vielfältige Art ihre feindseligkeit gegen die Christen bezeuget; doch schickte es eins mahls die wunderbahre Güte Gottes/ daß sie mit einer getaufften Türckin in einem Hoch=Gräfflichen Hause zu reden kam/ welche sie in einem Gespräch gantz geändert und auff einen bessern Sinn gebracht/ in dem sie ihr eigen Beyspiel angezogen/ wie nach der Tauffe an statt voriger Traurigkeit und wiederwillens eine solche freudigkeit und zufriedenheit in ihrem Gemüthe entstanden/ daß sie dem erkannten wahren Gott nicht gnugsam dafür dancken könte/[...]. Nach welcher Zeit unsere Ravis sich anders gehalten/ offt geseufftzet und endlich bey der andächtigen Hauß=Kirche und information willig und gehorsam bezeiget/ und gebethen/ man wolle ihr doch die Gnade erweisen und ihr Söhnlein mit ihr zugleich tauffen lassen. Welche Bitte auch statt gefunden."

69 Ibid., §3. 70 Ibid., C2v.

71 Franciscus Meineke, *Bericht/ Wie ein geborner Türckischer Knabe/ und ein gebornes Türckisches Mägdlein/ jhres alters im sechzehenden Jar/ zum Schermbeck im Fürstenthumb Lüneburgk/ in öffentlicher versammlung/ jres Glaubens bekäntnis gethan/ und darauff getaufft worden/ den 27. Septemb. Anno 1601. [...]* (Lüneburg, 1601), Biiiv.

72 Johann Niekamp, *Die göttliche Gnaden-Krafft Von dem Könige David Psalm. 71 v. 16.17.18: Gepriesen [...] am ersten Sontage nach dem Fest der H. Dreyeinigkeit Anno XCV. An dem [...] Fr. Elisabeth Juliane, Gebohrner Hertzoging zu Schleßwig-Holstein, Vermählter Hertzogin zu Braunschw.Lüneb. [... .] Gebuhrt- und eines Türckischen Aga, Mechmet genandt Tauff-Feyer* (Wolfenbüttel, 1696), 71; see for a similar observation of the situation at the court in Stuttgart, Anne Kuhlmann-Smirnov, *Schwarze Europäer*, 231.

73 Hahn, *Consilia*, 66. 74 Ibid., 65.

fiercely refused to become a Christian, as we have seen.[75] The Turkish widow in Memmingen seems to have either never really converted or just changed her mind again afterwards. Ten years after her baptism, rumours spread that she was mumbling in the direction of the rising moon while moving back and forth and also skipping Sunday services.[76] The Lutheran minister Johann Samuel Adami narrates the saddest story of all in his collection of baptism stories. He recounts the case of a Turkish baby baptized in the Brandenburg city of Wittstock in 1687. Immediately following the ceremony, the mother drowned herself and her child in the river.[77]

Baptism as Rite of Passage: Inventing a Lutheran Ritual

Baptisms were a key rite of passage.[78] Since the publication of Arnold van Gennep's research on the subject, we have known that rituals bring about a change in status and invariably rest on a combination of different elements.[79] The field of ritual studies has expanded greatly since the pioneering work of Van Gennep, Turner, and others.[80] According to Barbara Stollberg-Rilinger, a ritual is composed of five central elements, all of them relevant to the idea of baptism as a rite of passage.[81] First, there is a certain standardization and repetition or repeatability required in the ritual act. Secondly, rituals are solemn ceremonies that stand out from everyday life. Thirdly, they are laden with symbolism because they refer to an ordered context that transcends the act itself. This is connected, fourthly, to the performative quality of the rituals, which are not simply about display. Instead, they bring about a change in the social reality of the converted by requiring their future adherence to the commitments made during the ritual. This underscores, finally, their effect on the social

[75] See n. 68.

[76] In the minutes of the town council from July 3, 1699, one can read that there were complaints that "die Türggin in der Capellpfründe ganz vom Christenthumb kommen" and "das man sie bei aufgehendenem Mond hin und her in Winckhlen plappernd finden und komme wenig mehr zur Predigt," quoted in Christoph Engelhard, "Agenda für die Taufe einer Türkin zu St. Martin in Memmingen," in *Geld und Glaube. Leben in evangelischen Reichsstädten*, ed. Wolfgang Jahn et al. (Augsburg: Haus der Bayerischen Geschichte, 1998), 237.

[77] Adami, *Sonst Misanders Horae Succisicae*, 374.

[78] Friedrich, "Türkentaufen," 355; Theilig, *Türken*, 19, 61–66.

[79] Arnold van Gennep, *The Rites of Passage* (Chicago, IL: The University of Chicago Press: 1960).

[80] Jens Kreinath et al. eds., *Theorizing Rituals. Issues, Topics, Approaches, Concepts* (Leiden: Brill, 2008); Barbara Stollberg-Rilinger, *Rituale* (Frankfurt am Main: Campus, 2013); Pamela J. Stewart and Andrew Strathern eds., *Ritual: Key Concepts in Religion* (London: Bloomsbury, 2014).

[81] Stollberg-Rilinger, *Rituale*, 9–14.

structure. That Christian baptism meets this description of a ritual is immediately clear. Through baptism converts become members of the Christian church, thus distancing themselves from other religious communities while promising (via godparents in the cases of children) to adhere to the associated articles of faith and approach to life. Precisely because of the importance of this ritual for the self-conception of the Christian community, repeated efforts were made to clearly define the correct procedure for baptism.[82] This was true during the period of the Carolingian Empire as well as that of the Reformation.[83] As is well known, the correct handling of baptism was a central concern of the Reformation. People (or at least theologians) who lived in the sixteenth and seventeenth centuries were well aware of the transcendent symbolic meaning of rituals in general and baptism in particular. This was made abundantly clear by the care with which Lutheran pastors arranged every aspect of the *Türkentaufen* and *Mohrentaufen*, the detail with which they recorded each step in the process, and the solemnity with which they fine-tuned the symbolic meaning of the different elements. This does not, however, imply uniformity – nor, incidentally, was this the case in the Carolingian period. Indeed, recent scholarship about ritual in general no longer associates it with homogeneity, stability, and unambiguousness.[84] Below, we will see how Lutheran clerics appropriated elements of the Lutheran baptismal rite and adapted them to the particular needs and contexts of their individual congregations, a process that often led to difficulties in applying their chosen narrative approach. This, nevertheless, is exactly the reason why the *Türkentaufen* and *Mohrentaufen* of the seventeenth and eighteenth centuries should be interpreted as examples of Lutheran self-affirmation.

In line with Van Gennep's ritual theory, this painting (Fig 7.1) by an anonymous artist in the early seventeenth century emphasizes three

[82] Susan A. Keefe, *Water and the World. Baptism and the Education of the Clergy in the Carolingian Empire*, vol.1 (Notre Dame, IN: University of Notre Dame Press, 2002); see also Christian Lange et al. eds., *Die Taufe. Einführung in Geschichte und Praxis* (Darmstadt: Wissenschaftliche Buchgesellschaft, 2008).

[83] Robert W. Scribner, "Ritual and Reformation," in *Popular Culture and Popular Movements in Reformation Germany (1984)*, 2nd ed. (London/Ronceverte, WV: Hambledon Press, 2010), 103–22; Susan Karant-Nunn, *The Reformation of the Ritual. An Interpretation of Early Modern Germany* (London/New York: Routledge, 1997); Carine van Rhijn, *Shepherds of the Lord: Priests and Episcopal Statutes in the Carolingian Period* (Turnhout: Brepols, 2007).

[84] Robert Langer, "The Transfer of Ritual," *Journal of Ritual Studies* 20 (2006): 1–10; Ute Hüsken ed., *When Rituals Go Wrong. Mistakes, Failures, and the Dynamics of Ritual* (Leiden: Brill, 2007); Axel Michaels ed., *Ritual Dynamics and the Science of Ritual*, 5 vols. (Wiesbaden: Harrassowitz, 2010–2011); Adam B. Seligman, Robert W. Weller, *Rethinking Pluralism: Ritual, Experience, and Ambiguity* (Oxford : Oxford University Press, 2012).

essential elements of a *Türkentaufe*: below, the examination; in the middle, the introduction at the altar by the godparents and the local nobility; above, the baptism itself.[85] In the printed sermons, however, the liturgy is described in much greater detail. For example, the minister of the tiny village of Onolzbach, Andreas Geret, divided the ritual of baptism into seventeen separate activities.[86] The ritual obviously needed a lot of explanation, and much was written about it at the time. The problem was, namely, that although there was a baptismal rite for children, there was no standard liturgy for the baptism of adults. The Lutheran pastors' fear of being confused with Anabaptists also explains why the previous life of the baptismal candidate was described in such detail. These stories made it absolutely clear why these adults could not possibly have been baptized before. Lutheran pastors also had to differentiate themselves from both Catholics' alleged hastiness in baptizing converts and Calvinists' reluctance in baptizing adults in the first place.[87] This sandwich position between the Christian denominations was typical of early modern German Lutheranism.[88] Usually each parish invented or reinvented its own baptismal liturgy, provoking concern about the correctness of the baptismal act. For example, Hermann Müller, a pastor from Rostock, sought examples of successful *Türkentaufen* from several people, including Adam Olearius.[89] Similar uncertainty is palpable in a sermon from Erfurt, in which the pastor explains and justifies changing the passage of the baptismal rite pertaining to children to something more appropriate for adults. Instead of the invitation to the children in Mark 10:13–16, he called upon all those who faced trials and tribulations, as per Matthew 11:25–30.[90]

The meticulous details provided for each stage of the ritual was, first and foremost, intended to prove the orthodoxy of the baptism. Secondly, they illustrate how Lutherans experimented with different elements and how they conceived of baptism as a highly symbolic ritual. Finally, the descriptions show how different elements of the baptismal rite could sometimes conflict with one another, pushing the boundaries of what was acceptable. Improvisation and compromise were also part of the

[85] See below, p. 215. [86] Geret, *Das Neue Leben*.

[87] Samuel Huber, *Bericht und Antwort über die Frage, ob man der Türcken und anderer Ungleubigen Eltern Kinder teuffen solle. Darinn eines Theologen schädlicher Irrthumb/ darduch er gefährlichen Streit mit Verrichtung der Heiligen Tauff In der Kirchen Jesu Christi erweckt/ nach Notturff widerlegt wird* (Ursel, 1599); Müller, *Turca*, 40.

[88] Renate Dürr, "Prophetie und Wunderglaube – zu den kulturellen Folgen der Reformation,"*Historische Zeitschrift* 281 (2005): 3–32.

[89] Müller, *Turca*, 64; see also: Friedrich, "Türkentaufen," 352–53, see above p. 204–205.

[90] Klesch, *Christianorum Pikroglykytēs*, § 5.

proceedings.[91] The performative character of the entire ritual is visible even in printed versions. The authors retain the use of direct speech towards the audience, for instance, and often deliver their account in the present tense, including any unexpected turns in the proceedings. The ritual's performative character was enhanced by an audience consisting of distinguished members of the court or council acting as key witnesses and members of the local congregation, who participated in the ceremony through song and prayer. Sometimes, the size and enthusiasm of the crowd was such that soldiers were required to restore order.[92]

Transitions Underlined

Together the Lutheran *Türkentaufen* and *Mohrentaufen* were intended as visualized rites of passage. This manifested itself most clearly in the relinquishment of the old name and the adoption of a new Christian one. But there were additional elements in the transition. The baptism of a young boy in Lichtenstein am Lahm is the central theme of the painting (Fig 7.1) already briefly referred to in this chapter.[93] The importance of this baptism for the petty Franconian nobility in attendance is demonstrated by the fact that the painting was only commissioned in 1617 – fifteen years after the baptism had taken place. Moreover, the painting was considered so important that it underwent extensive restorations sixty years later. The three images of the convert form the centerpiece of the composition. The first two stations direct the viewer's gaze towards the central scene, in which the little boy, almost naked, is kneeling in front of the water basin. The contrast between the underdressed boy and the elaborately dressed clerics and members of the christening party is jarring. Nakedness served a practical purpose in late antique and early medieval Christianity, when baptisms involved three full immersions in water. However, nakedness is not integral to this scene. As was customary in Lutheran churches, baptism only required sprinkling the head with water. The lack of clothing here is more a symbol of the boy's transition from Islam to Christianity, I would suggest, and also represents the shedding of a religion considered illegitimate. The contrast of colors also supports the idea of a rite of passage. The boy starts out dressed in black, but then a white cloth is draped over his shoulders during the actual

91 For similar observations concerning Anglican England, see Matthew Dimmock, "Converting and Not Converting 'Strangers' in Early Modern London," *Journal of Early Modern History* 17 (2013): 457–78.

92 Klesch, *Christianorum Pikroglykytēs*, § 5.

93 Rosmarie Beier- de Haan, *Zuwanderungsland Deutschland – Migrationen, 1500– 2005* (Berlin: Edition Minerva, 2005), 168–69.

Fig 7.1 *Gemälde der Taufe eines türkischen Jungen*, 1617 Rittergut am Lahm

baptism; the open bible visible in the painting refers to Mark 7, concerning purity and impurity.[94] Similar symbolism is also found in sermons where the ministers often associated black with impurity (the old religion) and white with purity (Christianity).[95] Sometimes, the symbolic use of white was present in the baptismal name and date, as was the case of a ten-year-old girl, Maria Catharina Weißin (White), baptized on Alba (White) Sunday in 1692.[96]

The three central scenes are framed by two semicircles that emphasize the elegance of courtly society and the value of baptism. No less than three clergymen were needed for the baptism of a single boy: one to sprinkle water onto his head, one to read the baptismal formula, and one to receive him with a towel. The faces of those in attendance are turned towards the spectator, whose presence is thus incorporated into the event. But not everybody looks in the same direction. Some people listen intently to the examination while others look in different directions. While I do not wish to push the interpretation of this painting too far, it seems clear to me that the image shows an unrest within the christening party that contradicts the solemnity of the ritual.

Local Adaptations of the Ritual

In this way, the painting's iconography does not quite add up, perhaps reflecting the improvisational nature of inventing a ritual almost from scratch. The ceremony would typically begin with a festive procession into the church that functioned as a transition of sorts. The christening party often congregated at the home of the godparents before proceeding to the church, accompanied by the pealing of bells and sometimes even the sound of horns and trumpets. Such processions were carefully orchestrated but followed their own ordering principles. In Altdorf, the changing status of the female baptismal candidate was key: the men walked up front, the women stayed in back, and "the Moor, all alone" remained in the middle, separated from both groups.[97] After the baptism, the women allowed the new convert into their midst.[98] In Erfurt, it was not so much the status of the candidate as the prerequisites for the conversion that were emphasized during the procession.[99] Here godfathers led the way,

[94] Theilig, *Türken*, 114.
[95] Caspar von Lilien, *Das Christ-glaubige Mohren-Land/ Bey Angestelter Tauffe Einer Möhrin/ In der Pfarr-Kirche/ Der Hochfürstl. Residenz-Stadt Bayreuth/ am 13. Christmonats-Tag/ des 1668. Jahrs/ [...]* (Bayreuth, [1668]), 14; [Fussenegger], *Mohren Tauff*, appendix: Sequuntur Amicorum Carmina; Müller, *Turca*, 14; Klesch, *Christianorum Pikrglykytes*, § 7.
[96] Ruprecht, *Eigentlicher Verlauff*, 31. [97] [Reinhart], *Möhrin-Tauf [...]*, 4.
[98] Ibid., 16. [99] Klesch, *Christianorum Pikryglykytes*, § 6.

followed by godmothers. Then came the military commander who had brought the Turkish prisoners to the town, followed by the pastor and the deacon, each carrying a book; teachers of the catechism rounded out the procession. The three baptismal candidates dressed in white Turkish clothes walked between the different groups, followed by the military commander's daughter and wife, carrying wreaths for the candidates. Although the pastor regretted that two people would have to carry three wreaths between them, he explained that they had no other choice because the commander only had one daughter and asking a third person to carry one of the wreaths was apparently out of the question. Here we see how different actions were deliberately instilled with significance. In addition to the precedence of the noble godparents, the procession visualized both the military background of this baptism and the importance of instruction by teachers and pastors alike. The example from Erfurt shows, moreover, that the relatively straightforward color symbolism of black and white was not always used. Instead, many sermons make reference to the white Turkish costumes already worn by the converts as they approach the altar.

As these were all new traditions, the pastors clarified their significance to the community, emphasising their validity and venerable pedigree. Christoph Klesch, for example, told the Erfurt congregation in 1690 that the presentation of the white vestments and wreaths had a long history going back to apostolic times.[100] The white shirts, he said, signified innocence and justice; however, this symbolism was not always deemed strong enough for the baptisms of Muslims and adults. In Erfurt, candidates were wrapped in cloth of three different colours, each with a specified meaning. The red cloth tied around the belly was a symbol of love, peace, and the perfection of Christ's sacrifice of his own blood, Klesch explained. The black ribbon that bound the hands represented the cross and the convert's penitential status while the green cloth wrapped around the arms stood for hope, confidence, and strength. Finally, the wreath confirmed God's blessing. Here, the colours represented penance and repentance, both preconditions for baptism and attaining a new life as a Christian.

The removal of clothing was another way to symbolize transition, as we have already seen, but there were sometimes practical difficulties attached to this particular action. For example, once in Halle a convert stood "naked except for his undershirt," which was too big and almost slipped off his body entirely. This clearly threatened to disrupt the solemnity of the ritual, but the deacon quickly rectified the situation by wrapping one

[100] Klesch, *Christianorum Pikryglykytes*, § 7.

of his own ribbons around the Turk's loins.[101] Unsurprisingly, the difficulties involved in removing clothes were exacerbated when the converts were women. A pastor in Amberg highlighted the fact that a Turkish woman being baptized had not taken off her clothes, only her headwear.[102]

The Baptismal Examinations

Prior to the baptism was the examination – the other centerpiece of the ritual. Upon the procession's arrival to the church, the baptismal candidate would be led into the choir, accompanied by organ music and singing. In larger churches this meant that the convert was physically separated from the community and would sometimes have to stand on a wooden bench in order to be heard by everyone.[103] On other occasions, the pastors would ensure audience participation by loudly repeating the examinee's responses.[104] In one case, the examination was moved to the sacristy, where the candidate was examined for ninety minutes while the congregation sang one hymn after another.[105] Above all, the public nature of the baptismal examinations was designed to benefit the community. The preachers often emphasized the candidate's mastery of Christian learning – how quickly they had learned the tenets of faith by heart and how diligently they had renounced their former habits. The Muslim and African converts were made to serve as examples for the Lutheran parishioners. It is little wonder, then, that we rarely hear about complications arising during the process of instruction.

All of the sermons dwell on the fact that the baptismal candidate had already been examined multiple times before the actual baptism: by the pastor who instructed them, by impartial clergymen, and sometimes by the consistory, which might even include the duke on occasion. Nothing was left to chance. Because the examination in the church at Altdorf would be held in Italian, the questions were sent several days in advance to Johann Fabricius, a renowned professor of theology at the local university. This allowed him to translate them into Italian and practise them with his soon-to-be-baptized slave, as is documented in the printed sermon.[106] The actual examination in the church was thus a repetition of a previously rehearsed test, which meant that the proceedings were largely symbolic in nature. Despite the length of the tests and the multitude of questions – I have seen examinations with 147 or even 166

[101] Hahn, *Consilia*, 68–69. [102] Salmuth, *Bericht*, 53. [103] Ibid.
[104] Fussenegger, *Mohren Tauff*, Kiiiv. [105] Hahn, *Consilia*, 68.
[106] [Reinhart], *Möhrin-Tauf*, 6, 8–9.

questions – no candidate would have failed the exam. In one baptism, a thirty-year-old Turkish women answered questions delivered by the Rostock pastor Hermann Müller for three straight hours; that she did so while standing was commended by her examiner.[107]

The baptismal examinations varied in length and focus. Often pastors began by asking candidates to state their reasons for conversion. This question served two purposes: first, the candidates had to declare that they wanted to be blessed in Christ; secondly, candidates were given the opportunity to publicly renounce their old beliefs before witnesses. Indeed, their answers were often followed by strongly anti-Islamic remarks delivered by the Lutheran pastor.[108] In addition, the meaning of baptism itself was the subject of questions in some examinations. Christian Real, for example, was first asked "Where does baptism come from, and who introduced it?" In his pre-scripted answer he stated that neither an angel nor a human was responsible but, rather, that baptism had arrived from heaven like the Pentecostal wind and was then instituted by Christ; moreover, it should be carried out in the name of the Father, the Son, and the Holy Spirit.[109] Christian Real was then asked of what elements baptism consisted. In his well-rehearsed response, he said that it was composed of water, spirit, and the baptismal candidate's own faith. This prompted the pastor to expressly reject the use of other liquids, such as wine, oil, beer, milk, or brine, and to discuss the importance of faith as well as the spirit responsible for transforming the baptism into a sacrament. In good Lutheran form, he also pointed out that faith could not be a stand-alone component of the baptism, as this would imply that the act had a human basis. The third question related to the form of the baptism, which, as a symbol of a new member's acceptance into the community of believers, should be carried out in full view of parishioners. What was important was not whether the candidate was fully immersed in water or only sprinkled with it nor whether this happened once, twice, or three times. Discrepancies in the baptism ritual, the pastor argued, could instead be justified according to differences in climate and the number of candidates.[110] And so continued the pastor of Lindau: Who could be baptized? (everyone, regardless of sex, ethnicity, or age); what does one receive through baptism? (blessedness); what tangible benefits does one accrue? (acceptance into the Christian Church). Other baptismal examinations were organized around Luther's *Small Catechism*, which candidates were often required to reprise in full.[111] Still other examinations

[107] Geret, *Neues Leben*, 28–40, 147 questions in total; Müller, *Turca*, 65.
[108] Klesch, *Christianorum Pikroglykytēs*, § 7.
[109] Fussenegger, *Mohren Tauff*, Diiv–Diiir. [110] Ibid., Div. [111] Geret, *Neues Leben*.

were highly abstract in character. In Rückersdorff, for example, Tobias Gabriel Ruprecht asked Husin the meaning of the name Jesus and the word Christus before inquiring where the Holy Trinity was explained in the New Testament.[112]

The recorded examinations thus differed in their length and degree of abstraction. It is tempting for the modern-day reader to question whether the baptismal candidates had actually learned the answers to so many questions, some of them very detailed. Indeed, the primary sources show that the pastors all made a point of noting that the printed text faithfully recorded how the questions had been posed and answered. At times they also highlighted the work that went into learning so many answers by heart. One such example is Johann Samuel Adami's account of Hali, a man from Aleppo who was seemingly too old to learn to read or even speak new languages.[113] Over the course of many weeks, his pastor read the catechism word for word to him without much success; at some point Hali gave up and failed to appear for instruction. Even after he had resumed lessons, progress remained slow, so that Hali was spared public examination at church and tested at a private residence instead.[114] In other cases, one had to make do with the minister himself explaining the catechism during the baptismal service.[115] The community would then be asked to give due consideration to the difficult situation faced by the candidate. In one such case, Pastor Wilisch attributed the incomprehensible pronunciation of the former soldier Wolko to his great fear of being examined in front of the assembled community and in the presence of such noble godparents – however, this did not prevent him from interrogating the candidate with a full 100 questions.[116] Even at the burial of Wolko – baptized Gottlieb Christian Friedrich Wohlfahrt – the pastor deemed it necessary to mention his own difficulty in understanding the way Wolko had framed his thoughts and translated the concepts needed to understand his new faith. This illustrates just how demanding the process of instruction must have been for both parties.[117] Wolko, incidentally, was among the very few Ottoman prisoners of war or Africans

[112] Ruprecht, *Eigentlicher Verlauff*, 19–20.

[113] Adami, *Sonst Misanders Horae Succusicae*, 357–58. [114] Ibid., 360.

[115] Klesch, *Christianorum Pikroglykytēs*, § 2.

[116] Christian Gotthold Wilisch, *Predigt bey der Taufe Eines Türcken [. . .]* (Freiberg, 1746), Taufpredigt, 15; Catechetischer Unterricht für Wolko, den Türcken, 1–10.

[117] Christian Gotthold Wilisch, *Das Recht der Pilgrim, an den Gottesacker der Christen/ bey der öffentlichen und Christlichen Beerdigung eines gebornen Türcken/ Wolcko/ welcher in der Heil. Taufe genennet worden Gottlieb Christian Wohlfarth, und in die acht Jahr lang, ein Hütten=Arbeiter in Freyberg gewesen, den 1. Julii 1754 allda seelig gestorben, und den 4ten Julii auf den neuen Kirchhof begraben worden [. . .]* (Freyberg, 1754), 17–18.

allowed to pick their own baptismal name. Another was the nine-year-old Ahmet, who opted for the expressive name Gottfried (peace in God).[118]

Concluding Remarks: Global Lutheranism in Early Modern Germany?

How did this importation of global experiences impact Lutheran churches and parishes? That changes were afoot in the second half of the seventeenth century did not go unnoticed at the time. As early as the end of the 1660s, the general superintendent and court chaplain at Bayreuth, Caspar von Lilien, observed that many children from foreign lands could now be seen around the town, "something that was once seldom, or even not at all, seen by anybody in these parts."[119] This is not be surprising given that printed Lutheran sermons for so-called *Türkentaufen* and *Mohrentaufen* show that abduction, slavery, and forced immigration were part of the reality of early modern Germany, a fact often overlooked by contemporary scholars. Although some cases show that slaves could be freed, other examples suggest that not even baptism was a sure way out. The most striking point about these baptismal sermons is perhaps that the baptisms of particular individuals – women and men, children alone or with their mothers – were celebrated as a victory for universal Lutheranism. They were all called by their non-Christian names and their biographical information – parents, places of origin, former professions – divulged. I would argue that this is a particularly Lutheran manner of appropriating the world. It was the single believer who stood at the center of the entire feast. Thus it is perhaps no coincidence that these baptisms and their printed sermons best reveal the story of Muslims and Africans in Lutheran Germany. Lutheran Christian universalism was perhaps particularly glocal in character: anchored in small German villages and provincial towns, it facilitated the conversion of specific individuals, enacted and witnessed by a single parish while celebrating the local duke and duchess.

This emphasis on the curriculum vitae of baptismal candidates served multiple functions in the Lutheran church: it strengthened the idea of the baptism as a rite of passage because these accounts clearly belonged to the rhetoric of a before and an after, and it emphasized God's mercy in freeing these new Christians from unbelief and the devil's work. The authors of the sermons are especially explicit about this latter purpose. All sermons provide quite dramatic accounts of the cruelties of war and the

118 Adami, *Sonst Misanders Horae Succusicae*, 372.
119 Von Lilien, *Das Christ-glaubige Mohren-Land*, 7–8.

circumstances of abduction and slavery. The heavier the pain these men and women had suffered, the greater God's grace seemed to be.[120]

Through these stories of particular individuals, small-town Germans learned about the wider world. Responses by baptismal candidates to questions about their former religions provided one such source of information. It was from former Muslims that the Lutheran congregation learned, for example, about Muhammad as a *Mittler des Heils* (mediator of salvation), the importance of Christ in Muslim belief, and Islamic concepts of paradise – although answers were obviously pre-formulated. Some candidates were even explicitly asked if they had been circumcised.[121] Clearly this mise en scène strengthened the ritual of renunciation. The former Muslims themselves would tell of the many ways they had been subject to the devil's power. Nevertheless, detailed descriptions of candidates' individual fates sometimes encouraged identification with them. In many sermons, the ministers mention prejudices they held to be wrong.[122] Black skin was not a sign of depravity, argued Caspar von Lilien, for instance. In addition, he contradicted the common Christian belief of that time that connected skin colour to Ham, Noah's cursed son.[123] He also emphasized that black skin did not result from being burnt by the strong African sun, as Strabo had assumed. On the contrary, he continued – and here we get a glimpse of the influence of new experiences – even "Moors" who lived in the north gave birth to black children. Von Lilien was convinced that black skin colour should be interpreted as an act of God that human beings could never fully understand: "The natural black colour of the Moors is beyond doubt a work of the Most High, which is, however, completely inscrutable to us humans."[124] The Bayreuth cleric goes on to ridicule certain parishioners he had personally observed attempting to lighten the skin colour of their slaves through daily washing:

> And is the person not thus worthy of being heartily laughed at who imagined that the Moor they bought became so black through the carelessness and neglect of the previous owner, on account of which they tormented and nastily tortured the Moor with soap, other things for whitening, and with daily washing, in such a way that the poor Moor became very sick and still remained as black as they were before.[125]

[120] See also Friedrich, "Türkentaufen," 64.

[121] Niekamp, *Die göttliche Gnaden-Krafft*, 54. [122] Fussenegger, *Mohren-Tauff*, Jir.

[123] Von Lilien, *Das Christ-glaubige Mohren-Land*, 10–12.

[124] Ibid., 11: "Es ist ausser Zweiffel der Mohren natürliche schwarze Farbe ein Werk des Allerhöchsten/ welches aber uns Menschen ganz unerforschlich ist."

[125] Ibid., 12: "Und ist daher jener nicht unbillich Auslachens werth/ der Ihme eingebildet/ der von Ihme erkauffte Mohr wäre durch Unachtsam- und Nachlässigkeit seines vorigen Herren so schwarz worden/ weßwegen er den Mohren mit Seiffe/ auch andern

Other sermons read like brief treatises on the basic principles of Islam although an anti-Islamic impulse is always present. This is true, for example, of a lengthy sermon by Christoph Zeller emphasizing that Muslims also believe Christ is a prophet while launching a stream of invective against the Muslim – and, in passing, Jewish – faiths.[126] He speaks of an "accursed Koran," the arch-imposter Muhammad, and the damned Arians, among whom he counts the Jacobites and the Jews; elsewhere he claims that Jews, heathens, and Muslims were lost in the depths of the sea. Nevertheless, these detailed discussions of Islam prompted by the *Türkentaufen* are often more multifaceted than a simple anti-Islamic bias would imply. Christian Gotthold Wilisch, the pastor at Freiberg, in Saxony, who baptized Wolko in 1746, sermonized that those who do not wish to fight the Turks in vain should defeat them using their own weapons. In other words, they should read the Koran and debate with Muslims.[127] This sermon's discussion of Islam grew out of Wilisch's belief that blessedness could not be attained through the Muslim faith. He based his argument on the fact that Islam denies the existence of the Holy Trinity; therefore, he knew of no sacraments through which its believers could be blessed. He also contended that hell, the devil, and the fear of God's wrath in general were much too strongly emphasized within Islam, allowing no hope for salvation. Wilisch's views reveal a rather enlightened concept of God not generally shared by his Lutheran contemporaries. In any case, it may well have been through his deliberations on the subject that Lutheran parishioners were exposed to the Qur'an for the first time. Wilisch compared it to the Bible on a number of occasions and explained how Muslim believers cherished their sacred book. He compared Christian baptism to Muslim washing and purification rituals, describing the latter in great detail.[128] The pastor even cited particular surahs within his sermon.[129] He also argued that nowhere at all in the Qur'an was there any reference to required circumcision and that it was merely an ancient tradition rather than a divine command. This he had heard from Turkish teachers of the Qur'an, he explained to his congregation.[130] He also told the Freiberg community about the figurative nature of Arabic that must be taken into account when reading surahs.[131] Pastor Wilisch concluded

weismachenden Dingen/ und täglichen Waschen dergestalt zermartert und übel gequälet/ das der arme Mohr in eine schwere Krankheit gefallen/ und dennoch so schwarz/ wie er vorhin gewest/ geblieben ist."

126 Christoph Zeller, *Christliche Predigt über die Wort des 68. Psalms v. bei der Tauff [. . .] eines [. . .] gefangenen Türckischen Mägdleins in Stuttgart gehalten/ und / Sampt angehencktem Formular deß Tauffs/ auch deren bey solchem Actu angestelten Procession Beschreibung/ auß gnädigem Bevelch in den Druck gegeben* (Stuttgart, 1652), 14–27.

127 Wilisch, *Predigt*, Taufrede, 2. 128 Ibid., 4–5. 129 Ibid., 7. 130 Ibid., 5.

131 Ibid.

by referring parishioners to a new German translation of the Qur'an as well as German translations of publications by the Dutch orientalist Adrian Reland (1676–1716) on "Turkish religion," where they could learn more about these matters.[132] Because Wilisch delivered his sermon during the baptism of a Muslim, he did not put forth an objective analysis of Islam but rather an argument against the Muslim faith. This was, no doubt, also clear to the audience. Yet the possibility remains that numerous details about Islam, interpretations of the Qur'an, and comparisons between religious practices in Christianity and Islam opened up new horizons for Freiberg Lutherans.

The same can be said about the discourse on gender. During the 1691 baptism of a Muslim woman named Ayşe in Crailsheim, for example, Pastor Andreas Geret explained that the Islamic belief that women could not go to heaven was reason enough for a conversion to Christianity.[133] Geret went on to argue that women enjoyed equal status to men in Christianity, "both here in the realm of grace, and there in the realm of blessedness," an assertion that went far beyond the idea of equality before God espoused by Luther and most other theologians of the day. He further maintained that Adam and Eve were of equal status and pointed to the fact that an identical number of men and women had been saved by Noah's ark and that an equal number had also been freed from Egyptian captivity. Having mentioned the numerous women baptized in the Bible, he concluded by asserting that Christ had been "a saviour of the female sex" and that women had stood under his cross for this reason. It is very unlikely that the women in his congregation would have described their status within Christianity or in their hometown in quite the same way. In any event, Ayşe's baptism may have made arguments available to female Christians in Crailsheim that they would not normally have heard with such clarity, and in such depth, in their Sunday sermons.[134]

Clearly, baptisms of Muslims and Africans had an important impact on early modern German Lutheranism, and inhabitants at that time seemed to be quite aware of this, as evidenced by the famous illustrated Lutheran Merian Bible of 1630.[135] The only depiction of a baptism (aside from

[132] Ibid., 7. On Adrian Reland, see also Charles Parker's contribution in Chapter 6 of this book.

[133] Geret, *Das Neue Leben*, 24–26.

[134] Sabine Holtz, *Theologie und Alltag: Lehre und Leben in den Predigten der Tübinger Theologen, 1550–1750* (Tübingen: Mohr, 1993).

[135] Marion Keuchen, *Bild-Konzeptionen in Bilder- und Kinderbibeln. Die historischen Anfänge und ihre Wiederentdeckung in der Gegenwart*, vol. 1 (Göttingen: V&R unipress, 2016), 93,98; Bridget Heal, *A Magnificent Faith. Art and Identity in Lutheran German* (Oxford: Oxford University Press, 2017), 113–14.

Fig 7.2 *Taufe des Kämmerers aus Äthiopien*, in Die Kupferbibel Matthäus Merians von 1630 / durch D: Martin Luther verteutscht, Lachen 2002, Apg.7–26

Christ's baptism by John the Baptist) was that of an Ethiopian referred to in Acts 8 (Fig 7.2).[136] In this illustration, a travelling party dressed in Roman garb appears before the backdrop of a stylized central European landscape. The main event is the baptism of the black chamberlain of the queen of the "land of the Moors'"(Acts 8:27). Although the convert's legs are submerged in the water, Philip carries out the baptism in Lutheran fashion with a sprinkling of water on the head. While most of those depicted in the scene have central or northern European features, the realistic portrayal of the chamberlain as a black African is eye-catching. At the time, it was somewhat of a novelty to not simply depict an African as a European painted black, which makes it likely that Matthäus Merian had

[136] *Biblia, Das ist: Die gantze Schrifft Alten und Newen Testaments/ Verteutscht: Durch D. Martin Luther. Mit Vorreden [...] mit [...] Kupfferstücken Matthaei Merians gezieret [...]* (Strasburg, 1630), facsimile reproduction (Berlin: Coron bei Kindler, 2003), Act 8.

personal knowledge of black Africans.[137] If we look closely at the coffered ceiling of the Hospitalkirche at Hof in Franconia, it is clear that Merian's depiction is still quite provocative.[138] The magnificent ceiling completed in 1689 features ninety Old and New Testament scenes painted by Heinrich Andreas Lohe, who borrowed most of them from Merian's bible. The scene from Acts 8 is an almost perfect copy of Merian's depiction with the exception of the two Africans, whose brilliant white skin almost appears to be sending a signal. This reminds us of the multi-faceted nature of the still untold story of Muslims and Africans in the Holy Roman Empire: while some people utterly rejected the presence of Muslim prisoners and African slaves, others welcomed it. Likewise, while many Lutheran communities prided themselves on their participation in the conversion of Muslims or Africans, others rejected such universalist ambitions.

When black people were baptized, the story of the chamberlain was readily and frequently cited as an early example of a successful Christian mission in far-flung Africa as well as testament to the Christian universalism that encompassed Lutheranism.[139] Among clerics who expounded upon Philip's baptism of the Ethiopian in their sermons was Samuel Urlsperger (1685–1772), the Pietist chaplain at the court of Württemberg in Stuttgart. He explicitly emphasized the role of the chamberlain's baptism as an example of a universal Christianity relevant to the baptism of the African, Ebedmelech, who he was in the process of carrying out.[140] Yet Urslperger did not stop at general deliberations on the universal missionary mandate; he deduced from it a specific divine message. Just as Philip and the chamberlain's meeting was preordained, Stuttgart court society's participation in the conversion of this African man was product of a divine mandate.[141]

Should it have happened by chance that we have seen a converted Moor from among the heathen? Certainly not. God wants such examples to make us unconverted Christians together with our unchristian Christianity blush with shame, and to show us that Christianity exists not in name, words, gestures, reason or

[137] David Bindma, Henry Louis Gates Jr. ed., *The Image of the Black in Western Art*, vol. 3, part 1–3 (Cambridge, MA: Harvard University Press, 2010–2011).

[138] www.hospitalkirche-hof.de/ntgr/33.htm (accessed February 28, 2019).

[139] Johann G. Zeitz, *Der Aussätzige und wieder gereinigte Maeman* [. . .] (Cölln an der Spree, 1681), 13; Ruprecht, *Türken-Tauff*, 18; Samuel Urlsperger, *Philippus Und der Kämmerer. Wie solche In der Hoch=Fürstl. Würtembergischen Hof=Capelle in Stuttgart Bey Der Tauffe Eines Mohrenländischen Jünglings zusammen kommen/ Und in einer den 1. Martii 1716 gehaltenen jetzo aber auff Begehren zum Druck beförderten Predig zur Erbauung fürgestellet* (Stuttgart, [1716]); see also: Friedrich, "Türkentaufen," 52.

[140] Urlsperger, *Philippus*, 21. [141] Ibid., 23–24.

outward respectability but in divine power, wisdom, and certitude in the Holy Spirit, who drives us to all that is good and leads us away from evil.[142]

Thus, the African convert served as a role model for corrupt European Christianity. Shame on all the old Christians, Urlsperger preached. This was directed especially at Duke Eberhard Ludwig, explicitly addressed prior to the quoted passage. Sermons like this one show that encounters with the larger world helped provincial Germans gain new perspective on their own reality – at least sometimes.

[142] Ibid., 24: "Sollte es ohngefehr geschehen seyn/ daß wir einen aus den Heyden bekehrten Mohren angesehen? Mit nichten. GOtt will uns ohnbekehrte Christen samt unserm ohn=Christlichen Christenthum durch solche Exempel schamroth machen/ und weisen/ daß das Christenthum nicht bestehe in dem Namen/ in Worten/ in Geberden/ in der Vernunfft/ in äusserlicher Erbarkeit/ sondern in Göttlicher Krafft/ Weißheit/ und Gewißheit in dem Heiligen Geist/ der uns zu allem Guten treibet/ und von dem Bösen führet."

8 Conversion and Its Discontents on the Southern Colonial Frontier: The Pietist Encounter with Non-Christians in Colonial Georgia[1]

James Van Horn Melton

In November of 1733 the young Pietist pastor Johann Martin Boltzius, a recently ordained graduate of the University of Halle, boarded a ship in Rotterdam destined for the newly founded colony of Georgia in British America. Joining him was a transport of forty-two refugees from the prince-archbishopric of Salzburg, all of them men, women, and children expelled from their Catholic homeland on account of their Protestant beliefs. Most were peasants, farmhands, or miners from remote alpine districts that had become heavily Protestant in the Reformation. Since the sixteenth century, Protestants in the region had survived intermittent bouts of persecution by outwardly conforming to Catholic rites and practices, all the while retaining elements of their faith with the aid of Protestant Bibles, devotional handbooks, and clandestine conventicles. This survival strategy proved reasonably effective until the 1720s, when a new prince-archbishop, Leopold Anton von Firmian, authorized a series of investigations aimed at uprooting Protestant survivals in the alpine areas of his territory. His campaign culminated in the largest religious expulsion in eighteenth-century Europe, when more than 20,000 of Firmian's subjects were exiled in the wake of the archbishop's Emigration Patent of 1731.

Most of them found refuge in Brandenburg-Prussia and other Protestant territories of the Holy Roman Empire. A far smaller number, no more than a few hundred, made their way to Georgia during these years. They arrived in four successive transports and were settled on the Savannah River, where Boltzius and the exiles founded the community

[1] Parts of this essay previously appeared in James Van Horn Melton, *Religion, Community, and Slavery on the Colonial Southern Frontier* (Cambridge: Cambridge University Press, 2015).

they called Ebenezer. Its inhabitants later came to include immigrants from the Upper Rhine region of southwestern Germany, most of whom came to Georgia for economic rather than religious reasons.

Boltzius's Pietist superiors in Halle had originally recruited him to minister to the spiritual needs of the refugees. In time he also exercised temporal leadership, serving as the chief intermediary between the Ebenezer community and the Georgia Trustees (the London philanthropic body that had founded the Georgia colony and governed it until 1754, when it was formally incorporated as a royal colony). Along with his duties as Ebenezer's senior pastor, Boltzius was responsible for procuring and distributing supplies, adjudicating disputes, preserving discipline and morale, and conducting official correspondence with the Trustees and with Ebenezer's Pietist patrons in Germany.

The Trustees and Boltzius's Pietist sponsors also entrusted to him missionary duties aimed at Christianizing Georgia's indigenous peoples. James Edward Oglethorpe, the London-born social reformer, ex-soldier, and politician who had played a key role in designing the Trustees's plan for the colony, considered conversion of the natives essential for fostering peaceful relations between the newly arrived settlers and their indigenous neighbors. Conversion of the "Indians" was also part of the Pietists' global vision, a program – as Merry Wiesner notes in Chapter 12 – that aimed at nothing short of evangelizing the world and bringing forth the Kingdom of God.

During Boltzius's more than three decades on the Georgia frontier, his missionary efforts targeted not just Ebenezer's indigenous neighbors but also other non-Christian peoples he encountered in the colony. One was a small contingent of German-speaking Jews (or Ashkenazim) who had arrived in Georgia a year earlier. The other was the rapidly growing population of enslaved Africans who began arriving in Georgia after 1750, when the Trustees finally abandoned Oglethorpe's earlier efforts to ban the importation of slaves into the newly founded colony. Oglethorpe had designed Georgia not for a small planter elite living idly off the labor of an enslaved black majority – i.e., the slaveholding society that had by then emerged in South Carolina – but for a free, self-sufficient, and virtuous yeomanry able and willing to defend Britain's southern colonial frontier against the nefarious designs of the Spanish. Oglethorpe's efforts to keep slavery out of Georgia was ultimately abandoned after the Trustees, yielding to growing pressure from the colony's vocal pro-slavery lobby, rescinded their ban in 1750. Boltzius, who had formerly supported the ban, now set about expanding his missionary work to include slaves who had begun arriving in the Ebenezer area.

Focusing on his encounters with these three groups – Jews, Indians, and enslaved Africans – the remainder of this essay explores the respective challenges that Boltzius, like the Moravian missionaries Jacqueline Van Gent examines in Chapter 10, likewise confronted in his efforts at conversion. How did he view the various peoples he sought to convert? What obstacles did he face, and how did he respond when efforts at conversion met resistance or otherwise failed to measure up to his hopes? How did the Pietist project of converting the world fare in a local, non-European setting? Drawing on the research I conducted for my book on the origins and history of the Ebenezer settlement, my essay addresses these questions through the prism of Pastor Boltzius's diaries as well as the copious reports and letters he wrote for his Pietist correspondents back in Europe. The journals were edited and published by Samuel Urlsperger, the Augsburg Pietist and senior pastor, and an eighteen-volume American edition and translation (1968–1995) would include most of his diary as well.[2] This chapter also draws on the recent edition and translation of Boltzius's unpublished letters, along with manuscript sources housed in the Georgia section of the Archive of the Francke Foundations in Halle.[3]

The Global Context

Although the emigration of Salzburg refugees to Georgia was modest in number, their voyage and settlement were made possible by the financial and logistical support of a global Protestant network stretching from

[2] *Ausführliche Nachricht von der Königlichen Grossbritannischen Kolonie Salzburger Emigranten in America... herausgegeben von Samuel Urlsperger*, 3 vols. (Halle, 1735–1752); continuation as *Amerikanisches Ackerwerk Gottes; oder zuverlässige Nachrichten, den Zustand der amerikanisch englischen und von salzburgischen Emigranten erbauten Pflanzstadt Ebenezer in Georgien betreffend...*, 4 vols. (Augsburg, 1754–1767). The final volume was edited by Samuel Urlsperger's son, Johann August Urlsperger. For the American edition, see George Fenwick Jones et al., *Detailed Reports on the Salzburger Emigrants Who Settled in America...Edited by Samuel Urlsperger*, 18 vols. (Athens: University of Georgia Press, 1968–1993).

[3] More than 1,000 letters and reports from British America and Europe related to the Ebenezer community are housed in the Georgia section of the *Archiv der Franckeschen Stiftungen* (henceforth *AF/St/M, Georgia-Sektion*) in Halle, Germany. These include many of Boltzius's private letters, more than 150 of which were recently edited and translated by Russell C. Kleckley in a two-volume English edition. See *Letters of Johann Martin Boltzius, Lutheran Pastor in Ebenezer, Georgia*, 2 vols., ed. and trans. Russell C. Kleckley in collaboration with Jürgen Gröschl (Lewiston, NY: Mellen Press, 2009). An excellent guide to the Georgia section of the archives is *Salzburg-Halle-North America: A Bilingual Catalog with Summaries of the Georgia Manuscripts in the Francke Foundations*, ed. Thomas Müller-Bahlke and Jürgen Gröschl (Halle and Tübingen: Publishing house of the Francke Foundation, 1999).

eastern Germany to the southernmost frontier of British America.[4] Throughout Protestant Europe, the plight of the exiles quickly became an international cause célèbre. It started in Protestant towns and cities along the refugees' migration route through the Holy Roman Empire, where welcoming committees formed to greet the caravans of exiles. Published sermons and pamphlets celebrated them as Protestant martyrs, while the Hohenzollern elector of Brandenburg-Prussia, who offered free land and farm implements to exiles who chose to settle in his territory, scored a major public-relations coup through the acclaim he earned as leader of the imperial Protestant cause.[5] This outpouring of support quickly spread across the Channel, where published accounts described the sufferings of the refugees and funds were raised on their behalf.

The rapid internationalization of the Salzburgers' cause was made possible by a well-established network of links between Halle, the university town in Brandenburg-Prussia that by 1700 had become a center of the Pietist movement, and Anglican philanthropic organizations in London.[6] Dating back to the late seventeenth century, these ties grew stronger with the surge of British interest in Germany following the 1701 Act of Succession (the parliamentary measure that paved the way for the accession of a Hanoverian prince to the throne). By the time of the expulsions there had emerged a Halle-London axis of communication, the strength of which was attested by the cordial relationship that had evolved between the Francke Foundations (Franckesche Stiftungen) in Halle and the London-based Society for Promoting Christian Knowledge (SPCK).

The Francke Foundations were the eponymous creation of August Hermann Francke (1663–1727), one of the founders of German Pietism, under whose leadership Halle emerged as a Pietist stronghold. Francke, in addition to holding a professorship in the Halle theological faculty, devoted his energies to founding and funding the impressive complex of charitable enterprises that still bear his name today. By his death in 1727, they included his celebrated orphanage, schools for the poor, endowed stipends for needy theology students, and an elite boarding school. These assorted enterprises were subsidized partly through charitable donations as well as through the foundations' profitable

[4] See most recently the published dissertation by Alexander Pyrges, *Das Kolonialprojekt Ebenezer. Formen und Mechanismen protestantischer Expansion in der atlantischen Welt des 18. Jahrhunderts* (Stuttgart: Franz Steiner, 2015).

[5] See Mack Walker, *The Salzburg Transaction: Expulsion and Redemption in Eighteenth-Century Germany* (Ithaca, NY, and London: Cornell University Press, 1992), 204–22.

[6] See the standard work by Daniel J. Brunner, *Halle Pietists in England* (Göttingen: Vandenhoeck & Ruprecht, 1993).

publishing house and mail-order pharmaceutical trade. The pharmacy was the creation of the Pietist physician and Halle graduate Christian Friedrich Richter, head of the orphanage hospital. By 1710 it was successfully promoting and selling remedies for illnesses ranging from nervous disorders and gout to toothaches, dysentery, and venereal diseases. Agents in ports like Amsterdam and Rotterdam marketed them throughout North America and the East and West Indies, with annual profits averaging more than 20,000 talers by the 1730s.[7]

Founded in 1698, the Society for Promoting Christian Knowledge was a lay Anglican philanthropic organization dedicated to the cause of moral and religious reform. The Society's friendly ties to Halle dated back to 1699, when its members elected Francke a corresponding member of the organization. Francke and the SPCK shared a common interest in schools for the poor, and at the invitation of the Society, Francke sent two of his Halle schoolmasters to help with its charity school project. Francke's personal ties with the SPCK also had the effect of internationalizing the Society's philanthropical range. In 1710 he was able to enlist the organization's support for the Pietist missions in southern India, ultimately leading the SPCK to finance its own mission in Madras.[8] Relations between Halle and the SPCK continued to thrive with the influx of Hanoverian courtiers after 1714, which enabled Francke protégés like Anton Wilhelm Böhme and Friedrich Michael Ziegenhagen to rise to influential positions as court pastors. In this capacity they served as important intermediaries between the SPCK and the Francke Foundations.[9]

The Foundation's collaboration with the SPCK grew out of a shared religious sensibility that transcended whatever doctrinal differences might have otherwise divided the two. Both had an ecclesial (or churchly) orientation that resisted separatist tendencies within their respective confessions, a stance that facilitated cooperation by downplaying doctrinal differences in favor of a more practical focus on charity. Their specific blueprints for renewal varied, but all focused in one way or another on the need for Christian schooling for the poor, the reform of public morals, the

[7] A concise survey of the origins and development of the Francke Foundations is Helmut Obst, *August Hermann Francke und die Franckeschen Stiftungen in Halle* (Göttingen: Vanderhoeck & Ruprecht, 2002). On the Pietist pharmacy, see Renate Wilson, *Pietist Traders in Medicine: A German Pharmaceutical Network in Eighteenth-Century North America* (University Park: Pennsylvania State University Press, 2000).

[8] For a detailed account of the Pietist missions in southern India, see Andrew Zonderman, "Immigrant Imperialism: Germans and the Rise of the British Empire" (Ph.D. diss., Emory University, 2019), 25–155.

[9] Pyrges, *Das Kolonialprojekt Ebenezer*, 57–89; Brunner, *Halle Pietists in England*, 30, 57–58.

broader dissemination of Bibles and other devotional literature, and ultimately, foreign missions.[10]

The subsidized transports of refugee Salzburgers to Georgia was the fruit of these longstanding personal contacts and shared goals. In early 1732, the SPCK began receiving detailed reports on the expulsions from Friedrich Michael Ziegenhagen, the Halle-educated chaplain to the court of George II. Ziegenhagen, himself a member of the SPCK, read aloud from his English translation of Gotthilf August Francke's account of the expulsions at several successive meetings of the Society. The Society followed suit with a concerted publicity campaign on behalf of the refugees, including the printing and distribution of hundreds of copies of Francke's pamphlet to the Society's network of benefactors. In a matter of weeks, the SPCK raised almost 2,000 pounds sterling in contributions.[11] In the meantime, both Ziegenhagen in London and Francke in Halle stayed abreast of the exiles' status via their Pietist correspondent in Augsburg, Samuel Urlsperger, senior Lutheran pastor in the south German imperial city. Urlsperger was also a corresponding member of the SPCK, his ties to the Society dating back to his two years (1709–1711) in London as a vicar in a Lutheran chapel serving members of the city's German community. Already active in Augsburg organizing relief efforts on behalf of the refugees, he also worked with Henry Newman, secretary of the SPCK in London, to arrange sponsorship of their passage to Georgia.[12]

The SPCK had been involved from the outset in the founding of the Georgia colony.[13] The idea of chartering a philanthropic colony on the southernmost frontier of British America was first advanced by Thomas Bray, an elderly Anglican clergyman and founder of the Society. Bray had been involved in the campaign for prison reform, and in 1730 he and other members of the SPCK began discussing the possibility of populating the proposed colony with debtors recently released from London jails. Bray died the following year and James Edward Oglethorpe assumed leadership of the circle. It became the nucleus for the Georgia Trustees,

[10] On this point see Brunner, *Halle Pietists in England*, 46, and Eamon Duffy, "The Society for Promoting Christian Knowledge and Europe: The Background to the Founding of the Christentumsgesellschaft," *Pietismus und Neuzeit* 7 (1981): 28–41.

[11] *Archive of the Society for Promoting Christian Knowledge*, University of Cambridge Library (microfilm version in Pitts Theology Library, Candler School of Theology, Emory University), Miscellaneous Abstracts, 1723–1724: March 28–June 1, 1732. The English translation of Francke's pamphlet was entitled *An Account of the Sufferings of the Persecuted Protestants in the Archbishoprick of Saltzburg with Their Reception in Several Imperial Cities* (London, 1732).

[12] Urlsperger's correspondence with Newman is published in *Henry Newman's Salzburger Letterbooks*, ed. George Fenwick Jones (Athens: University of Georgia Press, 1966).

[13] For what follows, see Melton, *Religion, Community, and Slavery*, 105–13.

the philanthropic body chartered in 1732 as the governing board of the new colony. The Trustees were generally wealthy and influential men whose members included Anglican clergymen, Whig as well as Tory members of parliament, royal officials, and private philanthropists.

Oglethorpe soon abandoned the idea of settling the colony with debtors. What emerged instead was a more global and military vision of Georgia as a buffer colony, a design intimately tied to the defense of Britain's North American empire against the Spanish in Florida and the French and their Indian allies to the west. The colony's ban on the importation of enslaved Africans was an essential part of this vision. For almost two decades, Georgia was the only colony in British America that expressly excluded slaves. The prohibition grew out of Oglethorpe's conviction that a small-holding yeomanry could defend Britain's southeastern frontier far better than a small elite of slaveholding planters along the lines of what had evolved in South Carolina. He also believed that the exclusion of slaves would prevent the emergence of a potentially insurgent black majority whom the Spanish in Florida could instigate against British settlers. At a time when colonial rivalries were intensifying throughout the Atlantic world, Oglethorpe's military arguments were no doubt calculated to elicit parliamentary approval of subsidies to support the Trustees's plan. His imperial vision may also have hearkened back to Oglethorpe's previous career in Habsburg service, when he served as an adjutant to Prince Eugene of Savoy during the field marshal's successful 1715 campaign against the Ottomans in southeastern Europe. Oglethorpe's prior military service in a border region of the Old World may well explain the preoccupation with frontier security that later informed his vision of Georgia.

The Trustees had first proposed to parliament that settlers for the new colony be recruited from London's burgeoning poor, a plan that soon foundered on opposition from London manufacturers who objected that transporting unemployed young men to Georgia would siphon off a crucial source of the city's labor supply. It was at this point that plans for the transport and settlement of Salzburg Protestants began to crystallize. From the Trustees' perspective, the Salzburgers were ideal candidates for recruitment. As foreigners, their recruitment would allay concerns that the Georgia project would reduce domestic supplies of labor. Second, the SPCK's publicity campaign on behalf of the exiles had already made them a cause célèbre throughout Great Britain, and no less a figure than King George II, had endorsed the Society's efforts on their behalf. Finally, the idea of settling victims of "papist" persecution in the new colony resonated in a political culture in which anti-Catholicism was deeply ingrained. It thereby appealed to the sizable body of opinion inside and outside of parliament that had traditionally associated English national interests with the interests of Protestantism at home and abroad.

Enthusiastically endorsed by the SPCK, the proposal to recruit exiled Protestants played a critical role in persuading Parliament to approve the Trustees's request for an initial subsidy of 10,000 pounds. Informed by Henry Newman of the SPCK that funds were now available, Pastor Urlsperger in Augsburg set about recruiting the first transport of exiles from a caravan of refugees arriving in the city in August of 1733. On the recommendation of Gotthilf August Francke in Halle, with whom Urlsperger had been in steady contact regarding the scheme, he had also managed to recruit Pastor Boltzius to accompany the exiles to Georgia. Boltzius joined up with his flock of Salzburgers in Rotterdam, where they boarded a ship bound for Savannah.

Boltzius and the Jews of Savannah

Founded on a sandy coastal bluff overlooking the Savannah River, the town of Savannah had been settled just over a year when Boltzius and his first transport of exiles disembarked there in March of 1734. The first group of non-Christians they would have encountered were a Jewish couple, Benjamin and Perla Sheftall, who were waiting on the shore to greet the arriving ship. The Sheftalls were from the Prussian town of Frankfurt an der Oder and had migrated to Georgia the previous summer. They were fluent in German as well as Yiddish, and Benjamin Sheftall, who had lived for a time in London before emigrating to Georgia, also spoke some English.[14] That made him an ideal mediator between the Salzburgers and their Anglophone neighbors, a role Benjamin seems to have relished and one that the Salzburgers, struggling to adapt to an alien environment, must have appreciated. Boltzius's command of English was still rudimentary (he had begun learning it during the voyage to Georgia), so he too had reason to be grateful for Benjamin's services as interpreter and go-between. A few weeks after his arrival, Boltzius wrote that Benjamin Sheftall "has shown so much love and rendered so many services to us and the Salzburgers that no one could ask any more. And whenever he was offered some money for his troubles he refused to accept it."[15] The Salzburgers reciprocated by clearing the remaining trees from Benjamin's land and plowing his fields.

[14] On the Sheftalls, see Holly Snyder, "A Tree with Two Different Fruits: The Jewish Encounter with German Pietists in the Eighteenth-Century Atlantic World," *William and Mary Quarterly* 58 (2001): 862–82.

[15] *Detailed Reports on the Salzburger Emigrants* [henceforth *DR*], 1:70. Sheftall's role as intermediary continued during the early years of the colony, not only on behalf of the

Boltzius may also have ascribed a deeper, eschatological meaning to his encounter with the Sheftalls. A guiding theme throughout his journals was that of Exodus, the flight of the children of Israel from Egypt. Just as the Puritans described by David Hall in Chapter 2 had come to interpret their journey from England to Massachusetts as a re-enactment of the Old Testament's narrative of exodus and exile, so did Boltzius employ the same narrative as a metaphor framing his account of the Salzburgers' expulsion, transatlantic migration, and settlement. The exodus metaphor, which Boltzius's journal had first evoked on the eve of the sea voyage,[16] may well have inspired him to see his encounter with the Sheftalls in providential terms. By that time, the Jews and their history had become central to how Boltzius and the Salzburgers understood their own history. As he wrote in his journal in May of 1734: "We have often learned from experience that the travelogue of the Jewish people is no unfruitful history, but that one can learn very much of the trust, warning, and comfort, which have certainly been of incomparable value to our congregation, which has often been reminded of it."[17]

Underlying Boltzius's initially sympathetic account of the Sheftalls was also the belief – widespread among Halle Pietists – that renewed missionary work among Jews could hasten their conversion if it was conducted compassionately and with a deeper understanding of their traditions.[18] Pietist interest in Jewish conversion in some ways hearkened back to the young Luther. In the early years of the Reformation, Luther too had exhorted Christians to minister to Jews in a more charitable spirit. Insofar as he saw Jewish resistance to conversion as an understandable response to a corrupt Roman church, he was confident that Jews would embrace the Christian faith once the teachings and practices of the church had been reformed and purified. Luther's initial optimism, however, soon gave way to bitter condemnation when Jews failed to respond to Reformers' calls for mass conversions. Much of the virulent anti-Judaism later expressed in his writings grew out of this disillusionment, which led Protestants effectively to abandon missionary work among Jews for almost two centuries.

Salzburgers but other German-speaking colonists, with whom he sometimes appeared in court or in other venues where an interpreter was needed. See, for example, *DR* 5:226–7, 8:114, 275.

16 *AF/St/M*, Georgia-Sektion: 5A1:28, fol. 137. It is quite possible he borrowed the metaphor from contemporary Pietist accounts of the expulsions published in Germany. On this literature see Walker, *The Salzburg Transaction*, 202–3.

17 *DR* 1:167.

18 See the extensive discussion in Christopher M. Clark, *The Politics of Conversion: Missionary Protestantism and the Jews in Prussia, 1728–1941* (Oxford: Clarendon Press, 1995), introduction and chapters 1–2.

Like the early Luther, Halle Pietists of Boltzius's day were convinced that a spiritual awakening was at hand and that St. Paul's unrealized prophecy of Jewish conversion was imminent. This confidence in the coming conversion of the Jews bore traces of Pietism's millenarian origins. Born of the violence, pestilence, and destruction wrought by the Thirty Years' War, the movement came of age in a cultural and religious milieu teeming with apocalyptic visions and chiliastic hopes. Even with the return of peace in 1648, fresh catastrophes provoked continued calls for repentance and reform. Repeated invasions by the French from the 1670s through the early eighteenth century cut a destructive swath through areas of southwestern Germany, adding fuel to millenarian prophecies and jeremiads. Louis XIV's revocation of the Edict of Nantes (1685) and the attendant flood of Huguenot refugees into the empire bred fears that the Antichrist was afoot, as did the revived Ottoman threat occasioned by the siege of Vienna in 1683. Even though the more restrained variant of Pietism that subsequently arose in partnership with the Hohenzollern court toned down its earlier millenarian themes, elements of these had persisted. A notable example was the belief that the conversion of the Jews would usher in the 1,000-year era of peace that was to precede (or in some versions follow) the Second Coming. This presumed link between Jewish conversion and the advent of the millennium explains the urgency with which Pietists called for a dialogue with Jews, arguing that only through Christian guidance and instruction could the conversion of Israel and ultimately the salvation of humankind be achieved.

A key figure in Pietist efforts to bring Jews to the Christian Messiah was Johann Heinrich Callenberg (1694–1760). Callenberg studied theology and philology at Halle, during which time he also worked as a secretary in the household of August Hermann Francke. On Francke's recommendation he was appointed professor of oriental languages at the university, assuming his chair the same year (1727) that Boltzius had matriculated in the theology faculty.[19] Callenberg's classes in Greek, Arabic, Hebrew, and Yiddish aimed at training a future generation of missionaries able to propagate the Christian faith in Europe and in foreign lands. In 1728 Callenberg also founded Halle's Institutum Judaicum, a kind of institute for Jewish studies that served as the institutional center for the first organized Protestant mission to Jews in Germany.[20] The institute

[19] On Callenberg, see the recent study by Christoph Rymatzki, *Hallescher Pietismus und Judenmission: Johann Heinrich Callenbergs Institutum Judaicum und dessen Freundeskreis (1728–1736)* (Tübingen: Harrassowitz, 2004), passim.

[20] Callenberg's institute also had as its goal the training of missionary cadres to work among Muslims in foreign lands. In his correspondence he sometimes referred to the institute as

included a printing house and distribution center for Hebrew and Yiddish dictionaries, grammars, and translations of the gospels. Boltzius, who had studied with Callenberg in Halle, continued to correspond with him after the pastor's arrival in Georgia. In 1734, soon after his first encounter with the Sheftalls, Boltzius wrote to Halle requesting some of the institute's publications. Callenberg obliged and sent Boltzius one of his institute's Yiddish translations from the New Testament. Boltzius promptly passed it on to Benjamin Sheftall as a gift.[21]

Boltzius's expectations of conversion, however, proved misplaced. The Sheftalls never converted, and according to Samuel Quincy, who preceded John Wesley as Savannah's Anglican minister, the Jewish couple had never had any intention of doing so. Quincy, who know Boltzius well and was aware of his efforts to convert the Sheftalls, confided as much to a mutual acquaintance: "Their kindness shown to Mr. Boltzius and the Salzburgers was owing to the good temper and humanity of the people, and not to any inclination to change their religion." The Sheftalls, in other words, were just being polite.[22] As Benjamin Sheftall's steadfast adherence to Judaism began to dawn on Boltzius (Perla Sheftall died in 1736), his affection for Sheftall cooled accordingly. He was probably referring to Sheftall when he wrote in 1738 that "in their doctrine [the Jews of Savannah] remain stiff-necked, and little has been accomplished [with their conversion] to date."[23] His journals and diaries ceased referring to Sheftall by name, as Boltzius had done in earlier references. Following an encounter with Benjamin Sheftall some twenty years later, one of Boltzius's letters to Callenberg referred to Sheftall merely as "this Jew."[24] The pastor's references to Savannah's Jews grew less frequent, and where they did occur, the allusions were usually negative in tone.

Here one is reminded again of Luther, whose initial hopes gave way to hostile polemics once the expected conversion of German Jews had failed to materialize. The same pattern was to characterize Boltzius's encounter

the "Institutum Judaicum et Muhammedicum," and its publications included translations of catechisms into Arabic, Persian, and Turkish. Rymatzki, *Hallescher Pietismus und Judenmission*, 88–89.

21 *DR* 1:166; 2:98.

22 Quincy to Henry Newman, secretary of the Society for Promoting Christian Knowledge, in *Henry Newman's Salzburger Letterbooks*, ed. George Fenwick Jones (Athens: University of Georgia Press, 1966), 588. See *DR* 1:70 (April 3, 1734), for Boltzius's belief in the Sheftalls' imminent conversion.

23 *Letters of Johann Martin Boltzius*, 1:236.

24 Cited in Snyder, "A Tree with Two Different Fruits," 872, who notes Boltzius's growing disinclination to calling individual Jews by name. See elsewhere Boltzius's disparaging remarks on Savannah Jews in *Letters of Johann Martin Boltzius*, 2:646–7 (August 12, 1756).

with another non-Christian community he encountered in Savannah, one with its own history of exodus and exile.

Boltzius among the Natives

In 1732, not long before Oglethorpe and his first transport of British settlers arrived in Georgia the following year, a band of around 100 Creek Indians had migrated eastward to settle a quarter of a mile upriver from the site of what was soon to become Savannah. Guided by Tomochichi, their elderly but ambitious Creek leader, these were a group of banished members belonging to the so-called Lower Creek confederacy, a loose alliance of eight Native towns located along a fifty-mile stretch of the Chattahoochee River in present-day Georgia and Alabama. Their exile and resettlement grew out of colonial rivalries in the region. Tomochichi had been part of a delegation of Lower Creek leaders who had concluded a treaty with South Carolina's British governor in June of 1732, and his subsequent disgrace seems to have resulted from his opposition to their efforts at preserving simultaneous ties of friendship with French and Spanish colonists as well. The banishment of Tomochichi and his followers came after he had reputedly participated in the burning of a Catholic chapel erected by French missionaries. After settling on the Georgia coast Tomochichi's band came to be known as the Yamacraws (after Yamacraw Bluff, the name they gave to the site of their new settlement).[25]

Boltzius's first recorded encounter with a member of the Yamacraws occurred in Savannah some two weeks after his ship's arrival in March of 1734. Included in his account was a lurid description of an episode involving a Yamacraw man who had cut off the ears and hair of a Creek widow because she was said to have been "quite familiar in her conduct" with a white settler. Boltzius described the man walking through the town in a drunken state, brandishing the widow's severed ears and hair to passers-by, apparently as a warning to whites and Indians alike against transgressing the honor of a deceased husband.[26] Boltzius was, to be sure, appalled by the act, but he blamed it on drink and not on any Indian predilection for cruelty. As if to underscore his point, Boltzius's journal entry that day also recounted another incident involving a white settler who had been sentenced to 300 lashes for the crime of sodomy (Boltzius did not provide any further details, and the sodomy reference was edited

[25] On Tomochichi and his followers, see John T. Juricek, *Colonial Georgia and the Creeks: Anglo-Indian Diplomacy on the Southern Frontier, 1733–1763* (Gainesville: University Press of Florida, 2010), 39ff.

[26] *DR* 1:67; 3:314.

out of the published version of the entry). As the punishment was being administered, wrote Boltzius, "an Indian saw this [and] he felt pity for him, ran around the malefactor in a circle and cried: 'No Christian, no Christian!' that is, 'This is not Christian.' And since the lashing did not cease, he embraced the poor sinner and offered his own back to the lash. This caused the judges to end the affair and remit the rest of the rascal's punishment."[27] It is unclear whether the native was in fact a Christian convert – outright conversion was rare at this time among Indians on the southeastern frontier – but the rhetorical effect of Boltzius's account was to relativize the cruel treatment of the widow he observed on the same day. His juxtaposition of the two episodes implied that although Indians were capable of cruelty, especially when drunk, they were capable of Christian compassion and hence were potentially "convertible." This capacity for conversion mitigated their heathen barbarism, just as the prospect of conversion had initially served to bracket the Sheftalls' status as Jews. For the Pietist Boltzius, hope of imminent conversion transformed an alien, potentially hostile presence into a familiar and even benign one. Conversely, the dimmer the prospect of conversion, the more threatening non-Christians appeared in the pastor's eyes.

Conversion of the natives had been an explicit aim of the Georgia Trustees, just as it was for Boltzius's Pietist superiors back in Halle.[28] Boltzius had cause for optimism. Tomochichi and Oglethorpe, at that time the leader of the Georgia colony, had only a year earlier concluded a treaty of friendship. Their amicable relationship evolved out of mutual self-interest. Tomochichi, a shrewd diplomat, was intent on restoring his standing within the Lower Creek confederacy by carving out his status as chief mediator between the British in Georgia and Creek settlements to the west. Oglethorpe, nervously eyeing the threat posed by the French to the west and the Spanish to the south, was eager to win the friendship of the ambitious Creek chieftain. The result would be the first in a series of treaties ultimately ensuring that unlike Virginia and Carolina, Georgia would be spared serious Indian attacks in its early and most vulnerable years.[29]

27 *DR* 1:67.

28 Julie Anne Sweet, *Negotiating for Georgia: British-Creek Relations in the Trustee Era, 1733–1752* (Athens: University of Georgia Press, 2003), 78–96; Gotthilf August Francke to Boltzius (November 2, 1733), *AFSt/M*, Georgia-Sektion 5A1:10, fol. 51–2.

29 On Anglo-Creek diplomacy in colonial Georgia, see Juricek, *Colonial Georgia and the Creeks*, chapters 2 and 3. See also Jack P. Greene, "Travails of an Infant Colony: The Search for Viability, Coherence, and Identity in Colonial Georgia," in *Forty Years of Diversity: Essays on Colonial Georgia*, ed. Harvey H. Jackson and Phinizy Spalding (Athens: University of Georgia Press 1984), 278–309.

The following year, the first published installment of Boltzius's journals celebrated Tomochichi's London visit. The volume appeared in Augsburg in 1735 under the editorship of Samuel Urlsperger and had for its frontispiece a copper engraving of Tomochichi and Toonahowi, his grandnephew and heir. The Augsburg mezzotint was based on a London portrait executed the year before by the Flemish painter William Verelst, which had been occasioned by Oglethorpe's celebrated journey to England in the summer of 1734 with Tomochichi, his immediate family, and a retinue of other Creek dignitaries. With the exception of the 1616 sojourn to London of Pocohontas and her entourage, the Indian delegation of 1734 was the largest in the colonial era to visit England.[30] The affair included a royal audience and meetings with other British dignitaries, all aimed at bolstering the Anglo-Creek alliance. Tomochichi for his part skillfully used the occasion to showcase his own leadership and press for trade concessions on behalf of his Lower Creek allies.

Among his gestures of peace and friendship was a demonstrative interest in the Christian faith. While in England he attended Anglican services, reputedly discussed matters of faith with the archbishop of Canterbury, and requested that his people, including his heir Toonahowi, be given instruction in Christian doctrine. Urlsperger's preface to the volume quoted from Oglethorpe's description of the visit:

> ... it appears as though a door has been opened for the conversion of the Indians; because a superior or chief of the Indians, Tomocha-chi [sic], the Mecko [mico, or chief] of Yamacraw, a man with an excellent mind, is so desirous of having his young people instructed in the science and wisdom of the English, and consequently in the Christian religion, that he came over with me in spite of his advanced age in order to find ways and means for instructing his people. He is staying with me now, and he has brought with him a young boy whom he calls his nephew and immediate heir. This child has already learned the Lord's Prayer in the Indian and English languages.[31]

The visit also caught Urlsperger's attention because when Tomochichi and his retinue left England in November of 1734 to return to Georgia, his fellow passengers included fifty-five German-speaking passengers, all but five of them Salzburgers. They made up the second transport of exiles bound for Georgia who would join Boltzius and his community in January of 1735. There is no record of the Salzburgers' response to the natives aboard ship, but the spacious cabin the Trustees had arranged for Tomochichi and his retinue must have underscored their elevated status

[30] On the delegation see Alden T. Vaughan, *Transatlantic Encounters: American Indians in Britain, 1500–1776* (Cambridge: Cambridge University Press, 2006), 150–62.

[31] *DR* 1:19.

as friends and allies. The alliance forged by Oglethorpe and Tomochichi laid the foundations for peaceful relations between Salzburgers and natives in the years immediately following the arrival of the exiles.

Yet by 1738, fewer than five years after Boltzius and the Salzburgers had arrived in Georgia, the pastor had all but abandoned hopes of converting his Indian neighbors. What had happened to undermine his optimism? The demanding conditions of settlement, which left the pastor precious little time for missionary work, had much to do with it. Ebenezer's first site, founded in the summer of 1734 around twenty-five miles northwest of Savannah, proved unsuitable owing to the poor soil, and the settlers, most of them accustomed to a cooler alpine climate, suffered miserably in the hot, sticky, mosquito-ridden environment. Dysentery and recurrent outbreaks of malaria helped kill off around half of those who had arrived on the first transport. Conditions among the settlers gradually began to improve after they moved to a new site in 1736, where the soil was more fertile and the Savannah River more accessible. But meanwhile the struggle for survival on what was, in effect, the frontier of a frontier colony, sapped Boltzius's energies. Survival, not evangelization, was his top priority.[32]

As a pastor, of course, attending to the suffering of his parishioners included the spiritual and emotional distress occasioned by disease and material deprivation. Especially in the early years, much of Bolzius's time as a pastor was devoted to bedside visits to the sick and dying. For him, these occasions required more than comforting the afflicted; he valued illness as an occasion for eliciting contrition and precipitating the "conversion experience" (*Bekehrung*) that the Pietists, like their Puritan counterparts, considered essential to personal salvation. For Pietists the conversion experience was an event, a moment in which individuals, following a period of inner struggle, despair, and contrition – what Pietists called the atonement struggle, or *Busskampf* – shed their sinfulness and acquired the faith and confidence in God's grace.[33] In Boltzius's case the physical agonies of the sickbed became a metaphor for the internal anguish of the atonement struggle (*Busskampf*) that Pietists considered indispensable to spiritual rebirth. As Boltzius wrote in 1747: "The Lord also graced some of us with the insight that sickness. . .leads not only to contrition, but also to humility and shamefaced confession, as well as to a hunger and thirst for God's grace in Christ, to a true change of heart and

[32] On the difficulties Ebenezer settlers encountered in their early years in the colony, see Melton, *Religion, Community, and Slavery*, 151–57.

[33] For a useful analysis of the Pietist conversion experience, see Jonathan Strom, *German Pietism and the Problem of Conversion* (University Park: Pennsylvania State University Press, 2018), especially 1–70.

a mending of ways."[34] Instances of Boltzius's use of illness to spur conversion abound in his journals, testifying to the time and effort it consumed in his duties as a pastor. It left even less time for the other, quite different but equally demanding project of conversion that he was charged with undertaking. That was the task not of effecting a change of heart in nominal Christians, but of bringing to the faith peoples who had never been Christians in the first place.

Language was also a formidable obstacle. Boltzius had originally hoped to master the tongue spoken by Ebenezer's closest indigenous neighbors, the Yuchi people. The Yuchi were a small nation of no more than 800 members, far smaller than the roughly 4,000 Lower Creeks inhabiting Georgia at that time.[35] Although the Yuchi were loosely allied with the Lower Creek confederation, the two groups had warred in the past and the Yuchi had resisted cultural absorption by the Creeks.[36] Yuchi separatism may have stemmed from the singularity of their language, which ethnologists today reckon to be a linguistic isolate unrelated to any other native American tongue. Boltzius at first struggled to learn it but soon gave up in frustration. (He likened its bewildering clusters of consonants to Polish and Sorbish, both of which he would have occasionally heard spoken in his native Lusatia, a region in the electorate of Saxony.) Perhaps owing to their distinctive language, the Yuchi had a reputation for being closed to outsiders, whether native or European. Already resisting absorption by the Lower Creeks, they would have been even less open to assimilation into a white community. Aside from occasional forays into Ebenezer's fields and gardens under cover of night, the Yuchi kept their distance and showed little interest in sustained contact.[37]

All of this helps account for why Boltzius tacitly surrendered hopes of converting his Yuchi neighbors. A final half-hearted gesture came in August of 1738, when he tried to communicate to a visiting party of Yuchi his desire to raise and educate one of their children. Not surprisingly the idea was rejected: "they [the Yuchi] only laugh at this. Their love for their children is great, and therefore they allow them every freedom."[38] He now abandoned even sporadic efforts at conversion. In the process his comments on his Yuchi neighbors, as well as on other

[34] *DR* 11:2–3. Jürgen Helm, *Krankheit, Bekehrung, und Reform. Medizin und Krankenfürsorge im Halleschen Pietismus* (Tübingen: Max Niemeyer Verlag, 2006), examines in detail the Pietist link between sickness and conversion.

[35] Oglethorpe's estimate in 1734, see Juricek, *Colonial Georgia and the Creeks*, 56.

[36] On the Yuchi, see Jason Baird Jackson, "Yuchi," in *Handbook of American Indians*, ed. William C. Stutevant, vol. 14 (Washington, D.C.: Smithsonian Institute, 2004), 415–28.

[37] On Ebenezer's relations with the Yuchi, see Melton, *Religion, Community, and Slavery*, 157–63.

[38] *DR* 5:177.

indigenous peoples in the colony, grew less frequent and also less flattering. His scattered references to Indians employ adjectives like "bad-natured," "lawless," and "unbridled." "It is a blessing for us that the Indians seldom come to our place" wrote Boltzius in 1744, and he declared the following year that "these Indians are the worst of all... ."[39] His last reference to the Yuchi was in 1751, when a party of them took refuge in Ebenezer while fleeing from other Indians (likely Lower Creeks, with whom their relationship continued to be vexed): "they will presumably wish to remain here for a while, but this does not please us."[40]

As with the Jews of Savannah, then, Boltzius's perception of indigenous peoples was colored by his assessment of their capacity for conversion – their "convertibility," as it were. His initially positive view of both groups had been predicated on the expectation of conversion. In both cases, however, sympathy quickly changed to aversion when they did not heed the call.

From Abhorrence to Acceptance: Boltzius and Slavery

The same kind of dynamic structured his response to enslaved Africans, the last group examined in this essay. Here, however, expectations were reversed: in contrast to his encounters with Savannah's Jews and Georgia's Indians, Boltzius was at first pessimistic about the prospect of slave conversions. In part his doubts had to do with the timing of his arrival in the colonies. The ship bringing Boltzius and the Salzburgers to British America had briefly dropped anchor in Charleston before proceeding on to Savannah. Boltzius disembarked and spent a day in the South Carolina capital, where he immediately noted the presence of slaves. He could hardly have missed them: between 1700 and 1776 more than 40 percent of all enslaved Africans coming to North America probably passed through Charleston, where a robust market for rice and naval stores had stoked demand for slave labor. Already in 1700, 50 percent of the colony's population (excluding Indians) was black; by 1720 the proportion had risen to two-thirds.[41] In 1734 alone, the year of Boltzius's first visit to Charleston, close to 2,000 enslaved Africans would have arrived in the port. During the 1730s Charleston imported an average of 2,000 slaves per year, more than double the number arriving during the previous decade.

[39] *DR* 18:76; *Colonial Records of the State of Georgia*, ed. Allen D. Candler et al., 32 vols. (Atlanta: Franklin, 1904–89), 25:10.

[40] *DR* 15:70.

[41] Peter Wood, *Black Majority: Negroes in Colonial South Carolina from 1670 to the Stono Rebellion* (New York: Norton & Co, 1974), 146–47.

Boltzius spent only a day in the city, but the visit left him with a distinctly negative impression of slavery. As he wrote in his diary a few days later, "there are here many more black people than white people, all of whom are very much urged to work but never urged to become Christians. Very few, perhaps, have been baptized. The rest live like animals.... .Whole boatloads are brought here from Africa and offered for sale."[42] While in Charleston Boltzius also heard reports of violent slave insurrections in the Virgin Islands, where massacres of European planters and their families had just taken place on the sugar islands of St. John and St. Thomas.[43] Boltzius probably learned details of the massacre from Lewis Timothy, the editor of Charleston's *South Carolina Gazette*, whom Boltzius met during his brief stay in the city. The *Gazette*, which for two years had followed with concern lurid accounts of bloody insurrections in Jamaica, reported on March 2 – just a few days before Boltzius's visit – that the slaves of St. John's "had intirely [sic] massacred all the white People on that Island, consisting of about two hundred Families, and were very inhuman in the Execution of their Murders."[44] In noting the massacres, Boltzius wrote: "It is a great convenience to have many slaves to do the work, but this convenience is coupled with great dangers, for the blacks...are not faithful to the Christians and are very malicious."[45] Boltzius's first day in British America left him with a lasting impression of slaves as violent and menacing, an image that recurs throughout his diaries and journals for almost two decades. It goes far in explaining his firm support for the Trustees's ban on the importation of enslaved Africans.

Compounding the pastor's fear of slaves were the formidable obstacles he saw to their conversion. Since Boltzius, as an ordained Lutheran pastor, believed grace and redemption were potentially available to everyone, in principle he considered slaves capable of embracing Christianity. En route from Charleston following a brief visit in October 1742, Boltzius was surprised by the good behavior of slaves on a plantation where he was invited to spend the night: "I am sure that, by the grace of God, they could be brought not only to humanity and respectability but also to Christianity, if only the Masters themselves were Christian."[46] Yet his periodic visits to South Carolina, which lay just across the river from Ebenezer, convinced him that the conversion of slaves was impossible under their existing conditions of servitude.

42 *DR* 3:311. 43 *DR* 3:311. 44 Quoted in Wood, *Black Majority*, 222–23.

45 DR 3:311.

46 Quoted in George Fenwick Jones, "John Martin Boltzius's Trip to Charleston, October 1742," *South Carolina Historical Magazine* 82 (1981): 106.

Boltzius had grounds for pessimism. Most low country planters of the time, suspecting that ministers and preachers held antislavery views, were openly hostile to granting their slaves Christian instruction. There were exceptions, notably Jonathan Bryan, one of the wealthiest planters in the Lower South, whom Boltzius knew and considered a godly man for having been spiritually awakened by the preaching of the evangelist George Whitefield. In general, however, Boltzius was appalled at the planters' neglect of their Christian responsibilities. A clergyman visiting the Carolina low country in 1762 estimated that no more than around 1 percent of the colony's enslaved population had been baptized – an observation suggesting that Boltzius's impressions were well-founded.[47]

His outlook began to change after 1750, when Georgia's Trustees, finally bowing to pressure from the colony's proslavery lobby, repealed their earlier ban on the importation of slaves. Boltzius did his best to adapt. Easing his accommodation with slavery was his success in persuading the Trustees to include in the text of their repeal provisions aimed at mitigating some of the harsher aspects of the institution. He himself authored some of these, including one making it illegal to require slaves to work on Sundays; another enjoined masters to see that their slaves received proper Christian instruction. Boltzius was also consoled by the advice of fellow clergy like Samuel Albinus, a Halle-trained Pietist preacher at the German court chapel in London, who assured Boltzius that holding slaves was permissible as long as they were led to Christianity. George Whitefield, with whom Boltzius had maintained cordial relations despite his disapproval of the evangelist's earlier accommodation with slavery, wrote to him in a similar vein.[48]

Boltzius, consoled by such assurances and having himself authored provisions that urged masters to concern themselves with the salvation of their slaves, grew more hopeful about their prospects for conversion. His assessment of their character brightened accordingly. Responding in 1751 to a list of questions sent by an anonymous Augsburg benefactor regarding conditions in the lower-southern colonies, Boltzius wrote: "I have been told that the Negroes cannot be taught anything, that they are stupid and not inclined to learn, and that they abuse a Christian and soft treatment, but I consider all this to be an invention of such people who take no pains with the souls of these black people, nor want to keep them

[47] See Philip Morgan, *Slave Counterpoint: Black Culture in the Eighteenth-Century Chesapeake and Lowcountry* (Chapel Hill: University of North Carolina Press, 1998), 422. On the hostility of Carolinian planters to the conversion of slaves, see Jeffrey Robert Young, *Domesticating Slavery: The Master Class in Georgia and South Carolina, 1670–1837* (Chapel Hill: University of North Carolina Press, 1999), 23–29.

[48] *DR*: 15:44, 16:218.

in a Christian way regarding food, clothing, work, and marriage."[49] A visit the following year to a school for slaves founded in Savannah by the Anglican minister Reverend Joseph Ottotenghe, a Jewish convert from Italy, reinforced this belief: "I was amazed at the good understanding and native intelligence of the Negroes gathered in the school; and I was again convinced that they have as much good reason and ability as the Europeans to be led to the good and made capable."[50]

Hence the introduction of slavery – and the opportunities for conversion it seemed to promise – ironically served to bolster Boltzius's faith in the moral, spiritual and intellectual capacities of enslaved Africans. Their presence in Georgia changed his outlook in other ways as well. Prior to 1750, the pastor's exposure to slaves had been intermittent and limited to relatively sporadic visits to South Carolina. After 1750 the encounters grew more routine, whether in the Ebenezer region, where he was already baptizing slaves in 1751, or during visits to Savannah, where he saw them on the streets, at slave auctions, or in visits to Reverend Ottotenghe's school. The arrival of slaves and the prospect of his parishioners owning them spurred Boltzius to gain a deeper knowledge of their lives and customs. That in turn heightened an awareness of enslaved Africans not as an indiscriminate, potentially violent mass, but as distinct individuals with souls amenable to salvation.

This change was already visible in the aforementioned treatise he wrote for his anonymous Augsburg patron, still a valuable source on slavery in the lower-southern colonies.[51] Boltzius's tract is filled with information on matters like the price of slaves on the Carolina and Georgia markets, the cost of their upkeep, their diet, dress, and ethnic origins, how many were needed to run a well-appointed plantation, the amount of acreage a slave could harvest in a year, and the sexual division of slave labor. Much of this knowledge, like Boltzius's estimates of slave productivity or the cost of running a plantation, was doubtless acquired second-hand. Even so, the document evinces a level of ethnographic awareness absent from his previous references to slaves. Their presence in his community, and the sustained encounters with African men, women, and children this entailed, strengthened that attentiveness.

[49] Boltzius, "Reliable Answers to Some Submitted Questions Concerning the Land Carolina," *William and Mary Quarterly*, 3rd ser. 14/2 (April 1957): 240.
[50] *DR* 15:258.
[51] Boltzius, "Reliable Answers to Some Submitted Questions Concerning the Land Carolina."

Boltzius's Reconversion

By the mid-1750s, however, only a few years after the arrival of slavery in Georgia, Boltzius had once again come to question the prospects for slave conversions. He could not help but see that Georgia, now a slaveholding society, more and more resembled the Carolinian model that Georgia's founders had been so determined to shun. Nowhere was this more visible than in Georgia's 1755 slave code, which was virtually indistinguishable from South Carolina's. The earlier provisions that Boltzius had helped craft had fixed the permissible ratio of slaves to adult whites at 1:4. The 1755 code, one of the earliest measures passed by Georgia's new colonial assembly, dramatically increased the ratio to 20:1. The effect was to sanction a rapid growth of slave imports, from a few hundred in 1750 to around 15,000 in 1773.[52] Most egregiously from Boltzius's standpoint, the new code omitted any reference to the religious instruction of slaves, a provision the pastor had worked so hard to include in the Trustees's repeal. The omission suggested that Georgia planters had internalized attitudes akin to their slaveholding neighbors to the north, including the belief that the Christian instruction of slaves was dangerous because it made them less willing to bear their bondage.

Boltzius now harbored few illusions about the direction slaveholding had taken in Georgia. In a 1757 letter to Gotthilf August Francke in Halle, he castigated Georgia slaveholders for standing in the way of their slaves' conversion: "The most distressing thing is that these poor slaves as heathens spend their lives in the service of their so-called Christian masters and in the end as heathens must completely lose their souls. How indeed before the judgement seat of Christ will they look upon their masters and mistresses who certainly gave them enough work and vexation but no time and opportunity for the saving awareness of Christ and for the care of their souls!"[53] By this time Boltzius's physical capacities had waned considerably owing to recurring bouts with malaria, and his eyesight, weakened by cataracts and strained by the voluminous correspondence his duties entailed, had deteriorated. In 1760 he turned over responsibility for the *Detailed Reports* to his associate pastor, Christian Rabenhorst, who had come to Ebenezer in 1752 after being recruited for the post in Halle. The lightened workload, however, did little to mitigate his unease about the direction in which the Georgia colony seemed to be moving.

[52] Betty Wood, *Slavery in Colonial Georgia, 1730–1775* (Athens: University of Georgia Press, 1984), 112–30. The text of the 1755 code can be found in *Colonial Records of the State of Georgia*, 18:102–44.

[53] *Letters of Johann Martin Boltzius*, 2:662.

A particular cause for concern was Rabenhorst, who would ultimately succeed him as senior pastor after Boltzius's death in 1765. The son of a village schoolmaster in the Baltic province of Farther Pomerania (Hinterpommern), Rabenhorst had escaped his humble background by winning one of the scholarships available to poor but deserving students at Halle's Pietist orphanage. He was in some respects a talented and enterprising man, as Boltzius admitted even after their relationship had soured. He praised Rabenhorst's preaching abilities, his fluency in languages, and the ease with which he adapted to a foreign environment. But while on paper Rabenhorst's credentials were solidly Pietist (like Boltzius, he had studied theology at Halle), he was no missionary by temperament. Younger, more worldly and ambitious than Boltzius, who was twenty-five years his senior, Rabenhorst had none of the exacting austerity that Boltzius's Pietist generation had preached. Perhaps emulating the wealthy planters he encountered during visits to Savannah, or maybe recalling the Junker proprietors of his East Elbian homeland, Rabenhorst instead seemed intent on establishing himself as a landowner of substance, more interested in buying enslaved Africans than in converting them. His marriage to a wealthy widow enabled him to acquire a 500-acre plantation; by 1760 it had doubled in size, complete with overseer and with slaves producing rice, indigo, and corn. At his death Rabenhorst owned thirty-three slaves, making him the largest slaveholder in Ebenezer.[54]

Boltzius never owned slaves, either as domestics or on the glebe land he received as pastor. Neither his will, nor the inventory of his estate taken after his death in 1765, include any mention of them.[55] As he wrote in 1764 to Heinrich Melchior Mühlenberg, the Pennsylvania Lutheran leader, "I do not have the skill, the time, or the inclination for plantation affairs or the keeping of negroes."[56] By 1760 he had become openly critical of Rabenorst's acquisitiveness and charged that it left no time for the instruction of his slaves. As he wrote to Samuel Urlsperger in 1761: "What help is a teacher whose work is planting and harvesting, but whose side work is the teaching office?" Rabenhorst also drove his slaves hard, leading Boltzius to characterize him as a "severe taskmaster" so disliked by his slaves that they deliberately avoided having children. Years later, in fact, Rabenhorst appears to have been so hated by his slaves that one of

54 On Rabenhorst see Melton, *Religion, Community, and Slavery*, 250, 263–65.

55 *State Archives of Georgia*, Morrow, GA: Colonial Will Books, Record Group 049–01-005; Estate Records: Inventories and Appraisements, Book F, 1754–70.

56 *Die Korrespondenz Heinrich Melchior Mühlenberg aus der Anfangszeit des deutschen Luthertums in Nordamerika*, ed. Kurt Aland (Berlin and New York: De Gruyter, 1990), 3: 228.

them, a female domestic, was burned at the stake for trying to murder him and his wife by lacing their coffee with poison.[57]

A decade after the introduction of slavery into Georgia, then, Boltzius had seen little to sustain his earlier hope for a more Christian and temperate slaveholding regime. Not only did Savannah planters fail to attend to their slaves' spiritual needs; even in Ebenezer, Boltzius lamented, his own pastoral associate placed material gain over his Christian duties.

Disabused of his earlier faith that human bondage could be a path to conversion, Boltzius came to regret his accommodation of slavery. In the summer of 1763, two years before his death, the pastor underwent a conversion of his own and reaffirmed his earlier opposition to the institution. He described the occasion for his epiphany in an unpublished diary entry from 1763. Looking back on the Ebenezer community as it had evolved since the introduction of slavery, Boltzius observed:

> Because of the high price of silk [Ebenezer was by that time a leading producer of raw silk in the Lower South], some in our community attained sufficient means to purchase negroes. Seeking wealth, they surrendered to temptation, since greed is the root of all evil that leads them astray from their faith. An English-language pamphlet, published in Philadelphia, appeared last year [1762] which describes the injustice and cruelties arising out of the trade in African Negroes. If I had read it earlier, I would never have abandoned my previous belief that the importation and use of Negroes should not be permitted.[58]

Although Boltzius provided no further information about the pamphlet or its author, the work in question would almost certainly been the second installment of John Woolman's *Considerations on Keeping Negroes*, published by Benjamin Franklin in 1762 (the first part had appeared in 1754). Woolman, the grandson of English Quakers who had immigrated to the colonies and settled in New Jersey, was an itinerate tailor who spent much of his adult life preaching his abolitionist message to Quaker communities throughout the colonies. His writings and preaching are widely credited with forging the collective opposition to slavery that had become a hallmark of the Quaker movement by the American Revolution. David Brion Davis, who devoted the epilogue of his classic *Problem of Slavery in Western Culture* to Woolman, went so far as to write that "if the Western world became more receptive to antislavery thought between the time Woolman left for North Carolina in 1746 and when he arrived in

[57] The incident, which occurred in 1774, is recounted by Mühlenberg following a visit to the Rabenhorst plantation. *Journals of Henry Melchior Mühlenberg*, trans. Theodore G. Tappert and John W. Doberstein, 3 vols. (Philadelphia: Evangelical Lutheran Ministerium of Pennsylvania and Adjacent States, 1945), 2: 585.

[58] *AFSt/M*, Georgia-Sektion: 5D:13 (Boltzius Tagebuch, August 2, 1763), fol. 2.

England in 1772, the self-effacing Quaker was a major instrument of this transformation."

It is easy to surmise why the pamphlet would have resonated so deeply in Boltzius. Although Woolman's polemical target, the slave trade, was contemporary, his sources, language, and history were largely biblical. That was to be expected of a fervent Quaker, but more decisive is the fact that Woolman's reasoning, like Boltzius's narrative of his own religious community, drew copiously on the postexilic history of the Jews as described in the Old Testament. To contemporaries who invoked biblical justifications for slavery, he responded that yes, God's covenant with the Jews after leading them out of Egypt had permitted them to take slaves. But the laws of Moses had never sanctioned bondage for a slave's offspring, whether Hebrew or foreigner. And had not the prophet Jeremiah also reminded the people of Judah that the covenant had required each of them to set free any Hebrew slave who had served six years? Woolman charged that the Jews, by failing to heed God's word and free their Hebrew slaves accordingly, had corrupted Mosaic law and sealed their subsequent fate in Babylonian captivity.

In effect, then, Woolman's pamphlet integrated abolitionist discourse into the classic colonial jeremiad by placing slavery at the core of Old Testament's narrative of exile. Woolman tried to show that slavery was not a vehicle for fulfilling God's divine plan, but an obstacle. Therein lies another clue into why Boltzius would have been so moved by Woolman's tract, despite their confessional differences. The pastor's mounting unease with the direction in which Ebenezer was moving led him to fashion his own jeremiad, at the center of which also happened to be slavery. Slavery for Boltzius had become a symbol of how Ebenezer, once chosen and thus exceptional in God's eyes, had succumbed to worldly temptation. Woolman's *Considerations on Keeping Negroes* gave Boltzius a biblical framework for articulating his doubts, one that ultimately led him to renounce slavery on the eve of his death. One of his last letters, written shortly before his death in 1765, expressed thanks to God for the prosperity Ebenezer had come to enjoy. Yet as is clear from the letter, slavery and the prophet Jeremiah remained much in his thoughts.

> Our residents are coming to a good material sustenance, but in doing so the great God deals with many foes, as it were, in his own currency. The great love for Moorish slaves and for becoming rich ruins many, and nothing is devoted to the poor souls of these slaves except that the little Negro children are baptized, which does not happen at all in other places. The silk for several years has done well, which gives them [the people of Ebenezer] the means of buying Negroes. . . . God

also bestows to us yearly a good harvest, but also I wish that I would not need to apply to many among us the lamenting Word of God in Jeremiah.[59]

Conclusion

Boltzius's encounter with non-Christians in the Georgia colony yielded few if any conversions. The Sheftalls remained steadfast in their Jewish faith despite Boltzius's Pietist confidence in their impending conversion. His efforts among the Yuchi likewise came to naught, partly owing to cultural and linguistic obstacles, partly because the demands of Boltzius's ministry in his own community left little time for missionary work. The pastor's evangelical gaze remained fixed on his parishioners, which militated against the conversion of Indians who lived beyond the wooden palisades of Ebenezer. As Wolfgang Splitter has persuasively argued, this more narrowly intraconfessional focus was to be a characteristic of Halle's missions to indigenous peoples throughout colonial North America. Halle Pietists never developed a coherent missionary strategy for their conversion but remained primarily focused on maintaining internal order and conformity among their Lutheran co-religionists. This limited mission concept helps account for the declining importance of Lutheranism after the American Revolution. Lutheran churches in the new republic, while losing acculturated German Americans to other congregations, were never able to compensate for this attrition by attracting members of other Protestant groups.[60]

Although the arrival of slavery in Georgia after 1750 momentarily revived Boltzius's missionary impulses, there too his hopes proved misplaced. By Boltzius's death his Halle-trained associate pastor had emerged as the largest slaveholder in Ebenezer, and throughout the colony, as in South Carolina, most planters remained hostile to providing their slaves a Christian education. Only after the American Revolution, with the rise of evangelicalism and the sobering effects of Denmark Vesey's alleged slave conspiracy (1822), did this resistance give way to

[59] *Letters of Johann Martin Boltzius*, 2:778.

[60] Wolfgang Splitter, "Order, Ordination, Subordination: German Lutheran Missionaries in Eighteenth-Century Pennsylvania," in *The Creation of the British Atlantic World*, ed. Elizabeth Mancke and Carole Shammas (Baltimore, MD and London: John Hopkins University Press, 2005), 209–35; "Divide et impera: Some Critical Remarks on Halle Missionaries' Formation of a Lutheran Church in Pennsylvania," in *Halle Pietism, Colonial North America, and the Young United States*, ed. Hans-Jürgen Grabbe (Stuttgart: Franz Steiner, 2008), 45–92.

a belief that masters were responsible for the spiritual welfare of their slaves.[61]

Ebenezer's days were in any case numbered. Despite what Boltzius, with the prophet Jeremiah on his mind, might have predicted on the eve of his death, it was not slavery that precipitated the community's downfall. Since most inhabitants of Ebenezer and its outlying dependencies were smallholders who had to supplement subsistence farming with income derived from the sale of lumber processed in their community sawmill, slaveholding in the community was significantly less extensive than it was in the colony's rice-producing coastal areas.[62] Ebenezer owed its demise instead to the disastrous effects of the American Revolution, when the town, despite efforts by many of the inhabitants to stay out of the bitter and violent conflict that ensued between loyalists and rebels, changed hands four times and was repeatedly raided and sacked. The Revolution also had the effect of severing Ebenezer's ties with SPCK, long a dependable source of contributions, while Halle's interest dwindled as Ebenezer, depopulated and devastated by war, fell into irreversible decline. Ebenezer, the offspring of Britain's North American colonial empire, did not long survive its collapse.

[61] Young, *Domesticating Slavery*, 23–29, 167–82.

[62] The ratio of white settlers to enslaved Africans in the Ebenezer district was roughly 10:1 on the eve of the American Revolution, as opposed to 1.7: 1 in the colony as a whole. See Melton, *Religion, Community, and Slavery*, 249.

9 Globalizing the Protestant Reformation through Millenarian Practices

Ulrike Gleixner

Millenarianism is a global concept that has maintained its influential presence in many religions and different forms to this day.[1] In medieval and early modern times,[2] it referred to the belief-based on the Book of Revelation (20:4-6)–that after the second coming, Christ would establish his Messianic kingdom on earth and would reign over it for 1,000 years before the Last Judgment.[3] After the Thirty Years' War (1618-1648), the concept of millenarianism – often with apocalyptical overtones – developed into more cautious versions in Protestantism. Especially in intellectual and non-conformist circles in Britain and on the continent, the concept was used to articulate social and church reform programs, for example those advocated by intellectuals like Johann Amos Comenius, Samuel Hartlieb, Philipp Jakob Spener, and August Hermann Francke. But the concept was also common among non-intellectuals and was a driving factor in the process of the European colonization in North America. Beginning in the 1640s, the millenarian expectations of English settlers in the American colonies for example led to serious attempts to convert Indians to Christianity.[4] In his article on the millenarian approach of the young Gottfried Wilhelm Leibniz, Howard Hotson framed the millenarian aspirations of the seventeenth-century millenarians as follows: "The conversion

[1] Roland Robertson, "Global millennialism: a Postmortem on Secularization," in *Religion, Globalization and Culture*, eds. Peter Beyer and Lori G. Beaman (Leiden: Brill, 2007), 9–34; Sanjay Subrahmanyam, "Connected Histories: Notes towards a Refiguration of Early Modern Eurasia," *Modern Asian Studies 31* (1997): 735–62.

[2] Norman Cohn, *The Pursuit of the Millennium: Revolutionary Millenarians and Mystical Anarchists of the Middle Ages* (1st ed. 1957; repr. London: Paladin, 1970), 13.

[3] Martin Brecht, "Chiliasmus in Württemberg im 17. Jahrhundert," in *Chiliasmus in Deutschland und England im 17. Jahrhundert*, ed. Klaus Deppermann (Göttingen: Vandenhoeck & Ruprecht, 1988), 25–49; Hartmut Lehmann, "Pietistic Millenarianism in Late Eighteenth-Century Germany," in *The Transformation of Political Culture: England and Germany in the Late Eighteenth Century*, ed. Eckhart Hellmuth (Oxford: Oxford University Press, 1990), 267–79; Ulrich Gäbler, "Geschichte, Gegenwart, Zukunft," in *Glaubenswelt und Lebenswelten*, ed. Hartmut Lehmann (Göttingen: Vandenhoeck & Ruprecht, 2004), 4: 19–48.

[4] Carla Gardina Pestana, *Protestant Empire: Religion and the Making of the British Atlantic World* (Philadelphia: University of Pennsylvania Press, 2009), 91 ff.

of all the peoples of the earth to Christianity, the spread of Christ's kingdom throughout the whole world, the restoration of a golden age of apostolic piety, the instauration of man's domination over nature, the radical improvement of the art of medicine and of human health as a result, the perfection of law, justice, politics, civil life, morals, and above all of faith and charity."[5] This program included a positive vision for humankind that included all aspects of life – faith, politics, society, sciences, and the individual.

A contemporary of Leibniz, the German Lutheran theologian Philipp Jakob Spener (1635–1705) expressed his millenarian reform program without any apocalyptic references. In his *Pia Desideria* (1675), he turned the concept into an expectation of a positive future. His program advocated for church reforms, the conversion of the Jews, and the fall of a "Papal Rome."[6] Many church historians see the activities of Spener and his network of pious men and women as the beginning of the Pietist devotional movement extending from the last quarter of the seventeenth century to the end of the eighteenth. The Reformers took the view that both the Lutheran church and the believers paid too little attention to active piety in everyday life. As a minister in Frankfurt am Main, Spener arranged religious meetings in his house beyond the church services, which was officially prohibited since the state churches in the various German lands had a monopoly on the convening of religious gatherings. During the meetings, called conventicles, edifying literature and the bible were read aloud and subsequently discussed. Soon after, conventicles began to appear in Frankfurt organized by friends of Spener but without his presence in which women often took leading positions. The chronology shows that the conventicles developed dynamically. From the very beginning, there were separatist currents alongside those loyal to the church.[7] After the publishing of Spener's *Pia Desideria* in 1675, a lively debate on his suggested reform program began, and as a result of the theological controversy, the appeal of conventicles grew. From the city of Leipzig, a wave of conventicles spread into central and northern Germany through visits, correspondence, and testimonials. In March 1690, the elector of Saxony issued a ban on private meetings and the theological faculty of Leipzig's university set itself against university members involved in the

[5] Howard Hotson, "Leibniz and Millenarianism," in *The Young Leibniz and His Philosophy (1646–76)*, ed. Stuart Brown (Dordrecht: Kluwer Academic Publ., 1999), 169–98, see 171.

[6] Johannes Wallmann, *Philipp Jakob Spener und die Anfänge des Pietismus* (2nd revised and extended ed., Tübingen: Mohr, 1986), 324 f.

[7] Wallmann, *Philipp Jakob Spener und die Anfänge des Pietismus*; Johannes Wallmann, *Der Pietismus* (Göttingen: Vandenhoeck & Ruprecht, 2005).

movement. Its adherents were called Pietists, originally a derogatory term that nevertheless came to define the whole movement. Pietist students left Leipzig and carried the conventicle practice to other cities, including Eisenach, Erfurt, Halberstadt, Magdeburg, Helmstedt, Berlin, Arnstadt, Colditz, Quedlinburg, Jena, Gotha, and Altenburg. A super-regional sense of belonging grew from the experience of being part of a new Christian community.[8] Groups with separatist tendencies accorded particular significance to sensory experience and welcomed inspired visionaries as "instruments of the Lord." Accusations formulated in visions against the authorities as well as the official church had a particularly explosive potential. Conflicts over private gatherings grew increasingly bitter among participants, parish ministers, and local non-Pietists. As a result there were arrests, judicial examinations, and banishments. But the Pietist movement including the private gatherings was unstoppable and fell on fertile ground. One generation after the Thirty Years' War, Pietists took on pressing problems in church and society, as they found that the Lutheran church offered few solutions to a difficult social situation and poor educational and training opportunities.

Pietism represented the most significant Protestant renewal movement since the Lutheran Reformation. Its central features included new forms of sociability, social responsibility, and an optimistic vision of the future associated with an encompassing reform of church and society. Demonstrative penitence and techniques of self-improvement were designed to lead to individual awakening and rebirth. For the laity and particularly for women, Pietism offered new possibilities for religious communal formation as well as individuation. Charity, child-rearing, education, catechesis, religious text-production, mission and media policy as well as economic undertakings were considered necessary and compatible areas of Pietist activity. As part of the religious enlightenment, Pietism overcame class-bound conceptions and argued for the potential of human development.[9] Pietists turned away from the eschatology of Lutheran orthodoxy, with its emphasis on the impending end of the

[8] Ryoko Mori, *Begeisterung und Ernüchterung in christlicher Vollkommenheit: Pietistische Selbst- und Weltwahrnehmungen im ausgehenden 17. Jahrhundert* (Tübingen: Verlag der Franckeschen Stiftungen Halle im Niemeyer-Verlag, 2004); Katja Lißmann, *Schreiben im Netz: Briefe von Frauen als Praktiken frommer Selbst-Bildung im frühen Quedlinburger Pietismus* (Halle/Saale: Verlag der Franckeschen Stiftungen zu Halle/Wiesbaden: Harrassowitz, 2019).

[9] Jonathan Strom, *German Pietism and the Problem of Conversion* (University Park: Pennsylvania State University Press, 2018); Ulrike Gleixner, "Pietism," in *The Oxford Handbook of the Protestant Reformations*, ed. Ulinka Rublack (Oxford: Oxford University Press, 2016), 329–49; Douglas H. Shantz ed., *A Companion to German Pietism, 1660–1800* (Leiden: Brill, 2015).

world. Instead they cultivated a hopeful optimism about the future. Without this hopefulness, Pietism's social and missionary activism cannot be understood. Millenarian concepts served as the driving force for a practical approach to a pious society. Gradually, social, educational and missionary work was to lead to "God's Kingdom" (*das Reich Gottes*) on earth. In many respects, Pietism could appropriate Lutheran traditions. When it came to concepts of millenarian eschatology, however, there was a significant break. Until the second half of the seventeenth century, Lutherans placed their hope for a better future in another world and expected a near end of the present one. However, the Pietist vision of a better future focused on a realization on earth and its adherents saw themselves responsible for its efficient implementation. It is against this background that their global activities should be understood.

Based on the millenarian approach, the Pietist August Hermann Francke (1663–1727), who was a generation younger than Spener and the founder of the Halle Orphanage, campaigned for a "universal social reform."[10] With the support of the Prussian court, Francke and his colleagues succeeded in institutionalizing Pietism in Halle, developing the newly established university into a Pietist training center. The orphanage complex was quickly expanded into a school city, a campus, encompassing various educational institutions.[11] Piety, diligence, and personal responsibility were the educational goals. Orphanages and schools based on the Halle model were developed in the German-speaking lands, in Britain, Eastern Europe, North America, and India. Graduates of these institutions, influenced by Halle Pietism, saw themselves as active ambassadors for the expansion of the "Kingdom of God" on earth. Udo Sträter has described the millenarian frame of Halle very aptly. For the activists,

[10] Juliane Jacobi and Thomas Müller-Bahlke eds., "*Man hatte von ihm gute Hoffnung ...*"*: Das Waisenalbum der Franckeschen Stiftungen 1695–1749* (Halle/Saale: Verlag der Franckeschen Stiftungen Halle im Niemeyer-Verlag, 1998); Peter Menck, *Die Erziehung der Jugend zur Ehre Gottes und zum Nutzen des Nächsten: Die Pädagogik August Hermann Franckes* (Tübingen: Verlag der Franckeschen Stiftungen Halle im Max-Niemeyer-Verlag, 2001); Juliane Jacobi ed., *Zwischen christlicher Tradition und Aufbruch in die Moderne: Das Hallesche Waisenhaus im bildungsgeschichtlichen Kontext* (Tübingen: Verlag der Franckeschen Stiftungen Halle im Niemeyer-Verlag, 2007); Holger Zaunstöck, Thomas J. Müller-Bahlke and Claus Veltmann eds., *Die Welt verändern: August Hermann Francke – ein Lebenswerk um 1700*, exhibition catalog (Halle/Saale: Verlag der Franckeschen Stiftungen zu Halle/Wiesbaden: Harrassowitz, 2013).

[11] These included the German school as a primary school, the Latin school which prepared students for university, and the *Pädagogium regium* for the upper classes and nobility. Francke outlined the principles of his innovative education program in his pedagogical text *Kurzer und einfältiger Unterricht, wie die Kinder zur wahren Gottseligkeit und christlichen Klugheit anzuführen sind* (*Brief and Simple Instruction in How Children are to be Led to True Godliness and Christian Wisdom*, 1702).

the success of the Halle institutions demonstrated that the kingdom was already realized there. Halle was the bridgehead of "God's expanding Kingdom on earth."[12] Active conversion work would turn more and more sites to islands of "God's Kingdom" to finally be realized as a patchwork tapestry. Lutheran Pietists understood the realization as a gradual process. In his memorandum *Project for a Universal Seminary or the Planting of a Garden, in which a real improvement in all classes in and outside Germany, even in Europe and in all other parts of the world can be expected* (1701)[13], Francke framed his vision of a global Protestant mission:

> ... kein verständiger Mensch [wird] anders urtheilen können, als daß ein vortreffliches, ja das allervornehmste Mittel zu einer gründlichen Verbesserung in allen Ständen sein werde, wenn man ein rechtes Seminarium erlangen möchte, welches dergestalt eingerichtet wäre und unter göttlichen Segen so emsig, sorgfältig und weislich gepflanzet und gewartet würde, daß man aus demselben stets, und von Zeit zu Zeit wohlgerathene Pflanzen und Bäume herausnehmen, an andere Orte, und in andere Länder aller Theile der Welt und unter alle Nationes versetzen und von ihnen völlige Früchte erwarten, und mit Freuden genießen könnte.[14]

> ... no intelligent person [will] judge otherwise than that an excellent, indeed the most preferable device for the improvement of all classes will be to maintain a proper seminary, which would be arranged and planted so diligently, carefully and wisely under divine blessing, that we could remove from time to time mature plants and trees, to transplant them in other places, and in other countries in all parts of the world and among all nations, and to expect from them good fruits to enjoy. [trans. UG]

August Hermann Francke manifested his claim of a global conversion by defining the mission field as existing in and outside of Europe. This was one of the first times in German Lutheranism that an overseas mission was championed in public.

After the Chinese emperor Kangxi granted religious tolerance and freedom in 1692, the European call for a Protestant mission intensified.

[12] Udo Sträter, "Der hallische Pietismus zwischen Utopie und Weltgestaltung," in *Interdisziplinäre Pietismusforschung: Beiträge zum Ersten Internationalen Kongress für Pietismusforschung 2001*, eds. Udo Sträter et al. (Tübingen: Verlag der Franckeschen Stiftungen Halle im Max-Niemeyer-Verlag, 2005), 1: 19–36, here 32; Udo Sträter, "Spener und August Hermann Francke," in *Philipp Jakob Spener – Leben, Werk, Bedeutung: Bilanz der Forschung nach 300 Jahren*, ed. Dorothea Wendebourg (Tübingen: Verlag der Franckeschen Stiftungen Halle im Max-Niemeyer-Verlag, 2007), 89–104.

[13] August Hermann Francke, "Project zu einem Seminario universali oder Anlegung eines Pflanzgartens, in welchem man eine reale Verbesserung in allen Ständen in und außerhalb Deutschlands, ja in Europa und allen übrigen Theilen der Welt zu gewarten (1701)," in *August Hermann Francke: Ein Lebensbild*, ed. Gustav Kramer (first ed. 1882, repr. Hildesheim/Zurich/New York: Olms, 2004), 2: *Anhang*, 489–96.

[14] Kramer, *Ein Lebensbild*, 2: *Anhang*, 489.

Protestant scholars and theologians in particular stressed the need for a Protestant world mission. The enthusiasm of Gottfried Wilhelm Leibniz regarding the greater opening of China was accompanied by a grave concern about the growing spiritual and scholarly influence of Catholicism. In his correspondence to Francke, Leibniz strongly advocated the installation of a Protestant mission outside of Europe.[15] In his letter to Francke from April 16, 1699, written in Latin, he regretted seriously that the Protestant rulers were not doing anything about establishing missions in Russia and China instead leaving the field to the Jesuits. He framed his criticism in a laconic style:

Dum nos deliberamus, illi agunt: sed hoc interest, quod nostra privata sunt molimina, illi publica ope nituntur.[16]

While we are considering the matter, they are acting; the difference being that our efforts are private and theirs are based on public support. [trans. UG]

Protestant scholars were aware that new knowledge about foreign languages, religious and philosophical thought, geography, geology, flora and fauna were mostly recorded by Jesuits and then published within their Catholic network. Thus, Protestant academics requested that Protestant missionaries also process the new knowledge in their own scholarly circles. Whereas millenarianism had been one force in the Protestant mission endeavor, the demand of the Protestant scientific community to gain access to new disciplines outside of Europe became another. More than a few subscribers to the first Protestant mission journal, the *Hallesche Berichte,* had a stronger interest in reports on Tamil culture and lifestyle, animals, plants, and climate than in the narratives of conversions from Hinduism to Christianity.[17] The missionaries undertook

[15] Gerda Utermöhlen, "Die Rußlandthematik im Briefwechsel zwischen August Hermann Francke und Gottfried Wilhelm Leibniz," in *Halle und Osteuropa: Zur europäischen Ausstrahlung des hallischen Pietismus*, ed. Johannes Wallmann (Tübingen: Verlag der Franckeschen Stiftungen Halle im Niemeyer-Verlag, 1998), 109–28; Wenchao Li, "Leibnizens Plan einer protestantischen Mission in China," in *Neuzeitliches Denken: Festschrift für Hans Poser zum 65. Geburtstag*, ed. Günter Abel (Berlin: De Gruyter, 2002), 251–66; Thomas Fuchs, "Aufbruch in fremde Welten: Die Formierung der protestantischen Missionsbewegung im 18. Jahrhundert," in *Das eine Europa und die Vielfalt der Kulturen: Kulturtransfer in Europa 1500–1850*, ed. Thomas Fuchs and Sven Trakulhun (Berlin: BWV, Berliner Wiss.-Verl., 2003), 185–204; Markus Friedrich, "Gottfried Wilhelm Leibniz und die protestantische Diskussion über Heidenmission," in *Umwelt und Weltgestaltung: Leibniz' politisches Denken in seiner Zeit*, ed. Friedrich Beiderbeck, Irene Dingel, and Wenchao Li (Göttingen: Vandenhoeck & Ruprecht, 2015), 641–77.

[16] Gottfried Wilhelm Leibniz, *Sämtliche Schriften und Briefe*, ed. Akademie der Wissenschaften, Leibnizarchiv der Niedersächsischen, and Landesbibliothek Hannover (Berlin: Akademie Verlag, 2000), I/16: *Allgemeiner Politischer und Historischer Briefwechsel Oktober 1698–April 1699*, 714–16.

[17] Ulrike Gleixner, "Expansive Frömmigkeit: Das hallische Netzwerk der Indienmission im 18. Jahrhundert," in *Mission und Forschung: Translokale Wissensproduktion zwischen Indien*

the role as mediators of scientific news. They exchanged letters with European academics and published answers to the question catalogs of European scholars in the Halle mission journal. They also sent requested objects from South India to their correspondents. Theophil Siegfried Bayer, a philologist and historian, and an active member of the St. Petersburg Academy of Sciences, was born in Königsberg (presently Kaliningrad) in 1694 and died in St. Petersburg in 1738. He maintained an independent correspondence with the missionaries in India on various topics of regional studies and Indian languages. Since his research specialty was Asian languages, he requested information and books on the Tamil language for years and in 1734 he sent to the missionaries in Tranquebar his manuscript *Unterricht von der Brahmanischen Indostanischen Sprache* (Instructions of the Brahmanic Indostane language).[18] Indeed, many scholars obtained their knowledge about India from the mission magazines.[19] Johann David Michaelis (1717–1791), professor of theology and orientalist at the University of Göttingen and secretary of the Göttingen Academy of Science, was not primarily a Pietist although he had attended the Latin school at the orphanage in Halle and had studied at the university there. He was a leading German Enlightenment theologian and a precursor of the development of empirical social research. Michaelis not only subscribed to the mission journal on India from the 1770s onwards but also began a correspondence with the mission organizers in Halle and the missionaries in Tranquebar, some of whom he knew from his years in Halle.[20] There was a considerable transfer of knowledge in the correspondence, which lasted ten years, and he peppered the missionaries in southeast India with questions to which he often received answers. Michaelis reviewed the Bible text using a historical-critical approach. One question, he wrote to the missionaries in Tranquebar, concerned the capacity of elephants to carry humans to verify the biblical passage in 1 Maccabees 6:37 which says that an elephant can carry thirty-two people. The missionaries responded that an old mahout of the king of Tanjore had given the information that twenty-eight people could be accommodated on one elephant. Michaelis published the four-page transcript in 1778 as an appendix to the twelfth volume of his review.[21] Here we

und Europa im 18. und 19. Jahrhundert, eds. Heike Liebau, Andreas Nehring, and Brigitte Klosterberg (Halle: Verlag der Franckeschen Stiftungen Halle, 2010), 57–66.

[18] Archiv Frankesche Stiftungen/Mission (in the following AFST/M) ALMW/DHM 9/19, fol. 14).

[19] Rekha Kamath Rajan, "Der Beitrag der Dänisch-Halleschen Missionare zum europäischen Wissen über Indien im 18. Jahrhundert," in Liebau, Nehring, and Klosterberg eds., *Mission und Forschung*, 93–112.

[20] AFSt/M 3 L 23.

[21] See Britta Klosterberg, "How Many People Can an Elephant Carry?! Questions from Johann David Michaelis to the Missionaries in East India," in *Halle and the Beginning of*

can observe closely a practice in which mission-based knowledge from handwritten letters was transferred into printed scientific publications for a broader readership. Daniel Ernst Jablonski (1660–1741), a Reformed court preacher in Berlin and also president of the Prussian Academy of Science in that city, also subscribed to the mission journal.[22] We can find many overlaps in the networks of Pietism and science. Quite a few academics had leading positions in the mission steering committees as well as in the scientific community. Johann Ludwig von Holstein (1694–1763) was simultaneously president of the mission council at the Danish court and president of the Danish Academy of Science. Otto von Thott (1703–1785) was president of the mission council and rector of the University of Copenhagen.[23] For the transfer and generation of knowledge, mission and humanities as well as natural sciences worked together closely.

Besides the thirst for news from India in the Protestant scientific community, the millenarian hopes of a better future required practical engagement to realize "God's Kingdom" on earth. Millenarian expectations supported the drive for globalizing the Protestant Reformation and shaped the mission to southeast India in every respect, from the planning and communication, the medialization and fundraising, down to the local missionary work. My chapter will argue that the globalization of the Protestant Reformation was performed through millenarian practices in the Pietist mission project to southeast India. It will focus on millenarian practices in four fields: organization, knowledge transfer, transcultural interaction, and European religious identity.

Christianity has had polycentric structures since its beginning.[24] In the process of globalizing, Protestantism went through different stages of expansion. Single globalization impulses replaced, overlaid, or interacted with each other. They followed different dynamics of intercultural exchange, developed specific communicative and organizational structures and influenced a competition of denominational networks.[25] One force for the globalization of Protestantism through its missions was the concept of millenarianism. In the seventeenth century, this resulted in the catechization of indigenous groups in New England as well as in conversion efforts among Jews in Europe. At the beginning of the eighteenth

Protestant Christianity in India, eds. Andreas Gross, Y. Vincent Kumaradoss, and Heike Liebau (Halle: Verlag der Frankeschen Stiftungen zu Halle, 2006), 3: 1091–114.

22 AFST/M 3 L 14. 23 AFST/M 3 L 14 u. L 23.

24 Klaus Koschorke, "Christentumsgeschichte Asiens – Trends, Themen, Perspektiven," *Periplus: Jahrbuch für außereuropäische Geschichte 16* (2006): 8–34, here 12; Klaus Koschorke, "Einführung: Globale Perspektiven der Christentumsgeschichte," in *Etappen der Globalisierung in christentumsgeschichtlicher Perspektive*, ed. Klaus Koschorke (Wiesbaden: Harrassowitz, 2012), 1–36.

25 Koschorke, "Globale Perspektiven der Christentumsgeschichte," 3.

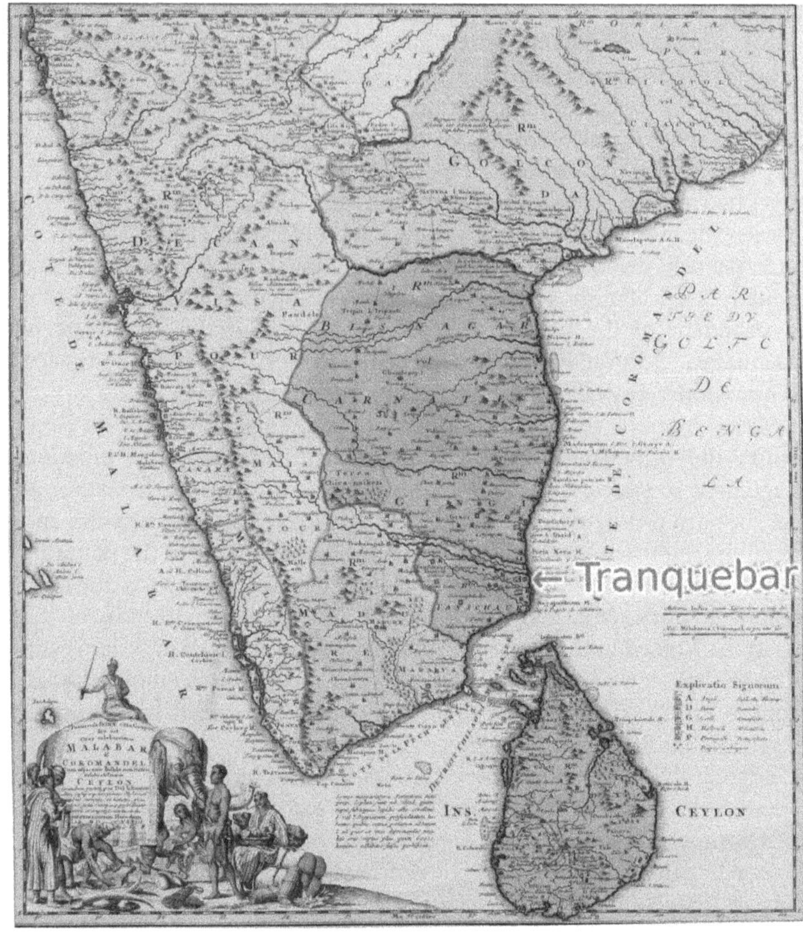

Fig 9.1 Detail Guillaume de Lisle: *Peninsula Indiae*, 1733, HAB: K 23,30a

century, millenarian hopes and expectations led to a Pietist mission in southeast India and over the years in other parts of the world as well. A transnational network existing of educational institutions, associations with Christian purposes, royal support as well as noble patronage, European missionaries and Indian mission helpers developed and financed the mission in India.[26] Nevertheless, Christianity in India can

[26] Michael Mann, "Ein langes 18. Jahrhundert, Südasien," in *Die Welt im 18. Jahrhundert*, eds. Bernd Hausberger, Jean-Paul Lehners (Vienna: Mandelbaum-Verl., 2011), 5: 274–301; Heike Liebau ed., *Geliebtes Europa – Ostindische Welt: 300 Jahre interkultureller*

by no means be reduced to European missionary efforts. An Indian Christian presence had existed continuously since the first century. The St. Thomas Christians, also called Syrian Christians[27], a community in South India, traced their origins to the evangelistic activity of Thomas the Apostle in the first century. With Portuguese colonization in the sixteenth century, European Catholicism came to India. In the seventeenth century, Protestantism arrived through the trade colonialism of Protestant countries but without any conversion intentions towards the Indian population. Much later, in the beginning of the eighteenth century, a Danish-German-British Lutheran mission started in the Danish trading port of Tranquebar in southeast India.[28] This transnational enterprise was the first major Protestant mission outside of Europe. The transnational character of the mission stood in contrast to the traditionally much more nationally oriented Lutheranism (Fig 9.1).

Transnational and Transconfessional Organization and Network Building in Protestant Europe

The mission to southeast India was a transnational (Prussia/Denmark/Britain) and transconfessional (Lutherans/Pietists/Anglicans) undertaking. The project started in 1706 and it lasted until 1845, initiated by the Pietistic Frederick IV of Denmark and maintained by a committee at the Danish Royal Court, the London "Society for Promoting Christian Knowledge (SPCK)" and the Halle Orphanage in Germany. The mission was founded on the southeastern Indian coast, in the Danish trading colony of Tranquebar – today Taragambadi – part of the federal state of Tamil Nadu. The colonial pattern in Tranquebar was that of a typical European trading port in India before the British Raj. The Danish East India Company leased the colony from the king of Thanjavur for an annual rent. The colony consisted of 40 square kilometers, with the town of Tranquebar on the coast of the Bay of Bengal and fifteen inland villages. The mission was part of a broader colonial system, but it was not directly connected with the Danish political authority in Tranquebar. The Europeans in the Danish colony were under the authority of the Danish governor, installed by the directors of the East India Company in Copenhagen. The mission itself was neither connected with the East India Company nor the Danish State Church, but only with the Danish

Dialog im Spiegel der Dänisch-Halleschen Mission (Halle/Saale: Verlag der Franckeschen Stiftungen, 2006).

27 The term *Syrian* relates not to their ethnicity but to their historical, religious, and liturgical connection to Syriac Christianity.

28 Koschorke, "Christentumsgeschichte Asiens," 8–34.

court. In the trilateral transnational network, the organizers had different responsibilities. The Danish crown held the colonial trading post, paid the salary of the missionaries and ran a supervisory committee of high-ranking officials. The SPCK in London provided money, material support, and promoted the project in England. The third player, the Halle institutions, educated the missionaries, established a wide network of financial supporters in the German-speaking Protestant lands and edited the mission journal. The Danish crown only paid the salary of the missionaries. Everything else had to be financed by donations. The mission work was based on a system of churches, schools, and charitable institutions.[29] The millenarian matrix of the conversion project transcended national and confessional borders. Millenarian practices were oriented towards like-minded people, less along territorial or inner Protestant church borders. Pietists worked within broader networks, which was in contrast to much more nationally oriented Lutheran activities.

The Halle Orphanage built up a network of supporters in the German Empire via letters and a constant flow of information. August Hermann Francke – and after his death in 1727, much more intensively his son Gotthilf August Francke (1696–1769) – established a network of middle-class and aristocratic female and male supporters. A mission journal was regularly sent to potential supporters, accompanied by a letter. Most of the recipients responded and sent money to Halle and in turn recruited other interested individuals. Halle also started a campaign for personal sponsorship of individual children in Tranquebar with 10 taler needed to maintain one child for a year.[30] Regular correspondence and the journal established reliable network connections.

[29] Johannes Ferdinand Fenger, *Geschichte der Trankebarschen Mission* (Grimma: Gebhardt, 1845); Anders Nørgaard, *Mission und Obrigkeit: Die Dänisch-hallische Mission in Tranquebar 1706–1845* (Gütersloh: Gütersloher Verl.-Haus Mohn, 1988); Daniel L. Brunner, *Halle Pietists in England: Anthony William Boehm and the Society for Promoting Christian Knowledge* (Göttingen: Vandenhoeck & Ruprecht, 1993); Harald Nielsen, “The Danish Missionary Society and Tranquebar,” in *It Began in Copenhagen: Junctions in 300 Years of Indian-Danish Relations in Christian Mission*, ed. George Oommen and Hans Raun Iversen (Delhi: ISPCK, 2005), 181–203; Andreas Gross, Y. Vincent Kumaradoss, and Heike Liebau eds., *Halle and the Beginning of Protestant Christianity in India*, 3 vols. (Halle: Verlag der Frankeschen Stiftungen zu Halle, 2006); Michael Mann, *Europäische Aufklärung und protestantische Mission in Indien* (Heidelberg: Draupadi-Verlag, 2006); Christina Jetter-Staib, *Halle, England und das Reich Gottes weltweit – Friedrich Michael Ziegenhagen (1694–1776): Hallescher Pietist und Londoner Hofprediger* (Halle: Verlag der Franckeschen Stiftungen Halle, 2013).

[30] The twenty-sixth issue of *Hallesche Berichte, preface* (2nd ed., Halle: Waysenhaus, 1730), I–XIV, https://digital.francke-halle.de/fsdhm/periodical/titleinfo/170756 (accessed July 13, 2018)

The middle class involved in the mission project consisted mostly of academics, city notables, and merchants. Maria Magdalena Böhmer (1669–1743), who lived in Hanover in the first half of the eighteenth century, was a poet of sacred hymns. She contributed two hymns to the famous Pietist song collection *Freylingshausen's Gesang-Buch* (1704, no. 655, 660)[31] and her songs continued to be listed in later Pietist song books until the mid-nineteenth century.[32] In an emotional language, the songs address the closeness between God and the believing soul as well as the longing for spiritual and physical love for Jesus. Böhmer came from a family of wealthy lawyers. Her brother Justus Henning Böhmer was Professor of Law and President of the Halle University and Chancellor of the Duchy of Magdeburg. Brother and sister read the mission journal and donated regularly to the Indian mission and to other Pietist projects.

The upper clergy formed another strong group of supporters. The court preacher Friedrich Wilhelm Berchelmann (1679–1754) in Darmstadt kept in close contact with Halle as a result of his time as a student at the *Pädagogium* and later at the University of Halle. At the court of Darmstadt, he collected money for the mission and was the distributor of the missionary magazine. He also campaigned for support of the Salzburg exiles and initiated large collections for this project.[33] Court preachers deployed their position at court to involve nobility and high-ranking civil servants in the millenarian project.

A third influential group was the nobility. Many dukes and especially duchesses were among the religious and financial supporters of the mission enterprise. The noble abbess of the Protestant convent of Gandersheim, Duchess Elisabeth Ernestine Antonie of Sachsen-Meiningen (1681–1766) who came from a small duchy in Saxony, corresponded with Gotthilf August Francke for thirty-four years concerning the India mission. The devout Lutheran abbess, inspired by the Pietist movement donated regularly and annually paid the tuition for two

[31] Johann Anastasius Freylinghausen (1670–1739) was a Pietist theologian, son-in-law and successor of August Hermann Francke as director of the orphanage in Halle and a poet of hymns. Freylinghausen published Pietist song books and was married to Sophie Anastasia Francke, twenty-seven years his junior.

[32] One song was even translated in English and published in John Wesley's Methodist songbook *A Collection of Hymns, for the Use of the People Called Methodist* in 1874 "Regardless now of things below." See Hymnary.org: https://hymnary.org/text/regardless_now_of_things_below (accessed April 18, 2019)

[33] AFSt/M3 H 31, fol. 133; AFSt/M 3 H 32, fol. 76; AFSt/M 3 H 34, fol. 185; AFSt/M 3 H 36, fol. 78; AFSt/M 3 H 37, fol. 135; AFSt/M 3 H 40, fol. 67; AFSt/M 4 C 2, fol. 21; AFSt/M 4 C 3, fol. 18. The Salzburger Emigrants were a group of German-speaking Protestant refugees from the territory of the Catholic Archbishopric of Salzburg (today Austria) that immigrated to the Georgia Colony. The 20,000 Protestants were expelled from their homeland from October 1731.

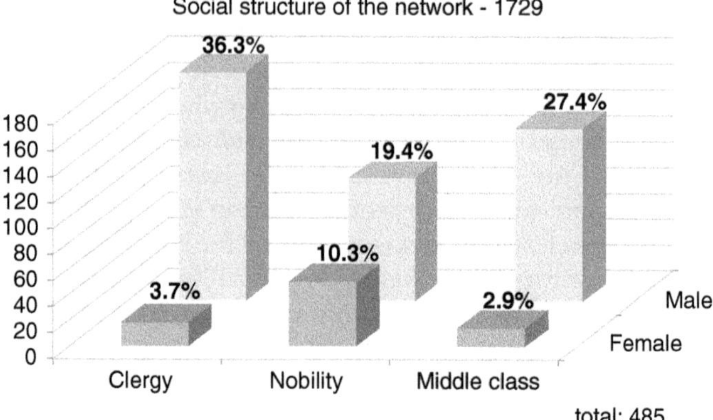

Social structure of the network - 1757

42.9%
27.6%
10.2%
9.9%
3.8%
5.7%
400
350
300
250
200
150
100
50
0
Clergy
Nobility
Middle class
Male
Female
total: 844

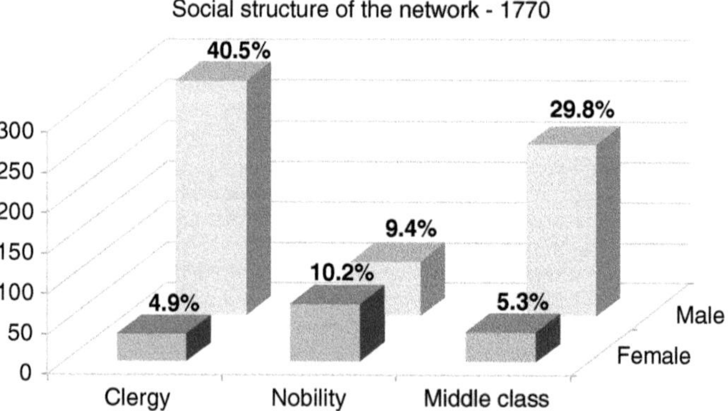

Fig 9.2 Overview of subscribers of the mission journal

schoolboys. The convent-administrator (*Oberhofmeister*) and other noble canonesses were also involved. Besides other support activities, the abbess established a "fund for widows" in her birthplace Meiningen, in Gandersheim (the abbey's location), as well as in Tranquebar in India. Through her endowment, she expanded the Protestant Empire geographically. The paralleled charitable activities made Europe and India appear as one territory in which she acted like a sovereign. Even kings and queens supported the mission project with money and personal empathy. Princess Charlotte Amalia (1706–1782), daughter of the reigning King Frederic IV of Denmark, was a major supporter of the India mission and other Pietistic projects. In December 1729, when two designated India missionaries from Halle, Gottlieb Richtsteig (1700–1735) and Andreas Worm, stayed in Copenhagen waiting to sail to South India, they were granted an audience with Charlotte Amalia and received a gift of 40 taler to finance their personal equipment for Tranquebar. The princess donated an additional 100 taler to the Halle Orphanage[34] (Fig 9.2).

Thus, the mission network consisted of men and women of mostly high-ranking social status from a wide range of the noble and professional elites, primarily the imperial aristocracy, military nobility, high government officials and high clergy/court preachers, and including a surprising number of noble women: middle-class widows and abbesses and canonesses of Protestant convents. The progress of the expansion of the "Kingdom of God" was reported in thousands of letters within the mission's network.

Transfer of Knowledge and Objects between Europe and India and Vice Versa

The transfer of knowledge and artifacts went in two directions: from Europe to India and from India to Europe. Knowledge and things were on the move.[35] Books, letters, medical and technical instruments, a printing press and basic equipment moved with the missionaries, physicians, and printers from Europe to India so that the missionaries could perform their work. Even wigs were part of the cargo, as were religious and pedagogical concepts and medicines.

[34] AFST/M 1 B 7, fol. 52.

[35] James Secord calls this "knowledge in transit." James Secord, "Knowledge in Transit,"*Isis* 95 (2004): 654–72. See also a similar description from an anthropological perspective: Arjun Appadurai, *Modernity at Large: Cultural Dimensions of Globalization* (8th ed., Minneapolis/London: University of Minnesota Press, 2008).

Another dynamic of transfer was initiated through the mission journal. Based on letters, work diaries, and reports from the missionaries in India, a journal was edited and published in Halle. This kind of reported content was a new and popular way of compiling journals in the early eighteenth century.[36] Pietists used the new media just as intensively as the Jesuits did, for example in the latter's *Lettres édifiantes et curieuses* (Fig 9.3).

The so-called Hallesche Berichte, which were published from 1710 until 1772 in 108 issues, exhibit a striking range of information. In addition to the topic of the conversion work – including schools, travels, and living conditions of the missionaries – the journal covered topics of science, astronomy, botany, climate, cartography, Indian religious practices, cultural anthropology, travel narratives, political conditions, and terrifying accounts of Catholic missionaries in the neighborhood. The contingent character of the journal relates its success to the readership and promises further progress in other text forms.[37] In the second half of the eighteenth century, items like the preparation of fish and mussels increasingly found their way to European collectors through missionaries as brokers.[38] With the medialization of the mission, news flowed constantly from India to a European readership.[39] The extended introduction of the journal framed the mission work as a millenarian project. For the mission organizers the knowledge transfer between Europe and India was a kind of millenarian practice. And for the Pietists the constant flow of

[36] Andrew Pettegree, *The Invention of News: How the World Came to Know About Itself* (New Haven, CT: Yale University Press, 2014); Markus Friedrich and Alexander Schunka eds., *Reporting Christian Missions in the Eighteenth Century: Communication, Culture of Knowledge and Regular Publication in a Cross-Confessional Perspective* (Wiesbaden: Harrassowitz, 2017).

[37] The comprehensive German and French representations of Indian Christianity (1724/1726) by Maturin Veyssière de la Croze are well known as is the compilation by Johann Lucas Niekamp, who used the "*Hallesche Berichte*" as his source material for "*Kurzgefasste Mißions-Geschichte*" (1740).

[38] Robert Eric Frykenberg ed., *Christians and Missionaries in India: Cross-Cultural Communication since 1500* (London: Routledge 2003); Monica Juneja, "Begegnung, Kommunikation, Sinnbildung: Deutsche Pietisten und südindische Tamilen im 18. Jahrhundert," in *Vom Weltgeist beseelt: Globalgeschichte 1700–1815*, eds. Margarete Grandner and Andrea Komlosy (Vienna: Promedia-Verlag 2004), 221–42; Liebau, Nehring, and Klosterberg eds., *Mission und Forschung*; Martha Ann Shelby and Indira Viswanathan Peterson eds., *Tamil geographies: cultural constructions of space and place in South India* (Albany: State University of New York Press, 2008); Thomas Ruhland, *Pietistische Konkurrenz und Naturgeschichte: Die Südasienmission der Herrnhuter Brüdergemeine und die Dänisch-Englisch-Hallesche Mission (1755–1802)* (Herrnhut: Herrnhuter Verlag, 2018), 244–382.

[39] Reinhard Wendt ed., *Sammeln, Vernetzen, Auswerten: Missionare und ihr Beitrag zum Wandel europäischer Weltsicht* (Tübingen: Narr, 2001); Mann, *Europäische Aufklärung*; Anne-Charlott Trepp, "Von der Missionierung der Seelen zur Erforschung der Natur: Die Dänisch-Hallesche Südindienmission im ausgehenden 18. Jahrhundert," *G&G* 36/2 (2010): 231–56; Kelly Joan Whitmer, "What's in a name? Place, Peoples and Plants in the Danish-Halle Missions, c. 1710–1740," *Annales of Science* 70/3 (2013): 337–56.

Der Königl. Dänischen Missionarien
aus
Ost=Indien
eingesandter
Ausführlichen
Berichten
Erster Theil,
Von dem Werck ihres Amts unter den Heyden, ange-
richteten Schulen und Gemeinen, ereigneten Hindernissen und schweren Um-
ständen; Beschaffenheit des Malabarischen Heydenthums, gepflogenen brieflicher Corre-
spondentz und mündlichen Unterredungen mit selbigen Heyden; des einen Missionarii Her-
aus-Reise nach Europa, auch glücklichen Zurückkunft in Ost-Indien; und übrigen Merck-
würdigkeiten, so von ihnen, seit ihrer Abreise nach Indien bis zum August des 1716ten
Jahres, heraus geschrieben, und hiernächst von Zeit zu Zeit in verschiedenen Fort-
setzungen ediret sind;
Vom Ersten ausführlichen Bericht an
bis zu dessen zwölfter Continuation mitgetheilet.
Nebst einem vollständigen Register

HALLE, in Verlegung des Waysen-Hauses. MDCCXXXV.

Fig 9.3 *Der Königl. Dänischen Missionarien aus Ost=Indien eingesandter Ausführlichen Berichten. Erster Theil, Von dem Werck ihres Amts unter den Heyden*, Halle 1735

information between Halle and Tranquebar, documented in the journal, connected both places as territories of the realized "Kingdom of God" on earth.

Transcultural Interactions

The Pietist efforts of realizing the "Kingdom of God" and their revitalized Lutheran concept of the "priesthood of all believers" constituted the reason why Tamil converts were included as co-workers from the very beginning in the mission efforts. Transcultural go-betweens, such as interpreters, translators, Tamil catechists, male and female bible helpers, and schoolteachers, were employed in large numbers.[40] In 1733 the first Tamil named Aaron was ordained. Only a few years after the mission started in Tranquebar, the missionaries developed a special training for Indian catechists by establishing a seminary for promising candidates, who came from the higher social classes. Indian pastors had the same duties as the missionaries had; they held services, preached, and baptized.[41] The mission strategy to integrate Indians as co-workers and even pastors had on the one hand an organizational goal as it furthered access to the local population. On the other hand the millenarian matrix of the mission demanded the establishment of an independent Indian Pietist community. A report about the barriers for the mission, printed in the journal *Hallesche Berichte*, discussed the lack of European missionaries for spreading the "Kingdom of God." There were not enough pastors to establish more parishes in the suburbs and villages around Tranquebar. Further it was mentioned that it would be possibly God's plan to arouse people from the "Indian nation" as pastors to establish national churches.[42] Today, Indian scholars regard the early participation of Tamils in the mission work as evidence for the Indianness of Protestant Christianity.[43] A Pietist kingdom required

[40] Heike Liebau, *Die indischen Mitarbeiter der Tranquebarmission 1706–1845: Katecheten, Schulmeister, Übersetzer* (Tübingen: Verlag der Franckeschen Stiftungen Halle im Max-Niemeyer-Verlag, 2008).

[41] Among the Indian co-workers in the eighteenth and early nineteenth centuries were fourteen pastors, eighty catechists (among them one woman), numerous schoolmasters (also women), assistants, prayer-leaders (among them many women, washer men, cooks, gardeners, grave-diggers, accountants, book-binders, see Heike Liebau, "The Indian Pastors in the Danish-Halle and the English-Halle Mission," in *Halle and the Beginning of Protestant Christianity*, 2: 719–34, 720.

[42] The twenty-seventh issue of the *Hallesche Berichte* (Halle: Waysenhaus, 1731), 191–96. https://digital.francke-halle.de/fsdhm/periodical/pageview/147444 (accessed April 18, 2019)

[43] Daniel Jeyaraj, *Inkulturation in Tranquebar: Der Beitrag der frühen dänisch-halleschen Mission zum Werden einer indisch-einheimischen Kirche (1706–1730)* (Erlangen: Verlag der Ev.-Luth. Mission, 1996); Frykenberg ed., *Christians and Missionaries in India*; Robert Eric Frykenberg, *Christianity in India: From Beginnings to the Present* (Oxford: Oxford University Press, 2008); Richard Fox Young ed., *India and the Indianness of Christianity: Essays on Understanding – Historical, Theological, and Bibliographical – in Honor of Robert Eric Frykenberg* (Grand Rapids, MI: William B. Eerdmans Publisher 2009).

stable Tamil Lutheran subject positions.[44] Baptized Lutherans should be able to resist in their faith against their non-Christian environment. The concept of a process of realization of the pietistic "Kingdom of God" had a universal, global character and required to make less distinction between European and non-European sites and people. The acquisition of allies and communicators was, therefore, the central Pietist mission approach.

The missionaries preached, translated texts, and ran the schools. The day-to-day conversion task, however, was the largest part of the basic missionary work and this was carried out by the Tamils themselves, that is Indian catechists, teachers, and bible-helpers. Of the registered official employees, about twenty-five were women. Wives of missionary workers, however, often collaborated without an official position. As a result, the actual number of Tamil women involved was much greater. Most women with official positions were widows. They worked as teachers in the girls' school and in missionary work as a prayer leader and Bible women. The higher positions as a catechist and the ordination as a minister were barred to them.[45] Nevertheless, it can be stated that the official participation of women in ecclesiastical work in Lutheranism was first realized outside of Europe in mission churches, long before it was possible in Europe.

The transcultural knowledge space in India was by no means new in the eighteenth century; it had existed for centuries. For the eighteenth and nineteenth centuries, the dynamic interactions of Protestant mission and south Indian society are well documented in the fields of education, philology, and science.[46] In the contact zones of the mission, the following fields can be identified as transcultural interactions: (a) conversion work and schools; especially in the expansion phase of the mission from the late 1720s when Indians and Europeans worked together in the mission stations; (b) philosophy: missionaries and Brahmins discussed philosophical questions and exchanged letters on ethical and religious subjects. The translated and printed ninety-nine letters of Tamil Brahmins sent to the first two missionaries, Bartholomew Ziegenbalg (1682–1719) and Johann Ernst Gründler (1677–1720), from 1712 to 1714 provide an insight into this

[44] For the concept of subject position, see Andreas Reckwitz, *Das hybride Subjekt: Eine Theorie der Subjektkulturen von der bürgerlichen Moderne zur Postmoderne* (1st ed. 2006, repr. Weilerswist: Velbrück Wiss., 2010).

[45] Liebau, "*The Indian Pastors*," 722.

[46] Frykenberg, *Christians and Missionaries in India*; Frykenberg, *Christianity in India*; Shelby, Peterson, *Tamil geographies*; Indira Viswanathan Peterson, *Poems to Śiva. The Hymns of the Tamil Saints* (Princeton, NJ: Princeton University Press, 1989).

conversation;[47] (c) joint translation activities for the Lutheran Canon: the Mission journal mentions the collaboration in translation as an established practice. Sometimes the missionary translated the text orally into Tamil and the translators wrote down and corrected what they had heard. Sometimes short texts like prayers were given to Brahmins for translation[48]; (d) the teamwork in school teaching: advanced students read Tamil philosophical and moral texts on Tuesdays and Thursdays and Christian texts on other days; (e) medical practice: an interweaving of cultural elements took place in the treatment of the sick.[49] Indian medicines were used by Europeans and European treatment methods were applied to Indians. In mission schools, Tamil healing methods were practiced and supplemented by European medications.[50] Intercultural collaboration in the mission field in India was a common practice.

The Consolidation of the European Religious Identity through the Narrative of Progress

The activities of the mission organizers in Europe took place in an economic framework of religious belief and financial resources. The mission was financed on the basis of a public-private mixture. The prosperity of the conversion enterprise proved the divine grace, which directed the mission. The growing group of converts in southeast India was evidence of the divine providence of the mission activities. Progress was interpreted as a divine sign. The editorial concept of the "Halle Reports" was intended to put the reader into a religious euphoria. Gotthilf August Francke wrote in April 1733 to the abbess of Gandersheim, Duchess Elisabeth Ernestine Antonie of Sachsen-Meiningen:

Euer Hochfürstliche Durchlaucht erachte mich schuldig hiermit auch die XXXIII. Continuation derer OstIndischen Missions Berichte in untertheinigsten respect zu überliefern, nachdem dieselben bißhero gnaedigst zu erkennen

[47] Johann Ernst Gründler, Bartholomäus Ziegenbalg, *Die Malabarische Korrespondenz: Tamilische Briefe an deutsche Missionare – Eine Auswahl*, ed. Kurt Liebau (Sigmaringen: Thorbecke, 1998).

[48] HB 20, 1726, 401–404; HB Cont. 20, 1726, 433, 487; HB Cont. 21, 1728, 612.

[49] For mission physicians, see Josef Neumann, "Tamil Medical Science as Perceived by the Missionaries of the Danish-Halle Mission in Tranquebar," in Gross, Kumaradoss, and Liebau eds., *Halle and the Beginnings of Protestant Christianity*, 3: 1135–154; Josef Neumann, "Medizinische Forschungen," in Liebau ed., *Geliebtes Europa*, 180–93.

[50] The missionary Johann Ernst Gründler (1677–1720) employed a Brahmin to put into writing the *Tamil system of medicine* as well as the *Tamil study of medicine*. Gründler translated the manuscript, calling it the "Malabarische Medicus" and sent it to Halle hoping to have it published, which did not materialize.

gegeben, wie Sie an der Ausbreitung des Evangelii unter denen Heyden Antheil nehmen und Sich mit denen die dero Wachsthum des Reiches Gottes wünschen, erfreüen wenn dieselben sehen daß dieser Wunsch in die Erfüllung gehe.[51]

Most respectfully, I am hereby taking it upon myself to send you the thirty-third Continuation of the East Indian Missions Reports after you have mercifully signified that you take an interest in the spread of the Gospel among the Heathens and rejoice with those who desire the growth of the Kingdom of God when they see that this desire is being fulfilled. [trans. UG]

Like a mantra, the progress of the expansion of the Pietist kingdom in India was communicated. The rhetoric of the letter subtly included the abbess in the group of those who championed the propagation of the "Kingdom of God." After receiving a mission journal, many of the mission supporters wrote back to Halle describing the edifying feelings that they had experienced during the reading process: "I have received the journal and read it with much edification and encouragement to praise God," "The kingdom among the pagans has to grow ..., " "May this donation serve to spread His kingdom .... ."[52] The calculated emotion throughout the printed reports created a functional connection. Practical support was extended on the basis of the millenarian conception in which India, Germany, and Europe were part of one Christian Empire.

The editorial model of the journal – advertisement, success, and information – followed Pietistic media patterns. The printed mission activities initiated an interactive process: the documented confirmation of the broadening of the Pietist Empire initiated religious emotions that resulted in financial support. The narrative mode was direct; often the reports from India were printed in direct speech enabling direct participation. And the stories were framed by calls to support the work of God financially. From their reading, the subscribers perceived the affirmation of the usefulness of their support. The journal conferred the illusion that the reader was directly involved in the realization of the Pietist Empire. This Kingdom-of-God-economy (*Reichgottesökonomie*) was the mainstay of the mission enterprise.[53] Inner-worldly economic contributions obtained eschatological meaning, and, vice versa, the Pietistic millenarianism was translated into economic practices which were embedded in a divine salvation economy. Support and donation offered participation in the "Kingdom of God."

[51] AFST/M 1 J 14, fol. 16. [52] AFST/M 1 J 14, fol. 16.

[53] Older research named the combination of Pietist profitable enterprises and religious salvation "*Reichgotteskapitalismus*," see Heinrich Bornkamm, *Mystik, Spiritualismus und die Anfänge des Pietismus im Luthertum* (Giessen: Töpelmann, 1926).

To conclude: Pietist educational, social and conversion projects, as well as conventicles and communities all campaigned for the realization of a Christian Empire on earth. Millenarian expectations became an essential element of the Pietist missionary campaign at the beginning of the eighteenth century. The millenarian matrix of the mission led to transgressive network-building, global expansion, and transcultural practices. Handwritten and printed media were used extensively in this process. Christian millenarianism traveled to India and linked Europe and India, and the global expansion of Protestantism into India emerged from the margins of state churches.[54] With state support and private money and with voluntary religious associations and Reform movements – like the SPCK and the Halle Pietists – cross-border mission projects were made possible. The assessment of the nature and impact of the Protestant Reformation, therefore, needs to integrate millenarianism in order to understand the interconnected religious change across Western and non-Western worlds. The core of millenarianism required social, educational, and religious creative initiative and activism; the concept resulted in practices which shaped the globalization of the Reformation to a high degree. An innovative framework in the study of Protestantism thus needs to integrate millenarianism as part of the globalizing character of the Protestant Reformation.

[54] For similar results for North America, see Alexander Pyrges, *Das Kolonialprojekt EbenEzer: Formen und Mechanismen protestantischer Expansion in der atlantischen Welt des 18. Jahrhunderts* (Stuttgart: Franz Steiner, 2015).

10 Global Protestant Missions and the Role of Emotions[1]

Jacqueline Van Gent

This chapter explores the vital role emotions played in the social practices of global Protestant missions and their connected histories in the early modern period. The empirical materials I draw on in this chapter are eighteenth-century global Moravian mission encounters. The Moravian Church is one of the oldest Protestant churches, with roots dating back to the Bohemian Reformation and the resulting Hussite movement in the fifteenth century. Fleeing the Catholic Counter Reformation in their homelands, a group of these Protestants fled from northern Moravia to Saxony where they were granted religious asylum and settled at the estate of the German Pietist nobleman Count Nikolas of Zinzendorf (1700–1760). This was the beginning of the so-called renewed *Unitas Fratrum* or Moravian Church.[2] Leading Protestant mission societies, such as the Moravian Church, had a strong Pietist background, which privileged personal emotional experiences over knowledge of the scripture. Culturally accepted emotions can be held to constitute "emotional styles," as William Reddy has argued, where social norms of emotions are promoted and group members are socialized accordingly, and where transgressions or non-compliance are usually punished.[3] Indigenous local

[1] Sections of this chapter have earlier been published in Jacqueline Van Gent, "Moravian Memoirs and the Emotional Salience of Conversion Rituals," in *Emotion, Ritual and Power in Europe, 1200–1920: Family, State and Church*, ed. Merridee L. Bailey and Katie Barclay (Basingstoke: Palgrave Macmillan, 2016).

[2] The historical literature on the Moravian Church and its religious practices is burgeoning. See for an excellent introduction Craig D. Atwood, *Community of the Cross: Moravian Piety in Colonial Bethlehem* (University Park: Pennsylvania State University Press, 2004); Craig D. Atwood, "Zinzendorf's Litany of the Wounds," *Lutheran Quarterly* 11 (1997):189–214; Craig D. Atwood, "The Mother of God's People: The Adoration of the Holy Spirit as Mother in the Eighteenth-Century Brüdergemeine," *Church History* 68 (1999): 886–909; Craig D. Atwood, "Sleeping in the Arms of Christ: Sanctifying Sexuality in the Eighteenth-Century Moravian Church," *Journal of the History of Sexuality* 8 (1997): 25–51; Aaron Spencer Fogleman, *Jesus is Female. Moravians and Radical Religion in Early America* (Philadelphia: University of Pennsylvania Press, 2007).

[3] For a discussion of the concept of "emotional styles," see William M. Reddy, *The Navigation of Feeling: A Framework for the History of Emotions* (Cambridge: Cambridge University Press, 2001). Reddy further develops his concept of "emotional styles" in his book, *The Making of Romantic Love* (Chicago, IL: University of Chicago Press, 2012).

cultures and Protestant mission societies had distinct emotional styles which differed significantly, and potential converts, actual converts, and those who "relapsed" engaged in many different ways with the emotional practices of "their" mission society as well as the wider colonial society.

The conversion of indigenous people to Protestantism was intended to fundamentally reshape their identities, moral systems and behaviour, and emotions were to play a vital role in aligning converts with Moravians, and – ideally – in integrating them into the Moravian emotional community, which was built at the local and at the global level.

Religious conversions on Protestant missions were a long and drawn-out process encompassing religious, social, and emotional changes. Formal conversions of indigenous people to Christianity constituted only a very small part of a much broader social process that was aimed at modifying converts' social behaviour. The performance of "appropriate" emotions was taken by missionaries as a reliable external indicator of successful internal conversion or, at least, a readiness for baptism.

Indigenous converts to the Moravian Church had to negotiate emotions as part of the conversion process, which was part of a much deeper, inherently colonial dilemma, where missionaries sought to promote a shared understanding of spiritual love and the experience of Christ's suffering, while also maintaining social distance and superiority by reinforcing shame and patriarchal obedience. Emotions became thus an important part of a wider colonial socialization process, and were indeed tools of social affiliation.[4] The socialization into particular emotional styles or even into emotional communities was a life-long process, where belonging needed to be re-affirmed and which did not take place without conflict, resistance, and contradiction – just like conversion.

Moravians and Emotions

Moravians perceived emotional experiences to be at the core of their religion and their identity. Merry Wiesner-Hanks has alerted us to the centrality of emotions in Moravian and Methodist religious practices: "Moravians spoke (and sang) about being swept away by love for the blood and wound of Christ, and dissolved into tears and near-ecstasy during their long Communion services. Among early Methodists, public testimonies of individual conversion experiences was often marked by weeping, crying-out, and other powerful emotional responses, for which

[4] For a very useful discussion on how emotions link the individual to the social sphere, see Joanne Bourke, "Fear and Anxiety: Writing About Emotions in Modern History," *History Workshop Journal* 55/ 1 (2003): 111–33.

both male and female Methodists were dubbed 'silly women' by their detractors."[5] From the beginning of the Moravian evangelical outreach in the 1730s, Moravian missionaries developed a very distinct set of rituals, language, and behavior in order to create a distinct Moravian identity and establish an "imagined community"[6] that had a specific emotional style. This community was centered on the love of Christ and his suffering, which had to be experienced individually by each believer in an "awakening" moment, causing a "moved heart," and the desire to change their spiritual path by handing over their heart to Christ. Moravians thus developed an elaborate "religion of the heart" (*Herzensreligion*) where the convert and believer comprehended the Christian message internally (*inneres Sehen*), and the heart was conceptualized as the spiritual center and the seat of all feelings.[7] The state of the heart then reflected the spiritual state of the believer in images of movement or bodily heat: a strong believer had a "warm," "moved," or "melted" heart, those who were untouched by the Moravian message were identified as possessing "cold" or "unmoved" hearts. Part of the conversion process was the close observation and the frequent discussion of the state of the convert's heart, to ascertain if their heart signaled a readiness for baptism. Moravian missionaries encouraged potential candidates for baptism (and in fact anyone they preached to) to report about the state of their hearts and to record their observations regularly in their diaries, reports, and letters. In a closely related trope, tears, which were believed to flow from the heart, similarly conveyed spiritual messages; tears and the ritual of weeping conveyed social meanings and interpretations as part of the conversion process, which reinforced power differences between Moravian missionaries and indigenous converts.[8]

[5] Merry Wiesner-Hanks, "Comparisons and Consequences in Global Perspective," in *Oxford Handbook of the Protestant Reformations*, ed. Ulinka Rublack (Oxford: Oxford University Press, 2016), 747–64, here 754 ff.

[6] The concept of an "imagined community" was developed by Anderson to explain the nature of the modern nation as a political body. I am suggesting that this concept is an excellent analytical tool with which to understand the nature of the global Moravian Church because they meet the criteria of Anderson's nation as an imagined community as their members "will never know most of their fellow members, meet them, or even hear of them, yet in the minds of each lives the image of their communion" and regardless of actual social and racial inequalities, the Moravian Church was always perceived by its members "as a deep, horizontal comradeship." Benedict Anderson, *Imagined Communities. Reflections on the Origin and Spread of Nationalism* (1983; London: Verso, 2006), 5–8.

[7] Craig D. Atwood, "Understanding Zinzendorf's Blood and Wounds Theology," *Journal of Moravian History* 1 (2006): 31–47.

[8] The link between the heart as seat of emotions and the social community has been discussed by a number of scholars for the Protestant European context. See for example Ulinka Rublack, "Fluxes: the Early Modern Body and the Emotions," *History Workshop*

Thus, the specific mission method of the Moravians favoured a personal spiritual awakening experience rather than catechetical instruction. Based on a Christ-centered theology and strong emotionalism, Moravians employed somatic metaphors of a moved heart, tears, and the wounds and blood of Christ to express their distinct identities.

My particular research interests are the local responses to a Protestant global Moravian mission enterprise and how to integrate the experiences of indigenous and slave converts who associated with the Moravians into our broader historical understanding of Protestantism and its global legacies. Global Protestantism in the early modern colonial world did not exist as an abstract concept, but as we have seen throughout this volume was constituted by a myriad of local histories with their specific gender, race, and social configurations. Religious encounters were a two-sided process in which indigenous people were not passive recipients but exercised considerable agency, a subject that has so far received insufficient scholarly attention. Protestant conversions linked to Moravian proselytization was a dynamic process in which different cultural meanings of the sacred were negotiated and the responses of local people ranged from rejection to acceptance and active involvement, depending on the local circumstances. One important observation here is that the actual ritual forms of conversions, including their emotional performances, were expected to be the same, no matter how different the converts' cultures were. Conversion meant also converting to a specific Moravian style. The similarities seen in such rituals, down to the utterances, gestures and emotions, in cultures that have very different ideas about the sacred, the self, or divine intervention, provokes necessarily critical questions about representations, sources, and the nature of religious change. Critical historical and postcolonial scholarship has shown convincingly how, at least in the first generations of indigenous conversions, the attraction to missions was rarely grounded in locals' theological acceptance of the Christian message. Indeed, missionaries' own letters and diaries are full of examples of misunderstandings and local misinterpretations of European Christian teachings. Instead, Christianity, and indeed the mission regimes themselves, were reinterpreted in light of local cosmologies and social networks by indigenous Christians.

Journal 53/ 1 (2002): 1–16 and for a discussion of Luther's understanding of the heart and emotions, see Susan Karant-Nunn, *The Reformation of Feeling: Shaping the Religious Emotions in Early Modern Germany* (Oxford: Oxford University Press, 2010).

Global Moravian Missions

The Moravians were the first and one of the most significant Protestant mission enterprises in the early modern Atlantic world, spreading fast during the eighteenth century to establish missions across three of the most important early modern colonial empires: the Danish colonies (1733 Greenland, 1734–1736 Lapland, 1737 Guinea and from 1758 Tranquebar); in Dutch colonies (1738 Surinam, 1737 South Africa and 1739 Ceylon); and the English colonies (from 1735 in Georgia and after 1740 in New York and Pennsylvania). As Dorinda Outram has observed, the Moravian missionary movement reflects the accelerated nature of global contacts during the Enlightenment, and was instrumental in creating encounter experiences across the Atlantic.[9] By the 1730s, when the Moravian mission outreach started, all of these indigenous societies had been touched by European colonialism, albeit in different forms and with different intensity and consequences for their identities. This global outreach is uniquely suited to an exploration of connected histories, which necessitates a comparison of different forms of local agency in cross-cultural encounters, because by the mid-eighteenth century, from New York to Tranquebar, the Moravians had practically covered the globe. Moravians can be understood as global "emotional communities" which the historian Barbara Rosenwein defined as communities characterized by "the emotions that they value, devalue, or ignore; the nature of the affective bonds between people that they recognize; and the modes of emotional expression that they expect, encourage, tolerate, and deplore."[10]

The global nature of Moravian communities was shaped to a significant degree by the specific Moravian gender arrangements which were a main factor in the social organization of these Protestant congregations. Eighteenth-century Moravian gender organization was distinct because it was based on radical sex-segregation in work, living arrangements, and spiritual practice which allowed women, including indigenous converts, a certain autonomy during the eighteenth

[9] Dorinda Outram, *The Enlightenment* (Cambridge: Cambridge University Press, 2004). For an excellent Moravian case study to illustrate this global connection in the life of one slave convert, see the study by Jon Sensbach, *Rebecca's Revival. Creating Black Christianity in the Atlantic World* (Cambridge, MA: Harvard University Press, 2005).

[10] The concept of "emotional community" has been developed most prominently by historian Barbara Rosenwein. See her article "Worrying about Emotions in History," *American Historical Review* 107/ 3 (2002): 821–45; see also Barbara Rosenwein, *Emotional Communities in the Middle Ages* (Ithaca, NY: Cornell University Press, 2006); and more recently, "Theories of Change in the History of Emotions," in *A History of Emotions, 1200–1800*, ed. Jonas Liliequist (London: Pickering & Chatto, 2012), 7–20.

century.[11] This represented a radical departure from contemporary social practices and was achieved through a consequent organization of all Moravian congregations into age- and sex-segregated groups, so called Choirs, between which Moravians moved according to their life stage (for example Children's Choir, Single Sisters or Single Brethren Choir, Choir for Widows or Widowers etc). These Choirs were led by women or men and enjoyed a relative spiritual autonomy, which meant that devotional practices and rituals such as Love feasts or Speakings, were conducted separately for each Choir. Choir leaders, including women, were members of the Church Council until 1760, and this provided women of all ethnic backgrounds in theory with a pathway to participate in the governance of the church.[12] But to what extent indigenous and slave women sought to engage with global Moravian missions, was determined significantly by their position and influence in their local communities, especially in the ritual sphere and in the socialization of children and adolescents.[13]

The performance of conversions and the shaping of identities in cross-cultural encounters at Moravian missions and in the memoirs of indigenous converts were strongly influenced by emotional experiences. Elsewhere I have argued that Moravian conversion rituals created emotional salience, that is the remembrance of "affective experiences of collective rituals" as one-off and significant self-shaping events which also became important for group formations.[14] In global mission contexts, the emotional salience of these Moravian conversion rituals was an important affective strategy for the integration of colonial converts into the Moravian mission stations across the globe.

Anthropologists have suggested that "strong emotional arousal" (such as in conversion rituals) can indeed be easily transmitted between cultures and this necessitates investigating "how universal features of human emotional systems might help to explain cultural transmission."[15]

[11] Craig D. Atwood, *Community of the Cross: Moravian Piety in Colonial Bethlehem* (University Park: Pennsylvania State University Press, 2004); Beverly Smaby, "No one should lust for power … women least," in *Pious Pursuits. German Moravians in the Atlantic World*, ed. Michelle Gillespie and Robert Beachy (New York: Berghahn Books, 2007), 159–73; Aaron S. Fogleman, *Two Troubled Souls: An Eighteenth-century Couple's Spiritual Journey in the Atlantic World* (Chapel Hill: University of North Carolina Press, 2015).

[12] Smaby, "No one should lust for power … women least."

[13] Gunlög Fur, *A Nation of Women: Gender and Colonial Encounters Among the Delaware Indians* (Philadelphia: University of Pennsylvania Press, 2009).

[14] For a discussion of this concept see Harvey Whitehouse, "From Mission to Movement: The Impact of Christianity on Patterns of Political Association in Papua New Guinea," *Journal of the Royal Anthropological Institute* 4/1 (1998): 43–63.

[15] Harvey Whitehouse, "Emotion, Memory and Religious Ritual: An Assessment of Two Theories," in *Mixed Emotions: Anthropological Studies of Feelings*, ed. Kay Milton and Maruška Svašek (Berg: Oxford, 2005), 91–108, here 92

Harvey Whitehouse proposes that imagistic rituals, which are associated with a singular event of revelatory character, such as conversions, are defined by high emotional intensity and therefore are remembered more vividly as profoundly self-shaping events.[16] Historians of early modern conversions have begun to explore the "contagious" nature of emotional arousal produced in conversion rituals. I would suggest that such emotionally intense and transformative events lend themselves especially well to becoming foundational events for the self-understanding of new communities like the Moravian Church and are transmitted in the collective memory. Drawing on Whitehouse's analytical categories of "strong emotions" and their associated "motivational effects" in imagistic rituals, we can see why ritual patterns might be transferred into new contexts and why indigenous people might engage with Christian missions that emphasized emotional rituals as mechanisms of bonding.[17]

The embodied nature of emotions was as evident in the European Moravian congregations as it was in the many mission stations that were rapidly established around the globe.[18] Indeed, the transformation of the convert was spoken of in Moravian texts as a somatic renewal process – converts had to acquire a new body, and in particular a "new heart," as the seat of a Christian spirituality. It was only when missionaries were satisfied that such a "new heart" was acquired that the conversion was seen as completed. Earlier indications of a willingness – or unwillingness – by indigenous people to accept and internalize the Christian message were spoken of in terms of them having "moved" or "unmoved hearts."[19] The emotional intensity that was conveyed in this performance of conversion rituals – the ritual weeping, kneeling, and praying – was frequently repeated and described as "infectious"; that is, the emotional arousal allowed others to join in.[20]

[16] Whitehouse, "Emotion, Memory." [17] Whitehouse, "Emotion, Memory," 99.

[18] For a discussion of the link between embodiment and emotions as a social practice, see Monique Scheer, "Are Emotions a Kind of Practice (and is that what makes them have a History)? A Bourdieuan Approach to Understanding Emotion," *History and Theory* 52 (2012): 193–220. I have elsewhere discussed the relationship between embodiment and the material force of emotions. See Jacqueline Van Gent, *Magic, Body and the Self in Eighteenth-Century Sweden* (Leiden: Brill, 2009).

[19] For a more detailed discussion of conversion experiences and emotions in the colonial contexts of Moravian missions, see Jacqueline Van Gent, "The Burden of Love: Moravian Emotions and Conversions in Eighteenth-Century Labrador," *Journal of Religious History* 39/4 (2015): 557–74.

[20] For an overview discussion of this topic, see Christian von Scheve, "Collective Emotions in Rituals: Elicitation, Transmission and a 'Matthew-effect,'" in *Emotions in Rituals and Performances*, ed. Axel Michaels and Christoph Wulf (London: Routledge, 2012), 55–77.

Moravian Conversions and Emotional Performance

The conversion rituals taken by Moravian missionaries to new global congregations originally developed in a 1727 revival movement in south-east Germany. In the founding conversions, which are still commemorated on August 17 in Moravian congregations every year, the ecstatic experiences of several young girls quickly extended to the whole community. The conversions resulted in the transformation of two recently founded religious communities belonging to the estate of Count Nikolaus Ludwig of Zinzendorf: the communities of Herrnhut and Berthelsdorf. These communities began with a socially heterogeneous population consisting of Pietist members of Zinzendorf's household, German peasants from his estates, and Protestant refugees from Bohemia and Moravia in the Habsburg Empire who fled violent re-Catholicization. Out of individual experiences of conversion a new sense of community and religious identity was forged, leading ultimately to the global outreach movement of Zinzendorf and his followers.

Moravian conversion rituals were instigated by a meditation upon Christ's wounds and suffering, which was held to result in a longing for his love and for repentance. In the 1727 religious revival, adolescent girls ritualized the components of Moravian conversion – crying, praying, prostrating oneself, sharing prophetic insights, expressing the need to receive a new heart, and admitting one's own worthlessness – for the first time publicly, and committed them to the social memory of future Moravian generations. Notably, the 1727 conversions drew on earlier revival experiences of Protestant religious refugees from Moravia, and particularly a "children's awakening" that occurred in 1724. Indeed, many of the girls who led the revival were from families who had recently arrived in Herrnhut after fleeing the violent re-imposition of Catholicism in Moravia. Along with their families, they had experienced existential crises triggered by incarceration and resistance to re-Catholicization. Acting as ritual leaders in a Protestant prophetic movement, the girls exhorted the new community on Zinzendorf's estate to repentance. The resulting spiritual revival transformed the socially fragmented communities into a unified religious congregation, while the emotional intensity of the conversion ritual persisted in the individual memories of participants and the collective memory of the Moravian Church as a whole.

The leadership of Anna Caritas Nitschmann in the 1727 revival exemplifies the transference of ritualized emotions through trans-regional migration at the very foundation of the Moravian Church. Anna Nitschmann was the daughter of the Hussite leader David Nitschmann, who had been persecuted and imprisoned in Bohemia – along with

Anna's brothers – for their adherence to Protestant belief. At the age of nine, Anna had witnessed the awakening movements that occurred in her native Bohemia in 1724, during which communal prayers involving hundreds of participants took place in her father's house.[21] Thus, by the age of twelve, when the 1727 Herrnhut revival took place, she had witnessed not only the trauma of her family's persecution and flight, but also the heightened emotions of collective spiritual revival. Anna Nitschmann's *Lebenslauf* records that in the year before the 1727 conversions, she had experienced a spiritual crisis:

This brought my heart and my eyes to many thousand tears and I began to seek Him with all of my heart. I asked Him to forgive everything and He did so, but I could not believe it and thought this was too soon.[22]

The elements of Anna Nitschmann's conversion – intense longing for Christ's love, somatic expression of repentance (tears) and the crucial role of her heart – are recognizable as founding features of Moravian conversion rituals. They also recall the earlier religious experiences of participants in the 1724 children's revival in Moravia. For instance, Anna Nitschmann's friend, Anna Gold, later recounted in her own *Lebenslauf*:

In the year 1724, an awakening took place among the children in Moravia. There I heard that one needs to have a new heart if one wanted to be blessed, and that one could receive such a new heart only from the dear God. This put me into new grief because I could see that I was lacking such, and this made me very sad. I sought out some friends with whom I could discuss my desire, and the Savior granted me eight peers who shared my thoughts. These fell down with me in lonely places and prayed with many tears for this new heart. I now received the hope that I would be given such a new heart, but I felt utterly undeserving of this.[23]

[21] "Lebenslauf der Anna Nitschmann von ihr bis 1737 in ihrem 22. Lebensjahre eigenhändig verfasst," *Nachrichten aus der Brüdergemeine* 26 (1844) (hereafter Anna Nitschmann), 577–611.

[22] "Das brachte mein Herz und meine Augen zu vielen tausend Thränen, und ich fing an, Ihn mit ganzen Herzen zu suchen, bat Ihm alles ab, und Er vergab mirs auch; aber ich konnte es nicht glauben und dachte, es wäre zu bald." Anna Nitschmann, 578. All translations are the author's own.

At the time of the revival, Anna was twelve. In 1729, aged only fourteen, she became the successor of Anna Quitt as the leader of the Single Women's Choir, a role that she retained for almost thirty years. Anna Nitschmann worked in the Zinzendorf household, tending to the Count's daughter Benigna, and she became Zinzendorf's constant, and closest, female travelling companion from the 1730s. In 1757, she married Zinzendorf after the death of his first wife, Erdmuth Dorothea von Reuβ.

[23] "Im Jahre 1724 entstand in Mähren eine Erweckung unter den Kindern. Da hörte ich, daβ man ein neues Herz haben müsse, wenn man selig warden wollte, und daβ man ein solches allein vom lieben God erhalten könne. Dies versetzte mich in neuen Kummer, da ich sah, daβ es mir daran fehlte und ich war darum sehr verlegen. Zugleich suchte ich einige Gespielinnen, denen ich mein Verlangen entdecken könnte, und der Heiland schenkte mir, acht Altersgenossen zu finden, die meines Sinnes waren, und mit mir an

Gold's account of the 1724 revival demonstrates unmistakable similarities to the ritual patterns found in the 1727 Herrnhut conversions, including the significant role of a peer group and the importance of physical isolation from the community, realization of spiritual failure, somatic forms of expressions (e.g., prostrating), and the notion of exchanging one's old heart for a new one. As persecuted Protestants, these migrants had ample experience in relying on emotional rituals with a strong agency of the laity because official clergy and churches were not allowed. As their memoirs show, both the experience of the trauma of persecution and the power of religious bonding rituals strongly shaped their identities. They would become instrumental in the emerging new Moravian communities in Germany and in the wider world.

Anna Gold also provides us with further evidence of the transmission of conversion rituals between dispersed groups through the performance of emotional scripts. Describing the emotional meaning the awakening had for the children, Gold recalled:

> At the time, when in Herrnhut the great awakening among the children began, Mr Krumpe [the teacher] once asked his pupils if they truly loved the Savior and if they were willing to give Him their hearts so that He could cleanse them with His blood? He then made with those, who showed a desire, a pact to love Him, who has loved us first and in whose eyes we are worth being loved. The Savior was so close to us that we could feel him.[24]

This emotional narrative indicates a required willingness to surrender, to feel the Savior, and joy. Somatic expressions are present in the form of crying and communal praying while adults in position of authority – here the teacher – supervise and guide the children through these stages of the ritual. Through these accounts of the 1727 revival we can see that ritual transmission follows an established pattern, confirming Whitehouse's suggestion that ritual actors are "rehearsing stereotyped procedures that have been fixed by others in advance."[25]

The ecstatic nature of the very first public Moravian conversion ritual shaped the emotional style of Moravian conversions in Europe and globally for the future: intense somatic experience, exchange of heart, and a

einsamen Plätzen niederfielen, und um dies neue Herz oft unter vielen Thränen beten. Ich erhielt nun auch die Hoffnung, daβ mir dies neue Herz zuteil warden würde, fühlte mich aber desselben ganz unwürdig." Anna Gold, 164–65.

[24] "Um die Zeit da in Herrnhut die groβe Erweckung unter den Kindern anging, fragte Herr Krumpe einmal seine Schüler, ob sie auch den Heiland lieb hätten, und Ihm seine Herzen hingeben wollten, auf daβ Er sie mit seinem Blute waschen möge? Er machte dann mit denen, die ein Verlangen danach bezeugten, den Bund, Ihn, der uns zuerst geliebt hat und in dessen Augen wir so wert seien, von ganzem Herzen wieder zu lieben. Dabei war uns der Heiland fühlbar nahe." Anna Gold, 166–67.

[25] Whitehouse, "Emotion, Memory," 92.

sequence of emotions from shame to joy. Thus, from the very beginning of the Moravian church the ritualization of conversion and performance of emotional scripts provided coherence and structure to religious experiences that had been shaped by social disruption and geographical dislocation. The immediate transferral of conversion rituals, and their associated emotions, across very different cultural contexts as part of the Moravian global missionary activities were in many respects a continuation of the trans-regional transmissions of ritual practices that came with the original religious refugees who settled in Herrnhut. As the next section will explore, peer associations – the sex- and age-segregated social units the Moravians called Choirs – formed the primary social ties within ritual groups and played a vital role in the reproduction of a Moravian emotional style, whether in Herrnhut or as far away as India, until at least the end of the eighteenth century.

Accepting Protestant Conversions: Maria Magdalena of Malabar and Globalized Moravian Emotions

Moravian reports about conversion experiences and their associated emotions were strikingly similar across vastly different societies.[26] The awakening experiences of Moravian converts, especially prominent converts whose experiences were recorded in detail and published in mission magazines, repeat key ritual elements of the 1727 events: the awakening takes place at night, in a place away from the settlement (a "wilderness" such as a forest or by a river), it is experienced in somatic forms through kneeling down or prostrating, accompanied by uncontrollable weeping and the acknowledgment, for the first time, of one's own "sinfulness" or moral worthlessness, and the need for redemption which is granted though a Savior. Let us now turn to the memoir of an Indian convert, Maria Magdalena Malabar, in Tranquebar (today Tharangambadi, India) who related in her memoir her own spiritual awakening and conversion directly back to the children's revival in distant Herrnhut, although this had taken place about fifty years before she was even born. Maria Magdalena led a truly transnational life that was not unusual for Moravian converts of this period. Her frequent moves between mission fields took her from India to Germany, from Germany to the Caribbean, and finally back to Europe, to the Danish congregation in Christiansfield where she died.

[26] I have discussed some of the methodological problems that letters and memoirs of indigenous converts pose in Jacqueline Van Gent, "Sarah and Her Sisters: Identity, Letters and Emotions in the Early Modern Atlantic World," *Journal of Religious History* 38 (2014): 71–90; see also Van Gent, "The Lives of Others."

Maria Magdalena Malabar – we only know her Christian name – was born on July 21, 1774 at the Moravian mission in Tranquebar, at the time a Danish colony on the southeastern coast of India, and she was baptized as an infant. She was the daughter of a slave woman named Aurora and only the third convert at that mission since its inception in 1760.[27] We learn nothing of her parents in the memoir, only that the child was immediately "devoted through the bath of baptism to the Savior."[28] In her memoir, dictated before her death, she begins her recollections, significantly, with the impact the stories of the 1727 children's awakening had on her when she was a child in Tranquebar:

> Already in my early childhood years the feeling of love for Jesus was alive in my heart, and I attached myself to Him in childish naivety [because of] the stories of the great awakening of the children in Herrnhut in the year 1727. [I] made a pact with other children to love only the Savior. This pact we renewed every week, for the lasting blessing of my heart, because the impression [it made on me] has lasted to this very hour.[29]

In this recollection, Maria Magdalena's awakening is triggered by and enacted according to the ritual example of the 1727 Herrnhut events: she makes her submission to Christ a priority, and she acts in collaboration with other children of her age through a pact which is periodically renewed to sustain its emotional power. Even the semantics of the centrality of the heart metaphor are the same: spiritual emotions are located in the heart, the blessing of the heart results in beneficial spiritual development, and there is a requirement to love the Savior. The salience of the emotions is simultaneously spiritual and somatic.

[27] Thomas Ruhland, "The Moravian Brethren and the Danish-Halle Mission in Tranquebar: 'The Garden of the Brothers' at the Centre of a European Conflict," in *Halle and the Beginning of Protestant Christianity in India*, ed. Andreas Gross, Y. Vincent Kumaradoss, and Heike Liebau, 3 vols (Halle: Verlag der Franckeschen Stiftungen, 2006), 2: 760.

[28] "durch das Bad der heiligen Tauffe Gott meinem Heiland geweiht worden." UA, R. 22.84.21, Memoir of Maria Magdalena of Malabar (hereafter Maria Magdalena). On the Moravian Tranquebar mission (1759–1795), see Johannes Ferdinand Feyer, *History of the Tranquebar Mission* (Tranquebar: Tranquebar Mission Press, 1863); Hartmut Beck, *Brüder in vielen Völkern: 250 Jahre Mission der Brüdergemeine* (Erlangen: Verlag der Ev.-Luth. Mission, 1981); Karl Müller, *200 Jahre Brüdermission. Vol. I: Das erste Missionsjahrhundert* (Herrnhut: Missionsbuchhandlung, 1931); Ruhland, "The Moravian Brethren."

[29] "Schon in meinen frühen Kinderjahren, regte sich das Gefühl der Liebe Jesu in meinem Herzen, u. ich hing an Ihn mit kindlicher Einfalt bey den Erzählungen von der großen Erweckung der Kinder in Herrnhut im Jahre 1727, schloß ich mit einigen anderen Kindern den Bund, nur einzig und allein den Heiland zu lieben. Diesen Bund erneuerten wir alle Wochen, meinem Herzen zum bleibenden Segen, denn der Eindruck davon ist mir bis in diese Stunde lebendig geblieben." UA, R. 22.84.21, Maria Magdalena.

Maria Magdalena describes two other important rituals that marked her spiritual development and retained a strong emotional salience judging by the way they are recalled (details of place, time, who spoke) in her memoir and the life-long moral insights they produced. One is a reference to the Moravian ritual of Speaking, which was a confessional conversation regularly undertaken with members of each Choir, including children.[30] One such devotional conversation with twelve-year-old Maria Magdalena was recalled by her later for its deep emotional and spiritual impact: "[H]e [a visiting Moravian Brother] spoke also individually with each of us older girls. With heartfelt intensity he admonished me to remain loyal to the Savior and to give myself to him as a reward for his suffering."[31] This episode reinforces the message from the awakening experience: to devote herself to the Savior and to remain loyal to him.

There is a strong thematic undercurrent again of suffering and pain. Maria Magdalena identifies her First Communion as a further ritual step in her emotional reorientation. This public entry into the congregation was an important ritual for every convert: "On April 13, 1789 I was gracefully received into the congregation and in the following year I enjoyed for the first time the Holy Communion. At this occasion I felt the utmost peace of God."[32] But this high point of positive experience and spiritual joy had another emotional subtext, that of sheer terror: "Now I got to know the fundamental depravity of my heart and everything that had brought the Savior to the cross [that is, the sinfulness of mankind] thoroughly."[33] The escape from this unbearable emotional state was the acknowledgement of Christ's authority and the submission to his guidance, here phrased in terms of friendship, trust, and redemption: "Whereas He, the most loyal friend of my soul, gracefully attended to me. He allowed me glances into His heart full of love and I felt his redemption forcefully inside me."[34]

The acknowledgement of Christ's authority was implicitly also an acceptance of the mission hierarchy – it was the visiting Moravian

[30] Faull, "Girls Talk," 183–96.

[31] "sprach er auch einzeln mit jeder von uns größeren Mädchen. Mit Herzens Anglegenheit ermahnte er mich dem Heiland treu zu bleiben u. mich Ihm auf ewig zum Lohne seiner Schmerzen zu weihen." UA, R. 22.84.21, Maria Magdalena.

[32] "Den 13. April 1789 ward mir die Gnade zu Theil, in die Gemeine aufgenommen zu werden, u. im folgenden Jahre genoß ich zum erstenmal das heilige Abendmahl mit derselben. Bey dieser feyerlichen Gelegenheit wurde ich dem Frieden Gottes auf das Fühlbarste inne." UA, R. 22.84.21, Maria Magdalena.

[33] "Nun lerne ich die Grundverdorbenheit meines Herzens und alles was den Heiland ans Kreuz gebracht hat, immer gründlicher kennen." UA, R. 22.84.21, Maria Magdalena.

[34] "wobey Er, der treuste Freund meiner Seele, sich gnädig meiner annahm. Er ließ mich diese Blicke in sein Herz voll Liebe thun, und ich fühlte Seine Vergebung in meinem Inneren kräftig," UA, R. 22.84.21, Maria Magdalena.

Brother's admonishments that Maria Magdalena took to heart. And within this mission hierarchy, she maintained a position that led to a transnational life as part of the missionary household: to look after the missionary children and even to accompany them across the Atlantic from the Caribbean to Europe where they would attend a boarding school. Maria Magdalena had not gained the same authority of the girl leaders of 1727; her conversion rituals had stayed within the frame of her peer group and did not expand to a more public event. The power that was available to the leading girls of the Herrnhut revival was out of reach for the female Indian convert.

In 1796, the Moravian mission at Tranquebar was dissolved. Maria Magdalena accompanied the missionaries initially to live in Europe but because the climate caused her to be sickly, it was decided that she would join Moravian Brethren and Sisters on St. Croix in the Danish West Indies.[35] She was trusted with the care of the missionary children and accompanied them on a second journey to Europe, where the children were taken for further education in the missionary boarding school. Finally, after twenty-five years in the West Indies, Maria Magdalena crossed the Atlantic again to retire to the Moravian congregation in Christiansfield, Denmark, where she had to join the Single Sisters in their communal house which she recalled in her memoir "was very hard for me, it was only after a whole year that I got used to it."[36]

In her memoir, Maria Magdalena modelled her life according to the main requirements of this literary genre: the emotional performance of conversion as a ritual of self-transformation (as a response to inner and outer terror) with a lasting emotional salience. As daughter of a female slave, she would have been no stranger to the experience of social disruptions and the need to remake one's identity. It was the conversion ritual and its narration in the literary genre of a memoir that enabled her to construct a new identity for herself and to integrate into a new social association of the Moravian Church. The ecstatic conversion ritual allowed female power to arise out of self-erasure: just as adolescent Moravian girls in Germany extended their emotional experiences to a community revival and gained leadership in this movement, Maria Magdalena emphasized the social bonding with her peers at the Tranquebar mission. It was their weekly ritual of the "pact" that mattered spiritually and socially, as her memoir emphasizes.

[35] UA, R. 22.84.21, Maria Magdalena.

[36] "Das Eingewöhnen im Schwesternhause wurde mir sehr schwer, erst nach Verlauf eines Jahres gewohnte ich mich ganz ein." UA, R. 22.84.21, Maria Magdalena.

In Tranquebar, the Indian girls were not able to initiate a public revival – the number of converts was too small – but did this mean Maria Magdalena had no aspirations for leadership? It is true that she did not acquire the political position of authority that her role models Susanne Kühnel and Anna Nitschmann had achieved. But we should remember that these two women also served initially in the household of the church leader before they advanced to public positions of leadership. Perhaps this gave rise to the hope for Maria to achieve the same? But by the end of the eighteenth century, the gendered structures of authority had changed in the Moravian Church and aspiring female converts were no longer able to gain political authority to the same extent that they had earlier. This change might have not been so clearly visible to the historical actors at the time. They still modelled the narratives of their spiritual paths and the emotional transformations conversions on the transmitted memory of the 1727 ritual, which continued to hold the appealing promise of a radical transformation of self and community.

Resisting Protestant Conversion and Emotions: Inuit Responses to Moravian Missions in Labrador[37]

Not all Moravian attempts to convert were met with approval by the local population. In many cases Moravian religious conversions, and their implied new emotional expressions, were resisted by local communities who preferred to follow their own religious beliefs and who found Moravian emotions and spirituality incomprehensible. One such example of cultural misunderstandings in global encounters are the early Moravian meetings with Inuit communities in Labrador.

The colonial context for Moravian missionary work in Labrador was quite different to that in India. While there had been trading exchanges between Inuit groups and European fur traders since at least the sixteenth century, there was much less social interruption and alienation to indigenous culture and identity than there had been in many other European colonies. European slave trading had not occurred here on a similarly devastating scale as in other places, and there had been no significant earlier Catholic proselytization, as was the case in India where many new Protestant converts had been Catholic and were often drawn from the lower social castes and especially from the slave population. In Labrador, Inuit groups still followed their traditional hunting economy, and their shamanic religious and social structures remained largely intact. Shamanic ritual leaders had significant social authority and were often

[37] This section draws on an earlier discussion in Van Gent, "The Burden of Love."

also leaders in the local trade enterprise that catered to the European markets for fur.

Moravian mission stations in Labrador were only established in 1771, after a failed attempt twenty years earlier when several Moravian missionaries had been killed by local Inuit.[38] Some years earlier, Moravian missionaries were hired by governor Hugh Palisser on the grounds of their language skills to mediate in increasingly violent conflicts between Inuit and the British colonial administration in Labrador. The. missionary Jens Haven had previously worked among Inuit groups in Greenland, where he had learned Inuktitut, and Palliser was hoping that this would lead to more successful political negotiations. A closer tie to the British government suited Moravian interests as well. After the establishment of the church's headquarters in London, they had lobbied unsuccessfully for some time to receive permission to expand their proselytization efforts into British colonial territories such as Labrador. Following the expedition in the 1760s, they finally received a land grant from the British government and the first Moravian mission station was established in Nain in 1771. The encounters between missionaries and Inuit, discussed below, were not part of regular mission work, but occurred slightly earlier in the context of the expeditions undertaken in the 1765. Nevertheless, the Moravians used the opportunity to attempt some proselytization work and to find suitable places for future mission stations.

The missionaries' attempts were met with little success and it was with disappointment that the Moravians noted the Inuit response to Brother Drachardt's question: "Listen, do you understand this: 'I feel now that the Savior is close to my soul?' … They repeated the words one after the other until they knew them by heart, but they did not reflect on the matter."[39] The missionaries expected that their emotional message of Christian love would stimulate an appropriate emotional performance of "feeling something," in response. Repetition of words alone were simply not enough to indicate conversion: responses were required in the Moravian emotional style, by showing that hearts were warm or that new hearts had been acquired from Christ.

Inuit responses to Moravian proselytization were shaped by very different cultural norms of emotional expression. While it is difficult to

[38] Hans Rollmann, "Johann Christian Erhardt and the First Moravian Exploration of Labrador in 1752," in *Moravian Beginnings in Labrador: Papers from a Symposium Held in Makkovik and Hopedale*, ed. Hans Rollmann, Newfoundland and Labrador Studies, Occasional Publications No. 2. (St. John's: Faculty of Arts Publications, Memorial University of Newfoundland, 2009), 53–68.

[39] UA, R.15.K.a.5.2.b, "Journal der Brüder Hill, Haven, Drachardt, Schloezer 1765" (hereafter "Journal der Brüder"), 50–183, here 107, entry for August 26, 1765. All translations are mine unless otherwise noted.

reconstruct Inuit emotional regimes during the eighteenth century, ethnographic studies suggest that the social performance of emotions was complex and highly codified. For instance, the performance of love was a delicate matter, since strong attachments were perceived to be dangerous and therefore the Inuit did not seek to be "loved" intensely.[40] From a Moravian perspective, love was vital to conversion and the intense experience of overwhelming emotion was to be sought through somatic rituals and welcomed as the beginnings of spiritual transformation. For the Inuit, such intense emotion was to be avoided because it was understood as potentially socially disruptive. Thus, the global aspirations of Protestant conversions and religious empire-building were hindered by very different local cultural concepts of what emotions mean.

In particular, the persistent emphasis on Christ's blood flowing from his side-wound and a "warm heart," that was so central to Moravian imagery and teaching, created significant difficulties for the Inuit. The open Moravian discussion of the power of Christ's blood to effect conversion conflicted with Inuit spiritual norms and taboos concerning blood. These deeper dimensions of emotional conflicts stemming from the Moravians' violation of Inuit cultural taboos is hinted at in the following episode, when Drachardt asked adolescent Inuit girls and boys first if "they also wanted to learn something." When they did not respond, he scolded them by saying that Inuit children in Greenland, where he had previously worked, were able to pray:

> In Greenland the children are able to pray to the Savior, I will teach you a prayer. They said: "Pray." So he prayed: "O Savior! Give me a drop of blood into my heart!" Some young men repeated the words, but the unmarried ones were embarrassed. After that they did not want to stay anymore.[41]

One can imagine that it was difficult to understand why one would have to ask Christ to receive his blood in one's own heart as part of this Christian learning. The embarrassment of the unmarried men also points to the emotional impact of these words on Inuit adolescents who were brought up in a society with strong gendered taboos connected to death, menstruation, and blood.[42]

40 For an anthropological discussion of Inuit emotional socialization, see, for example, Jean L. Briggs, *Never in Anger: Portrait of an Eskimo Family* (Cambridge, MA: Harvard University Press, 1970); Jean L. Briggs, *Inuit Morality Play: The Emotional Education of a Three-Year-Old* (New Haven, CT: Yale University Press, 1998); Jean L. Briggs, "Emotions have many Faces: Lessons from the Inuit," in *Psychological Anthropology: A Reader on Self in Culture*, ed. Robert A. LeVine (Malden, MA: Wiley-Blackwell, 2010), 60–67.

41 UA, R.15.K.a.5.2.b, "Journal der Brüder,"107, entry for August 26, 1765.

42 See, for example, Ernest William Hawkes, *The Labrador Eskimo* (New York: Johnson Reprint Corp, 1970), 133–34.

In response to the Moravians' somatic ideas of conversion, the Inuit were unambiguous about their inability to understand the missionaries' teaching. When Drachardt tried to pray with them: "O Savior give us ears to hear how your body is wounded everywhere and how you have purchased us with your blood," the Inuit answered: "We don't have any ears, we don't understand these things."[43] For the Inuit, the somatic elements of Moravian religious teaching seemed increasingly and perhaps unnecessarily complicated. At this stage of early contact between Inuit and Moravian missionaries the Inuit had yet to be socialized into the Moravian emotional regime and did not perceive a need to change. This clear Inuit refusal to "hear" was a strong refusal to conform to the required Moravian emotional somatic style and a rejection of the missionaries' claims to spiritual authority.

The missionaries' records posit that being emotionally moved and "understanding" were quite distinct from "knowing the words," or the repeating phrases. As one missionary remarked in a disappointed manner "But they don't really want to understand it, and there was no difference to saying these words to a parrot who repeats them."[44] The Inuit also seemed to recognize the contrast, but their perception of the contrast reveals different cultural values. For the Moravians, strong emotions signified genuine religious conversion, so a lack of evidence of deep feeling was to be mourned. The Inuit, on the other hand, reiterated that they understood the Moravian teaching as they could repeat the words: in their view, "understanding" did not require demonstration through ritualized forms of emotional expression. The different perspectives are clear in the following example, which records how one missionary chastized the Inuit:

> "Your hearts are as cold as ice, but the Savior's blood and his wounds can help." They repeated it as usual and then said, "Now we know everything!" He [the missionary] answered: "It is not enough that you know it, the Savior wants to possess your hearts."[45]

The somatic and emotional nature of a Christian conversion is here explicitly linked to questions of authority and power: Christ demands to possess their hearts and the missionaries expect to see evidence of this. At this point, the Inuit declined further cooperation, implicitly denying missionary authority to teach new forms of emotional, as opposed to semantic, expression:

[43] UA, R.15.K.a.5.2.b, "Journal der Brüder," 117, entry for August 29, 1765.
[44] UA, R.15.K.a.5.2.b, "Journal der Brüder," 117, entry for August 29, 1765.
[45] UA, R.15.K.a.5.2.b, "Journal der Brüder," 159, entry for September 13, 1765.

They called: "Hearts, souls," but there was not the slightest movement to feel. The men in particular did not want to hear very much today, and they said that they already knew it.[46]

The Inuit refusal of Moravian conversion attempts is similar to other first-contact situations, where indigenous worldviews retained their coherence and validity, before colonial intrusions caused serious social and cultural dislocation.[47]

The Inuit resistance to Moravian emotions of conversion was an ongoing site of struggle.[48] The meaning of conversion as the submission to Christ, through the metaphor of giving one's old heart and acquiring a new one, could be viewed as an emotional and somatic colonization of the Inuit. Shortly before the missionary Drachardt left Labrador the following exchange was recorded by a fellow missionary:

When they came to the shore, one of the Esquimaux said to Brother Drachardt: "The day before yesterday Brother Jens Haven did ask us if we thought of that which we had heard from you. We talk about it amongst us, but we do not know more than: Creator, Savior, blood and wounds." Brother Drachardt said: "You should keep this in your hearts. The Savior wants to have your hearts. You shall receive new ones. We cannot tell you more for the time being." An old man said: "A new heart, what is this? We don't understand this either."[49]

This cultural miscommunication between Inuit and Moravian missionaries demonstrates how not only different religions, but also different emotional styles and concepts of body and self, came into conflict when global Protestant missions encountered local indigenous cultures. For the Inuit, refusing to understand and enact Moravian emotions of conversion was a form of resistance to a Protestant spirituality that involved intense somatic performances.

After the initial Inuit resistance to Protestant Moravian teachings in Labrador, there was later a slow but increasing uptake of their teachings. The agency of Inuit converts was significant here, as it had been earlier in Greenland.[50] Thus the decisive change in the willingness to convert came

[46] UA, R.15.K.a.5.2.b, "Journal der Brüder," 159, entry for September 13, 1765.

[47] A similar point has been observed for a Lutheran mission in central Australia in the mid-nineteenth century, when Arrernte elders saw no need to incorporate the missionary teachings. For a discussion of this case, see Peggy Brock and Jacqueline Van Gent, "Generational Religious Change Among the Arrernte at Hermannsburg, Central Australia," *Australian Historical Studies* 33 (2002): 303–18.

[48] See, for example, a letter from Brethren in Nain mission station, dated September 16, 1791 printed in *Periodical Accounts relating to the Missions of the Church of the United Brethren established among the Heathen* (hereafter *Periodical Accounts*), vol. 1 (1790): 88–91, here 89.

[49] UA, R.15.K.a.5.2.b, "Journal der Brüder," 117, entry for August 29, 1765.

[50] On "national helpers" on Moravian missions in Labrador, see Hans Rollmann, "'So That in This Part You Should Not Lag behind Other Missionary Congregations … ': The

much later, when local Inuit converts took the initiative to spread the Christian message to their people. In general, it was often the work of these "national helpers" that was instrumental in the spread of Protestantism.[51] Also, it is worth noting that on this earlier "exploration journey" of the Moravians in 1765, there were no Moravian women in the party. Very often, indigenous and enslaved people responded especially positive to the work of Moravian women missionaries, who developed a good rapport with local women and children.[52] This was aided by the fact that Moravian women functioned not only as wives, but often as more independent missionaries in their own right because of the sex-segregated nature of Moravian communal and spiritual life.

Conclusion

Emotions played a crucial role in the spread of early modern global Protestantisms and in the cultural and religious encounters which they entailed. Missionary intentions of creating an emotional community of Protestant believers was met by a wide range of emotional and social responses – from emulation to open rejection – which illustrate how local cultural contexts shaped encounter histories and the transformation of Protestant beliefs and practices in very different ways.

Global Protestant churches, like the Moravians, placed a strong emphasis on the role of emotions in the conversion experiences as well as in their devotional culture. In some respects, this made it easier to reach potential converts since emotions did not rely solely on language but were performed in somatic ways, such as kneeling, crying, and so on. In societies that were affected by significant colonial disruptions, such as slavery, Moravian conversions offered the possibility of a transformation of emotions such as fear, grief, terror, or distrust into trust, joy, and acceptance as part of a "religion of the heart" that was able to connect to the suffering of Christ. In areas not yet significantly altered by European colonialism, such as Labrador, on the other hand, the Moravian brand of Protestantism was rejected for much longer.

The emotional intensity of Moravian devotional culture that placed a high emphasis on communal and embodied emotions and practices

Introduction of National Helpers in the Moravian Mission among the Labrador Inuit," *Journal of Moravian History* 17/2 (2017): 138–59.

[51] See for example Peggy Brock, Norman Etherington, Gareth Griffiths and Jacqueline Van Gent, *Indigenous Evangelists and Questions of Authority in the British Empire, 1754–1940* (Leiden/Boston: Brill, 2015).

[52] Rachel Wheeler, *To Live Upon Hope. Mohicans and Missionaries in the Eighteenth-Century Northeast* (Ithaca, NY and London: Cornell University Press, 2008).

singing, praying, Speakings, and love feasts allowed believers to join this new religion without too much time spent on learning the Lutheran Catechism.[53]

The active inclusion of converted indigenous and slave women and men in mission proselytization practices allowed Moravian missions to connect very quickly with local populations in places where colonial intrusions had disrupted the social and cultural worlds of colonized people to the extent that they sought support, protection, and hope in the new Protestant missions. Indigenous converts could negotiate their belonging to the emotional community of Moravians in careful expressions of shared religious identity, symbols, and emotions. When indigenous religious practices and their associated emotional styles remained strong, however, people did not see any need for conversion. As in the European reformations where the new Protestant religion caused strong emotional responses, the global spread of Protestant churches was shaped by emotional dynamics that reflected local power relations.

[53] This power of embodied and sensual experiences to create imagined communities was not restricted to early modern Moravians. Similar observations have been made by modern anthropologists for other religious groups and their emotional bonding mechanisms. See, for example, Birgit Meyer ed., *Aesthetic Formations: Media, Religion and the Senses* (New York: Palgrave Macmillan, 2009).

11 The Sacred World of Mary Prince

Jon Sensbach

The History of Mary Prince holds an exalted place in the canon of ex-slave narratives. The first such autobiography by a woman, published in London in 1831, Mary Prince's revelation of slavery's enormities, especially towards women, shocked the British public, galvanized the anti-slavery movement, and contributed to Parliament's passage of the Slavery Abolition Act in 1833. As slavery's everywoman, Prince spoke for the unvoiced millions. "I have been a slave myself," she famously wrote. "I know what slaves feel – I can tell by myself what other slaves feel, and by what they have told me. The man that says slaves be quite happy in slavery – that they don't want to be free – that man is either ignorant or a lying person." Rebut her account, attack her character, discredit her reliability as they might, British slaveholders and their defenders in the end could only capitulate before Mary Prince's witness.[1]

Like most autobiographies of former enslaved people in the eighteenth- and early nineteenth-century British Empire, *The History* is also a religious narrative. Prince structured her tale as the intertwined accounts of physical liberation and emancipation from sin, portraying conversion to Christianity as an essential milestone on the path to spiritual and bodily freedom. Her narrative staked a claim to Christian universalism and to her own stature as a moral being while advancing abolitionists' assurances that enslaved West Indians were eagerly embracing Christianity to prepare for emancipation. Establishing the authenticity of her experience to an English reading public accustomed to the conventions of evangelical confessional writing, Prince asserted her spirituality as a redemptive counterpoint to the sacrilegious cruelty of the slave masters.[2] That affirmation – the slave as suffering servant – forms the ethical bedrock of the narrative. As the only true

[1] Mary Prince, *The History of Mary Prince, a West Indian Slave Related by Herself*, ed. Moira Ferguson (Ann Arbor, MI: University of Michigan Press, revised ed. 1997), 94 (hereafter *HMP*); Mary Jeanne Larrabee, "'I Know What a Slave Knows': Mary Prince's Epistemology of Resistance," *Women's Studies* 35 (2006): 453–73.

[2] On the role of religion as a narrative and strategic framing device in *The History*, see Ferguson, "Introduction," in *HMP*, 19–20; Gilliam Whitlock, "Autobiography and Slavery: Believing the *History of Mary Prince*," in *The Intimate Empire: Reading Women's Autobiography*, ed. Gilliam Whitlock (London: Continuum, 2000), 20–24; and

Christians, enslaved people must endure persecution and death to restore humankind. Like other slave narratives, Prince's story bursts out of the core of the black prophetic tradition. For enslaved people, as theologian James Cone has written, "Christ crucified manifested God's living and liberating presence ... in the lives of black Christians that empowered them to believe that *ultimately*, in God's eschatological future, they would not be defeated." At heart, *The History of Mary Prince* is a passion story rooted in sacrifice and redemption. Putting enslaved women at the forefront of the antislavery campaign, Prince demonstrates that religion is a crucial weapon in their arsenal.[3]

And yet, although scholars have widely recognized the importance of religion in Prince's narrative, the deeper role of spirituality in her life, and its resonances, both written and unwritten, in her autobiography, remain largely unexplored. As literary historian Sue Thomas points out, many critics perceive Prince's Christianity as "inauthentic ... a role-playing on Prince's part for a British Christian audience [and] an empty signifier" in the scholarship. In ways that historians have barely begun to explore, Prince, as the product of a larger culture of West Indian slavery, was immersed in several overlapping sacred worlds in conversation, and often at odds, with her providential narrative. A fresh reading of *The History of Mary Prince* points towards a new examination of the fusion of religion and antislavery and of women's spiritual lives in the Caribbean outpost of the Protestant Reformation.[4]

The circumstances that called *The History* into being are familiar to students of the slave narrative genre. Born enslaved in Bermuda in 1788 to a domestic servant mother and a sawyer father named Prince, Mary Prince was sold several times in subsequent decades to a succession of

Jenny Sharpe, *Ghosts of Slavery: A Literary Archaeology of Black Women's Lives* (Minneapolis: University of Minnesota Press, 2003), 120–51.

[3] James H. Cone, *The Cross and the Lynching Tree* (Maryknoll, NY: Orbis, 2011), 2. For comparative scholarship on religion in antebellum US slave narratives, see Joycelyn Moody, *Sentimental Confessions: Spiritual Narratives of Nineteenth-Century African-American Women* (Athens: University of Georgia Press, 2003); Yolanda Pierce, *Hell Without Fires: Slavery, Christianity and the Antebellum Spiritual Narrative* (Gainesville: University Press of Florida, 2005); Yolanda Pierce, "Redeeming Bondage: Captivity Narratives and Spiritual Autobiographies in Slave Narrative Tradition," in *Cambridge Companion to the African American Slave Narrative* (New York: Cambridge University Press, 2007), 83–98; Albert Raboteau, "The Blood of the Martyrs is the Seed of the Faith: Suffering in the Christianity of American Slaves," in *The Courage to Hope: From Black Suffering to Human Redemption*, ed. Cornel West and Quinton Hosford Dixie (Boston: Beacon, 1999), 22–40; Sue Thomas, *Telling West Indian Lives: Life Narrative and the Reform of Plantation Slavery Cultures, 1804–1834* (New York: Palgrave Macmillan, 2014), 119–66, esp. 121. On enslaved women's resistance as antislavery struggle, see Hilary Beckles, "Taking Liberties: Enslaved Women and Anti-Slavery in the Caribbean," in *Gender and Imperialism*, ed. Clare Midgley (Manchester, UK: Manchester University Press, 1998), 137–60.

[4] Thomas, *Telling West Indian Lives*, 121.

owners in the Caribbean, first in Grand Turk Island, then again in Bermuda, and finally, by 1815, in Antigua, as the slave of Mr. and Mrs. John Wood of St. John's. When the Woods traveled to England in 1828, Prince went with them, leaving behind her husband, Daniel James, a free man she had married in 1826. Once on English soil she herself became free by law, and after continuing to work for the Woods as a laundress and household servant for several months, she ran away to a local missionary organization which directed her to the Anti-Slavery Society. Abolitionists quickly realized the public relations value of her story, which she narrated to a poet, Susanna Strickland, who shaped it into publishable form; Thomas Pringle, an Anti-Slavery Society official, edited and pruned the narrative further. Instantly popular with an English antislavery public eager for first-hand testimony of slavery's atrocities, the narrative went through three editions in the first year alone. The Woods sued Pringle for libel; he countersued, and in several trials Prince was called as a witness, submitting to humiliating interrogation by Wood's attorney. Proslavery writers challenged the truthfulness of her account, denouncing her as a sexually promiscuous ingrate incapable of appreciating the Woods' kindness to her.[5]

Indeed, *History* contains precious little kindness, at least among the slaveholders. Prince did recall a happy childhood on Bermuda in the household of a benevolent mistress, Mrs. Williams, living carefree as the friend and playmate of Miss Betsey, the mistress's daughter. As critics have pointed out, the kind-hearted master or mistress, particularly during an author's childhood, was a conventional trope in ex-slave narratives to show that not all slaveholders were irredeemably wicked. After being sold from the household, however, Prince's life quickly became a nightmare. Each of her subsequent owners superseded the previous in fiendishness; being exchanged from one set of hands to the next simply meant going "from one butcher to another." Just as planters' inventories listed the names and value of their human property, Prince catalogued the atrocities on which the slaveholders built their fortunes. All of them beat and tortured slaves, sometimes even to death, for trivial offenses or for no reason at all. In her graphic revelation of the casual routinization of slavery's sadism, blood flowed unchecked from whippings, backs were scarred, bodies maimed, anguished cries for mercy ignored. One owner "often stripped me naked, hung me by my wrists, and beat me with the cow-skin, with his own hand, till my body was raw with gashes," she wrote. "Yet there was nothing very remarkable in this; for it might serve as

[5] On the publication and post-publication history of the narrative, see Ferguson, "Introduction," *HMP*.

a sample of the common usage of the slave on that horrible island." Slaves were merely work engines, unfit for a compassionate word, a humanitarian gesture. On Grand Turk, Prince was assigned to a labor crew, raking mounds of salt crystals on the shore for the local salt industry. Her description of standing in saltwater for days on end, her legs filling with "dreadful boils, which eat down in some cases to the very bone," debilitating her with lifelong rheumatism, are some of the most memorable in British antislavery literature.[6]

Prince's narrative is charged with the sexual morality of slavery, even though it carefully cloaks the subject in early Victorian euphemism and strategic silence. In deference to readers' sensibilities, Prince did not directly refer to sexual abuse by masters, but she hinted at it. Every bit as destructive as slavery's physical rapacity, she contended, was its psychological violence, the worst aspect of which was being exposed to the "indecency" of masters. "Worse to me than all the licks" was being forced to see one of these men naked while she bathed him. Recoiling from this "man with no shame for his servants, no shame for his own flesh," she refused to perform the duty any longer. Part of the rhetorical strategy of *History* is its framing of the enslaved female body as a repository of modesty and decorum vulnerable to the disgusting predations of unchristian masters. The metaphoric violence of immodesty stands in for the actual violence of rape, to acknowledge which would have undercut Prince's morality, and with it, her credibility among evangelical antislavery activists. The strategy also required her to conceal the fact that, like many enslaved women, she had entered into a years-long relationship with a white man – in her case, a Captain Abbot, in Antigua – to earn money and improve her fortunes. The relationship was revealed publicly only during the post-publication libel suits, when proslavery lawyers depicted her as an immoral "prostitute" whose testimony was worthless. Prince's entire story seemingly rested on the slender, and contested, thread of her upstanding character.[7]

The extent to which Prince narrated, or was allowed to narrate, her own story has been the central motif of scholarship on the history of *History*. Virtually all critics agree that the document is a highly mediated text formed from some compound of Prince's own words and strategic emendations by Strickland and Pringle to make her story fit their own antislavery imperatives. Pinpointing which is which has proven difficult. Some critics argue that Strickland and Pringle's editorial heavy-handedness – despite their insistence that the narrative was "related by herself"– undermines Prince's authorial voice while forcing her into their

[6] *HMP*, all quotations on 72–73. [7] Ibid., 77–78; Sharpe, *Ghosts of Slavery*, 133–34.

ideological straitjacket. They transformed her West Indian patois into standard English, injected conventional elements of sentimental literature into the narration, and crafted a persona not entirely Prince's. Other scholars contend that Prince's own voice shaped the narrative in ways that eluded and transcended these interventions. For the first time, readers of the *History* met, not a helpless female victim, but a woman who protested mistreatment, disobeyed orders, defended herself and others, and ultimately emancipated herself by running away. By framing her narrative as a lifetime project of resistance to oppression, Prince claimed for herself an "emergent West Indian subjectivity in the gendered space of a black woman and a slave." In this vein, for example, one recent critic has argued that Prince's subversion of colonial slaveholding authority worked within the African oral tradition of the trickster.[8]

Her image endlessly reflected in a hall of mirrors between her own narrative intent, the editorial ventriloquism of her day, and modern literary exegesis, Mary Prince herself remains a riddle trussed up in an enigma. Debates about *The History of Mary Prince* have almost always centered on its status as a text and on the hermeneutics of Prince's narrative authority. Literary scholars and historians have seldom used the *History* as an entry point to the broader African-Caribbean cultures in

[8] Contours of this debate may be followed in Sharpe, *Ghosts of Slavery*; Whitlock, "Autobiography and Slavery"; Sandra Pouchet Paquet, "The Heartbeat of a West Indian Slave: *The History of Mary Prince*," *African American Review* 26 (1992): 131–45, quote on 131; Jessica L. Allen, "Pringle's Pruning of Prince: *The History of Mary Prince* and the Question of Repetition," *Callaloo* 35 (2012): 509–19; Rachel Banner, "Surface and Stasis: Re-Reading Slave Narrative via *The History of Mary Prince*," *Callaloo* 36 (2013): 298–311; Barbara Baumgartner, "The Body as Evidence: Resistance, Collaboration and Appropriation in *The History of Mary Prince*," *Callaloo* 24 (2001): 253–75; Rosetta Haynes, "Voice, Body and Collaboration: Constructions of Authority in *The History of Mary Prince*," *Literary Griot: International Journal of Black Expressive Cultural Studies* 11 (1999): 18–32; Larrabee, "I Know What a Slave Knows." More recently scholars have built upon debates about the multivocal construction of Prince's narrative to place the author in larger contexts of black Atlantic subjectivity and narrative self-fashioning. See, for example, Michelle Gadspaille, "Trans-colonial Collaboration and Slave Narrative: *The History of Mary Prince* Revisited," *English Language Overseas Perspectives and Enquiries* 8 (2001): 64–77; Babacar M'Baye, "African and Caribbean Patterns in Mary Prince's Resistance," in *The Trickster Comes West: Pan-African Influence in Early Black Diasporan Narratives*, ed. Babacar M'Baye (Jackson: University of Mississippi Press, 2009), 178–205; K. Merinda Simmons, "Sites of Authentication: Migration and Subjectivity in *The History of Mary Prince*," in *Changing the Subject: Writing Women Across the African Diaspora*, ed. K. Merinda Simmons (Columbus: Ohio State University Press, 2014), 23–49; Alan Rice, *Radical Narratives of the Black Atlantic* (London: Continuum, 2002); Ifeoma Kiddoe Nwankwo, *Black Cosmopolitanism: Racial Consciousness and Transnational Identity in the Nineteenth Century* (Philadelphia: University of Pennsylvania Press, 2014); Nicole Aljoe, *Creole Testimonies: Slave Narratives from the British West Indies, 1709–1838* (New York: Palgrave Macmillan, 2011); Nicole Aljoe and Ian Finseth eds., *Journeys of the Slave Narrative in the Early Americas* (Charlottesville: University Press of Virginia, 2014).

which Mary Prince moved, overlooking opportunities to learn more about Prince from archival sources that can broaden the contexts in which highly scripted ex-slave narratives like hers are read.[9]

Death and Rebirth

Her story begins with a ritual killing – her own. "The great God above alone knows the thoughts of the poor slave's heart." These words, from an early scene in *History,* contain two important cues about the struggle ahead. Prince leaves it to God to understand that which cannot be understood: the experience, as a child, of being posted on the auction block with her mother and siblings and watching her family atomized by sale after kindly Mrs. Williams's death. The narrative device signals God's immanence in her story: he cannot prevent the family's destruction, but in his omniscience, he can make the slaves' cause his own. Prince must first step on the emotional killing floor of the auction block – quite literally entering a heart of darkness. Describing this experience, Prince (perhaps aided by Strickland and Pringle) steeps her prose in the language of sentiment, urging readers to understand the enslaved as people with thoughts, feelings, and emotions. The word "heart" pulses through the text over and over, dozens of times, five times alone in a single paragraph. On the block her "heart throbbed with grief and terror so violently, that I . . . thought it would burst out of my body." The trauma of the auction block epitomizes what historian Nell Painter calls the "soul murder" of slavery. Careless white bystanders ignored "the pain that wrung the hearts of the negro woman and her young ones." Though not all the onlookers were evil, "slavery hardens white people's hearts towards the blacks"; their unfeeling comments about the enslaved merchandise before them "fell like cayenne on the fresh wounds of our hearts." Here, then, is a double murder, or rather a murder-suicide, by white people whose failure to acknowledge black pain destroys their own souls.[10]

[9] Natasha Lightfoot, "*The History of Mary Prince* as a Historical Document of Slavery in Antigua and the British Empire," *Antigua and Barbuda International Literary Festival Magazine* 2 (2011): 28–32; Margot Maddison-MacFadyen, "Mary Prince, Grand Turk and Antigua," *Slavery and Abolition* 34 (2013): 653–62.

[10] *HMP,* 61–62; Nell Irvin Painter, "Soul Murder and Slavery: Toward a Fully Loaded Cost Accounting," in *Southern History Across the Color Line* (Chapel Hill: University of North Carolina Press, 2002), 15–39. On the connections between religion, emotion and the antislavery movement, see Brycchan Carey, *British Abolitionism and the Rhetoric of Sensibility: Writing, Sentiment and Slavery, 1760–1807* (London: Palgrave Macmillan, 2005); David Brion Davis, *The Problem of Slavery in the Age of Revolution, 1770–1823* (Ithaca, NY: Cornell University Press, 1975), 45–48, 213–54; Christopher Brown, *Moral Capital: Foundations of British Abolitionism* (Chapel Hill: University of North Carolina Press, 2006); and the essay by Jacqueline van Gent in Chapter 10 of this volume. On the

The battleground of the heart forecasts the impending conflict as not simply between slavery and freedom but between belief and unbelief. In this, the slaves are the righteous, and the whites are blasphemous tyrants. She describes one of her several violent enslavers as a "cruel son of a cruel father" with "no heart – no fear of God." On Grand Turk, slaves are not even allowed to pray. When enslaved worshipers on the island build a "place with boughs and leaves, where they might meet for prayers," whites destroy it twice. A flood that later washed away many white people's homes, Prince concludes, was God's punishment for this wickedness, though she carefully reins in any temptation to rejoice. Without Prince's knowledge, God intervenes in her troubled life. After another master fatally beats her friend Hetty, Prince, withering under the increased workload, longs to join her in death, but "the hand of God whom I knew not, was stretched over me, and I was mercifully preserved for better things." Similarly, God "ordained" her sale to yet another master, John Wood, which she believes (wrongly, as it turned out) would ease her burden; and after she is crippled by rheumatism while in Wood's service, God inspires her fellow slaves' kindness to care for her in her misery.[11]

These narrative maneuvers foreshadow the great turning point in her life – her adoption of Christianity. By 1817, Prince had been in Antigua as a household servant with the Woods for several years, and life was miserable. They beat her when rheumatism kept her from working and beat her again for protesting. When she quarreled with another slave woman about a pig, Mrs. Wood sent her to the "Cage," the jail in St. John's, to have her flogged. She does not explicitly say she turned to religion as a refuge from these troubles, but readers may infer that intent from the narrative's sequence of events. In August 1817, she was baptized by James Curtin, an Anglican clergyman with the Society for the Propagation of the Gospel in Foreign Parts. After Curtin "told her to learn the Lord's Prayer," according to a later court deposition by Wood, "she got some of her neighbours to teach her it, and paid them." Prince was at first "too wild" to receive instruction in reading, according to this account, but Wood's younger daughter later gave Prince her first reading lessons. Prince herself recalls that she needed Wood's permission to attend Curtin's Sunday school but never asked him "from the belief that it would be

psychological trauma of the slave auction block, see Anne C. Bailey, *The Weeping Time: Memory and the Largest Slave Auction in American History* (New York: Cambridge University Press, 2017).

[11] *HMP*, 67–68, 75, 76, 78, 79.

refused; so that I got no farther instruction at that time from the English Church."[12]

During a Wood family stay at Date Hill, a plantation in the countryside, Prince was invited by an enslaved domestic housekeeper to attend a Methodist meeting at another plantation, Winthorp. "I went; and they were the first prayers I ever understood," she recounted. "One woman prayed; and then they all sung a hymn; then there was another prayer and another hymn; and then they all spoke by turns of their own griefs as sinners." Henry, a plantation driver and the husband of the woman who invited her, testified of his shame and sorrow at having to punish slaves under his supervision, and he prayed that they, and God, would forgive him. These testimonies triggered an awakening in Prince:

> I felt sorry for my sins also. I cried the whole night, but I was too much ashamed to speak. I prayed God to forgive me. This meeting had a great impression on my mind, and led my spirit to the Moravian church; so that when I got back to town, I went and prayed to have my name put down in the Missionaries' book; and I followed the church earnestly every opportunity. I did not then tell my mistress about it; for I knew that she would not give me leave to go. But I felt I *must* go. Whenever I carried the children their lunch at school, I ran around and went to hear the teachers.

The "Missionaries' book" in which Prince yearned to have her name written was a registration list of church members on Antigua. The list has survived, and it confirms that part of her account. On one line amid a list thousands of names long is the entry "12/19 Mary Wood," accompanied by the notation "none" for spouse. Because of the West Indian practice of identifying enslaved people by their owner's last name, there is no question this is the woman later known as Mary Prince. As further proof, a few years later, after she had left Antigua with the Woods, someone wrote "in England" over her name. At the time, Prince could not have known that she would one day write a famous memoir, and her desire to have her name inscribed in the mission ledger testifies to a determination to leave some archival record of herself, to have her name known somewhere.[13]

So began Prince's years-long association with the Moravian Church, or Renewed Unity of Brethren, the evangelical Protestant fellowship based

[12] Ibid., 83–84; *Wood v. Pringle,* in ibid., 147. Wood disputed Prince's account, claiming that it was he who had sent Prince to Curtin in the first place. He "always desired his servants and slaves to attend church, and recommended Mary Prince in particular for the religious instruction of the Rev. J. Curtin," according to a defense of Wood published in 1831. *Bermuda Royal Gazette* 22 Nov. 1831, in *HMP,* 154.

[13] Ibid., 82–83; "Estate Book," East West Indies Collection, A6, no. 6, Moravian Archives, Northern Province, Bethlehem, Pa. (hereafter EWIC).

Fig 11.1 Mary Prince's Church: Mission Station at Spring Gardens, Antigua, from Johann Heinrich Stobwasser, *Ansichten von Missions-Niederlassungen der Evangelischen Brüdergemeinde,* 1832

in Germany that established its first missions among enslaved Africans in the Danish West Indies nearly a century earlier and extended them throughout the British Caribbean in subsequent decades. Thousands of pages of seldom-studied manuscripts from the Antigua mission, preserved in the Moravian Archives in Bethlehem, Pennsylvania, open new perspectives on Prince's relationship to this emergent Afro-Christian fellowship and its central place in her narrative. Prince describes how she gained a footing in the congregation at Spring Gardens, in St. John's (Fig 11.1):

The Moravian ladies (Mrs. Richter, Mrs. Olufsen, and Mrs. Sauter) taught me to read in the class; and I got on very fast. In this class there were all sorts of people, old and young, grey headed folks and children; but most of them were free people. After we had done spelling, we tried to read in the Bible. After the reading was over, the missionary gave out a hymn for us to sing. I dearly loved to go to the

> church, it was so solemn. I never knew rightly that I had much sin till I went there. When I found out I was great sinner, I was very sorely grieved, and very much frightened. I used to pray to God to pardon my sins for Christ's sake, and forgive me for everything I had done amiss; and when I went home to my work, I always thought about what I had heard from the missionaries, and wished to be good that I might go to heaven. After a while I was admitted a candidate for the holy Communion.

Here, too, the documentary record corroborates her account. Next to her name in the membership list is the notation "8/21" for her confirmation date. Church records also clearly identify the "Moravian ladies" as the wives of missionaries, all of them born in Germany and resident in Antigua for many years: Johanna Elizabeth Richter, from Witzenhausen, near Kassel; Anna Margaretha Olufsen, from Böhl, near Speyer; and Mary Sautter, from Upper Lusatia. Naming these women, who played vital roles as assistants in the Antigua mission, provided verifiable evidence that enhanced the authenticity of Prince's narrative.[14]

From Prince's description, British readers would take away three main impressions of her religious experiences to this point: her admission of sinfulness; her seeking out of several Christian organizations, ending with acceptance in the Moravian Church; and her instruction by dedicated white female mission assistants. Each of these was calibrated to evoke a certain emotional and intellectual response. Prince's account fell somewhat short of a classic conversion narrative in the transatlantic evangelical and Pietist traditions, in which narrators recounted, often at great length, a restless, ungodly life as the prelude to spiritual doubt and crisis, recognition of sinfulness, catharsis in an emotional relationship with God, and shedding of an old self for a new life in Christ. She fulfilled enough of those criteria to gain readers' empathy, however, and in particular, her quest for redemption from sin would have found a receptive audience among evangelicals (many of them antislavery) who supported West Indian missions to overcome national guilt for the slave trade and slavery and to erase what they considered enslaved Africans' inherent heathen debauchery. Especially after the closing of the slave trade in 1807, Christianization became the linchpin of Britain's "amelioration" program to humanize and soften slavery while supposedly preparing the slaves for gradual – and very distant – emancipation. The Anglican, Methodist, and Moravian churches all claimed great success in this campaign, and British women, who provided the popular impetus and organizational heft for both the antislavery and evangelical movements, would have recognized

[14] *HMP*, 83; "Complete Catalogue of All the Brethren and Sisters on Antigua & of Their Children born on this Island," EWIC A7, no. 2.

and appreciated the efforts of Sisters Richter, Olufsen and Sautter, German though they were, on the Caribbean frontlines.[15]

Sisters and Helpers

But these hardworking women were not alone. Though there had been missionaries all over the British West Indies since the eighteenth century, the relatively high percentage of enslaved people in Antigua who affiliated with one version of Protestant Christianity or another made the colony the "favorite of heaven," in Methodist churchman Thomas Coke's words. When Moravians and Methodists arrived in the 1750s, both depended for their success on Afro-Caribbean evangelists, many, or most, of them women, to spread the egalitarian appeal of Christianity through the slave quarters. Methodist founder John Wesley visited Antigua in 1758, reporting that two enslaved women on the plantation of Nathaniel Gilbert "appear to be much awakened" by his words. Those women, Mary Alley and Sophia Campbell, became recruiters, lay preachers, and organizers in the mission, assembling a congregation and raising money and "an army of women workers" to clear land for a church. "But for their exertions the name of Methodist would have been extinct in this country," concluded one observer in 1814. By the early nineteenth century, the Methodists claimed 3,516 adherents on Antigua, including "many women … in Society" who have "good gifts in Prayer and hold prayer meetings," making the island the epicenter for Methodism's spread throughout the Caribbean.[16]

[15] Clare Midgley, *Women Against Slavery: The British Campaigns, 1780–1870* (London: Routledge, 1992), including a discussion of Mary Prince on 87–91; John Coffey, "'Tremble, Britannia!': Fear, Providence, and the Abolition of the Slave Trade, 1758–1807," *English Historical Review* CXXVII/527 (2012): 844–81; Stiv Jakobsson, *Am I Not a Man and a Brother? British Missions and the Abolition of the Slave Trade and Slavery in West Africa and the West Indies, 1786–1838* (Lund, Sweden: Gleerup, 1972); Mary Turner, *Slaves and Missionaries: The Disintegration of Jamaican Society, 1787–1834* (Urbana: University of Illinois Press, 1982); Christa Dierksheide, *Amelioration and Empire: Progress and Slavery in the Plantation Americas* (Charlottesville: University of Virginia Press, 2014).

[16] Sylvia R. Frey and Betty Wood, *Come Shouting to Zion: African American Protestantism in the American South and British Caribbean to 1830* (Chapel Hill: University of North Carolina Press, 1998), 104–6; John W. Catron, "Evangelical Networks in the Greater Caribbean and the Origins of the Black Church," *Church History* 79 (2010): 77–114; and Catron, *Embracing Protestantism: Black Identities in the Atlantic World* (Gainesville: University Press of Florida, 2016). On Mary Alley and Sophia Campbell, see also Anne Hart Gilbert to Richard Pattison, June 1, 1804, in *The Hart Sisters: Early African Caribbean Writers, Evangelicals, and Radicals*, ed. Moira Ferguson (Lincoln: University of Nebraska Press, 1993), 63; Natasha Lightfoot, "The Hart Sisters of Antigua: Evangelical Activism and 'Respectable' Public Politics in the Era of Black Atlantic Slavery," in *Toward an Intellectual History of Black Women*, ed. Mia Bay, Farah J. Griffin, Martha

It was much the same with the Moravians, who by 1823 claimed 11,680 members, more than a third of the colony's approximately 29,000 enslaved workers.[17] In the Danish West Indies, the Moravians had pioneered the technique of using "helpers," or black assistants, to translate Christianity to Africans, hold small gender-segregated prayer groups or classes, counsel and reprimand backsliders, and maintain congregational order. As with the Methodists, female helpers and exhorters were essential in this work because in Moravian liturgical practice women learned best from women, as men did from men, and most West Indian congregants were women. Through these techniques African-Caribbean Moravians essentially indigenized Christianity by and among themselves, refuting the idea, as Sylvia Frey and Betty Wood point out, "that the Christianization of slaves was a weapon wielded by planter-slaveholders to make their bondpeople more pliant." In the hands of itinerant black preachers and organizers, Christianity became a seaborne, circum-Caribbean religion. Historian John Catron has documented more than 300 enslaved Moravian Antiguans who, when sold or otherwise transported out of the colony, largely against their will, carried their faith with them to black communities throughout the British and Danish West Indies, North America, and even England between 1757 and 1833. "Accommodating as best they could to local religious practices while bringing their own brand of Afro-Caribbean spirituality with them," Catron contends, they "influenced the development of African American Christianity."[18]

S. Jones, and Barbara Savage (Chapel Hill: University of North Carolina Press, 2015), 53–72.

[17] Thomas, *Telling West Indian Lives,* 124; Barry W. Higman, *Slave Populations of the British Caribbean, 1807–1834* (Baltimore, MD: Johns Hopkins University Press, 1984), 77.

[18] Catron, *Embracing Protestantism,* 91–94. A church ledger lists fifty-five "Helper Brethren" and sixty "Helper Sisters" between 1789 and 1832; see Estate Book, A6, no. 6. On Moravian missions in Antigua, see also Michael Mullin, *Africa in America: Slave Acculturation and Resistance in the American South and British Caribbean, 1736–1831* (Urbana: University of Illinois Press, 1992), 243–49. On the role of helpers and the origins of Moravian missions in the West Indies, see Jon F. Sensbach, *Rebecca's Revival: Creating Black Christianity in the Atlantic World* (Cambridge, MA: Harvard University Press, 2005), and Katharine Gerbner, *Christian Slavery: Conversion and Race in the Protestant Atlantic World* (Philadelphia: University of Pennsylvania Press, 2018). On Moravianism and slavery in other settings, see also Sensbach, *A Separate Canaan: The Making of an Afro-Moravian World in North Carolina, 1763–1840* (Chapel Hill: University of North Carolina Press, 1998); Richard S. Dunn, *A Tale of Two Plantations: Slave Life and Labor in Jamaica and Virginia* (Cambridge, MA: Harvard University Press, 2014), 224–70; Katharine Gerbner, "'They Call Me Obea': German Moravian Missionaries and Afro-Caribbean Religion in Jamaica, 1754–1760," *Atlantic Studies* 12 (2015): 160–78; Jan Hüsgen, *Mission und Sklaverei: Die Herrnhuter Brüdergemeine und die Sklavenemanzipation in Britisch- und Dänisch-Westindien* (Stuttgart: Franz Steiner, 2016). On Moravians in post-emancipation Antigua, see Natasha Lightfoot, *Troubling*

That system was still in place when missionaries wrote Mary Prince's name in their registry. She would have been assigned to a class of women of roughly comparable life circumstances – unmarried, of similar age, relatively new to Christianity, under the leadership of a female helper, probably enslaved but perhaps free, who would guide her through the initiation process and meet with her in "speakings," individual or small group sessions where acolytes expressed concerns or raised other questions about their spiritual state. With only three ministers and their wives to direct the mission and oversee the administrative load for thousands of congregants across the island, most of the day-to-day supervision fell to the helpers, the eyes and ears of the fellowship who operated, in effect, as proxy pastors. Although Sisters Richter, Olufsen, and Sautter were crucial to the mission and to Prince's own development, her account makes no mention of black initiative and leadership, especially by women, within a virtually all African-Caribbean gathered community. Whether this oversight reflected a strategic choice by Prince or her editors is unknown, but it did reinforce a sense of white benevolence and patronage on behalf of the enslaved while diminishing Africans' ability to do for themselves. That same conviction, after all, had produced the antislavery insignia of a chained, kneeling African woman helplessly pleading "Am I Not a Woman and a Sister?" that embodied the public image of the movement. Black Antiguans had long since answered for themselves: yes, they were women and they were sisters.

Sisterhood and brotherhood, however, produced their own tensions within the slave society whose exploitative violence the church, in fact, supported. Planters wanted no troublemakers, and since the 1740s Moravian missionaries had earned their trust by refusing to challenge slavery. One missionary urged planters in 1806 to "have their Negroes instructed in the Christian religion [because] such a general respect prevails in the minds of the Negroes, as to constitute one powerful means to preserve them from the pernicious principles of insurrection and rebellion." As another explained in 1821, "meddling with the outward circumstances of the Negroes is not practicable," and unless missionaries refrained from "interfering with the slaveowners in a manner that would ... defeat the object of the mission," slaveowners would "never submit to any authority vested in the missionary." In fact, Moravian missionaries themselves owned plantations and slaves throughout the British and Danish West Indies, including Antigua, combining religious proselytization with sugar production among the same

Freedom: Antigua and the Aftermath of British Emancipation (Durham, NC: Duke University Press, 2015).

workforce. Planters had come to accept the missionaries as partners in maintaining the slaves' submission. As a result of "cordial cooperation" between planters and missionaries in Antigua, "the Negroes are become more intelligent and their treatment better and more systematical, than in any of the neighboring islands. Flogging with the drivers whip has in great measure given way to the more humane punishment by solitary confinement, which is more dreaded by the Negroes." Though Mary Prince's account contradicts the last assertion, neither does her account acknowledge the strains within a religious culture that championed the slaves' humanity while endorsing their captivity.[19]

Those strains made the helpers lightning rods for others' discontent. Helpers commanded prestige, responsibility, respect and power, which often produced intimidation, resentment, and fear among congregational brothers and sisters, implicating them in the enforcement apparatus for slavery itself. Stationed on many prominent plantations, they were usually appointed from among figures of authority such as drivers and rangers (head drivers). As go-betweens for congregants and missionaries, helpers fielded complaints and mediated disputes, but as disciplinarians and informants they also investigated allegations of misbehavior and reported regularly to the ministers. It was a helper, Walter, for instance, who found out that another man on his plantation, Jacob, had "got Cate a young woman with child" and consulted a conjuror to "get something to drink to cast her belly away – or to make her miscarry, but it did not [have] the intended purpose. He saith Jacob hath been twice before, for the same wicked work."[20]

Though her narrative does not mention the role of helpers, Mary Prince understood their role and participated in the Moravian disciplinary chain of command, as she revealed on the witness stand during the post-publication libel trial of 1833. Under cross-examination by John Wood's lawyer, she said – in testimony that drew laughs from titillated spectators – that she found another woman in bed with her lover, the white Captain Abbot. Pretending to be her friend, the woman had pursued the relationship with Abbot to "plague" Prince, who beat her in retaliation. Prince took her to a Moravian helper for adjudication, but the woman denied the charge, so Prince beat her again. Though

[19] Letter to Governor of Antigua, ca. 1806, EWIC, Box 22, item 7; Br. Stobwasser to Br. Hueffel, April 24, 1821, Mission West Indies Papers, no. 160, Moravian Archives, Northern Province, Bethlehem, Pa.; "Remarks" book, 1814–1819, A11, no.7, under 1815 heading, "Beneba," EWIC. Plantation ownership by Moravian missionaries is discussed in Jan Hüsgen, *Mission und Sklaverei: Die Herrnhuter Brüdergemeine und die Sklavenemanzipation in Britisch- und Dänisch Westindien* (Stuttgart: Franz Steiner, 2016).

[20] "The Remarkable Book," April 1, 1807, p. 1, EWIC A11, no. 5 (this and all subsequent citations to Moravian mission documents in EWIC, Bethlehem, unless noted otherwise).

courtroom spectators fastened onto salacious details about Prince's personal life, her testimony revealed a far more important detail about how the Christian congregational order actually worked that her narrative had not disclosed – namely, the centrality of black congregational leadership, especially among women.[21]

Church disciplinary records are filled with the clashes emanating from the helpers' conflicting roles. One congregant, Elizabeth, "abused" another, Julia, after the latter told helpers about Elizabeth's two lovers. Helpers reported misdeeds, but they took abuse too. After being reprimanded by a helper, Louisa, Sister Cloe "behave very bad towards Louisa H[elper], flying up into her face, when she speak to her when going on in a bad way." Similarly, "Quashy made a dance and abused Anthony H when he exhorted him not to do it" – an instance of a helper meeting resistance when trying to forbid an African cultural expression. Helpers were targeted for revenge: a congregant, George, beat up helper Agnes after she reported his quarrel with another man that brought him a suspension. As intermediate focal points of power in a society riven by extreme imbalances of power, helpers were in a difficult position. On the other hand, they were the key figures in a religious community largely controlled by enslaved people themselves, one that delegated authority, and provided avenues for redress, to Caribbean women.[22]

Whatever spiritual or theological attractions Christianity may or may not have held for enslaved Antiguans, the Moravian Church's strong appeal lay in the sense of community and spiritual family it provided, as well as in the possibility of gaining literacy, both aspects emphasized by Mary Prince. Exclusion, or the threat of exclusion, from that community therefore became the missionaries' chief mechanism to enforce moral order. In egregious cases like assault, rape, or murder, or for repeated infractions, offenders could be banished permanently, in addition to whatever punishment was meted out by the state or the planters, but usually they could gain readmission after a suitable absence, a declaration of contrition, and a heartfelt promise to change. Some, or perhaps many, congregants naturally became cynical about this system even as they learned to navigate within, manipulate, or reject it. When the helpers

[21] Wood v. Pringle, March 1, 1833, in *HMP*, 147.

[22] "Remarks" book, 1814–1819, A11, no. 7 (Elizabeth and Julia); "The Remarkable Book," April 20, 1807, p. 3, A11, no. 5 (Cloe and Louisa); "Remarks" book, 1814–1819, A11, no. 7, under 1815 heading (Quashy and Anthony); Exclusions, 1803–1812, A11, no. 2, under "Weatherell's" heading (George and Agnes); "Remarks" book, 1814–1819, A11, no. 7, p. 44 (Alice and Agnes); "Remarkable Book," May 1820, p. 35 (Magdalena and Ann); Exclusions, 1803–1812, A11 no. 2, under "St. John's" heading (William and Christiana); "Remark Book," 1805–1806, July 1805, p. 39, A11, no. 3 (Hubert and John Anthony).

admonished brother Peter for never coming to church, "He said, I do not care, they may turn me out." Similarly, after Harriet complained to the church that her husband Gabriel had taken another wife, Gabriel replied that he did not care: "tho' he shall be turn'd out, he will have Harriett no more – if one door shut another will open – he even go in the big Church [of England]." As these cases show, congregants sometimes responded defiantly or indifferently to the prospect of suspension. The power of exclusion in the church's disciplinary culture meant, though, that the missionaries spent an enormous amount of time adjudicating and reporting alleged wrongdoing. The archive they left, consisting of thousands of cases, documents their effort to maintain order as well as Antiguans' participation in, and resistance to, that project. Of course, the documents are one-sided: they are written from the missionaries' perspective, and they portray protest and dissent rather than cooperation or quiescence. But from punishments for sexual misconduct to domestic abuse, violence, insubordination, African spiritual practices and slave festivities, the church "court" proceedings take us inside the world of religion and slavery that shaped *The History of Mary Prince.*[23]

Contrary to the missionaries' confident assertion that Christianity made slaves more pliant, the exclusion records show constant opposition towards discipline and humility. The sacred battleground remained a proxy for the larger struggle over slavery and freedom, a conflict that burns in the records with desperate intensity. Working as stewards of the sugar economy, missionaries excluded congregants for all manner of infractions that threatened the plantation order. They banished for running away, stealing, talking back to masters and overseers, refusing to work and inciting trouble. Samuel forged his wife's manumission papers; Susanna used "abusive language for which she was flogged at the Cage"; Noah sold "poison to a Mulatto woman to kill Mrs. Nugent." John Peter "cut off his fingers on purpose" – an offense to God and to the plantation by diminishing his value as a laborer. While such examples could be multiplied many times over, they show enslaved Antiguans' resistance to the Moravian moral order and the intertwining of sacred and profane punishment employed to enforce that order, a point that black parishioners understood. To defy slavery was to defy the slaveholders'

[23] "Remarks" book, 1814–1819, A11, no. 7, under 1815 heading (Peter); "Remarkable Book," April 20, 1807, A11, no. 5, p. 3 (Harriet and Gabriel), and June 20, 1807, p. 12 (Elizabeth and Mary). On the role of church "courts" and slavery in the American South, see Betty Wood, "'For Their Satisfaction or Redress': African Americans and Church Discipline in the Early South," in *The Devil's Lane: Sex and Race in the Early South*, ed. Catherine Clinton (New York and Oxford: Oxford University Press, 1997), 109–23. On punishments for backsliding Moravian parishioners in Jamaica, see Dunn, *Tale of Two Plantations*, 251–54.

Christianity, even to use that Christianity against its practitioners. Nancy "behaves very bad to her mistress, uses unbecoming language, and said among the rest: she will not be received in heaven, if her late father did not leave the house to her." With this lacerating theological taunt, Nancy pointed out white women's vulnerability in patriarchal society, connecting dispossession in property to a loss of personhood, the death of a soul condemned to wander in eternity – a condition enslaved people knew a great deal about.[24]

Black congregants directed an enormous amount of disregard for Christian morality against each other. Not surprisingly, a system of human imprisonment born of, and sustained by, violence reproduced that violence – emotional, verbal, spiritual, physical – among the enslaved towards friends, neighbors, children, lovers, and co-religionists. Competition for power and resources in a society that denied them generated hostility, jealousy, and, fear – normal human emotions that erupted when survival was at stake. People poisoned and stole from each other, raged at one another, destroyed others' belongings, fought desperately in church or in the fields, attacked friends and family members for reporting them. Judith and her daughter Grace carved out a provision ground on a plantation, taking part of a plot belonging to a neighbor, Felix. When he complained about it to church authorities, the women beat him up. Jonas killed Pegg "because she broke his Pott." Violet accused Elsy of stealing "a trifling thing which outraged her so much that she broke everything in Violet's house and miscarried with 5 months." Mary "in a passion put her own child's hand in the fire and burnt it dreadfully because the child (for hunger) picked some eatable from the Neighbor." Plantation drivers and other authorities came in for retribution. Daniel "cut the driver for which he was flogged at the Cage"; after James, a watchman, killed Venus's pig, which had destroyed a patch of cane, enraged workers beat him and threatened to "burn the cane peace belonging to his watch." In this world of fear and retribution, it is no wonder Mary Prince beat the woman who slept with her lover.[25]

[24] Exclusions, 1795–1806, A11, n. 1, under "St. John's" heading (Samuel and Susanna); under "G. Thomas" heading (Crispin); under "Willocks Folly" heading (Noah); under "Dickinsons" heading (John Peter); under "St. John's" heading (William); "Remarks" book, 1814–1819, under 1815 heading (Nancy Blizzard).

[25] "Remarks" book, 1814–1819, A11, no. 7, under 1815 heading, and "The Remarkable Book," A11, no. 5, p. 32 (Judith, Grace, Felix); Exclusions, 1795–1806, A11, no. 1, under "Clearhall" heading (Jonas and Pegg), under "Blackmans" heading (Elsy and Violet), under "St. John's" heading (Mary and child; Daniel); "The Remarkable Book," June 20, 1807, p. 12 (James and Venus).

The Conjuror's Art

Buffeted by malign forces, people sought help from the spirit world. The Christian church, with its talismanic Bible and its martyred prophet, was one source of power. But *The History of Mary Prince* is silent on the influence of African spiritual practices in the author's Caribbean. It is not hard to explain why – the narrative of Christian progress that anti-slavery activists wanted to project had to downplay the lingering power of African-derived spiritualities in the West Indies. Yet church records document Christian congregants' continued reliance on what colonial authorities condemned under the umbrella term "obeah" (or obia), defined by modern scholars as "a wide variety and range of beliefs and practices related to the control or channeling of supernatural/spiritual forces." Never a "unified, coherent system," obeah commonly involved "the recitation or casting of spells and the manipulation of material objects that have been endowed with spiritual qualities" for the purpose of "bringing good fortune, diagnosing illness and healing, finding lost or stolen goods, protecting from harm," and occasionally to direct harmful spirits towards others. "I am sorry to say that too much of this diabolical work still exists in the West Indies," lamented Anne Hart Gilbert, a Methodist free woman of color in early nineteenth century Antigua, identifying obeah with the "sin of witchcraft." Obeah was linked to major slave insurrections throughout the British Caribbean, including a foiled plot in Antigua in 1736, and all the colonies passed statutes – Antigua in 1809 – making the practice a crime.[26]

Diabolical or not, obeah, or conjury, remained as much a part of the spirit world that Prince knew as was the Moravian Church. Though she herself was not born in Africa, Prince, a product of African-Caribbean culture, interacted with Africans every day, some of whom she

[26] Jerome S. Handler and Kenneth M. Bilby, *Enacting Power: The Criminalization of Obeah in the Anglophone Caribbean, 1760–2011* (Kingston, Jamaica: University of the West Indies Press, 2012), 4–5, Anne Hart Gilbert to Richard Pattison, June 1, 1804, in Ferguson ed., *Hart Sisters*, 60. Essential recent works on obeah also include Diana Paton, *The Cultural Politics of Obeah: Religion, Colonialism and Modernity in the Caribbean World* (New York and Cambridge: Cambridge University Press, 2015); Diana Paton and Maarit Forde eds., *Obeah and Other Powers: The Politics of Caribbean Religion and Healing* (Durham, NC: Duke University Press, 2012); Margarite Fernández Olmos and Lizabeth Paravisini-Gebert, *Creole Religions of the Caribbean: An Introduction from Vodou and Santería to Obeah and Espiritismo* (New York: New York University Press, 2nd ed., 2011); Kenneth M. Bilby and Jerome S. Handler, "Obeah: Healing and Protection in West Indian Slave Life," *Journal of Caribbean History* 38 (2004): 153–83; and Randy M. Browne, *Surviving Slavery in the British Caribbean* (Philadelphia: University of Pennsylvania Press, 2017). On the similar practice of conjuring in the American South, see Yvonne Chireau, *Black Magic: Religion and the African American Conjuring Tradition* (Berkeley: University of California Press, 2003).

occasionally mentioned. Despite its relatively small size, Antigua was a major destination for the transatlantic slave trade, receiving some 138,000 Africans between 1670 and 1820, even after Britain ended the legal trade in 1807. High mortality among these captives meant not only that the population struggled to reproduce itself but that African and African-derived cultures were constantly replenished by new arrivals. As with many slave societies in the Americas, Antigua received enslaved laborers from an enormous swath of west and west-central Africa, including Senegambia, Sierra Leone, Windward Coast, Gold Coast, the Bight of Biafra, Angola, and Kongo. A thick Moravian baptismal ledger from Antigua that recorded the ethnic origins or embarkation point of African congregants provides a revealing profile of this group. Of 11,180 brothers and sisters baptized between 1757 and 1833, almost 8,000 were born in the West Indies and 3,255 in Africa. Among the latter group, the largest ethnic concentrations were Igbo (894), Kongo (427), and Coromantee (390), along with significant representations from Popo (200), Mocco (128), Soko (236), Malinke (71), Senegal (50), and Fulbe (47). By the early nineteenth century, the majority of Antiguans, and the majority of Moravian Antiguans, were creole. Though the proportion of African Antiguans continued to decline, their numbers remained significant well into the 1820s when Prince lived there, augmented by the presence of nearly one hundred "apprentices," Africans taken from illegal slave ships and resettled in British colonies as nominally freed people.[27]

Whether African themselves or the descendants of Africans, dozens of Moravian congregants earned banishments for seeking out obeah practitioners and for practicing obeah themselves. In the great majority of cases, people sought answers to mysteries, protection against misfortune and theft, practical gain or the healing of ailments. Catharina "consulted a conjuror man to make her husband to return to her." Christian went to a fortune teller "to hear from him, why his Son would no more go to school." Lucy was flogged at the Cage for trying to find out "who has killed Charles who died on the Consumption." Hannah was punished "for employing Thomy Crosbie a conjurer man to procure a safe delivery for her daughter Louisa; who notwithstanding died in childbirth." Collin wanted to know who stole his goat; Ann Phoebe wondered whether "her

[27] Natasha Lightfoot, "Africa's Legacy on Antigua's Shores: The African Presence in Antiguan Cultural Identity," in *A Herança Africana no Brasile no Caribe: The African Heritage in Brazil and the Caribbean*, ed. Carlos Henrique Cardim and Rubens Gama Dias Filho (Brasilia: Fundação Alexandre de Gusmâo, 2011), 17–32; John W. Catron, "Slavery, Ethnic Identity, and Christianity in Eighteenth-Century Moravian Antigua," *Journal of Moravian History* 14 (2014): 153–78. African "apprentices" in Antigua are enumerated in "The Remarkable Book," A11, no. 5.

Daughter Dinah is pregnant with a black or with a coloured Child." After Maria quarreled with Hagar, accusing her of wanting to take part of her provision ground, she "got some Coals and a Pot from John Drewshill a conjuror Man, which she buried in the ground for that Purpose that Hagar should not take any of her Ground." Though the precise African provenance of any particular practice is impossible to trace, the use of coal buried in a pot to protect a plot of land closely resembles the west-central African use of *minkisi,* ritual objects such as statues, figurines, amulets, and even sacred spaces endowed with divine power to ward off harm.[28]

The Bible itself served as just such an object of mystical divination. In particular, a ritual called "turning the Bible," or "Bible and key," apparently of medieval European origin and widely used in English folk tradition, was believed to reveal the identity of thieves. A congregant, Melinda, was suspended for having gotten another woman "to turn the Bible to know who had stolen her Boards." After Brother Joseph Daniels complained in 1805 that he had been unfairly targeted by a turning of the key, a church report described how the practice worked. "The beard of the key was put into the Bible, then the Bible was tied together by John Jeffrey and his wife Nan: held the key so, that the handle or eye of the key did rest on two of their fingers – each holding the key's eye by one finger – then they called out: 'By St. Peter and St. Paul – was A.B. the thief?' No sooner was Joseph Daniels name mentioned, but the Bible turned in such a manner that it was almost fallen to the ground! O what darkness!" Daniels was cleared of wrongdoing, but the ritual revealed practitioners' ready blending of religious traditions in the use of Christian scriptures and "biblical characters who assumed the roles of the otherworldly arbiters of divine judgment" for magical purposes. As a "conjure book," a "magical formulary for prescribing cures and curses, and for invoking extraordinary powers to reenvision, revise, and transform the conditions of human existence," the Bible fit easily into their constellation of power objects.[29]

[28] Exclusions, 1795–1806, A11, no. 1, under "Boon" heading (Catharina), under "Mackinnens" heading (Christian), under "Ottos 5 Islands" heading (Lucy), under "St. John's" heading (Simon), under "Weatherell" heading (Hannah); "Remarks" book, 1814–1819, A11, no. 7, under 1815 heading (Collin and Ann Phoebe), under 1817 heading (Maria). On *minkisi,* see Chireau, *Black Magic,* 46–49. Obeah items forbidden by West Indian legislation quoted in Handler and Bilby, *Enacting Power,* 20–21.

[29] Exclusions, 1795–1806, A11, no. 1 (Melinda); "Remark Book," 1805–1806, A11, no. 3, Jan. 1805, p. 5 (Joseph Daniels). On "Bible and key," see Handler and Bilby, *Enacting Power,* 130 n. 53. A similar ritual called "turning the sifter" also invoked the names St. Peter and St. Paul; see Ann Hart Gilbert letter to Pattison, June 1, 1804, in Ferguson ed., *Hart Sisters,* 61. On the Bible and key in European tradition, and related rituals in Jewish tradition, see Gideon Bohak, "Catching a Thief: The Jewish Trials of a Christian Ordeal," *Jewish Studies Quarterly* 13 (2006): 11–12. On the Bible as a thief-detection

Graves, and grave dirt, were common themes in obeah accusations. West and west-central African traditions shared a belief in the continued involvement of ancestors and deceased kin in the affairs of the living, and Africans captive in the Americas regarded graves as locations of particular sacred power. Richard "took the Dirt from his Mother's grave," and Jane "called on the Grave of her Brother to make return a Callabash of Corn Flower which was stolen from her, and abused the H Sister Bella who had mentioned it to her." Unfinished conversations between family members resumed at gravesites, where the living blamed and beseeched the dead. "Ann Rosina, hearing that her son Theodore was accused of having stolen some Guineafowl eggs," according to a disciplinary report, "went to her late husband's grave, poured rum upon it, knocked it well with a stick and then reproved the dead man (Philip) for having given her so little when he was alive, but now she wanted him to stand always behind Theodore, until he should see all his enemies dead before him." In the search for practical solutions to everyday problems, the protective supernatural abilities of the departed proved a powerful continuity from Africa to the Caribbean.[30]

Spirits could be placated, manipulated, and deployed in multiple ways, and Moravian congregants also sought and practiced conjuring techniques for punishment and vengeance. Sister Susanna "is constantly quarreling and talking of Obeah work for putting Smiths Coal in her ground to hurt Rebecca who took them and throwed them in the See. When she did it she was frightened, got sick and died soon after." Skilled in African, European, and Indian pharmacological techniques using a variety of medicinal plants, obeah practitioners demonstrated that healing and harming were part of the same circum-Caribbean epistemological universe. Frederick was accused of going to "an obia man to get something to bring his Master away"; after consulting a conjuror to poison cattle on their plantation, Solomon and Frank were punished by being "sold off to a Guineaman." "Caribbean practices did not reference a specific system of belief," explains Pablo Gomez, "but rather embodied a new common ground among many traditions in which the experiential" helped create new ideas about how "power over bodies could be wielded."[31]

method in the US South, see Chireau, *Black Magic,* 26, 62 (quote). On the Bible as "conjure book," see Theophus H. Smith, *Conjuring Culture: Biblical Formations of Black America* (New York: Oxford University Press, 1994), 6, 14–15.

30 "The Remarkable Book,'"A11, no. 5, Jan. 1808, p. 33 (Richard); Exclusions, 1795–1806, A11, no 1, under "St. John's" heading (Jane); "Remark Book, 1805–06," A11, no. 3, Oct. 1805, p. 54 (Ann Rosina).

31 Exclusions, 1795–1806, A11, no. 1, under "James Langt Nibbs" heading (Susanna, and Rebecca); Exclusions, 1803–1812, A11, no. 2, under "York's and Tullideph's" heading (Frederick); "Remark Book, 1805–1806," A11, no. 3, March 1805, p. 9 (Solomon and

No specific evidence in her narrative or in the congregational records connects Mary Prince to obeah; to admit having anything to do with it would have undercut her pious self-portrayal. But obeah very likely formed some element of her spiritual outlook, as her antislavery patron Thomas Pringle hinted in his own supplement to her *History*. Prince, he admitted, was no orthodox Christian: "Her religious knowledge, notwithstanding the pious care of her Moravian instructors in Antigua, is still but very limited," though he considered her imperfect professions of Christianity sincere. Prince's claim to authority rested on her typicality, on knowing what enslaved people thought and felt. By that standard she would have done as millions did – selected, interwove, and rearranged beliefs and practices from multiple sources to fortify herself spiritually in a cruel and capricious world. Historians and anthropologists have applied several terms to the processes by which African cultures intersected and absorbed new influences to reinvent themselves throughout the world of Atlantic slavery – hybridity, creolization, syncretism, and so on. To these we might also add a linguistic term, "code-switching," whereby bilingual or multilingual speakers intersperse words and phrases from two or more languages in speech. The term also connotes the modification of behavior or cultural practices to adapt to specific situations. By both these definitions, Mary Prince's sacred cosmos depended on the daily, flexible shifting between, and splicing of, spiritual and ethical vocabularies in her dealings with white people, fellow slaves, and free people of color.[32]

From this perspective, moreover, the entire *History of Mary Prince* can be construed as an exercise in code-switching. It conceals as much as it reveals. Like all powerless people, Prince would have been skilled in verbal misdirection and evasion, in dissembling to the powerful, in discerning and saying what they wanted to hear while hiding the rest. What black narrators kept to themselves can be termed the "articulate silences" of self-preservation – the rhetorical subterfuge, the deliberate obscuring of the self to divert the prying white gaze. Prince put these skills to good use in her story, lifting the veil covering her spiritual personality only partly in some instances, and not at all in others. She revealed Afro-Caribbean religiosity as British readers imagined it, giving the reassuring impression that black people were becoming more Christian as the result of whites' philanthropic labors. She did not disclose the strong, if disputed, leadership roles of Caribbean women in the church hierarchy, the

Thomas); Pablo F. Gomez, *The Experiential Caribbean: Creating Knowledge and Healing in the Early Modern Atlantic* (Chapel Hill: University of North Carolina Press, 2017), 80.

32 "'Supplement to the *History of Mary Prince*,' By the Original Editor, Thomas Pringle," in *HMP*, 116. For an overview of code-switching, see Penelope Gardner-Chloros, *Code-Switching* (New York: Cambridge University Press, 2009).

religious sphere as a battleground of slave resistance and discipline, and the interplay of deities, traditions, and revelations from multiple transatlantic sources. In the highly selective portrait she provided of her own spirituality and of the devotional world that nurtured her, she drew a sharp distinction between her own morality and the slaveholders' corruption, and she emphasized the need for right-thinking white people to give the slaves Christian guidance and to end slavery. Her editors helped her frame this message, but in its understanding of how to appeal to white readers through words and silences alike, the *History* bears a heavy imprint of Prince's authorship.[33] Emanating from "an African American tradition that is simultaneously conjurational and Christian," her testimony performed what the historian of religion Theophus H. Smith calls an act of "conjuring culture."[34]

In her discussion of religion and Sunday markets, for example, Prince straddled a political line between an evangelical view, popular in abolitionist circles, and the opposite opinion of enslaved West Indians. Throughout the Caribbean, slaves flooded in from the countryside on Sunday bringing produce from their provision grounds to urban markets. As a centerpiece of their amelioration program, evangelicals wanted to promote church attendance by prohibiting both markets and gardening in provision grounds on Sunday. The result of such a ban, one Methodist missionary claimed, "would be to suppress the greatest Moral Evil in the W. Indies and to confer the greatest blessing that England could at present bestow upon her Colonies." Apprehending no such evil, Caribbean slaves opposed the policy, pointing out that it would deprive them of a source of extra cash and that the burdens of plantation labor left Sunday as their only free day. Prince, who earned money selling coffee and yams to ship captains, took both positions. "It is very wrong, I know, to work on Sunday or go to market," she admitted, "but will not God call the Buckra men to answer for this on the great day of judgment – since they will give the slaves no other day?" While seeming to toss a bone to white readers, she turned

[33] I adapt the term "articulate silences" from King-Kok Cheung, *Articulate Silences: Hisaye Yamamoto, Maxine Hong Kingston, Joy Kogawa* (Ithaca, NY: Cornell University Press, 1993). For further development of the idea, see Jon Sensbach, "Born on the Sea from Guinea: Women's Spiritual Middle Passages in the Early Black Atlantic," in *Toward an Intellectual History of Black Women*, 17–34. In this vein, according to Sasha Turner, Prince "gave the appearance of disclosure, of openness about herself, while concealing the deepest parts of herself." Sasha Turner, "The Nameless and the Forgotten: Maternal Grief, Sacred Protection and the Archive of Slavery," *Slavery and Abolition* 38 (2017): 232–50.

[34] Smith, *Conjuring Culture*, 226.

the issue into a judgment against the slavers, showing that enslaved West Indians operated on a higher moral plane.[35]

The Passion of Mary Prince

And yet, that higher plane required Prince to hide the ultimate truth. Her antislavery manifesto did not reveal that the Christianity her readers longed to believe in, at least the version practiced by white missionaries, pirouetted a dance of death with slavery. In emphasizing her own sins, she covered up the sins of Christianity. Specifically, she protected the Moravian Church, and mission Christianity broadly, from public embarrassment by concealing its complicity with slavery. This deception preserved the providential arc of her narrative, but it deflected criticism away from institutions like the church, and the British state itself, towards cruel individuals like the Woods to personalize the fallenness of humankind.

Christianity defined Mary Prince's literary persona, opened a gateway to self-emancipation, and validated her antislavery testimony. And the church betrayed her in the end. Upon learning, in 1826, that by law she was free in England, she fled the Woods' house in London to seek refuge with "the only persons I knew in England," the Moravian missionaries in Hatton Garden. They took her in and directed her to the Anti-Slavery Society, indicating that, despite the church's official refusal to condemn slavery, some congregants sympathized with the antislavery position. This introduction set in motion the chain of events that brought forth *The History*. But Prince paid dearly for her witness. John Wood no longer owned her body, but he still had a say in how the public judged her body. He and his allies in the proslavery press sought to destroy her carefully scripted reputation. An article in the *Bermuda Gazette* in late 1831 ridiculed the Anti-Slavery Society for seeing "purity in a prostitute because she knew how and when to utter the name of the Deity, to turn up the whites of her eyes, and to make a perfect mockery of religion." A long article in *Blackwood's Magazine* in 1832 vilified Prince as a "wretched tool" of antislavery whose immoral character invalidated her claims. And during Wood's libel suit against Pringle the next year, Prince was forced to acknowledge on the witness stand her relationships in Antigua with a free man of color, one Oyksman, and with the white sea captain

35 *HMP*, 82; David Barry Gaspar, "Slavery, Amelioration, and Sunday Markets in Antigua, 1823–1831," *Slavery and Abolition* 9 (1988): 1–28, 3. When markets were finally abolished in March 1831, after Prince had left Antigua, enslaved workers rose in rebellion, setting fire to twenty-two sugar plantations before martial law was imposed and the uprising suppressed.

Abbot, for which she had been excluded from Spring Gardens for seven weeks.[36]

Character assassination became the second soul murder of Mary Prince. She again turned for comfort to the Moravians in London, asking to join their congregation, a request that suggests she retained a sense of genuine spiritual kinship with the group. But after looking into her case, church officials responded: "Mary Prince a Negroe woman from the island of Antigua, has made application to be readmitted to our connexion. It appears she was belonging to the congregation at St. John's, but she was suspended or excluded for immoral conduct. It was decided to tell her, that we could not entertain her request for readmission." Dangling on a scaffold of public shame, shunned even by the Moravians, who forgot or were unaware that she had protected their reputation from public ridicule, she lived out the dénouement of her own passion story foreshadowed by *The History of Mary Prince.* Taking up the sins of the world, she had sacrificed herself to end slavery, yet she could neither sit on a church bench with people who once claimed an interest in her soul, nor even return to her husband, Daniel James, in Antigua without being re-enslaved. Did she seek companionship from London's black community? Was her spirit, in the end, as broken as her body? No one knows. As the Slave Abolition Act, which her testimony had done so much to inspire, took effect in 1834, Prince disappeared from the record and is presumed to have died, in obscurity, soon thereafter.[37]

"They will have work – work – work, night and day, sick or well, till we are quite done up; and we must not speak up nor look amiss, however much we be abused," she testified at the end of *The History*. "And then when we are quite done up, who cares for us, more than for a lame horse? This is slavery." Who cared for Mary Prince, whose passion produced some of the most stirring lines in all antislavery literature? "I tell it to let English people know the truth," she wrote, "and I hope they will never leave off to pray God, and call loud to the great King of England, till all the poor blacks be given free, and slavery done up for evermore."[38]

[36] *HMP,* 94; *Bermuda Royal Gazette,* November 22, 1831, in *HMP,* 155; James Macqueen, "The Colonial Empire of Great Britain. Letter to Earl Grey, First Lord of the Treasury, etc., etc.," *Blackwood's Magazine* (November 1831): 744–64.

[37] Sue Thomas, "New Information on Mary Prince in London," *Notes and Queries* 58 (2011): I: 83.

[38] *HMP,* 102.

12 New Perspectives on Gender and Sexuality in Global Protestantism, 1500–1800

Merry Wiesner-Hanks

This essay discusses three trends in the scholarship on gender and sexuality within Protestant belief and practice around the world: First, the "emotional turn" and its focus on emotional communities, in which Protestants figure prominently, but which also examines emotional genealogies in other cultures, thus allowing for what world and global historians call "reciprocal comparison" in which each case is viewed from the vantage point of the others.[1] Second, processes of migration and movement that are part of the "spatial turn," including the creation and critique of the "Atlantic World" as a site of complex interactions among gender cultures, and various diasporas, a type of movement that over the last decade has become a favorite concept in world and global history. Third, the inclusion of a wider range of actors, including European women and indigenous people of all sexes, in processes of the expansion of Christianity and the transcultural exchange, blending, indigenization, and hybridity that sometimes resulted.

Studies that reach beyond Europe build on those of the process of social discipline within Europe that resulted in part from the religious reformations of the sixteenth century. Such research, which began in the 1990s, increasingly focused on issues involving gender and sexuality, including marriage and divorce, fornication and illegitimacy, clerical sexuality, same-sex relations, and moral crimes.[2] Work on Protestant gender and sexuality from

[1] This methodology was first proposed in Kenneth Pomeranz's *The Great Divergence: China, Europe, and the Making of the Modern World Economy* (Princeton, NJ: Princeton University Press, 2000). For a fuller description, see Gareth Austin "Reciprocal comparison and African history: tackling conceptual Eurocentrism in the study of Africa's economic past," *African Studies Review* 50/3 (2007): 1–28. For examples of its use in the early modern period, see Victor Lieberman, *Strange Parallels: Southeast Asia in Global Context, c. 800–1830, Vol. 2: Mainland Mirrors: Europe, Japan, China, South Asia, and the Islands* (Cambridge: Cambridge University Press, 2009).

[2] R. P-Chia Hsia, *Social Discipline in the Reformation: Central Europe 1550–1750* (London: Routledge, 1992) provides an early general overview. Other works from this era include: Lyndal Roper, *The Holy Household: Women and Morals in Reformation Augsburg* (Oxford: Oxford University Press, 1989); Rosalind Mitchison and Leah Leneman, *Sexuality and Social Control: Scotland 1660–1780* (London: Basil Blackwell, 1989); Eric Josef Carlson, *Marriage and the English Reformation* (Oxford: Oxford University Press, 1994); Joel F. Harrington, *Reordering Marriage and Society in Reformation Germany* (Cambridge: Cambridge University

a global perspective also builds on studies of women and the Reformations, which began in the 1970s and now include hundreds of books and articles, and on the smaller but still substantial number of works that discuss religion and masculinity in the early modern era.[3] Beginning in the 2000s, scholars reached across the Atlantic to examine social discipline and gender issues in the colonial Americas, and a few studies had an even wider geographic range.[4] Since then new theoretical perspectives and new emphases have developed.

The Emotions

Protestants figure prominently in the new scholarship on the history of the emotions, as Jacqueline van Gent explores in Chapter 10 of this volume.[5]

Press, 1995); James R. Farr, *Authority and Sexuality in Early Modern Burgundy* (New York: Oxford University Press, 1995); Michael F. Graham, *The Uses of Reform: "Godly Discipline" and Popular Behavior in Scotland and Beyond 1560–1610* (Leiden: Brill, 1996); Marjorie Keniston McIntosh, *Controlling Misbehavior in England 1370–1600* (Cambridge: Cambridge University Press, 1998); Susanna Burghartz, *Zeiten der Reinheit, Orte der Unzucht: Ehe und Sexualität in Basel während der Frühen Neuzeit* (Paderborn: Schoeningen, 1999); David Turner, *Fashioning Adultery: Gender, Sex, and Civility in England, 1660–1740* (New York: Cambridge University Press, 2002); Garthine Walker, *Crime, Gender and Social Order in Early Modern England* (Cambridge: Cambridge University Press, 2003); Helmut Puff, *Sodomy in Reformation Germany and Switzerland, 1400–1600* (Chicago, IL: University of Chicago Press, 2003).

[3] For an overview of older work on women and gender and the Reformation, see my "Reflections on a quarter century of research on women," in *History Has Many Voices*, ed. Lee Palmer Wandel (Kirksville, MO: Sixteenth Century Journal Publishers, 2003), 93–112. For a comprehensive bibliography, see the website that accompanies my *Women and Gender in Early Modern Europe:* www.cambridge.org/womenandgender, which now features the fourth edition of this book. On masculinity, see Elizabeth Foyster, *Manhood in Early Modern England: Honour, Sex and Marriage* (London: Longman, 1999); Alexandra Shepard, *Meanings of Manhood in Early Modern England* (Oxford: Oxford University Press, 2003); Todd W. Reeser, *Moderating Masculinity in Early Modern Culture* (Chapel Hill: University of North Carolina Press, 2006); Scott H. Hendrix and Susan C. Karant-Nunn eds., *Masculinity in the Reformation Era* (Kirksville, MO: Truman State University Press, 2008); Susan Broomhall and Jacqueline Van Gent eds., *Governing Masculinities in the Early Modern Period* (Aldershot: Ashgate, 2011).

[4] For Protestants in North America, see: Richard Godbeer, *Sexual Revolution in Early America* (Baltimore, MD: Johns Hopkins University Press, 2002); Debra Meyers, *Common Whores, Vertuous Women, and Loveing Wives: Free Will Christian Women in Colonial Maryland* (Bloomington: Indiana University Press, 2003); Dwight Bozeman, *The Precisionist Strain: Disciplinary Religion and Antinomian Backlash in Puritanism to 1638* (Chapel Hill: University of North Carolina, 2004); Thomas A. Foster, *Sex and the Eighteenth-Century Man: Massachusetts and the History of Sexuality in America* (Boston: Beacon, 2006). For an early global work, see Merry E. Wiesner-Hanks, *Christianity and Sexuality in the Early Modern World: Regulating Desire, Reforming Practice* (London: Routledge and Kegan Paul, 2000, 2nd ed. 2010, 3rd ed. 2020).

[5] Overviews of the field include Eiko Ikegami, "Emotions," in *A Concise Companion to History*, ed. Ulinka Rublack (Oxford: Oxford University Press, 2011), 333–353; Barbara H. Rosenwein and Riccardo Cristiani, *What is the History of Emotions?* (London: Polity, 2018).

Barbara Rosenwein's *Generations of Feeling: A History of the Emotions, 600–1700,* for example, expands an idea she had developed earlier, of "emotional communities," which she defines as "groups – usually but not always social groups – that have their own particular values, modes of feeling, and ways to express those feelings."[6] Rosenwein's own specialty is monastic life in the early Middle Ages, so monasteries are one of the "emotional communities" she explores, but so are the people who left them, Martin Luther and Katharina von Bora among them. Susan Karant-Nunn's *The Reformation of Feeling* takes up Rosenwein's idea of "emotional communities," and also builds on her own work on the changes in ritual in the Protestant Reformation to examine the emotional tenor in the programs that Catholicism, Lutheranism, and Calvinism developed for their members, as clergy explicitly and implicitly encouraged their parishioners to make an emotional investment in the faith.[7] To her study of sermons and consideration of the decorative, liturgical, musical, and disciplinary changes made by authorities, Karant-Nunn adds an analysis of the much smaller body of surviving sources from laity that speak to their reception of these instructions and admonitions.

Along with these two major monographs, there are many collections of essays published over the last decade that focus on the interplay between emotion and religion or other aspects of society among Protestants in this era.[8] Almost all of these are about Europe, or sometimes one country in Europe, but Susan Broomhall has just edited a major handbook, *Early Modern Emotions: An Introduction,* with more than fifty brief essays, of which seven go beyond Europe to consider global trading companies, colonies, indigenous/European encounters, and Catholic and Protestant missions.[9] This collection thus begins to examine the emotions in a way recommended by the medical historian of Africa Julie Livingston, who in a 2012 "Conversation" on the historical study of emotions in the *American Historical Review* noted that "if we understand emotions as necessarily social processes, then we must contemplate them within socially complex and dynamic historical worlds. These worlds are linked

[6] Barbara Rosenwein, *Generations of Feeling: A History of the Emotions, 600–1700* (Cambridge: Cambridge University Press, 2015), 3.

[7] Susan Karant-Nunn, *The Reformation of Feeling: Shaping the Religious Emotions in Early Modern Germany* (New York: Oxford University Press, 2010). Karant-Nunn's earlier book was *The Reformation of Ritual: An Interpretation of Early Modern Germany* (London: Routledge, 1997).

[8] See, for example, Susan Broomhall ed., *Gender and Emotions in Medieval and Early Modern Europe: Destroying Order, Structuring Disorder* (London: Routledge, 2015); Susan Broomhall ed., *Spaces for Feeling: Emotions and Sociabilities in Britain, 1650–1850* (London: Routledge, 2015).

[9] Susan Broomhall ed., *Early Modern Emotions: An Introduction* (London: Routledge, 2017).

and at times densely connected through movements of people, goods, ideas."[10]

Much of the early work on gender and sexuality in Protestantism discussed emotions, including envy, fondness, hate, jealousy, love, fear, anger, shame, concern, pride, caring, and friendship, and my own *Christianity and Sexuality in the Early Modern World* even had an emotion in its subtitle – desire. Rarely was this overtly noted, however, but now that some scholarship on religion has begun to frame itself explicitly as the history of the emotions, studies of gender and sexuality can take their own emotional turn. Such a turn should not only frame itself in theories of the emotions based on Western evidence and Western models of feeling, however, particularly in studies that have a comparative or global dimension. In that same 2012 AHR Conversation, both Julie Livingston and the historian of China Eugenia Lean warned about the tendency to use European emotional genealogies as the norm, a result, in part, of the fact that so much of the theorizing about the emotions to date has been based on the West. Thus, along with European theories of the emotions, new work should also consider theoretical formulations and ideas regarding affect, moods, mind, heart, and other concepts (including those for which there are no easy English translations) from other cultures to allow for reciprocal comparison. As van Gent and Jon Sensbach show in this volume, this is particularly important for studies that examine missionary work and colonial Protestantism, both to allow reciprocal comparison and to set up the discussion of the hybrid and blended ideas and practices that resulted when those who converted to Christianity in colonial areas brought their ideas in with them.

For such reciprocal comparisons there is also new scholarship, such as Dror Ze-Evi's *Producing Desire: Changing Sexual Discourse in the Ottoman Middle East,* which analyzes medical, religious, legal, literary, and travel texts, and Walter Andrews and Mehmet Kalpakli's *The Age of Beloveds: Love and the Beloved in Early-Modern Ottoman and European Culture and Society,* one of the few cross-cultural studies of an emotion that directly compares Muslim and Christian works, and has a chapter on love and religion.[11] John Corrigan has edited several collections on religion and emotion that reach across religious traditions to consider the ways in

[10] Nicole Eustace, Eugenia Lean, Julie Livingston, Jan Plamper, William M. Reddy and Barbara Rosenwein, "AHR conversation: the historical study of emotions," *American Historical Review* 117/5 (2012): 1487–1531. The quotation is on p. 1520.

[11] Dror Ze-Evi, *Producing Desire: Changing Sexual Discourse in the Ottoman Middle East* (Berkeley: University of California Press, 2006); Walter Andrews and Mehmet Kalpakli, *The Age of Beloveds: Love and the Beloved in Early-Modern Ottoman and European Culture and Society* (Durham, NC: Duke University Press, 2005).

which emotionality and performances of religious feeling express, reinforce, are shaped by, and challenge social and moral orders.[12]

For East Asia, Paolo Santangelo has used the huge database of Ming and Qing sources that he has developed to examine in several books how emotions and states of mind were expressed.[13] Santangelo's research is not comparative, but this situation offers many parallels with Calvinism. For example, Santangelo finds contradictions between official Confucian values with rigid ethical codes that promoted "virtuous sentiments" and social control, and personal desires for wealth and pleasure. Such contradictions were similar to those of Dutch Calvinists, who, as Simon Schama put it, "lived in constant dread of being corrupted by happiness."[14] Although there were not many Calvinists in China, there were Chinese in many places that the VOC went, so Confucian ideas shaped ideas of the emotions there, at least among merchants and other Chinese immigrants.

In Africa, though most scholarship on the emotions is ethnographic and focuses on the twentieth and now twenty-first centuries, Rhiannon Stephenson has examined the emotions associated with motherhood in Uganda before and after the introduction of Christianity, and David Schoenbrun has explored those associated with experiences of loss and sadness in sixteenth-century Bunyoro, a kingdom in today's Uganda.[15] Here tradition holds that a man named Rukidi established a new dynasty and social order in the sixteenth century after the trauma of a major famine, restoring birth to people and animals in this society where cattle were important currencies in marriage negotiations. Here as well as in China there were emotional valences that can be compared with those of Calvinists who were establishing new social orders at the same time: "Rukidi's traditions deployed affective language, told of emotional events, and depicted bodily displays of emotions that respected silent, calm self-control in the service of a radical change in ritual practice."[16]

[12] John Corrigan ed., *Religion and Emotion: Approaches and Interpretations* (Oxford: Oxford University Press, 2004); *The Oxford Handbook of Religion and Emotion* (Oxford: Oxford University Press, 2008); *Feeling Religion* (Durham, NC: Duke University Press, 2018).

[13] Paolo Santangelo, *Sentimental Education in Chinese History: An Interdisciplinary Textual Research on Ming and Qing Sources* (Leiden: Brill, 2003); *From Skin to Heart: Perceptions of the Emotions in Traditional Chinese Culture* (Wiesbaden: Harrasowitz, 2006); Paolo Santangelo and Donatella Guida eds., *Love, Hatred, and Other Passions: Questions and Themes on Emotions in Chinese Civilization* (Leiden: Brill, 2006).

[14] Simon Schama, *The Embarrassment of Riches: An Interpretation of Dutch Culture in the Golden Age* (New York: Vintage, 1997), jacket summary.

[15] Rhiannon Stephens, *A History of African Motherhood: The Case of Uganda, 700–1900* (Cambridge: Cambridge University Press, 2015); David L. Schoenbrun, "A mask of calm: emotion and founding the Kingdom of Bunyoro in the 16th century," *Comparative Studies in Society and History* 55/3 (2013): 634–64.

[16] Schoenbrun, "A mask of calm," 639.

In South Asia, the traditions of personalized affective piety generally known as *bhakti* have also been examined from the perspective of the emotions, especially in the Vaishnavism of the spiritual teacher Chaitanya Mahaprabhu (1486–1534), which advocated loving devotion to an avatar of Vishnu (often Krishna), in which Krishna's divine acts were understood to evoke intense love and spiritual delight.[17] Chaitanya Mahaprabhu's most fervent followers believed that he became the goddess Radha, and, like her, glowed golden in his longing for Krishna. Although to my knowledge no Protestants glowed golden, the Society of Friends quaked (or were accused by their opponents of doing so), the Methodists wept and yelled (or were accused by their opponents of doing so), and the Moravians expressed delight in crawling inside Christ's side wound to bathe in his blood. Followers of Chaitanya Mahaprabhu may well have grasped the power of these notions of intense joy.

Emotions are at the heart of religious conversion, as Jacqueline van Gent and Spencer Young have argued eloquently in a special issue of the *Journal of Religious History*.[18] Although the new *Oxford Handbook of Religious Conversion* oddly does not have a chapter that discusses emotions and conversion, some new scholarship on the process of conversion does examine how emotional practices and feelings shaped relationships between missionaries and prospective converts and among converts themselves.[19] The essays in *Emotions and Christian Missions* examine how external emotional practices such as hymn-singing or prayer so fervent that it led to tears, along with interior feelings such as pity, joy, and frustration, shaped relationships between missionaries and prospective converts, both European and indigenous.[20] Methodists on both sides of the Atlantic, for example, were criticized for overly emotionalized pious practices, in the words of the bishop of London, of "sudden Agonies, Roarings and Screamings, Tremblings, Droppings-down, Tavings, and Madnesses." Such criticisms were often gendered, as in the comments of an English observer of German Methodists in Philadelphia, who noted that there was "a hue and cry from all sides, particularly from the wenches."[21] Because of such behavior, both male and female

[17] Guy L. Bek, *Alternative Krishnas: Regional and Vernacular Variations on a Hindu Deity* (Albany: State University of New York Press, 2012).

[18] *Journal of Religious History* 39/4 (2015): 461–630, special issue on "Emotions and Conversion," ed. Jacqueline Van Gent and Spencer Young.

[19] Lewis R. Rambo and Charles E. Farhadian eds., *Oxford Handbook of Religious Conversion* (Oxford: Oxford University Press, 2014).

[20] Karen Vallgårda, Claire Mclisky, and Daniel Midena eds., *Emotions and Christian Missions: Historical Perspectives* (London: Palgrave, 2015).

[21] Quoted in Monique Scheer, "German 'shouting Methodists': religious emotion as a transatlantic cultural practice," in *Emotions and Christian Missions*, 53, 54.

Methodists were dubbed “silly women” by their detractors. Whether in colony or metropole, and in whatever language they worshipped, Methodists formed a shared emotional community, demonstrating Eugenia Lean’s point: “throughout history, emotions do not solely develop over time, but move and traverse over space, small-scale and large, and in messy, unexpected ways that do not conform to civilizational, regional, national, or local boundaries.”[22]

The Spatial Turn

Lean’s comment points to the second major trend that has begun to shape scholarship on gender and sexuality in global Protestantism and could do so more explicitly in the future: the spatial turn. Over the last several decades, scholars in many disciplines have examined borders and their permeability, connections and interactions, cities and frontiers, actual and imagined spatial crossings, migration and displacement, and the natural and built environment. Within world and global history, scholars have developed history with many shapes: the ball that is the world, long thin trade routes, the barbells or triangles of comparative studies, the fuzzy lines of borderlands, the daisy-like shapes of diasporas and the spread of ideas, the knotted webs of networks, the tangles of migration and trade. Sometimes these shapes are unacknowledged, but sometimes they are explicitly highlighted; the spatial turn has made us aware of all of them. Some of these shapes have become their own sub-fields of world and global history, such as diasporic history, *histoire croisee,* and borderlands history.

Implicit in this scholarship is an awareness that spatialization is as much a cognitive process and epistemological strategy – that is, a way of perceiving, producing, and organizing knowledge – as it is a geo-political formation.[23] For example, Ann Christensen notes that two genres of advice books designed for the same audience of bourgeois English merchants, guides to married life and guides to travel, prescribe very different proper places for the married man. In the domestic conduct manuals, he is to be at home, asserting patriarchal order, with only occasional

[22] “AHR conversation,” 1518.

[23] For a brief introduction to the spatial turn in many disciplines, see Jo Guldi, “What is the spatial turn?” at Spatial Humanities: A Project of the Institute for Enabling Geospatial Scholarship, University of Virginia Library http://spatial.scholarslab.org/spatial-turn (accessed April 7, 2018). Her discussion of the spatial turn in history notes that scholars consider various developments in the Renaissance and early modern period, such as linear perspective, invented utopias, geometric gardens, the building of dikes and canals, and extensive sea travel, as essential in creating the modern understanding of landscape and the place of humans in it.

absences, and in the travel guides he is to be at sea or in a foreign destination, overseeing trade and business. Such manuals, many of which went through multiple editions so were clearly read, ignore each other just as they ignore potential conflicts between business and family life in a globalizing economy.[24]

Of the shapes in early modern history, the "Atlantic world" has been arguably the most important; once viewed as a radical departure from separate histories of Europe and North America, it is now seen as self-evident, and thus also open to revision and critique.[25] The overwhelming dominance of Britain in Atlantic world studies led Kenneth Mills and Allan Greer to point out about a decade ago that there was a Catholic Atlantic as well, though Jorge Cañizares-Esguerra has argued both in *Puritan Conquistadors* and an article in a recent issue of the *Archive for Reformation History* that the idea that there were separate Catholic and Protestant Atlantics is itself a product of the Reformation, and that "the histories of Protestants and Catholics in the Americas are in fact deeply entangled."[26]

In a series of articles on gender, Susan Amussen and Allyson Poska have also used the word "entangled" to describe the Atlantic world, arguing that trans-imperial approaches allow one to develop a more complex understanding. They note that "the Americas became the stage for complex interactions among gender cultures with competing norms and standards, more informed by the realities of daily life and the gender expectations of non-European peoples than by European patriarchal ideals ... This dialectic ultimately limited the influence of European patriarchy and contributed to the creation of the rich cultural

[24] Ann Christensen, "Guides to marriage and 'needful travel' in early modern England," in *Mapping Gendered Routes and Spaces in the Early Modern World*, ed. Merry Wiesner-Hanks (Aldershot, UK: Ashgate, 2015), 271–90.

[25] Atlantic history began at Johns Hopkins University under Jack Greene in the 1970s and under Bernard Bailyn at Harvard in the 1980s, and now has its own scholarly journal, *Atlantic Studies* (www.tandfonline.com/toc/rjas20/current), print and online handbooks, companions, and bibliographies (e.g., www.oxfordbibliographies.com/page/atlantic-history#4) and even a Wikipedia page: https://en.wikipedia.org/wiki/Atlantic_history. Reviews and critiques of the idea of the "Atlantic world" include: William O'Reilly, "Genealogies of Atlantic history," *Atlantic Studies* 1 (2004): 66–84; Alison Games, "Atlantic history: definitions, challenges, opportunities," *American Historical Review* 11/3 (2006): 741–57; Peter A. Coclanis, "Atlantic World or Atlantic/World," *William and Mary Quarterly* 63/4 (2006): 725–42; Philip D. Morgan ed., *Atlantic History: A Critical Appraisal* (New York: Oxford University Press, 2009).

[26] Allan Greer and Kenneth Mills, "A Catholic Atlantic," in *The Atlantic in Global History, 1500–2000*, ed. Jorge Cañizares-Esguerra and Erik R. Seeman (Upper Saddle River, NJ: Pearson Prentice Hall, 2007), 3–19; Jorge Cañizares-Esguerra, *Puritan Conquistadors: Iberianizing the Atlantic, 1550–1700* (Stanford, CA: Stanford University Press, 2006) and "How the 'Reformation' invented separate Catholic and Protestant Atlantics," *Archiv für Reformationsgeschichte* 108 (2017): 245–54(quotation 247).

tapestry of the Atlantic world."[27] Male travel was not simply a recommended activity, as it was in the advice books Christensen studies, but a reality. This resulted in a large proportion of female-headed households, a high level of births out of wedlock, and interracial marriages in which indigenous practices regarding property and child-rearing were followed, none of which fit with the European norms of patriarchal families.

Several article collections on women and religion reach across the Atlantic and consider both Protestants and Catholics, but most of the monographs and articles about colonial Christianity published in the last decade are still about Protestants *or* Catholics, and usually only about one colonial power.[28] Mark Häberlein opens his chapter on Protestantism outside Europe in the new *Oxford Handbook of the Protestant Reformations* with the statement that "for a long time, the study of a single religious movement – New England Puritanism – has dominated the literature on Protestantism outside Europe . . . but during the last three decades historians have moved beyond this 'Puritan paradigm' to explore the transatlantic and global connections of early modern Protestantism."[29] Carla Pestana's *Protestant Empire* and Scott Dixon's *Protestants: A History from Wittenberg to Pennsylvania* are the only monographs in Häberlein's notes to actually do this, however, and five of the eleven books in his brief list of further reading are about Puritans in New England.[30] Thus the move beyond Puritanism and exploration of connections may remain more of a goal than an accomplishment, a situation Philip Benedict also discusses in an article in the *Archiv für Reformationsgeshichte*, "Global? Has the Reformation even gotten transnational yet?"[31] Benedict points to the continuing weight of national histories, language barriers, and the fact that German history is often the privileged point of reference as powerful

27 Susan Amussen and Allyson Poska, "Restoring Miranda: gender and the limits of European patriarchy in the early modern Atlantic World," *Journal of Global History* 7/3 (November 2012): 342–63 and " Shifting the frame: trans-imperial approaches to gender in the Atlantic World," *Early Modern Women: An Interdisciplinary Journal* 9/1 (2014): 3–23. Quotation from "Restoring Miranda," 346, 363.

28 The collections are Susan E. Dinan and Debra Meters eds., *Women and Religion in Old and New Worlds* (London: Routledge, 2001); Daniella Kostroun and Lisa Vollendorf eds., *Women, Religion and the Atlantic World, 1600–1800* (Toronto: University of Toronto Press, 2009); Emily Clark and Mary Laven eds., *Women and Religion in the Atlantic Age* (Farnham, UK: Ashgate, 2013).

29 Mark Häberlein, "Protestantism outside Europe," *Oxford Handbook of the Protestant Reformations*, 350.

30 Carla Pestana, *Protestant Empire: Religion and the Making of the British Atlantic World* (Philadelphia: University of Pennsylvania Press, 2010); Scott Dixon, *Protestants: A History from Wittenberg to Pennsylvania* (London: Wiley-Blackwell, 2010).

31 Philip Benedict, "Global? Has the Reformation even gotten transnational yet?" *Archiv für Reformationsgeschichte* 108 (2017): 52–62.

structural forces that work against broader views of the Reformation, though he highlights histories of tolerance as an area in which there has already been good transnational work and ends by calling for more work that uses a wider lens. Benedict's opinion is countered somewhat by a forum on globalizing early modern German history in *German History*, in which the participants note ways in which early modern Germanists frequently write history that crosses borders, both territorial and confessional, including studies of shared infrastructures of communication, transoceanic/transcontinental flows of goods and ideas, and missionary ventures.[32] It is also countered by new comparative and transatlantic work on Quakers, Pietists, and Moravians, about which more below.

Along with the Atlantic world, another spatial configuration that is becoming more widely adopted is the diaspora, that is, any movement, migration, or scattering of a people away from an established or ancestral homeland. Over the last decade diaspora has become a favorite concept in world and global history, as, to quote Rogers Brubaker, there has been a "'diaspora' diaspora, a dispersion of the term in semantic, conceptual and disciplinary space."[33] Diasporic studies is now its own field, with a transnational research center – The International Institute for Diasporic and Transcultural Studies – and two journals, *Transtext(e)s-Transcultures: A Journal of Global Cultural Studies* and *Diaspora: A Journal of Transnational Studies*.[34] Understanding early modern migrations for religious reasons, such as those in the new collection *Religious Diaspora in Early Modern Europe* or in Nicholas Terpstra's *Religious Refugees in the Early Modern World*, as diasporas offers new ways to think about how certain kinds of movements and the experience of exile shaped many aspects of life, including sexual relations and social structures.[35] For example,

[32] " Forum: Globalizing early modern German history," with Renate Dürr, R. Po-Chia Hsia, Carina Johnson, Ulrike Strasser, and Merry Wiesner-Hanks, *German History* 31/3 (2013): 366–82.

[33] Rogers Brubaker, "The 'diaspora' diaspora," *Ethnic and Racial Studies* 28/1 (2005): 1–19. Quotation on p. 1.

[34] The International Institute for Diasporic and Transcultural Studies (IIDTS) – a transnational institute incorporating Jean Moulin University (Lyons), the University of Cyprus, Sun Yat Sen University (Guangzhou), and Liverpool Hope – describes itself as "a dedicated research network operating in a transdisciplinary logic and focused on cultural representation (and auto-representation) of diasporic communities throughout the world." It sponsors the trilingual publication *Transtext(e)s-Transcultures: A Journal of Global Cultural Studies* (https://journals.openedition.org/transtexts/). *Diaspora: A Journal of Transnational Studies* is published by the University of Toronto: https://utpjournals .press/loi/diaspora.

[35] Timothy Fehler, Greta Grace Kroeker, Charles H. Parker, and Jonathan Ray eds., *Religious Diaspora in Early Modern Europe: Strategies of Exile* (London: Pickering and Chatto, 2014); Nicholas Terpstra, *Religious Refugees in the Early Modern World: An Alternative History of the Reformation* (Cambridge: Cambridge University Press, 2015).

diasporic religious communities, including Protestant ones such as French Huguenots in the Americas, English Puritans in Massachusetts, and Salzburg Lutherans in Prussia, all had to decide how they would handle marriage with those not in the group, balancing group cohesion and common traditions against demographic and political realities.

Among the various diasporas that have been part of this expansion of the concept has been the "queer diaspora," which scholars use to describe the movements of those whose sexual and/or gender identities and presentation may be seen by some as non-normative.[36] Studies of queer diasporas have so far focused on the era after World War II, but the movement of the Moravians in the eighteenth century from their homelands in central Europe was certainly a diaspora, and many of their marital practices and sexual ideas were regarded by most of their contemporaries as non-normative. Decisions on marriage partners for the Moravians were made by a combination of the Elders' Conference and a lottery seen as guided by the hand of God, not by families or the individuals themselves. Nicolas von Zinzendorf, the founder of the Moravians, taught that union with Christ could be experienced through sexual intercourse between husband and wife who were true believers, a physical re-enactment of marriage with Christ. In the late 1740s, some Moravians, including Zinzendorf's son Christian Renatus von Zinzendorf, interpreted this to mean intercourse outside of marriage as well. Christ was proclaimed as the "dear husband" of all believers by Moravians on both sides of the Atlantic, and in 1748, Christian declared all the single men in the Moravian community at Herrnhaag in Germany to be women, thus more open to marriage with Christ. As Paul Peucker has suggested, desire for Christ was not simply an erotic metaphor, but for a brief period was expressed through single men kissing one another and perhaps even engaging in same-sex intercourse. Moravian devotion at this point focused on the side wound of Christ, the wound left by the spear of a Roman soldier as Christ hung on the cross, with hymns, sermons, and writings urging believers to lick or bathe in its blood and go inside the side wound to gain access to Christ's heart. As men sang that they wanted to enter the side wound and walked through a giant papier-maché model of the wound, they may have also engaged in ritualized same-gender sex as a way of representing love and marriage with Christ.[37] Such ideas and

36 Cindy Patton and Benigno Sánchez-Eppler eds., *Queer Diasporas* (Durham, NC: Duke University Press, 2000), and Gayatri Gopinath, *Impossible Desires: Queer Diasporas and South Asian Public Cultures* (Durham, NC: Duke University Press, 2005).

37 On Moravian marriage and gendered theology, see Aaron Spencer Fogleman, *Jesus is Female: Moravians and the Challenge of Radical Religion in Early America* (Philadelphia:

practices quickly came to be seen as non-normative by Moravians themselves as well as by other Protestants, and the leaders tried to erase all memory of them. Stories of Moravian sexual and gender peculiarities and excess did not disappear, however, so that thinking about the movements of the Moravians as a "queer diaspora" might not be too far a stretch.

Not all travels are diasporas, of course, and the spatial turn has led to more consideration of all types of movements, especially in looking at the early modern period, that era when unprecedented numbers of people traveled new routes, all of which were gendered. Voluntary and forced migrations shifted gender balances, necessitating new forms of marriage and other social and sexual relationships. Travel and commerce generally involved more men than women, which affected the families left behind at one end of a route, and those formed at the other end or somewhere along the way. But women traveled as well, and they did so more than has previously been recognized. Gender also figured in understandings of spatialized activities, from dissecting the interior of the body to traveling across the globe. Recent scholarship has examined all of these.

Within the scholarship on movement and migration there are also new twists, including an emotional turn within the spatial turn. The essays in Tony Ballantyne's and Antoinette Burton's *Moving Subjects,* for example, assess ways in which distance and movement shaped intimacy, and in which intimacy, the prospect of intimacy, or the desire for intimacy, influenced the formation of imperial power. The intimate served, in the words of the editors, "not merely as a domain of power but as one of the technologies available to colonizer and colonized alike in the struggle over colonial territory, imperial goods, and the meanings of global aspirations."[38] Some of these struggles involving intimate relationships were about religion as well as empire. For example, in the late seventeenth century Protestant ministers and officials in the English colony of Fort St. George on the east coast of India became alarmed that merchants and soldiers were taking wives and sexual partners from among Eurasian families in the nearby Portuguese colony of St. Thome, families that had themselves resulted from earlier marriages between Portuguese men and local women. These women were Catholic and their children

University of Pennsylvania Press, 2007) and Paul Peucker, *A Time of Sifting, Mystical Marriage and the Crisis of Moravian Piety in the Eighteenth Century* (University Park: Pennsylvania State University Press, 2015). On same-sex relations, see pp. 124–28 in Peucker and also Paul Peucker, "Inspired by flames of love: homosexuality, mysticism, and Moravian brothers around 1750," *Journal of the History of Sexuality* 15 (2006): 30–64.

[38] Tony Ballantyne and Antoinette Burton eds., *Moving Subjects: Gender, Mobility, and Intimacy in an Age of Global Empire* (Urbana: University of Illinois Press, 2009), quotation on p. 12.

were baptized as Catholic by French and Portuguese friars, which the English Protestant clergy and officials saw as a threat to maintaining both religious and imperial boundaries. The English East India Company urged such women to convert or risk expulsion, and also promoted marriages between Englishmen and "native women," encouraging financial rewards be paid to the women as long as the resulting children were baptized Protestant. In the minds of English officials, fears of the "popish menace" to English Protestant identity represented by the Portuguese Eurasian women's Catholicism were stronger than anxieties about skin color or racial background.[39]

In *Intimate Strangers: Friendship, Exchange and Pacific Encounters,* Vanessa Smith explores the meaning of friendship in the Pacific in the late eighteenth century, when a whole series of European explorers reported that the first word they heard from the various peoples they encountered was *taio,* friend.[40] She engages in reciprocal comparison, unpacking general ideas about intimacy, friendship, gift-giving, and emotions that Pacific Islanders and Europeans carried with them, and then examines particular individuals in situations that brought these emotional communities together. This includes Oceanians who joined European voyages, such as Ajutoru who accompanied Bougainville to France, and missionaries such as William Crook, who came to the Marquesas in 1797 as part of the first London Missionary Society voyage to the Pacific. Crook's Christian views of friendship, captured in the most influential early modern work on the subject, the Anglican cleric Jeremy Taylor's *Discourse of the Nature, Offices, and Measures of Friendship, with Rules of Conducting It* (1657), emphasized disinterestedness and charity, and his desire as a missionary to spread the Word meant he was more interested in effecting cultural transformation than engaging in cultural exchange. Thus, Crook saw the Oceanic practice of ceremonially exchanging names to seal friendship as too instrumental and particular, and so did this only rarely. He ultimately left the Pacific in disappointment after less than two years, having made no friends or converts, retrospectively reporting that there was little conjugal or paternal affection and that "real disinterested friendship, or even genuine compassion, is almost literally unknown."[41]

39 Adrian Carton, " 'Faire and well-formed': Portuguese Eurasian women and symbolic whiteness in early colonial India," in Ballantyne and Burton, *Moving Subjects,* 231–51.

40 Vanessa Smith, *Intimate Strangers: Friendship, Exchange and Pacific Encounters* (Cambridge: Cambridge University Press, 2010).

41 William Pascoe Crook, *An Account of the Marquesas Islands 1797–1799,* quoted in Smith, p. 277.

Intimacy has also emerged as a common way to frame studies of intra-family relations within the context of colonialism. In *The Inner Life of Empires,* Emma Rothschild examines intimacy among family members, as she surveys the ideas, sentiments, and values of a large Scottish family, the Johnstones, the male members of which lived around the globe in the eighteenth century, and all of whom wrote often to one another "continually evaluating their own and other people's inner sentiments in the light of their outer circumstances." Rothschild sets this microhistory within the context of the larger story of empire and Enlightenment, but pays great attention to what the brothers and sisters were thinking and feeling, noting that "the distinction between the inner and the outer life, or between an interior, private existence of the mind and an exterior universe of events and circumstances, is very difficult to identify in the lives of the Johnstones (as it is in our own lives)."[42] Although several male members of the family were elders in the Church of Scotland or vicars in the Church of England, and a number of family members married into clerical families, most of the Johnstones say very little about religious observance or belief except at points when someone had died or they were contemplating their own death. Thus in terms of emotions, in Rothschild's view, "the Johnstones were a family in whose lives religion played an inconspicuous role."[43]

In *Atlantic Families: Lives and Letters in the Later Eighteenth Century,* Sarah Pearsall argues that the ideal of a loving family life emerged because of the "grim reality" that many families were separated by overseas ventures, which restructured and reconstituted families and societies.[44] Like Rothschild, she finds that by the late eighteenth century letters only barely mentioned religion, and were instead couched in the language of sentiment and sensibility. By contrast, seventeenth-century letters emphasized faith more than feeling, invoking the need to depend on God, who will protect family members far away and assist in hoped-for reunions. Margaret Winthrop, for example, writing from Massachusetts to her husband John in England in 1630, opened the letter, "Deare Husband, I received thy sweet letter, and doe bless God for all his mercys to us, in the continuation of thy healthe and welfayre." She included a prayer, "I beseech the Lord to send us a comfortable meetinge, and

[42] Emma Rothschild, *The Inner Life of Empires: An Eighteenth-Century History* (Princeton, NJ: Princeton University Press, 2011), quotations p. 9 and 7–8.

[43] Rothschild, *Inner Life of Empires*, 231.

[44] Sarah Pearsall, *Atlantic Families: Lives and Letters in the Later Eighteenth Century* (Oxford: Oxford University Press, 2008). For examples of transatlantic Catholic family life, see Jane E. Mangan, *Transatlantic Obligations: Creating the Bonds of Family in Conquest-era Peru and Spain* (New York: Oxford University Press, 2016).

thus with my best love to thy self... and all the rest of our friends, I desyre the Lord to send thee a good end to all thy troubles."[45]

One of the key developments in the study of movement over the last decade is a recognition that there were more women travelling than we had assumed earlier.[46] Among Protestants, Quaker women have long been recognized as peripatetic, preaching throughout England, Ireland, the English colonies in the New World, and occasionally elsewhere in the world.[47] English Quakers are well represented among the hundreds of women discussed in the German anti-Pietist clergyman Johann Feustking's polemical *Gynaeceum Haeretico Fanaticum* (1704), with its 700 pages describing, as his full title reads, the "false prophetesses, Quakeresses, fanatics and other sectarian and frenzied female persons through whom God's church is disturbed."[48] In *Daughters of Light,* Rebecca Larson examines sixty-four Quaker women who journeyed across the Atlantic as ministers and several hundred who preached in either North America or Britain, discussing who they were, how they understood their religious authority, where they traveled, and the role they played in the Quaker and wider communities. She argues that they had a strong sense of inward assurance and godly calling, which allowed them to overcome patriarchal gender expectations of domesticity and silence. They were supported in their travels by women's monthly meetings, sometimes over the objections of the women's spouses.[49]

45 Margaret Winthrop to John Winthrop, "Groton, ca. February 15, 1629/30" quoted in Pearsall, *Atlantic Families*, 83.

46 Recent scholarship on this includes Allyson Poska, *Gendered Crossings: Women and Migration in the Spanish Empire* (Albuquerque: University of New Mexico Press, 2016); Patricia Akhimie and Bernadette Andrea eds., *Travel and Travail: Early Modern Women, English Drama, and the Wider World* (Lincoln: University of Nebraska Press, 2019).

47 Catherine M. Wilcox, *Theology and Women's Ministry in Seventeenth-Century English Quakerism: Handmaids of the Lord* (London: E. Mellen, 1995); Margaret Hope Bacon ed., *Wilt Thou Go on My Errand?: Journals of Three 18th Century Quaker Women Ministers: Susanna Morris 1682–1755, Elizabeth Hudson 1722–1783, Ann Moore 1710–1783* (Wallingford, PA: Pendle Hill Press, 1994).

48 Johann Heinrich Feustking, *Gynaeceum Haeretico Fanaticum, Oder Historie und Beschreibung Der Falschen Prophetinnen, Quäkerinnen, Schwärmerinnen, und anderen sectirischen und begeisterten Weibes-Personen...* (Frankfurt, Leipzig 1704). For more on Feustking, see my "Confessional histories of women and the Reformation from the eighteenth century to the twenty-first," in *Archaeologies of Confession: Writing the German Reformation, 1517–2017*, ed. Carina L. Johnson, David M. Luebke, Marjorie Plummer, and Jesse Sponholz (New York: Berghahn, 2017), 89–110. Feustking's book is a largely untapped source for the history of the Atlantic world, as for some of the women he mentions no other source provides their names or describes their ideas and travels in such detail.

49 Rebecca Larson, *Daughters of Light: Quaker Women Preaching and Prophesying in the Colonies and Abroad, 1700–1775* (Chapel Hill: University of North Carolina Press, 2000).

Similarly, in *Female Friends and the Making of Transatlantic Quakerism, 1650–1750*, Naomi Pullin examines the lives and social interactions of Quaker women in the British Atlantic between 1650 and 1750, both those who traveled and those who did not, focusing in particular on bonds of companionship among women in the household, community, and mission ventures.[50] Katharine Evans and Sara Cheevers, for example, who were held captive together by the Inquisition on Malta between 1658 and 1662, emphasized in their joint account of their imprisonment the way their intense connection with one another and spiritual unity had allowed them to prevail over their captors. Because male as well as female Quakers generally traveled in same-sex partnerships modelled on those of the early apostles, this language of shared spiritual alliance and close bonds was expressed by Quaker men as well, making their masculinity somewhat distinctive from that of other Protestants.[51] In contrast to earlier scholarship on women's roles in Quakerism, which point to increasing restrictions, both Larson and Pullin argue that Quaker women ministers enjoyed greater acceptance in both the Quaker and wider non-Quaker world by the middle of the eighteenth century.

Quaker women who traveled have recently been joined as objects of study by Calvinist Dutch women, who, as Susanah Shaw Romney has demonstrated in *New Netherland Connections*, formed an essential part of the networks created by religion, family, trade, friendship, neighborhoods, and godparentage that bound together the Dutch Atlantic.[52] Unmarried servants, soldiers' and sailors' wives, middling-status artisans' wives, poor young widows, and many other women bounced from one port and one ship and sometimes one spouse to another, loaning money, serving as business partners, and trading in goods as they forged a new imperial society. In New Amsterdam and the Hudson Valley, for example, Dutch Protestant women traded the baked goods and beer they produced with their Munsee, Mahican, and Mohawk neighbors for beaver pelts and maize. One Dutch woman, Sara Kierstade, repeatedly served as a go-between and translator at business and treaty negotiations between the Dutch and the Munsee; she had become fluent in Munsee and was trusted by both sides.

[50] Naomi Pullin, *Female Friends and the Making of Transatlantic Quakerism, 1650–1750* (Cambridge: Cambridge University Press, 2018).

[51] Other new scholarship on gendered friendship includes Amanda E. Herbert, *Female Alliances: Gender, Identity and Friendship in Early Modern Britain* (New Haven, CT: Yale University Press, 2014) and Amyrose McCue Gill and Sarah Rolfe Prodan eds., *Friendship and Sociability in Premodern Europe: Contexts, Concepts, and Expressions* (Toronto: Centre for Reformation and Renaissance Studies, 2014).

[52] Susanah Shaw Romney, *New Netherland Connections: Intimate Networks and Atlantic Ties in Seventeenth-Century America* (Chapel Hill: University of North Carolina Press, 2015).

German Pietist women were also involved in global endeavors, generally as suppliers of funds and prayers of support from Europe, but occasionally also as travelers and settlers. As the work especially of Ulrike Gleixner is showing, women were active participants in the Pietist project of universal conversion outlined by August Francke in his "Project for a *Seminario Universale*" in 1701, which called for conversion "inside and outside Germany, indeed everywhere in Europe and all other parts of the World."[53] Francke's call to global evangelism, combined with new colonial ventures by Protestant powers, allowed well-off women to extend their longstanding patterns of support of pious pursuits beyond Europe. With the opening of the Jesuit mission in China in 1692 and a number of high-profile conversions to Catholicism among the princely classes at home, German Protestant women felt their efforts in support of their own confession were even more important. Their networks of social patronage could extend across the seas as they became godmothers for newly-baptized believers in India – whose names they learned in mission newsletters – and paid for the schooling of able indigenous pupils who could eventually become catechists. These new citizens in the Kingdom of God would in turn expand the global mission even further, evangelization that would not simply lead people to Christ but could help bring about Christ's second coming as well.

And then there are the Moravians! As other essays in this volume make clear, discussion of almost any aspect of Protestantism outside of Europe, including gender and sexuality, would have to include significant discussion of the Moravians. Moravian women traveled as migrants and missionaries throughout the Atlantic world, sometimes working as a team with their husbands, but sometimes independently, in communities that included Europeans, Africans, and indigenous people. Rebecca Protten is the best known of these, and she probably traveled the furthest, but she was not alone.[54] Jane Merritt has examined Moravian women in

[53] Ulrike Gleixner, "Remapping the world: the vision of Protestant empire in the eighteenth century," in *Migration and Religion: Christian Transatlantic Missions, Islamic Migration to Germany*, ed. Barbara Becker-Cantarino (Amsterdam: Rodopi, 2012), 77–90. See also Ulrike Gleixner, "Mäzeninnen im Reich Gottes: Frauen hohen Standes im Netzwerk der protestantischen Indienmission im 18. Jahrhundert," *L'Homme. Themenheft: Geschlechtergeschichte global* 2 (2012): 13–31, and "Fürstäbtissin, Patronage und protestantische Indienmission: Das Stiften sozialer Räume im 'Reich Gottes,'" in *Der Hof: Ort kulturellen Handelns von Frauen in der Frühen Neuzeit*, ed. Susanna Rode-Breymann, Antje Tumat (Cologne: Böhlau, 2013), 157–76. There are also several essays on women and gender in Jonathon Strom, Hartmut Lehmann, and James van Horn Melton eds., *Pietism in Germany and North America 1680–1820* (Burlington, VT: Ashgate, 2009).

[54] For Rebecca Protten, see Jon F. Sensbach, *Rebecca's Revival: Creating Black Christianity in the Atlantic World* (Cambridge, MA: Harvard University Press, 2005). For other

Pennsylvania, where German immigrants learned Native languages and held separate services for indigenous women.[55] More Delaware and Mahican women converted than did men, a situation that even male Moravian missionaries openly admitted was the result of their wives' efforts.

Moravians in Pennsylvania established mission communities for Native converts, believing, as did Spanish Catholic missionaries in the Americas and the Philippines, that they would remain true to the faith only if they lived together under the watchful eye of Europeans. But in contrast to Catholic missions, where there was no formal role for indigenous women, baptized Native women became elders (*Arbeiter Schwestern*) in Native congregations, where they blessed children, heard other Native women's professions of faith, and proselytized. Their dreams and visions were told as part of the life stories about spiritual longing and crisis that were related after baptism, were written down, distributed, and read by Moravians and others in Pennsylvania and beyond. Thus, as Native Americans accommodated their spiritual language somewhat to Moravian idioms – or the missionaries recorded them as doing so – German and English audiences read about vision quests, hunting magic, and miraculous healings, which fit well with their own worldview, in which prophecies, apparitions, and portents were regularly reported and interpreted. The similarities among these were evidence of God's global providence and the coming Kingdom of God, just as similarities between witches' sabbaths and indigenous American rituals were evidence of Satan's global reach for demonologists and witch-hunters.[56]

women, see Beverly Prior Smaby, "Female piety among eighteenth-century Moravians," *Pennsylvania History* 64 (1997): 151–67; Ray Kea, "From Catholicism to Moravian pietism: the world of Marotta/Magdalena, woman of Popo and St. Thomas," in *The Creation of the British Atlantic World*, ed. Elizabeth Mancke and Carole Shammas (Baltimore, MD: Johns Hopkins University Press, 2005), 115–36; Michele Gillespie and Robert Beachy eds., *Pious Pursuits: German Moravians in the Atlantic World* (New York: Berghahn, 2007); Aaron Spencer Fogleman, *Two Troubled Souls: An Eighteenth-Century Couple's Spiritual Journey in the Atlantic World* (Chapel Hill: University of North Carolina Press, 2013).

55 Jane T. Merritt, *At the Crossroads: Indians and Empires on a Mid-Atlantic Frontier, 1700–1763* (Chapel Hill: University of North Carolina Press, 2003).

56 Gerhild Scholz Williams has emphasized that the language of the witch hunts provided a vocabulary for educated Europeans to describe the Natives of the New World. In 1585, for example, the French explorer Jéan Lery described religious rituals of Brazilian women in words he had taken from a contemporary French demonological guide. Like women in Europe, the women of the New World were regarded as especially likely to give in to demonic suggestion; linking their practices with those of European women charged with witchcraft also made European witches appear even more exotic and dangerous, representatives of a truly worldwide conspiracy. Gerhild Scholz Williams, *Defining Dominion: The Discourses of Magic and Witchcraft in Early Modern France and Germany* (Ann Arbor: University of Michigan Press, 1999). Williams has also translated and edited one of the

A Wider Range of Actors

The role of European and Mahican *Arbeiter Schwestern* in family life among Moravian immigrants and of indigenous Christians in Pennsylvania are examples of the third trend in recent scholarship that I wish to highlight in this essay: the inclusion of a wider range of actors, including European and European-background women and indigenous and mixed-race people of all sexes. Twenty years ago, it was evident that the older view of indigenous people's acceptance of Christianity as a "spiritual conquest" in which missionaries acted on passive Natives – either destroying or saving them, depending on one's view – was incomplete. Historians of the Americas developed what scholars of Latin America referred to as the "new mission history," in which indigenous peoples became historical agents in religious encounters, transforming Christianity in the process.[57] Historians of Africa, most prominently John Thornton, asserted that African religious cosmology and practices shaped African and Afro-American Christianity throughout the Atlantic world, a development that began in the fifteenth century when the kings of Kongo and many of their subjects embraced Christianity.[58] This process was not conceptualized as "conversion" – some scholars chose to reject that word completely – but instead as indigenization, creolization, cultural translation, appropriation, *mestizaje*, hybridity, and/or syncretism.[59]

longest and most important demonological treatises that argues this, *On the Inconstancy of Witches: Pierre de Lancre's Tableau de l'inconstance des mauvais anges et demons (1612)* (Phoenix, AZ: ACMRS Publications, 2006).

57 One of the first books to make this argument was James Axtell, *The Invasion Within: The Contest of Cultures in Colonial North America* (New York: Oxford University Press, 1986). Other early studies on North America include Richard White, *The Middle Ground: Indians, Empires, and Republics in the Great Lakes Region, 1650–1815* (Cambridge: Cambridge University Press, 1991) and Carol Devens, *Countering Colonization: Native American Women and Great Lakes Missions, 1630–1900* (Berkeley: University of California Press, 1992). For overviews of Latin America, see Erick Langer and Robert H. Jackson eds., *The New Latin American Mission History* (Lincoln: University of Nebraska Press, 1995); Susan Deeds, "Pushing the borders of Latin American mission history – review article," *Latin American Research Review*, 39/2 (2004): 211–20.

58 John Thornton, *Africa and Africans in the Making of the Atlantic World, 1400–1800* (Cambridge: Cambridge University Press, 1st ed. 1992, 2nd ed. 1998) and *The Kongolese Saint Anthony: Dona Beatriz Kimpa Vita and the Antonian Movement, 1684–1706* (Cambridge: Cambridge University Press, 1998).

59 On problems with "conversion," see Jean and John Comaroff, *Of Revelation and Revolution: Christianity, Colonialism, and Consciousness in South Africa, Vol. 1* (Chicago, IL: University of Chicago Press, 1991); the introduction to Kenneth Mills and Anthony Grafton eds., *Conversions: Old Worlds and New* (Rochester, NY: University of Rochester Press, 2003); Neal Salisbury, "Embracing ambiguity: native peoples and Christianity in seventeenth-century North America," *Ethnohistory* 50/2 (2003): 247–59; Katharine Gerbner, "Theorizing conversion: Christianity, colonization, and consciousness in the early modern Atlantic world," *History Compass* 13/3 (2015): 134–47. Peter Burke has an excellent discussion of the origins and uses of the newer

Such scholarship situates this process of negotiation and mixing within the context of colonial conquest and enormous power differences, so it generally recognizes the limits of choice for individuals and groups, though some scholars have criticized it for not emphasizing this enough.[60]

The "new mission history" is not so new anymore, which means it has also been critiqued and revised, as scholars have debated terminology, conceptualizations, and methods, but its central point has been made even more strongly over the last several decades. A large body of scholarship has emerged in which non-European and mixed-race people, including the women among them, are actors rather than victims in religious encounters. They shaped beliefs and practices, including but not limited to those related to gender and sexuality, such as marriage, divorce, and same-sex relations.

Here scholars of global Catholicism have taken the lead. Among Africanists, John Thornton has been joined by many others who also emphasize the persistence of African traditions in African, Caribbean, and Latin American Catholic Christianity.[61] George Brooks, for example, traces the ways in which European and local notions about acceptable marriage partners and practices combined in the colonies of West Africa to create distinctive patterns. Wealthy female traders – termed *nharas* in Crioulo and *signares* in French – often married Portuguese, French, or English traders, sometimes in Christian ceremonies and sometimes in what French commentators called "in the style of the land." Whatever the ceremony, if the husband returned to Europe, the *signare* was free to marry again, as, we assume, the husband understood himself to be as

terms in *Cultural Hybridity* (Cambridge: Polity Press, 2009). On syncretism, see Anita Maria Leopold and Jeppe Sinding Jensen eds., *Syncretism in Religion: A Reader* (New York: Routledge, 2004).

60 Davíd Carrasco, "Borderlands and the 'Biblical Hurricane': images and stories of Latin American rhythms of life," *The Harvard Theological Review* 101/3,4 (2008): 353–76.

61 James Sweet, *Recreating Africa: Culture, Kinship and Religion in the African-Portuguese World, 1441–1770* (Chapel Hill: University of North Carolina Press, 2003); J. Lorand Matory, *Black Atlantic Religion: Tradition, Transnationalism, and Matriarchy in the Afro-Brazilian Candomblé* (Princeton, NJ: Princeton University Press, 2005); Herman L. Bennett, *Africans in Colonial Mexico: Absolutism, Christianity, and Afro-Creole Consciousness, 1570–1640* (Bloomington: Indiana University Press, 2005); Yvonne P. Chireau, *Black Magic: Religion and the African American Conjuring Tradition* (Berkeley: University of California Press, 2006); Linda M. Heywood and John K. Thornton, *Central Africans, Atlantic Creoles, and the Foundation of the Americas, 1585–1660* (Cambridge: Cambridge University Press, 2007); Stephan Palmié, *Africas of the Americas: Beyond the Search for Origins in the Study of Afro-Atlantic Religions* (Leiden & Boston: Brill, 2008); Mariza de Carvalho Soares, *People of Faith: Slavery and African Catholics in Eighteenth-Century Rio de Janeiro* (Durham, NC: Duke University Press, 2011). For a look at this persistence in a Protestant area, see Jason R. Young, *Rituals of Resistance: African Atlantic Religion in Kongo and the Lowcountry South in the Era of Slavery* (Baton Rouge: Louisiana State University Press, 2011).

well.[62] In *Christians, Blasphemers, and Witches*, Joan Bristol uses Inquisition documents to examine the ritual lives of some of the hundreds of thousands of Africans brought to Mexico as slaves to bolster native labor. Some had already adopted Christianity in Africa, and many more did so in Mexico, participating in mass, confession, and communion, while others engaged in various magical practices the Inquisition regarded as blasphemous or demonic.[63] Many did both, providing an example of the type of mixture that Neal Salisbury has noted "the Euro-American tradition could and can comprehend only as ambiguity."[64] Increasingly using sources in native languages, Latin Americanists have pointed to many examples of similar processes of *mestizaje* involving indigenous and mixed-race women and men, which shaped family life, notions of morality, and religious practices.[65]

Like historians of Africa, historians of French North America have looked at indigenous women and men as active agents in the creation of new religious practices, and at the ways intermarriage facilitated cultural exchange, including religious ideas and practices. Allan Greer's studies of Kateri Tekakwitha, one of a group of young Mohawk women in the Jesuit community of Kahnawake near Montreal who adopted austere penitential practices, note the ways in which she combined traditional Christian practices, such as fasting and flagellation, with those that may have come from Native American rituals of healing and war preparation, such as voluntary exposure to cold and burning.[66] Tracy Neal Leavelle examines

62 George E. Brooks, *Eurafricans in Western Africa: Commerce, Social Status, Gender, and Religious Observance from the Sixteenth to the Eighteenth Century* (Athens: Ohio University Press, 2003). See also Hilary Jones, *The Métis of Senegal: Urban Life and Poltics in French West Africa* (Bloomington: Indiana University Press, 2013).

63 Joan Cameron Bristol, *Christians, Blasphemers, and Witches: Afro-Mexican Ritual Practice in the Seventeenth Century* (Albuquerque: University of New Mexico Press, 2007).

64 Salisbury, "Embracing ambiguity," 257.

65 Chapter 4 of the third edition of my *Christianity and Sexuality* has a long bibliography of older and recent works. Newer studies include Pete Sigal, *The Flower and the Scorpion: Sexuality and Ritual in Early Nahua Culture* (Durham, NC: Duke University Press, 2011); David Tavárez, *The Invisible War: Indigenous Devotions, Discipline, and Dissent in Colonial Mexico* (Stanford, CA: Stanford University Press, 2011); Matthew Restall, *The Black Middle: Africans, Mayas, and Spaniards in Colonial Yucatan* (Stanford, CA: Stanford University Press, 2013); David Tavárez ed., *Words and Worlds Turned Around: Indigenous Christianities in Colonial Latin America* (Boulder: University Press of Colorado, 2017).

66 Allan Greer and Jodi Bilinkoff eds., *Colonial Saints: Discovering the Holy in the Americas, 1500–1800* (New York: Routledge, 2003); Allan Greer, *Mohawk Saint: Catherine Tekakwitha and the Jesuits* (New York: Oxford University Press, 2004). Tekakwitha's confessors hoped to make her a saint, but this was a slow process; she was made venerable in 1943, beatified in 1980, and canonized in 2012, when the Congregation for the Causes of Saints and Pope Benedict XVI certified a second miracle through her intercession. The last step happened largely through the pressure of the Tekakwitha Conference, an

interactions between Jesuits and the Algonquian-speaking Illinois and Ottawa men and women, analyzing rituals, speech, song, and behavior to argue that both Jesuits and Native Americans were transformed by their interactions and the complicated cross-cultural religious practices that developed.[67] A number of authors have examined intermarriage between French men and indigenous women, through which French officials and missionaries in their policy of *Fransication* hoped the women would be "made French," but in which women and their children blended cultures in their work patterns, choices in clothing and material objects, distribution of property, and spiritual practices.[68]

Kateri Tekakwitha's story comes to us only through the words of her Jesuit confessors and hagiographers, but Haruko Nawata Ward has recovered the words and ideas of female converts on the other side of the world in *Women Religious Leaders of Japan's Christian Century*. Female converts to Christianity, some of whom had been abbesses and other types of religious teachers in the Buddhist and Buddhist-Shinto traditions, preached, translated and wrote religious works, disputed with Buddhist priests, and taught catechism. Nawata Ward investigates the actions of many women and concludes that these were the major reason for Japan's total rejection of Christianity and what is using termed the "closing of Japan," a shift in politico-religious ideology that has previously been seen only as a story of men.[69]

Scholarship on early modern Protestants has a way to go to catch up with that on Catholics, but it also increasingly emphasizes European women and indigenous and mixed-race people of all sexes as active agents, instead of focusing only on European men.[70] Evangelical and

organization of Native American Catholics, and she became the first North American Native American woman to be made a saint.

67 Tracy Neal Leavelle, *The Catholic Calumet: Colonial Conversions in French and Indian North America* (Philadelphia: University of Pennsylvania Press, 2011).

68 Susan Sleeper-Smith, *Indian Women and French Men: Rethinking Cultural Encounter in the Western Great Lakes* (Amherst: University of Massachusetts Press, 2001); Gilles Havard, *Empire et métissage: Indiens et Français dans le Pays d'an Haut 1660–1715* (Sillery: Septentrion, 2003); Jennifer M. Spear, *Race, Sex, and Social Order in Early New Orleans* (Baltimore, MD: Johns Hopkins University Press, 2009); Sophie White, *Wild Frenchmen and Frenchified Indians: Material Culture and Race in Colonial Louisiana* (Philadelphia: University of Pennsylvania Press, 2012); Saliha Belmessous, *Assimilation and Empire: Uniformity in French and British Colonies, 1541–1954* (New York: Oxford University Press, 2013), Part I.

69 Haruko Nawata Ward, *Women Religious Leaders of Japan's Christian Century* (Aldershot, UK: Ashgate, 2009).

70 Studies of Protestant missionary ventures in the nineteenth and twentieth centuries increasingly emphasize the importance of indigenous women and men and the centrality of gender issues as well. For just one example, see Hyaeweol Choi and Margaret Jolly eds., *Divine Domesticities: Christian Paradoxes in Asia and the Pacific* (Canberra: Australian National University Press, 2014).

experiential Protestantism offered some Euro-American women expanded opportunities for leadership, perhaps not as dramatic as that among the Quakers or early Moravians, but still significant. Catherine Brekus tells the story of Sarah Osborn, for example, a married schoolteacher in Rhode Island, who led a revival in the 1760s that brought hundreds of people, including many slaves, regularly to her house, and left thousands of pages of spiritual memoir.[71]

Charles H. Parker's articles in the volume and elsewhere include indigenous linguists and teachers who instructed children and adults in Dutch Indonesia, and Jon Sensbach's essay in this volume, as well as his earlier work, explores religious practices among many groups in the Caribbean.[72] Chiu Hsin-hui's *The Colonial "Civilizing Process" in Dutch Formosa, 1624–1662* highlights the role played by Taiwan's indigenous peoples rather than simply the VOC in creating new institutions and new practices, in what she views as a dynamic encounter.[73] For example, several Dutch military victories and an outbreak of smallpox that both the Dutch and the indigenous Sirayan people attributed to the "Dutch god" led local inhabitants to destroy their idols, agree to be baptized, and support the construction of churches and schools. A delegation of headmen promised (as reported by Dutch authorities) that "henceforth the people were to desist from all lewdness and fornication; that the women when pregnant should no longer practise abortion; and that polygamy, which is most shamefully practised, should be done away with. Further, that the men should cover their nakedness, and henceforth live as Christians and not as beasts."[74] The headmen had clearly recognized that conversion involved sexual, bodily, and marital practices as well as notions of the divine. Some couples did marry in Christian ceremonies, a few local men became teachers, and consistories of Dutch and Sirayan men were formed, with disciplinary powers for moral infractions that

[71] Catherine A. Brekus, *Sarah Osborne's World: The Rise of Evangelical Christianity in Early America* (New Haven, CT: Yale University Press, 2013). For the story of a woman who began life as Protestant but ended it as the abbess of a French Canadian Ursuline convent, with five years among the Wabanaki in between, see Ann M. Little, *The Many Captivities of Esther Wheelwright* (New Haven, CT: Yale University Press, 2016).

[72] Charles H. Parker, "Converting souls across borders: Dutch Calvinism and early modern missionary movements," *Journal of Global History* 8/1 (2013): 50–71; Sensbach, *Rebecca's Journey*.

[73] Chiu Hsin-hui, *The Colonial "Civilizing Process" in Dutch Formosa, 1624–1662* (Amsterdam: Brill 2008). For another look at indigenous converts on Formosa, see Natalie Everts, "Siraya concepts of marriage in seventeenth-century Sincan: impressions gathered from the letters of two Dutch missionaries," in *(En)gendering Taiwan: The Rise of Taiwanese Feminism*, ed. Ya-chen Chen (Berlin: Springer, 2018): 13–24.

[74] *Dagregisters Zeelandia*, I, K fos. 459–60, quoted in Hsin-hui, *The Colonial "Civilizing Process,"* 195.

included fines and whipping. But underlying these conversions and religious institutions, as Hsin-hui points out, were indigenous practices of gift giving, with the headmen expecting food and Dutch military support against their enemies and indigenous teachers expecting rice and cash. Despite the promises of the headmen, divorce and multiple wives continued, as indigenous converts filtered and blended Christian teachings with their own cultural values.

In the Atlantic world, studies of indigenous Christians include Linford Fisher's *The Indian Great Awakening*, which examines ways in which previously unevangelized Native Americans adopted Christian practices as a result of the First Great Awakening of the mid-eighteenth century, and then asserted cultural autonomy by establishing their own churches, schools, and even a few settlements. As was true among white settlers, Native American women affiliated themselves with Congregational and other types of Protestant churches – through adult and infant baptism, Christian marriage ceremonies, and full membership in communion – at about twice the rate of men. Some converts, however, such as the Montaukett Mary Occam, insisted on continuing to wear traditional Indian clothing and speak their native languages, though Occam was reported to be able to speak English well. Mothers and grandmothers brought children to be baptized, in part because this might give them access to Euro-American education, but also because both Native and Euro-American Christians believed that the ritual of baptism itself gave the children physical and spiritual protection, even though ministers tried to dissuade them of this notion.[75] Edward Andrews's *Native Apostles* focuses on the many black and Indian men, and a few women, for whom records of their missionary work in the Atlantic world survive, often from white missionaries, but a surprising number from their own hands.[76] Laura Chmielewksi's *The Spice of Popery* looks at the entangled Christianities in the Province of Maine, using material culture as well as written sources to examine the range of experience of its diverse inhabitants, including accused witches, indigenous religious thinkers, and voluntary and involuntary converts.[77]

[75] Linford D. Fisher, *The Indian Great Awakening: Religion and the Shaping of Native Cultures in Early America* (New York: Oxford University Press, 2012). These examples are on pp. 100–2. See also David J. Silverman, *Faith and Boundaries: Colonists, Christianity, and Community Among the Wampanoag Indians of Martha's Vineyard, 1600–1871* (New York: Cambridge University Press, 2005) and Joel W. Martin and Mark A. Nicholas, *Native Americans, Christianity, and the Reshaping of the American Religious Landscape* (Chapel Hill: University of North Carolina Press, 2010).

[76] Edward E. Andrews, *Native Apostles: Black and Indian Missionaries in the British Atlantic World* (Cambridge, MA: Harvard University Press, 2013).

[77] Laura M. Chmielewski, *The Spice of Popery: Converging Christianities on an Early American Frontier* (Notre Dame, IN: University of Notre Dame Press, 2011).

Jenny Shaw's *Everyday Life in the Early English Caribbean* analyzes ways in which Irish indentures and laborers and enslaved Africans created communities and categories of difference through practices and rituals of daily life, including religious ones. She finds that the Irish and Africans most likely to become members of the Church of England were those who saw advantages in doing so, including free and newly freed people of color who thought that marrying within the church and baptizing their children could help to bolster their status as free colonial subjects, and social-climbing Irish men hoping to become members of the planter elite. As with recusants in England, Irish women in the English Caribbean often continued to engage in Catholic practices (including baptizing infants) while their husbands went to Anglican services, and oversaw their husbands' burials in private ceremonies, thus having a say in the final destiny of their souls.[78]

Travel across the Atlantic went in all directions, with Native Americans, Africans, and Asians moving to Europe as well as Europeans moving away. Church records and other sources are beginning to be analyzed for what they can tell us about the religious experiences of non-Europeans living in Europe. In *Exceeding riches of grace* (1647), a report of the transformation in London of the fasting girl Sarah Wight into a spiritual medium written by the Independent clergyman Henry Jessey, one of the witnesses is described as "Dinah the Black." In a later publication, Jessey includes details about Dinah's (or a woman who was most likely Dinah) baptism and baptismal records elsewhere in England that include a handful of other non-European adults as well, occasionally mentioning something about their motivation.[79] Much of this was formulaic and unsurprising, but no matter how brief, such sources remind us that the global reach of Protestantism was sometimes visible in the bodies gathered for worship in London and other European cities, as well as in the colonies.

While Protestant Christianity increased the possibilities for agency and independent action for some indigenous and black individuals in the Atlantic world, Christian works and teachings were also used as justifications for slavery, a link being analyzed in a growing body of scholarship that also traces the shift from constructions of difference based on religion and culture towards models of difference based on

[78] Jenny Shaw, *Everyday Life in the Early English Caribbean: Irish, Africans, and the Construction of Difference* (Athens: University of Georgia Press, 2013).

[79] Kathleen Lynch, "What happened to Dinah the Black? and other questions about gender, race, and the visibility of Protestant saints," in *Conversions: Gender and Relgious Change in Early Modern Europe*, ed. Simon Ditchfield and Helen Smith (Manchester, UK: Manchester University Press, 2017), 258–80. See also Imtiaz Habib, *Black Lives in the English Archives, 1500–1677: Imprints of the Invisible* (Aldershot, UK: Ashgate, 2008).

race.[80] Much of this focuses primarily on the works of European or European-background learned men, but some newer studies also include the ideas and practices of ordinary people. Heather Miyano Kopelson's *Faithful Bodies: Performing Religion and Race in the Puritan Atlantic*, for example, examines changing ideas and practices in southern New England and Bermuda, two areas settled by dissenting Protestants intent on creating godly societies.[81] Difference was increasingly defined racially rather than religiously in these colonies, often through laws and cases about unlawful sex that marked a racialized definition of womanhood, a pattern similar to that in the plantation colonies of the south or other parts of the Caribbean. But this transformation happened at a slower pace and more irregularly than it did in plantation colonies, and "Christian" continued to be an identity claimed by people of color and interracial people. Kopelson recounts the story of a young enslaved interracial woman named Doll Allen, who in 1658 petitioned for the freedom to seek her own indenture based on her father/owner's status as a white English man and on her Christian identity, noting, "since it hath pleased God to sett a distinction between her and heathen Negros by providence [in] [a]lotting her birth among Christians and making her free of the Ordinances [of C]hrist." She had followed these "ordinances," that is, religious practices of Protestant Christianity, "from her Cradle unto fifteene yeares of age" living with "the priviledge of Christian people."[82] Allen was not successful, as the notion that the legal status of a child was based on that of its mother was already well established in Bermuda, but her petition suggests that her understanding of herself as Christian was not simply instrumental, but part of her identity. Kopelson's book weaves religion with the more common categories of gender, sexuality, and race in an intersectional analysis, providing a model for future studies of early modern Protestants in other parts of the world.[83]

[80] Colin Kidd, *The Forging of Races: Race and Scripture in the Protestant Atlantic World 1600–2000* (Cambridge: Cambridge University Press, 2006); David M. Whitford, *The Curse of Ham in the Early Modern Era: The Bible and the Justifications for Slavery* (London: Blackwell, 2009); David N. Livingstone, *Adam's Ancestors: Race, Religion, and the Politics of Human Origins* (Baltimore, MD: Johns Hopkins University Press, 2011); Rebecca Anne Goetz, *The Baptism of Early Virginia: How Christianity Created Race* (Baltimore, MD: Johns Hopkins University Press, 2012). For an examination of this process in the Indian Ocean rather than the Atlantic, see Adrian Carton, *Mixed-Race and Modernity in Colonial India: Changing Concepts of Hybridity Across Empires* (London: Routledge, 2015).

[81] Heather Miyano Kopelson, *Faithful Bodies: Performing Religion and Race in the Puritan Atlantic* (New York: New York University Press, 2014).

[82] General Court, Bermuda (1652), quoted in Kopelson, *Faithful Bodies*, 203–4.

[83] For recent discussions of intersectionality as a theory and method, see the special issue of *Signs*, "Intersectionality: theorizing power, empowering theory," 38/4 (Summer 2013):

Conclusions

All three of these newer perspectives – the emotional turn, the spatial turn, and the inclusion of a wider range of actors – separately and intertwined, offer ways to broaden and deepen our understanding of early modern Protestant movements, including patterns of gender and sexuality within them. As this essay has noted, much of the intertwining is already beginning to occur, as scholars focus on the emotions of people who moved, those they encountered, and those that were produced through such encounters, whether this was the physical production of "mixed blood" children or the spiritual production of indigenous Christians. Although much scholarship on the Reformation continues to be national or even sub-national and local in scope, there is beginning to be a great deal of fascinating work that uses a wider spatial lens, particularly if we take a broader chronological purview and incorporate the first part of the eighteenth century into our understanding of "Reformation culture." In the same way, though some scholarship on the Reformations continues to avoid considerations of gender and sexuality, of the many biographies of Luther produced for the 500th anniversary of 2017 – hardly a cutting-edged genre of historical writing – few lacked at least some discussion of his marriage, sexual life, and ideas about women.

Twenty years ago I wrote a global book on sexuality in early modern Christianity, in part because I had no good answer to the question posed by friends who were specialists in areas outside of Europe: "Why are you just looking at Europe?" If there was no good answer then, there is truly no good answer now. Had I included all the new research, perspectives, and ideas in that book's third edition, it would have weighed more than twenty pounds.

785–1055 and "Forum: rethinking key concepts in gender history," *Gender and History* 28/2 (August 2016): 299–366, which also discusses agency, gender crisis, and gender binary.

Index

Milton Keynes UK
Ingram Content Group UK Ltd.
UKHW050628150424
440973UK00017B/209

9 781108 794978